RECOGNIZING PERSIUS

MARTIN CLASSICAL LECTURES

The Martin Classical Lectures are delivered annually at Oberlin College through a foundation established by his many friends in honor of Charles Beebe Martin, for forty-five years a teacher of classical literature and classical art at Oberlin.

John Peradotto, *Man in the Middle Voice: Name and Narration in the Odyssey*

Martha C. Nussbaum, *The Therapy of Desire: Theory and Practice in Hellenistic Ethics*

Josiah Ober, *Political Dissent in Democratic Athens: Intellectual Critics of Popular Rule*

Anne Carson, *Economy of the Unlost (Reading Simonides of Keos with Paul Celan)*

Helene P. Foley, *Female Acts in Greek Tragedy*

Mark W. Edwards, *Sound, Sense, and Rhythm: Listening to Greek and Latin Poetry*

Michael C. J. Putnam, *Poetic Interplay: Catullus and Horace*

Julia Haig Gaisser, *The Fortunes of Apuleius and the Golden Ass: A Study in Transmission and Reception*

Kenneth Reckford, *Recognizing Persius*

RECOGNIZING PERSIUS

Kenneth J. Reckford

PRINCETON UNIVERSITY PRESS

PRINCETON AND OXFORD

Published by Princeton University Press, 41 William Street, Princeton, New Jersey 08540

In the United Kingdom: Princeton University Press, 6 Oxford Street, Woodstock, Oxfordshire OX20 1TW

Reckford, Kenneth J.

  Recognizing Persius / Kenneth J. Reckford

     p. cm. — (Martin classical lectures)

  Includes bibliographical references and index.

  ISBN 978-0-691-14141-1

  1. Persius—Criticism and interpretation. 2. Satire, Latin—History and criticism. I. Title.

PA6556R43 2009

871'.01—dc22   2008048717

British Library Cataloging-in-Publication Data is available

This book has been composed in Janson Typeface

Printed on acid-free paper. ∞

press.princeton.edu

Printed in the United States of America

10 9 8 7 6 5 4 3 2 1

CONTENTS

ACKNOWLEDGMENTS

THIS BOOK began as four Martin Classical Lectures at Oberlin College in April, 1999, under the auspices of Jim Helm and Tom Van Nortwick. I laid the groundwork for these lectures in Fall, 1998, as a pampered Resident in Classical Studies at the American Academy in Rome. Versions of sections 1.1 and 4.3 were given at the University of North Carolina at Chapel Hill, the University of Florence, and Washington and Lee University. Parts of 1.1 and especially 2.6 appeared earlier, in my 1998 *Arethusa* article; part of 1.2, in my Introduction to Cynthia Dessen's *The Satires of Persius* (2 ed., 1996). The book's eventual midwives were Tom Van Nortwick (again) for Oberlin and Rob Tempio for the Princeton University Press, aided by Heath Renfroe and Jon Munk, and earlier by two attentive readers who have since identified themselves as Dan Hooley and Cedric Littlewood. They will see for themselves how much I have profited from their generous advice and criticism.

My excitement about Persius goes back to Robert A. Brooks's Roman Satire course at Harvard in Spring, 1951. A multitalented teacher, scholar, poet, and (later) businessman and administrator [see my Introduction to Brooks 1981], Rab Brooks remarkably, and fatefully for me, preferred Persius to Horace and Juvenal. At UNC, between 1960 and 2003, I had the privilege of teaching Roman satire frequently to bright and gifted students, for whose interest, support, and friendship, together with that of my former UNC colleagues, I am forever grateful. More recently, the Department of Classics at Florida State University has welcomed me as a neighbor and allowed me to use the Strozier Library.

Scholars to whom I am indebted include, but are by no means limited to, the following: Susanna Braund, Marcia Colish, Nancy de Grummond, Sheila Dillon, Barbara Gold, Margaret Graver, Lois Hinckley, Nicholas Horsfall, John Kirby, Anthony Long, Mark Morford, Glenn Most, Jeanne Neumann, Michael Putnam, Gretchen Reydams-Schils, Niall Slater, Philip Stadter, Nicola Terrenato, and Jessica Wolf. Special thanks are due to Trevor Luke and Allen Romano at FSU, who helped me with elusive references and bibliography, and with inter-library loans; and to David Orth Reckford, for his unstinting assistance with computer problems, needs, and formatting, and his constant encouragement.

To Charlotte Orth—who, amid so many other generous gifts, has *bade me welcome* to her vast treasure house of fiction and nonfiction, and creative ideas; who has often improved my wording; who has teased me into reading theoretical studies beyond my habitual comfort zone, and thinking more modernly; who has prodded me to travel to places—Oxford, London, Rome, Florence—where I could listen to other scholars, study, and talk; and who, beyond all this, has done me the honor of believing that I could transcend my academic persona and become, or try to become, more of a person—this book is gratefully dedicated.

RECOGNIZING PERSIUS

Prologue

▣ ▣ ▣ ▣ ▣ ▣ ▣ ▣ ▣ ▣ ▣ ▣ ▣ ▣ ▣ ▣

IN SEARCH OF PERSIUS

> The first impression of an unbiassed reader who dips into the poems . . .
> is unfavorable. He is repulsed by the intolerably harsh and crabbed
> versification, by the recondite choice of theme and expression, and by
> the oddity of the thought. In time, however, he perceives that behind
> the fantastic garb of language there is an earnest and vigorous mind, an
> imagination that harbours fire within its cloudy folds, and an insight
> into the mysteries of spiritual life which is often startling.
> —E. G., in the *Encyclopedia Britannica* (1911)

THE TWO missing words in the first line are, "of Donne." Omit these,
and Edmund Gosse might as well have been writing about Persius, who
much influenced the "harsh and crabbed" late Elizabethan style of Hall,
Marston, and Donne in their satires, and whose notorious obscurity they
may have adopted, in some part, for their own protection. To the literary
scholar, Donne's *Satyres* represent a high-water mark in the appreciation
of Persius, who more than holds his own alongside Horace and Juvenal.
Let me push the comparison further, as prologue to my account.

First, some external similarities. The little book (*libellus*) of Persius's six
satires plus their choliambic preface adds up to 664 verses (14 + 650). He
wrote them as a young man of around twenty-four to twenty-seven years;
they were only published, perhaps for safety's sake, after his death. Donne's
five satires add up to 669 verses. He wrote them between, roughly, twenty-
one and twenty-seven, but withheld them from publication ("to my Satyres
there belongs some fear . . . "). They were published eventually, but never
as a collection.

Then, style: "Persius evidently taught Donne much about concise ex-
pression and complexity of syntax, rigorous argumentation, abrupt transi-
tions in thought, hyperbolic and catachretical imagery, the drama and
forcefulness of second-person address—much, in short, that readers have
associated with Donne in general." James Baumlin points out that Donne
adopts Persius's style—"the protreptic zeal, the homiletic tone"—when it
suits his needs.[1] The "deliberate harshness of style and tone" serves both

satirists in their struggle for sincerity and truth, as against the usual, always tempting complicity in the rhetorical and linguistic corruptions and elegant flatteries of the time. Note, however, that Donne also satirizes "Gloriosus" in *Satyre* 4, the crude, careless fellow who has the roughness without its inner meaning—a shadow figure of the satirist, much in the manner of Horace or Persius.

All satire, whether Roman or English, involves self-fashioning, usually in the sense of fashioning an effective self-image or persona for the outside world, and sometimes in the deeper sense of fashioning, exploring, and educating the inner self to which, as poor old Polonius ironically says, one must be true. Most "Renaissance self-fashioning" in modern critical accounts has been of the former type: what Polonius and Laertes, not Hamlet, really had in mind.[2] Living as we do in understandably cynical times, we most easily imagine someone like Donne as a man on the make, a subtle courtier, with far more worldly wisdom than his *Satyres*, taken in isolation, would suggest. Might we also take his youthful self-searching seriously? How much was it stimulated, encouraged, even shaped in some part by his reading of Persius? How much may we bring back, for purposes of comparison, from Donne's Christian satires to our modern reading and interpretation of Persius's Stoic ones?

In his five satires Donne explores three interrelated topics: how he should write Christian satire, and how he should live an effective Christian life both inwardly and in dealing with the world(s) around him. His religious beliefs and struggles are central. As a Christian, he learns to acknowledge his own sinful failures, to accept God's grace and forgiveness, and to persevere in life's struggles without losing either heart or soul; and he learns to hate the sin but love the sinner, with "Kinde Pity and Brave Scorn," which bears strongly on his redefinition of satiric aims and methods. But there is more. His Christian beliefs and loyalties are tested to the bone by the Catholic-Protestant split; hence the special, tightrope-walking intensity of *Satyre* 3 (which comes closest to Persius in style and thought):

> To' adore, or scorne an image, or protest
> May all be bad; doubt wisely; in strange way
> To stand inquiring right, is not to stray;
> To sleepe, or runne wrong, is. On a huge hill,
> Cragged, and steep, Truth stands, and hee that will
> Reach her, about must, and about must goe;
> And what th' hills suddennes resists, winne so;
> Yet striv' so, that before age, deaths twilight,
> Thy Soule rest, for none can worke in that night.
> To will, implyes delay, therefore now doe:

> Hard deeds, the bodies paines; hard knowledge too
> The mindes indeavours reach, . . .[3]

Donne must struggle hard to rediscover his own spiritual integrity and then to maintain it amid pressures, temptations, and obstacles, both external and internal. His typical movement in the *Satyres* is inward, then outward again. He repeatedly fails, or "sins," in the outer world of social and political ambition; each time, he moves back into a meditative stance, reorganizes his thoughts, deepens his sense of devotion, self-awareness, and purpose, and reemerges with new resolve and authority to recommence the struggle. *Satyre* 5 is finally confident, as his achieved self-reform equips him, now in the service of Sir Thomas Egerton, to root out bribery and corruption in the public realm.[4]

Like Horace and Persius, Donne plays brilliantly with the different voices that he dramatizes. (Much of the mimicry and fun emerges as we read them aloud.) The idiotic, worldly, would-be courtier of *Satyre* 1, derived from the Bore of Horace's *Satires* 1.9, seems a simple antagonist and foil; but he also embodies the very real temptations to which a cloistered scholar like Donne is subject, a shadow side that he must grasp imaginatively in order to reject. Amid these many seductive, distracting, or (momentarily) confusing voices, the poet pursues single-mindedness of purpose as best he can. As Thomas Hester well says,

> The *Satyres* are, of course, excellent examples of Donne's status as a "witty" poet, as the creator in English literature of a poetry of wit; but their animating principle is the poet's profound contempt for sham and pretense, falsehood, affectation, and intolerance—in himself as well as his satiric victims. Such an attitude necessitates above all his own discovery or creation of a voice appropriate to the conditions in which and about which he writes, a voice able to address and to admit the variety of human failures he confronts. . . . So, as the sequence depicts the satirist's discovery of a various world of folly and crime it also details his expanding awareness of the variety, strengths, and limitations of his powers as man and as poet.[5]

We think again of Hamlet, Donne's close contemporary, playing out his wild impersonations in order to root out dishonesty and corruption, self-ignorance and self-deception, his own not least, and emerging finally from a web of pretenses and counterpretenses into a world of self-affirmation and action. To be reported honestly is his last request.

Suppose now that Donne had died, like Persius, at twenty-seven, that we had none of his writings besides the youthful *Satyres*, and no outside information about his life and thought. How might we have guessed that this intense young writer was, in those same years, a courtier, lover, and writer of elegies; a military adventurer in Spain; and a man who would lose his position and be thrown into prison for secretly marrying his patron Egerton's niece? Or that the youth who walked an intellectual tightrope between Catholicism and Protestantism in *Satyre* 3 would abandon Rome, albeit with dangerous reluctance; would embark on what proved a splendid career as priest, chaplain, dean, and superb preacher of sermons in the Church of England; would die, much honored, at fifty-nine—and would be remembered, after all this, and taught in schools mainly as a metaphysical poet? But, again: knowing Donne's story as we do, how seriously can we take what I have envisioned as his struggle for integrity in the *Satyres*?

By one view, Donne's higher aspirations disappear, together with his religious innocence, beneath the alchemy of quite ordinary "Renaissance self-fashioning." By another—indeed, as was foreshadowed in precisely those youthful *Satyres*—what might have been "a fugitive and cloistered virtue" (Milton) is tested, time and again, by worldly involvements and pressures, yet passes the test, is constantly renewed, and provides the world (as Polonius never could) with yet another paradigm of intellectual and spiritual maturity. Between the two views, are there any criteria for deciding? And would it be foolish to try?

And do I feel emboldened to speak as I will about Persius's search for integrity in his *Satires*, which so much influenced Donne, not although but because we know so very little about the man, his work, and his life?

᠁ ᠁ ᠁

The title of this Prologue, "In Search of Persius," is deliberately ambiguous. If I, despite all the usual warnings ("Pay no attention to the man behind the curtain!") am tracking this elusive, especially private author through and even behind the text, my subject, it seems, was no less in search of himself. But how, as a Roman and Stoic, might he have conceived of that self? How might the fashioning of words in satire have been played off against, or consorted with, the fashioning of a life?

Here is a starting-point. Persius is describing his debt to his teacher, the Stoic philosopher Cornutus:

>   tum fallere sollers
> adposita intortos extendit regula mores
> et premitur ratione animus vincique laborat
> artificemque tuo ducit sub pollice voltum.   (5.37–40)

> [The tricky rule straightens out twisted habits;
> impressed by reason, the mind struggles to
> surrender, producing an artful countenance
> beneath your thumb.]

As Persius masters the tricky rule of reason under Cornutus's tutelage, his mind increasingly cooperates in a paradoxical effort of active submission, letting itself be informed as a statue is shaped from clay by the sculptor, and therewith "taking on a face." The standard of reason is universal and unchangeable, an infallible guide to right action, though tricky, as Persius implies, in its particular applications. Yet his language, with its striking metaphors and bold, playful conceits, is as individualistic as the moral and philosophical lesson is general. What is education? An application of rule and measure; an imaginative and artistic pressure that shapes our humanity and allows it, in turn, the intellectual and moral autonomy to shape itself (and others).

The "artificial face" reminds us, too, that poetry can deceive even as it describes the construction or self-construction of a genuinely human life. Persius is too self-ironic, like his other teacher, Horace, or perhaps too honest, to let us forget that we are dealing with an authorial persona, a literary "mask" assumed by the writer in a recognizable literary and rhetorical tradition.[6] The more naïve he appears, the more suspicious we should be. Yet we might usefully distinguish two types of Roman self-fashioning invoked by the metaphor persona, literally meaning "mask," but metaphorically, by extension, the role someone plays onstage or (by further extension) in the theater of life. The first, more familiar type, then as now, is well described by Seneca in his essay on *Tranquillity of Mind*:

> And this, too, affords no small occasion for anxieties—if you are bent on assuming a pose (*si te anxie componas*) and never reveal yourself to anyone frankly (*simpliciter*), in the fashion of many who live a false (*ficta*) life that is all made up for show; for it is torturous to be constantly watching oneself and be fearful of being caught out of our usual role. And we are never free from concern if we think that every time anyone looks at us he is always taking our measure, for many things happen that strip off our pretence against our will, and, though all this attention to self is successful, yet the life of those who live under a mask (*sub persona*) cannot be happy and without anxiety. But how much pleasure there is in simplicity that is pure (*sincera*), in itself unadorned, and veils no part of its character! (*De Tranq.An.* 17.1–2, trans. Basore)

How much energy we spend "getting ourselves together" (*componas*, taken literally) for public view, keeping up appearances, and worrying about whether our mask might slip. Would it not be simpler and better just to be ourselves?

Satire strips away the mask, exposes the baseness beneath. Persius will go further, exposing his every pretension of "sincerity" and "simplicity," and indicating the real difficulty and complexity of "getting yourself together" in a philosophical, not superficial, sense. At the same time, Stoic teaching and social habit enforced a more positive notion of role playing, most carefully described in the so-called four-personae theory developed by Panaetius, a philosopher of the Romanizing Middle Stoa, in the mid-second century B.C., and splendidly reworked for a broader audience by Cicero in his *De Officiis* ("On Duties") in the first. Here, we are assigned four personae or roles in life. The first, and by far the most important, is that of our common humanity (a). Its inner core and guiding principle is the power of reason—the same power that steadies the great universe on its course. The other three personae include our individual differences and capabilities (b), the circumstances of life in which we find ourselves (c), and the careers or life-styles that we choose (d). In Christopher Gill's view, Panaetius's innovation was at once individualizing and socializing, putting less emphasis on the Stoic sage, the ideally wise man (*sapiens*), and more on the realization of individual differences of character and circumstance, but also locating the individual more surely than before in a network of social relationships and responsibilities.[7] Gretchen Reydams-Schils goes further, envisioning the Roman Stoic self as "a mediator between philosophic norms and the demands of society, ranging from those of spouse, children and kin to those of the political community."[8]

Might we, then, reimagine Persius's search for himself—for self-realization and integrity—in terms of the gifts and challenges of the four personae?[9] We think first of his satire-writing, a distinctive gift and calling (b, d), supported by privileged circumstances of money, status, and leisure (c); yet, in the Stoic hierarchy of values to which he subscribed, it cannot have taken precedence over the more general requirements of the rational human nature we all share (a), or the social, economic, and familial responsibilities (c) of a Roman-Etruscan landowner. What did these further roles entail for Persius's life and thought? For his poetry-writing?

First, again: our common human nature. In Stoic terms—going back in orthodox succession to the old Stoa, especially Chrysippus, but creatively reinterpreted in or shortly after Persius's time by Seneca, Musonius Rufus, and Epictetus—we are all called:

1. to cultivate and follow reason: for each one of us is endowed with a unitary rational soul, a small "torn-off fragment" of the world-soul, or world-*logos*, or god, which is our rightly ruling part (*hêgemonikon*);
2. to cultivate and exercise our power of moral choice (*prohaeresis* or *iudicium*, what in later times might be called the "will"), the inalienable faculty by which our integrity is maintained, whether in the face of tyrants' threats, or Fortune's trickery, or the everyday "presentations" of pleasure and pain, desire and fear;
3. to practice mindfulness and self-awareness, and to pursue consistency of life (*constantia*), through various exercises and disciplines, in-

cluding self-observation, testing, and criticism, memorization of basic ontological and moral axioms, and the internalization of good teaching and good advice; and

4. to recognize that we are all, at best, "progressives" (*proficientes*) who fall far short of the ideal sage (*sapiens*) in our thoughts and actions, and who, even if we seem to have reached a moral plateau, can always fall back into folly and vice: hence the urgency, now and always, of unremitting watchfulness and study.

Taken together, these precepts constitute a Stoic version of the call to self-realization enjoined by the god at Delphi ("Know Thyself"), and by Socrates ("Care for your soul"), or, in one of my own favorite quotations from Pindar, "Learn what sort of person you are, and become that person" (*genoi' hoios essi mathôn*, *Pythian* 2.72).

My epigrammatic teacher John Finley used to say, "It doesn't matter whether you're a poet or a squire; what matters is whether you're a saint or an egotist." Evidently, Persius followed his poetic bent, achieving (as he intended) a high degree of perfection in his art, and also (beyond his self-permitted hopes?) remarkable success in later ages. What is less obvious is that he was also a "squire," much of whose time and energy was probably spent not in writing poetry, but rather in carrying out everyday duties, *officia*.[10] Did he treat his tenants well? Did he abuse his slaves? We cannot know. Good people may profit from unjust systems. What we are told, in a surviving and largely reliable *Vita*,[11] is that Persius had "most gentle manners, modesty like a maiden's, a beautiful reputation," and showed "exemplary devotion (*pietas*) towards his mother, his sister, and his aunt. An honest fellow, and chaste." This is no small praise. It was once the fashion among (predominantly male) scholars to speak patronizingly of Persius as a bookish poet surrounded by adoring female relatives, "his sisters and his cousins and his aunts." Happily, that time is past—though prejudices linger. It seems reasonable, in the end, to imagine a good poet who was also trying, in accord with his best Stoic principles, to be a good man, and whose achieved perfection of the art of Latin verse satire may, in its own peculiar way, have provided a working model—or better, *a playing model*—for the life he felt called to lead, and a way of mediating between his joyfully individualizing talent, his social responsibilities, and the underlying demands of his god-given, rational human nature.

Readers over the centuries have found in Persius's satires a moral seriousness and sincerity that they missed, despite their other, often greater merits, in Horace and Juvenal. I would rather speak not of his sincerity, but of his *will to sincerity*, conditioned by a more profound awareness of interior obstacles than Seneca, for example, pauses to acknowledge; and not of his moral seriousness, but of the peculiar mix of Stoic seriousness and imaginative play in the *Satires*. Here is another key passage:

> verba togae sequeris iunctura callidus acri,
> ore teres modico, pallentis radere mores
> doctus et ingenuo culpam defigere ludo.   (5. 14–16)

> [You go for ordinary words, keenly and shrewdly
> combined in a moderate style; you are skilled at
> scraping pale-sick habits, nailing down faults in
> free-spirited play.]

Against a comically depicted background of grandiose epic and tragic effusions of contemporary poetasters, an inner or internalized voice of sanity and taste—perhaps Cornutus's admonitory voice—reauthorizes Persius, reminding him of his true objectives in writing satire. His style (following Horace's) is unpretentious. He uses ordinary words, though shrewdly and strikingly conjoined; he bites off no more than he can chew. The metaphors, typically, recall Horatian definitions and twist them in unexpected directions, relating them now to the "mouthings" of bad poets described earlier. Metaphorically, too, Persius compares his satire's moral aim to the doctor's diagnostic method ("You're looking pale.") and the surgical practice of scraping away diseased flesh. We can say that he writes diagnostic satire about the ills of contemporary society—and self-diagnostic satire, too, examining his own faults as representative of others' but prior in their demand for treatment. Finally, the satirist has learned "to nail down faults in free-spirited play" (or, "in a free man's play"). The time-honored purpose and justification of satire, to denounce vice and folly, to pin down blame, putting it firmly where it belongs, is circumscribed, verbally and figuratively, by play. What is this play, and what does it imply about the writer?

Forms of *ludere/ludus* and related terms of playing and leisure are themselves used playfully and ironically by poets writing in minor genres like lyric, pastoral, and satire who contrast their "fooling around in verse" to the higher tasks of epic and tragic poets. Thus Lucilius, the founder of Roman satire as we know it, speaks of his "playful discourses" (*ludo ac sermonibus nostris* [1039 M], a hendiadys for satire). The irony, of course, is that Hellenistic poets of minor genres like Callimachus and Theocritus, or the Roman Catullus and his fellow-Moderns *(Neoteri)* after them, write for educated readers who will appreciate the enormous amount of skill and labor, revision and polishing, that has gone into these light, seemingly effortless effusions. So here, for Persius: his satire-writing is serious in ways that bad contemporary epic and tragedy are not. Secondly, however, the now-trite commonplace of artistic "play" reverses itself, becoming true in a different sense, for in relation to the serious demands (*seria*) of Stoic philosophy—the call to intellectual, moral, and spiritual self-refashioning, not to mention life's more ordinary duties—poetry-writing might indeed seem a trivial diversion, a mere "fooling-around in words," after all. But then again—in a second reversal of ironies—Persius's play with words may complement and abet his philosophical homework. His savage humor probes faults, weaknesses, pretensions—his own, not least. For example, by questioning the "persona of sincerity" developed by Lucilius and Horace, by putting his own deepest claims to sincerity in quotation marks, as it were, and undercutting them with a certain residual self-mockery, Persius conveys a powerful new sense of sincerity, joining the intense seriousness of Stoic intentionality with an equally powerful humor that strips away pretension, acknowledges limitation and failure, and tests the practical realization of integrity and spiritual freedom.[12]

To call Persius a Stoic poet is misleading. His poetry, though infused with Stoic concepts and values, is not didactic (though it shares important human insights with Lucretius's didactic epic, *De Rerum Natura*). As satire, it asserts its own special autonomy, its own originality of exploration. And what it discovers is often surprising. Among other things, it acknowledges powerful and dangerous feelings of desire and fear, anger and grief, scorn and rebellion and self-disgust, that Stoic theorists and teachers too easily dismiss. The poetry does not, I think, contradict the philosophy, but it tests its results in the person of one unusually sensitive and self-aware human being. Given his own play with the term *componere*, "to put together," we might speak of Persius's attempts at poetic composition and Stoic self-composure as parallel, reciprocally self-clarifying experiments in "getting things together" in a world replete with folly, vice, and general disintegration.

▣   ▣   ▣

Persius is a notoriously difficult author.[13] Even Isaac Casaubon, his most zealous and influential defender, who praised his moral vigor, the thematic coherence and urgency of his satires, and his "obvious sincerity," was hard-pressed to explain what seemed his deliberate obscurity: through difficulties inherent in the genre, the passing of time, and the author's (presumable) intention.[14] Few professors today, let alone students, will read Persius—or Juvenal, for that matter—without a translation and commentary at hand. But let me change focus. Let me ask not why Persius is so difficult, but why he is so *demanding*—what he expects of his readers. And here we find help. In *Satire* 1, Persius develops an opening question, " '*Quis leget haec?*' " (" '*Who will read this stuff?*' ") into a reflective self-challenge to his artistic and personal integrity. He will write what and as he must. He accepts the loneliness that comes, in part, from refusal to worry about pleasing an audience. Yet, after working through the causes and implications of that refusal, he feels free toward the end of *Satire* 1 to reverse course, to revert to the familiar topic (after Lucilius and Horace) of the reader he wants, or does not want:

> audaci quicumque adflate Cratino
> iratum Eupolidem praegrandi cum sene palles,
> aspice et haec, si forte aliquid decoctius audis.
> inde vaporata lector mihi ferveat aure, . . .   (1. 123–26)

[Whoever you are, who have been inspired by a blast from bold Cratinus; who grow pale over Eupolis's anger and the Great Old Man, then look at these things too, if by chance you're able to listen to something quite concentrated. I want a reader who, with his ear steamed open, can come to a good slow boil.]

The key word is *palles*, "grow pale." It indicates, first, the long hard work of study, of reading into the night by lamplight, necessary now if one is to understand and enjoy the canonical three great poets of Athenian Old Comedy—Cratinus, Eupolis, and (climactically) Aristophanes—for Old Comedy, unlike New, is marked by strange old forms and conventions, references to things and persons and transient political events and concerns, that require careful elucidation. But secondly, it suggests what it feels like for an attentive and sensitive reader to experience the sheer power and inspiration (*adflate*) of the Old Comedy, which bursts upon one like a mighty storm. If you restage Aristophanes in the theater of your own mind, you will "grow pale" from the greatness and power of that ancient laughter, the gut-felt conviction it still can bring after all these years. So, too, with Persius's satire, which returns (after Horace's deviation) to an Old Comic allegiance; which requires, in its turn, careful study and explication; and which, too, should be read "with fear and trembling." It requires a reader with openable ears, one who can accept the cleansing bite of strong satire, which diagnoses and operates upon our individual and social sickness (*palles*, again); a reader who, in an implicitly punning change of metaphor, will not "favor" Persius (*foveat*) as a wished-for partisan, but will "seethe" (*ferveat*) from reading his poetry, like an old man in Aristophanes, maybe, recooked into youthful vitality and healthy-mindedness.

Yes, Persius is difficult. But so are Donne and Herbert, and Milton, and Dryden and Pope (especially for students ignorant of the Bible and the Classics), and Hopkins and Yeats, and Eliot, whose expression of personal, social, and cultural fragmentation "in different voices" I shall use as a touchstone for Persius's somewhat Modernist subject-matter and style.[15] But Persius's difficulty, though poetically and culturally explicable like theirs, may offer special advantages that we would not find, say, in Horace or Juvenal. For one thing, it resists familiarity. Readers over the ages may have succumbed, as I once did, to the illusion that Horace was their friend, that he invited them into his confidence, into his inner circle; not so with Persius. For another thing, because Persius died young, leaving only six satires, people generally grapple, as best they can, with his entire opus—but how many read all of Horace's *Satires* and *Epistles*, or Juvenal's *Satires*?

The philologians' efforts to clarify Persius's famous "obscurity" have been continuous and cumulative, from the ancient scholiasts to the present day. We are privileged inheritors of a long and unbroken textual tradition—of old manuscripts copied and recopied, corrected and recorrected, and printed texts of unusual accuracy—against which most textual problems affect our reading only in very minor ways. I work with three excellent texts before me: Wendell Clausen's *editio maior* of Persius (1956), his *Persius and Juvenal* (1959), and Domenico Bo's *Persio* (1969). I have also benefited from many fine commentaries, from Conington (1893) to Harvey (1981) and Kissel (1990, almost nine hundred pages in German). If a few lines still remain obscure, it is not from scholarly inertia.

The critics' work, too, is cumulative. Much of what we do today builds on older foundations, and especially on practices of close reading established, roughly, between 1955 and 1970, when the "New Criticism" (new only to Classics) took hold: when a few brave pioneers traced patterns of diction and rhetorical style, explored metaphorical continuities, identified speaking voices, asserted the poetic coherence and closed unity of the individual satire, and distinguished the satirist persona from the inaccessible poet behind the scenes, who tended to fade, not unlike the eighteenth-century Deity, into a critical limbo of mere authorial implication. Only the text was real and accessible, to be mastered by sophisticated critics like ourselves.[16]

Now a younger generation weaned on postmodernist theory has grown up; and, just as we old-timers once rebelled against the strictures of philological positivism, so our successors in turn have reveled in the manifold pleasures of questioning New-Critical assumptions and dogmas, playing outside the white lines, and implicating their own readings and ours in a vertiginous regression of meanings. Yet even as I grow pale over, say, John Henderson's essays on Roman satire, I realize how appropriate their naughty playfulness, their radical questioning and self-questioning, and their multiple perspectivity are to Persius—indeed, how they turn criticism itself into a form of satire. At the same time, I feel reassured by the sense of shared enterprise and mutual support in a lonely world that I continue to find among Persius scholars, and by their careful assimilation and acknowledgment of earlier work on which they have built. How much I have learned from them all, in turn—from Freudenburg, Hooley, Keane, and

Relihan; from Braund and Henderson; from Citroni, La Penna, and Pasoli, and so many others—will be evident from my many grateful citations.

Amid all these changes, I have watched the ongoing, rapidly shifting "negotiations" between author, text, and reader with some fascination. Although the text as we have it remains, as it must, a primary focus of study, we have come to realize as never before the radical contingency of poetry-reading, as it changes in every moment of reception (or what, for Persius, I shall call "reperformance"); and we have begun to ask whether the loud-trumpeted "death of the author" has not been—as Mark Twain once said about reports of his death—"somewhat exaggerated."[17] But what interests me most today is how these postmodern studies may also, as the cycles turn, help us find our way back, through distraction and fragmentation of perspectives, to a reconsideration of older, still vital questions about poetry and poets: not least, how they speak to us (if indeed they do), and how, through time and change, we may still enjoy and appreciate their work. I give three examples.

1. Reader-response theory, back in the 1970s, brought new, playful awareness of reading as a dynamic process, a moving event. As we read, we form impressions, which, even if they prove mistaken, still matter; indeed, the writer may have intended them to matter (Fish, on Milton). Reading is "a process that occurs linearly through time"; it evokes "a series of provisional responses"; it should not just be judged teleologically, from the end-point (Slater, on Petronius). Jauss's three readings, each containing a multitude, are highly suggestive for classicists (cf. Edmunds on Horace, *Odes* 1.9). With George Steiner, I would put even more emphasis on the (somewhat naïve) enthusiasm of the first, "aesthetic" reading, which has a special delight and energy of its own, not unlike the time of courtship before couples settle down to more serious business.[18]

2. Reader-reception theory has added new dimensions to the older study, so basic to my work, of Persius's allusions to Horace—or, more modernly, of "the way in which intertextuality creates meaning in texts through a dialectic between resemblance and difference" (Fowler).[19] It always was, and remains, so very helpful to study Persius's *Satires* against the background of Horace's *Satires* and *Epistles*, whose presence there is reassuringly pervasive and unchallenged (compare Homer behind Virgil, and contrast Lucilius behind Horace, so largely unavailable to us).[20] It is this omnipresence of Horace that gives us confidence when we perceive any one allusion or cluster of allusions as intentional—or better, as drawn from half-unconscious memory and consciously welcomed and reshaped into new poetry. We see much of Persius's debt to Horace, and something of his competitive anxiety, as he echoes key words, phrases, even passages from his predecessor and rings his own self-defining changes on these. A running definition

of Persius: he is not Horace. But Horace will not be satisfied today to play the passive foil. He keeps changing as we read him through Persius's eyes. We see what Horace was not, but also what he might have become under different conditions (Nero for Augustus, Cornutus for Maecenas); so we may study "Persius's influence on Horace," conducting a kind of shuttle diplomacy between the two. [21] Furthermore, once we have read Juvenal (see my epilogue), we can never read Persius in the same way again. And there are still more complications, involving myself as over-reader. Not only does Persius change on my every reading ("You cannot step into the same text twice"); not only is my reading of Persius conditioned by all my other reading, my cultural and educational baggage, my entire life so far, but I am also allowing this poet to read *me*, to challenge my habitual perceptions, to turn me pale.[22] So we are, both of us, in flux. All very exciting— but not an easy tangle for the postmodern critic to unravel.

3. My argument draws heavily on performance theory. Roman oratory, whether in court or senate or military assemblies, was a performative art, most skillful when it seemed most spontaneous; and so was Roman poetry, from its inception, when the poet first mouthed or subvocalized his or her words; through various revisions, as s/he dictated them to a skilled slave, and tried them out on a friend or a small, select audience of friends; to first publication, when they passed beyond the poet's control into the hands of an unknown, promiscuous variety of readers and listeners. So, too, with Persius: although he wrote very privately, left publication to his executors, and had, as will be seen, no illusions about his poetic afterlife—although, indeed, he foresaw that same radical dependence of poetry on future readers, who would be perfectly capable of turning his *Satires* into a mockery of themselves at one bad dinner-party or another—still, his poetry grew out of private creative performance, and it was aimed finally at those who could *hear* it: that is, could reperform it well to themselves and then to others. I want to argue that, despite all those famous "difficulties," if we will just read Persius's *Satires* aloud as they were meant to be read—declaiming them, for a start, to our own initially half-uncomprehending selves—then we shall recover more than we might expect of the pleasure of the performance, the delight that balances out pain, the old-and-new *jouissance* that initiates us into the company of Persius's listeners and admirers over the centuries.

But pleasure, they say, is never innocent.[23] What function, New Historicists and cultural materialists might ask, did the performance of Roman satire serve, and to whose profit (*cui bono*)? To disciples of Bourdieu, Roman satire would function as an enhancement of "cultural capital," reinforcing the status of a socially and economically privileged elite against outsiders, redefining and perpetuating their shared values, while also affording a new field of play for old male competitiveness.[24] What such ideological interpretations occlude in their turn is, first, the pervasive ambiguity of satire, which, like its ancestor, the Greek Old Comedy, now reaffirms, now subverts inherited *mores*—a special case now of the Hellenistic Greek culture, at once admired and distrusted, that "conquered its fierce Roman conqueror." Secondly, Roman satire criticizes self as well as others; it presses, sometimes Socratically, toward self-knowledge; in Horace's hands and, still more, in Persius's, it becomes a self-consuming artefact. And, thirdly: Roman satire shows the modern-day critic, as in a mirror, the moral and intellectual limitations of his or her critical metaperformance, so that the joke, as Persius will insist, is now on us, the challenge passes to us. How should we respond in our criticism, and in our lives?

My overall approach in this book is not (intentionally) ideological, but intuitive and empirical; I like hermeneutical circles and Jaussian rereadings; I subscribe to the larger ideals of aesthetic criticism, involving form and content together, that Charles Martindale, for one, has persuasively defended against neoreductionist attacks.[25] At the book's core is still the excitement I felt when I first encountered Persius in Rab Brooks's Roman Satire course back in Spring 1951, an excitement often rekindled through subsequent decades of study and teaching. "The communication / of the dead," wrote Eliot, "is tongued with fire beyond the language of the living."[26] So I believe, and will argue in this difficult test case; but my argument, however many times rewoven to accommodate new insights, approaches, and criticisms, in the end remains personal and subjective, a multileveled excavation report that I hope others who come after me will find instructive, and even encouraging.

Plan of the Book

Recognizing Persius is a revised and expanded version of my 1999 Martin Classical Lectures at Oberlin College. Because this book is aimed primarily at students, teachers, and others interested in Roman satire, and only secondarily at specialists in Horace and Persius, I have deliberately kept my presentation informal, as in the Lectures. The following plan indicates my main directions and concerns.

Chapter 1, *Performing Privately*, traces the movement in *Satire* 1 from Persius's initial rejection of anxiety about his poetic reception, a rejection based on the total corruption, as he sees it, of aesthetic and moral standards in poetry-writing and criticism, to his about-face, re-entry into the literary fray, and redefinition of his preferred audience. *Satire* 1 also introduces the *Satires* as dramatic monologues "in different voices" (Eliot) that must be performed, if only inwardly, to be appreciated, and sets Persius's paradoxical "non-performance" against the performative background of the satires of Lucilius and Horace. The *Choliambics*, also heralding his "nonpoetry," are discussed in appendix 1.

Chapter 2, *Seeking Integrity*, moves from the multiple challenge of spiritual corruption and religious hypocrisy in *Satire 2* to the horrific images of decomposition in *Satire 3*, which seem to overwhelm, even as they reinforce, the usual philosopher-doctor comparison. As Persius reactualizes themes and techniques of the Cynic-Stoic diatribe, deconstructing Horace's parodies in his *Satires* but also developing strong though only tentative initiatives in his *Epistles*, he brings a powerful new inwardness and intensity to satire's dramatic monologue, reshaping it as an effective diagnostic and, still more, self-diagnostic instrument. Similarities to Epictetus's teaching, in the next generation, are striking (appendix 2).

Chapter 3, *Exploring Freedom*, moves down, in *Satire 4*, to an abyss of self-ignorance and slander where philosophy fails, or seems to fail, and satire becomes its own vilest object, and then up again, in *Satire 5*, as Persius recalls his youthful Stoic conversion under Cornutus's tutelage, which in turn reauthorizes him to resume the Quixotic struggle—but confidently, and in good humor—against the vices and follies of humankind. The last section moves outside the text to ask, with the aid of Václav Havel, what effectiveness, if any, Persius's "dissidence" may have had in Nero's Rome.

Chapter 4, *Life, Death, and Art*, speculates further on the relation between Persius's art and life, the poet and the squire; proceeds through a reading of *Satire 6*, so near to Horace and yet (passionately) so far; and reviews the *libellus*, the little book of poems, as a whole, emphasizing the "Ages-of-Man" theme, the challenge of personal growth, and satire's response to its almost universal failure. A final section, again about art and life, broaches the idea of satire as "emotional recognizance."

The Epilogue, *From Persius to Juvenal*, gives examples of how Juvenal adapted Persius's language and motifs, especially in *Satires 1* and *7*, and argues that his "strong readings" can still bring us back to Persius with renewed appreciation.

Chapter One

𝔉 𝔉 𝔉 𝔉 𝔉 𝔉 𝔉 𝔉 𝔉 𝔉 𝔉 𝔉 𝔉 𝔉 𝔉 𝔉

PERFORMING PRIVATELY

Hᴇʀᴇ, more or less, are the facts, according to the unusually reliable *Vita* that has come down to us. Persius was born in Volaterrae (modern Volterra) in northwest Etruria on 4 December ᴀ.ᴅ. 34. He died of a stomach ailment on 24 November ᴀ.ᴅ. 62, shortly before his twenty-eighth birthday. A Roman knight with blood ties to senatorial families, he came from a rich old Etruscan family and received a first-class education in literature and rhetoric in Rome from two distinguished teachers, Remmius Palaemon and Verginius Flavus. Persius's father died when he was around six and his stepfather died not long afterwards. He was, says the *Vita*, "a person of gentlest ways, of virginal modesty, handsome repute, and exemplary devotion (*pietatis . . . exemplo sufficientis*) to his mother, his sister, and his aunt." He was related to the younger Arria, whose parents were forced to commit suicide under the emperor Claudius after a failed conspiracy, and from the age of ten he enjoyed a close friendship with her husband, Thrasea Paetus, the best-known Stoic dissident under Nero. Persius's friends also included the poet Caesius Bassus and some older men who served as foster-fathers and mentors: Servilius Nonianus, a man of affairs; two philosopher-doctors from Greece and Asia; and most important, the learned Annaeus Cornutus, a freedman and scholar who wrote Greek treatises on theology and literature—the Stoic role model par excellence of Persius's *Satire 5*.

Although orientation in time and place is useful, I might better have let Persius speak for himself from the start. Biographical criticism in his case is always so tempting, and so misleading: partly, because we still know so little about his life and work; and partly, because that little has all too often produced a distorted, itself easily satirized image of a sheltered poet with little experience of the world, surrounded by philosophical treatises and adoring female relatives. The modernist reaction, as said earlier, redirected us to the safely bounded space of the text, the postmodernist to the unbounded vagaries of readers' imaginations. But now, I wonder: has the time come round to pay renewed attention to the author? Not just the "implied author" safely embedded in the text, but the person behind the text who lived and died; who fought hard, as it seems, for his integrity and moral freedom; and who, amid his many duties and concerns (to which I shall return in chapter 4), wrote Satires.

But why did he write satire? He was well-born, rich, and independent, with no need to secure a patron or consolidate his position in society. His own version in *Satire* 1 develops traditional lines of defense: he writes because he must; because truth will out; because if he doesn't cry out against the world's follies, he will simply burst. On closer inspection, it seems likely that Persius regarded his writings at once as playful self-indulgence, as a competitive bid for mastery in the field of Roman satire, and as a means of unusually intense self-scrutiny and self-debate, freely conducted but ultimately reinforcing the aim of living honestly and well. His satire attacks vice and folly, to be sure, and with greater urgency than ever; but it also affords a special kind of emotional self-recognizance, giving voice to powerfully distracting thoughts and feelings that require, even as they resist, Stoic reorganization and control—which will never in his lifetime be quite complete. In turn, I suggest, Persius felt enabled to compete with Lucilius and Horace, his predecessors, the "scourger of vice" and the master-ironist, not least because his satire had something new and exciting to discover, and to proclaim.

My first chapter focuses on *Satire* 1 and the theme of performance. In earlier Roman tradition, satire was usually performed at elite dinner-parties for a sympathetic audience of friends and allies before it was circulated and/or published. Against this background, and confronted now with bad performances of epic and tragedy, and also criticism, in a world increasingly hostile to free and honest speech, Persius gives his own very private nonperformance or metaperformance of satire, speaking his passionate findings into the as yet secret "hole" of his little book.

"Who'll Read This Stuff?" (*Satire* 1)

The beginning of *Satire* 1 plunges us into intense dialogue between undefined voices:

> **O curas hominum! o quantum est in rebus inane!**
> *"quis leget haec?"* <u>min tu</u> istud ais? nemo hercule. *"nemo?"*
> vel duo vel nemo. *"turpe et miserabile."* quare?
> ne mihi *Polydamas et Troiades* Labeonem
> praetulerint? nugae. non, si quid turbida Roma
> elevet, accedas examenve improbum in illa
> castiges trutina, nec te quaesiveris extra.
> nam Romae quis non—a, si fas dicere—sed fas
> tum cum ad canitiem et nostrum istud vivere triste

aspexi ac nucibus facimus quaecumque relictis,
cum sapimus patruos. tunc tunc—ignoscite (nolo,
quid faciam?) sed sum petulanti splene—cachinno.   (1–12)

**O cares of men! O how much emptiness
there is in things!** *"Who'll read this stuff?"*
You're asking *me* that? No one, by Hercules.
"No one?" Maybe two people, maybe no one.
"Shameful and pathetic." Why? Afraid
Polydamas and the Trojan Women might prefer
Labeo to me? Nonsense. If muddled Rome
makes light of something, you shouldn't join in;
you shouldn't blame the faulty tongue of the scale
or look outside yourself. For at Rome, who
[is? or does?] not—ah, if it's right to speak—
but of course it's right, when I look at those gray hairs
and the grim, "grown-up" front we display, though living
in any way whatsoever—it's then, it's then
(sorry, can't help it, my spleen compels me), I have
to roar with laughter.

Editors help, and commentators, going back to Persius's own time. Wendell Clausen's careful punctuation reflects his own interpretive efforts and, in turn, shapes mine, which I convey through different fonts on my Macintosh. The old scholiasts tell us that Persius quotes Lucilius in line 1—or is it line 2?—but we don't have the context, or much of Lucilius, for that matter.[1] We learn that Labeo wrote a Latin *Iliad* (apparently, an overliteral translation): how is this relevant? We must recreate for ourselves the conventions of Prologue Satire that Persius inherited from Lucilius and Horace, the expectations of the audience for whom he refuses to write. Still more, we must recreate for ourselves from reading and rereading Persius the tone and rhythm of this passage: the quick, passionate exchanges; the scornful rejection of contemporary Roman criticism, wonderfully represented by *"Polydamas and the Trojan women"* out of the *Iliad*, once Homer's, now the wretched Labeo's; the great, dangerous Question that desperately wants to be posed but can't be, yet; and the renewed, now doubly intense build-up of scornful indignation, with its premature climax (so to speak) of wild, helpless laughter.

In the usual reading of these lines, Persius announces his great satiric theme of human folly (in a line probably taken from his satiric grandfather Lucilius and enriched with Lucretian resonances of "the void in things"; the result is something like the opening of *Ecclesiastes*, where the Preacher proclaims, "Vanity of Vanities, all is vanity" [or "vapor"]);[2] but he is interrupted by an interlocutor, perhaps a concerned friend. " '*Who'll read this stuff?'* " A good, practical question, then as now. It also hints at a warning that will be made explicit later in the satire, one that was well established in satiric tradition and in readers' expectations, and that acquires new urgency under Nero: "Why offend tender little ears with the biting truth? Be careful, or important people's doors will freeze you out." Satire is offensive, and the satirist will pay.

"Who am I? In what genre am I writing, and why, and for whom?" A Prologue Satire usually answers these questions, however ironically or obliquely; Lucilius started the trend of conveying the answers rhetorically as a response, whether to kindly warnings, importunate suggestions, or outright attacks. (In other genres, too, real or imagined attacks provide an excellent excuse for the writer's *apologia*, a reasoned account of his life and work.) Fragments of Lucilius's satires, scattered lines or groups of lines, show him debating with adversaries. "You are malicious," they say, "You like to hurt people. And you'll be sorry." They want him to keep quiet, perhaps only "mutter," if he must, under his breath. To which he answers that he is a good, honest man who speaks from the heart, unlike flatterers and hypocrites, and who must speak out: it is his way, and it benefits society.[3] Differently, a respected older friend advises and warns Lucilius: writing satire is dangerous; wouldn't it be better, say, to write historical epic? That would "bear fruit" (*fructum*, implying usefulness, money, success). In response, Lucilius presumably explains why he writes, and for whom. We have the second part. He writes, not for just anybody, but for an educated minority, neither philistines nor pedants, who will appreciate what he has to say.[4]

Horace develops similar arguments in his literary satires 1.4 and 1.10, polishing them with wonderfully teasing irony as he turns Lucilian statements against the very critics who would defend their beloved Lucilius, their classic satirist, against this interloper. His satire (he alleges) is not malicious, or dangerous, or even public; he only shows it (unlike Lucilius?) to a few very select readers and critics, men of true discrimination for whom, in the end, he writes. And if he criticizes Lucilius for his stylistic faults and the generally rough carelessness of his satire writing, he is only following the master, who criticized epic and tragic poets in his time, and bringing him up to date. The attacks on Horace, real or imagined or a mixture of both, once again provide the rhetorical impetus for the poet's full, if ironic, statement of his aesthetic and moral standards and intentions in writing satire. Differently, in *Satires* 2.1, the prologue to Book 2 (and Persius's chief model), an older friend, the lawyer Trebatius, warns Horace that satire is dangerous: better an epic praising Caesar! Horace replies with wonderful excuses. He writes because he has to; it is his bent, or hobby; a weapon, yes, but only for self-defense, or Lucilian self-revelation—not antisocial, in the end, but beneficial. The satire ends jokingly, or not so jokingly, with Horace receiving Caesar's seal of approval. So much for law!

When, therefore, Persius's interlocutor asks " '*Who'll read this stuff?*' " we quickly envision the speaker as a helpful friend concerned with Persius's practical success and, still more, with the riskiness of satire writing. Again, as with Lucilius and Horace, the warning provokes Persius to say why he writes, and for whom. He writes, as we learn later, because he has to—has to voice the truth, somehow, about a society whose moral and aesthetic standards are totally corrupt. But he is silenced, or almost silenced, for the same reason. Unlike Lucilius and Horace, he has virtually no audience left. "Maybe two people, maybe no one." The riddle remains unsolved,[5] but Persius will show us, in this first satire, why he can't write for an audience like Lucilius's or Horace's. Those reasonable, moderately educated people are gone. But the danger is more real than ever, the warning more necessary, the challenge greater. Why, and how, and for whom (ultimately) should one write satire in the age of Nero?

As it turns out, Persius's first question, " '*quis leget haec?*' " is integrally involved with the second, "nam Romae quis non . . . ," broken off at line 8 and only completed at 121: "auriculas asini quis non habet?" "Who [at Rome, maybe in the whole world] hasn't asses' ears?" The reference is to the Midas story. Asked to judge a musical contest between Apollo and Pan (or, in some versions, the satyr Marsyas), Midas chose Pan and was given asses' ears for his bad taste.[6] He hid them under a cap. His barber learned the secret, could not speak out, but desperately wanted to tell it, so he dug a hole in the ground and whispered the truth into that hole, which he covered up; but reeds grew up, and when a breeze blew, you could hear the reeds saying, "King Midas has asses' ears." So Persius will whisper the truth, the dread secret, into his little satire book. It looks as if some early commentator, meaning to be helpful, wrote in the gloss, "auriculas asini Mida rex habet" ("King Midas has asses' ears"), and someone else then probably explained this gloss by means of a new story: evidently, Persius's friend and mentor, the Stoic philosopher Cornutus, had induced him to substitute the generalizing "quis non habet" ("who hasn't . . . ?") for the direct mention of Midas, which might strike Nero's ears as too personal.[7] Obviously, the story is foolish. In Nero's world, any reference to Midas's story, however indirect, was quite sufficient to get one exiled or killed (and there was no shortage of informers ready and willing to serve as amateur literary critics).[8] Obviously, too, the punch line, "auriculas asini quis non habet," precisely completes the revelation broken off much earlier, "nam Romae quis non . . . ?"

I propose that Persius's two questions are interdependent. It is a case of "the reciprocal clarification of two unknowns." Let x stand for Persius's readership and y for the dangerous, unspoken truth about Rome. Persius teases us by delaying his revelation; he plays games of desire and constraint, pressure and (self-)censorship, and explosive bursts of uncontrollable laughter; but the delay also gives him time to show us the corruption of taste at Rome, building (when we are ready) to the full revelation of the second question, and clarifying the acute problem of the first.

So far my reading of Persius's opening lines has been fairly traditional. Let me now try a different reading, which I prefer. I suggest that line 1, probably taken from Lucilius, presents human folly as the satire book's general theme; and that the first half of line 2, probably also taken from Lucilius, introduces the specific theme of *Satire* 1. In part, then, it serves as a subtitle. But the old warning given by an opponent or external adviser has now become internalized, a voice from within the poet himself, anxious about his effectiveness.[9] Will his satire be read? Will it make a difference? This is the voice of common sense—a rather Horatian voice, in fact. But a second, stronger voice rejects the very question, with all its implied concerns. It rejects, contemptuously and decisively, any imagined compromise with what will turn out to be a world of flattery, falsehood, and bad taste. "You know better," it says, "than to take popular opinion seriously, to measure the worth of anything by public standards. Don't look outside yourself."

From line 2, then, Persius brings himself (and us, with him) into a passionately intense inner dialogue. The words "*min tu* istud ais" (*"You're* asking *me that?"*) are an inside joke. And the culminating advice, "nec te quaesiveris extra," is grammatically ambiguous: more obviously, it means, "Don't look outside yourself," but there is an important secondary suggestion: "Don't look for yourself outside." In his writing, as in his life, Persius is primarily in search of himself. Good writing, for him, requires good self-criticism, which in turn cannot be separated from self-knowledge such as Socrates and the Stoics advocated, or from the pursuit and expression of truth. That is why he begins by shutting out the public—shutting out all of us—so very emphatically. He can't afford to let himself be distracted by all those inane concerns, doubts, warnings, and expectations (including, most emphatically, his own). He has to slam the door: "vel duo, vel nemo." Yet he will explain himself, if we will listen, during the course of *Satire* 1, and by its end, his no will turn to yes, and he will define his satiric aims, after all, and even his wished-for audience, as Lucilius and Horace did before him.

"In Different Voices"

When I used to teach a passage like *Satire* 1.1–12, I would read it aloud twice: once before working through it in detail and once afterwards, for my main purpose in teaching was to bring my students to read Latin poetry with understanding and enjoyment. The two work reciprocally. Without understanding—which requires looking up unfamiliar words like *examen* and *trutina* and *cachinno*, and picking up allusions (*Labeonem*) and peculiarities of idiom (*nostrum istud vivere triste*) from translations and commentaries, and trying to sort out these baffling voices and ideas, at least in a preliminary way—you cannot enjoy Persius. But you won't understand Persius, either, unless you enjoy him, even at first, by what might be called poetry's prevenient grace of seduction as you read out those striking phrases and lines. "O curas hominum! o quantum est in rebus inane!" They need, before anything else, to be heard.[10]

When we read Persius aloud, in the classroom or elsewhere, we reperform his satires. We recreate, that is, the dramatic and rhetorical effects of poems that grew out of a performance genre, even if, as Persius will demonstrate, they cannot be performed now for a general audience. Reading *Satire* 1, we recreate (as best we can) the clash of voices, the tension and excitement of internal dialogue within this powerful dramatic monologue.[11] We recreate the rise and fall of Persius's rhythms: the build-up, with enjambment, to the dismissive "nugae" (3–5); the build-up to a preliminary conclusion, "nec te quaesiveris extra," at 7, followed by the grave, deliberate, monosyllabic and heavily spondaic new beginning at 8 ("nam Romae quis non," each word heavily weighted); then the breaking-off, itself interrupted; the audial representation of slow, hypocritical, senile pretenders to morality, when really (in a quickening rhythm) old men fool around just like children; and then the climax, the unbrakeable slide into wild satiric laughter. An opening of extraordinary variety and power.

Widu-Wolfgang Ehlers has argued that orality is the missing dimension in interpretations of Persius. Many so-called obscurities, he believes, and especially the difficulty of distinguishing different speakers, would have been clarified by the early teachers, the *grammatici*, who used punctuation and other distinguishing marks (*distinctio*) in the texts from which they read aloud and taught. In Ehlers's view, our very difficulties prove the necessity of such illustrative oral readings.[12] I would go further and say that reading aloud not only tests and completes our interpretation of passages like *Satire* 1.1–12: it also reminds us that, despite satire's habitual disclaimers, we are reading poetry. And recreating what was once, if only in the private auditorium of Persius's mind, the pleasure of the performance.

That is why, before reviewing what we know about Lucilius, Horace, and the performance tradition of Roman satire up to Persius's time, I want to suggest the analogy of Eliot's *The Waste Land* with its abruptly introduced voices and scenes, its conflicting levels of style, and its inset dramatic sketches, what one early unappreciative critic called "the mingling of willful obscurity and weak vaudeville." It begins, famously, with incantation and mystery:

April is the cruellest month, breeding
Lilacs out of the dead land, mixing
Memory and desire, stirring
Dull roots with spring rain.
Winter kept us warm, covering
Earth in forgetful snow, feeding
A little life with dried tubers.
Summer surprised us, coming over the Sternbergersee
With a shower of rain; we stopped in the colonnade,
And went on in sunlight, into the Hofgarten,
And drank coffee, and talked for an hour.
Bin gar keine Russin, stamm' aus Litauen, echt Deutsch.
And when we were children, staying at the archduke's,
My cousin's, he took me out on a sled,
And I was frightened. He said, Marie,
Marie, hold on tight. And down we went.
In the mountains, there you feel free.
I read, much of the night, and go south in the winter.

The uncertain, shifting pronouns (who is the "us", the "we", the "you," the "I"?) surprise us, transporting us all too quickly from the grand, enigmatic and impersonal pronouncements of lines 1–4 to those curious images of European travel and society, those snatches of conversation or recollection. Who is speaking, asks the critic, and when, and with what authority? How are the parts connected in time and space? And why does Eliot borrow a bit of memoir by Marie Larisch, Empress Elizabeth's niece? Is it that the proud reality of the Austro-Hungarian empire has been reduced by the late war to nostalgic chatter? Or does the child's vivid experience of excitement and fun set off the jaded pretensions of ordinary grown-up life, with its timid evasions of seasonal reality, terror and passion, the burial of the dead and the renewal of life? In answering these questions, we can build now on eighty-plus years of scholarly annotation and interpretation, increasing knowledge of Eliot's life and work both before and after *The Waste Land*, and a theoretically informed criticism that not only accepts but positively welcomes connective gaps and celebrates the reader's role in creating meaning. Yet all this cumulative knowledge and critical sophistication may prove futile, may turn to dust and ashes in the mouth, unless it is balanced by the enjoyment that comes of listening to the poem—which means, reading it aloud and hearing it read by others. Only in this way can we recover, rather than evade, the weirdly mixed feelings of "excitement, bafflement, and terror" that ordinary readers experienced on its first appearance.[13] And, I would especially add, of laughter.

Originally, the poem was entitled, "He Do the Police in Different Voices," a title taken from Dickens's *Our Mutual Friend*. ("You mightn't think it," says the old woman, Betty Higden, "but Sloppy is a beautiful reader of a newspaper. He do the Police in different voices.")[14] An earlier draft of *The Waste Land* begins with a very funny sketch of some drunken gentlemen around town: "First we had a couple of feelers down at Tom's place . . ." Had Eliot not, by Ezra Pound's advice, red-penciled through this scene, *The Waste Land* would have been read more as a comic/satiric poem, less mysterious than it later became, and not demanding, or seeming to demand, so much reverence.[15]

Parallels between *The Waste Land* and Persius's *Satires* are striking. Both poets, to put it simply, are Modernists, reacting with fragmented vision to what they perceive as a fragmented culture, a spiritually bankrupt society.[16] Both ironize that vision, refracting it through "different voices." Both shift abruptly between different linguistic registers, echoing and parodying high epic, lyric, and tragedy, which evoke lost worlds of belief and value, even as they drop comically into the banal. Both depict a spiritual waste land crying out for redemption. And of course, both question the meaning and value of their own writing in such a broken world.

Other parallels involve the difficulty of the poetry and/or the excitement. Many readers feel frustration with a poet who seems to be trying their patience with deliberate, uncalled-for obscurity. One set of difficulties, wrote E. M. Forster, may be "due to our own incompetence or inattention," but the other is Eliot's fault, for he misleads us. From his personal suffering, his wish for stability, come

> the attempted impersonality and (if one can use the word here) the in-hospitality of his writing. Most writers sound, somewhere or other in their scale, a note of invitation. They ask the reader in, to co-operate or to look. . . . Mr. Eliot does not want us in. He feels we shall increase the barrenness. . . . He is difficult because he has seen something terrible, and . . . has declined to say so plainly.[17]

Contrast Eliot's own statement in his 1921 essay, "The Metaphysical Poets," contemporary with *The Waste Land*:

> We can only say that it appears likely that poets in our civilization, as it exists at present, must be difficult. Our civilization comprehends great variety and complexity, and this variety and complexity, playing upon a refined sensibility, must produce various and complex results. The poet must become more and more comprehensive, more allusive, more indirect, in order to force, to dislocate if necessary, language into his meaning.[18]

Just so, Persius might have responded to frustrated readers who complained, like the witty Scaliger, that he wanted his writings *"legi, non intellegi"* ("to be read, not understood"). Fortunately, others reacted differently. A powerful, lone sentence in the *Vita* describes how Persius's poetry was first received, after his death: *editum librum continuo mirari homines et deripere coeperunt.* "Straightway, when the book was published, people marveled at it and snatched it up."[19] It seems unlikely that these first enthusiasts understood the *Satires* very fully—though many references to people, things, and events would have been more immediately familiar to them than to later readers. But they lived in what was still largely an oral/aural environment, where poetry was read aloud and enjoyed. Although they missed the chance to hear their poet recite in person, they had skilled slave readers (*anagnôstai*) to read on demand from crabbedly written, unpunctuated manuscripts. And their children, if they were lucky, had teachers (*grammatici*) who enjoyed and understood Persius's *Satires* and passed that enjoyment and understanding on to later generations.

The present chapter is largely about "different voices" in performance. Its thesis is that Persius's satire belongs, after Lucilius and Horace, to a genre of dramatic entertainment in which the pleasure of the performance is essential, even for private readers. The antithesis, introduced by Persius in *Satire* 1, is that good satiric performance—as it involves good, honest criticism—becomes impossible when the ears of society are corrupted and clogged with dirt. What audience is left, and why (if at all) should one write? The synthesis, I shall argue, is *Satire* 1 itself: a satiric and comic metaperformance that both parodies bad literary and social performances and advertises itself, paradoxically, as a nonperformance, or better, as a very private performance whispered into a book, as into that barber's hole in the ground, and awaiting the right sort of reader to "dig it up again" (Eliot)—to reperform it well and appreciatively some day and bring it back to life.

Performing Satire (1): Lucilius and the Greek Background

Nothing has hurt the study of Roman verse satire more than the loss of Lucilius's satires, now reduced to scattered fragments. Not one satire that Horace uses, let alone Persius, can be reconstructed convincingly. Brave scholars who tried, like George Fiske, became trapped in circular argument, reconstructing Lucilius out of Horace and explaining Horace out of Lucilius. Yet fragments can speak, as the "mute stones" of archaeology are said to do. We can still hear Lucilius's voice as he proclaims himself a friend of virtue and an enemy of vice, or else, in a lower register, tells funny stories about himself or others. He calls his satires "playful conversations," *ludo ac sermonibus nostris* (1039M); the Latin *sermo* means not "sermon" but "talk": conversation, gossip, narrative presentations, and editorializing on a wide variety of social and literary subjects, usually in the "plain style," though its tone rises sometimes to great rhetorical heights. And Lucilius wrote these talks to be heard, not just read. They were dramatic pieces, sophisticated entertainment in the Hellenistic fashion, whether performed for friends at dinner parties and other festive occasions in private houses, or read aloud and reperformed by the moderately educated readers for whom Lucilius wrote, and then, after the poet's death, preserved in continuing performance by the teachers and critics of literature, the *grammatici*. I give a few examples, to illustrate Lucilius's dramatic range and his close affinity to comedy and mime.

His satiric defense, mentioned earlier, emerges from a dramatic *agôn*, a clash of voices. An adversary speaks:

> nunc, Gai, quoniam incilans nos laedis, vicissim . . . (1089M)
> gaudes, cum de me ista foris sermonibus differs. (1090M)

> [Now, Gaius, since you hurt us with lashing, in turn . . .
> You rejoice in spreading this gossip about me in your *sermones*.]

Satire, in this view, is malicious slander; the satirist delights in hurting people, attacking them personally (Greek *mnêsikakia*; Horace's *laedere gaudes*; German *Schadenfreude*). The later image of the satirist as a "lasher of vice," picked up by Persius in *Satire* 1,

>   secuit Lucilius urbem,
> te Lupe, te Muci, et genuinum fregit in illis,   (1.114–15)

> [Lucilius lashed the city, you, Lupus, and you, Mucius, and broke
> his back tooth on them,]

may come from this line where, if we listen carefully, the satirist is playing on his own name, Gaius Lu*cil*ius. He can't help it, he was born with a "cutting" way about him.

Elsewhere, Lucilius appears in the third person singular, whether (in a hostile report) someone is said to have assembled his friends for counsel, including "that wicked Lucilius" (821–22M; the name is deferred for special emphasis), or whether he represents himself as haranguing the general public in high Roman style:

> Rem populi salute et fictis versibus Lucilius
> quibus potest, impertit, totumque hoc studiose et sedulo.   (688–89M)

> [Lucilius greets the Commonwealth, bearing good news and
> made-up verses: all this with serious and constant purpose.]

The loose trochaic meter, the mock-serious use of a political-religious formula, the comic zeugma, the mix of casual speech and high poetic seriousness, with alliterative emphasis: all this could come from a Plautine prologue or, behind Plautus, from a parabasis of Aristophanes.

Differently, Lucilius relates a funny story, turning it into casual (for Horace, much too casual) verse:

conicere in versus dictum praeconis volebam
Grani.   (411–12M)

[I wanted to throw a clever saying of Granius, the
advertising man, into verse.]

The "dictum" is a "clever saying," very likely the punch line of a contest of *dicacitas*, or scurrilous wit, for which Granius was notorious. Lucilius made a specialty of reporting such contests, which range from gladiators' exchange of insults before their fights to mutual vilification in the lawcourt, an expected but dangerous side of oratory. In Book 2 he described the trial of Mucius Scaevola for embezzlement. Albucius, the prosecutor, attacks Scaevola as a bully, a glutton, and a lecher (the obscenity is unusually vivid, and very funny), but Scaevola has, it seems, the last word, making fun of Albucius's rhetorical extravagances and his exaggerated philhellenism, which invited a practical joke. Since Albucius wanted to be regarded as more Greek (that is, more cultured and sophisticated) than Roman, Mucius and his staff greeted him with a chorus of Greek: *Chaere Tite* ("Bonjour, Tite"). That is why, says Scaevola, Albucius became his personal enemy.

We would like to know more. Was Lucilius, as Erich Gruen has suggested, making fun of the feuding Roman nobility?[20] Or playing with old Italic versus new Greek styles of oratory? Even without the entire satire, we can see why Lucilius's (actually indirect) "lashing of Mucius" became a touchstone of his aggressive freedom and outspokenness, his satiric *libertas*, for Persius (quoted above) and later for Juvenal. Differently, our fragments tell us something about performance, with the help of Cicero's comment in *De Oratore* 3.43.171, where, speaking of smoothness of stylistic composition, the orator Crassus remarks that "on this point Lucilius, who could do it most elegantly, played amusingly in the character of my father-in-law" (*lepide soceri mei persona lusit*). Lucilius, that is, assumes the persona of Mucius Scaevola, mimics his voice, and parodies his style as part of a dramatic entertainment that his contemporaries and, by extension, his far-flung readers will enjoy.

I insist on this notion of dramatic entertainment for two reasons. First, it makes us aware of the performability of Roman satire, as of other kinds of poetry, and the kinds of meaning it acquires through performance. And second, despite Quintilian's famous dictum that "Satire is entirely ours"

(*Satira quidem tota nostra est*)—entirely Roman, that is, with no apparent Greek ancestry—if we look more closely, we find that Roman satire bears a family resemblance not only to the Greek Old Comedy of Aristophanes and the Greco-Roman New Comedy of Menander, Plautus, and Terence, but also to such other dramatic or quasi-dramatic entertainment-forms, popular in the Hellenistic Age, as *iambos*, mime, and pastoral. Indeed, the old notion of a "dramatic *satura*," mentioned by Livy, and long since exploded as a probably Varronian invention to fill out a neo-Aristotelian scheme of the development of Roman drama, may prove useful after all, for early Roman satire resembles nothing so much as a "variety show" covering many unrelated subjects (the basic meaning of *satura* being "fullness and variety," though Lucilius gave it what afterwards became its defining character of aggressiveness and indecency).[21] Consider, briefly, satire's relation to comedy and to the *iambos*.

Horace derives Lucilius's satire directly from the Greek Old Comedy of Eupolis, Cratinus, and Aristophanes, who "marked down" evildoers "with much freedom" (*multa cum libertate notabant*; *Satires* 1.4.1–5). The verb *notare* implies that these writers assumed a function that at Rome belonged properly to the censor, an official magistrate. Lucilius may have represented himself as a self-appointed censor of morals, as well as a literary "critic" or judge; there is also a play on "making people known," or notorious. Horace's own view of satiric *libertas* in *Satires* 1.4 is ambivalent. Although he partly admires, and surely envies, that older Aristophanic and Lucilian outspokenness to which this freedman's son today must not aspire, he also refines the notion of true freedom (*libertas*) in his own personal life and in Roman society, modifying candor with tact, and self-expression with consideration for others. He endorses Aristotle's theory of "liberal" or gentlemanly humor as a mean between scurrility and stiffness, and he subscribes to Aristotle's theory of the evolution of comedy at once from lawless, indiscriminate aggressiveness to socially edifying humor and from casual improvisation to ordered structure—a consummation that, we come to feel, might just possibly be realized for Roman satire too under his personal direction. The move, that is, from Lucilius to Horace would parallel the move from Aristophanes to Menander and Terence—though Aristophanes continued to exemplify many fine stylistic qualities, including especially the interplay of high and low styles, that a good satirist might well imitate, and that Lucilius's self-styled champions, who disdained Horace, would never understand.

Athenian Old Comedy, which attacked individuals (and worse, public figures) by name, could not be revived on the Roman stage. The poet Naevius went too far, and was sent to prison.[22] Plautus, who brilliantly combined Greek New Comedy with Italic farce, took the warning and kept his satire general. But Lucilius brought Aristophanes' indecency, invective, and free-spirited reporting onto the private stage of satire, where—in private houses, at dinner parties, with friends—we may imagine his entertainment-pieces to have been performed, before the jokes and the individual satires were circulated, informally and perhaps dangerously, and the satires collected in book form, in the Hellenistic manner, and published.

Some features of Roman satire go back even before Aristophanes, to the Greek *iambos* of Archilochus and Hipponax (itself a major influence on the development of Greek Old Comedy). Although this *iambos* became known primarily as blame poetry, specializing in invective and obscenity (hence Aristotle's *iambikê idea* and the use of the term *iambisdein* to mean "to lampoon or satirize"), it was more broadly a serio-comic entertainment form, to be performed at private symposia and sometimes, too, from a public platform, preferably on religious occasions that licensed its broad humor and scurrility. The dramatic elements in the *iambos* are striking, even in the surviving fragments, and influential. Archilochus may assume a persona such as "Charon the carpenter" in a dramatic monologue, breaking abruptly into personal or social comment ("I don't want Gyges' riches"), and perhaps only identifying his speaker toward the end; or he may speak in his own persona; or he may present an amusing narrative of his erotic adventures, with lively internal dialogue ("I said," "she said"), as in the *Cologne Epode*. We have learned not to take Archilochus's satirical comments and narratives at face value as autobiographical self-revelations. They are a mix of fact and fiction, personal experience and generic convention. Their audience is aware that it is watching a performance, and one that includes self-satire together with satire of others. Centuries after Archilochus's death, the Greek rhapsodes, those professional reciters, continued to perform and interpret (*hypokrinesthai*) his poems, adding a further dimension of impersonation to the satiric *mimesis*.

Callimachus revived the *iambos* in the third century B.C., adapting it to new poetic and critical purposes and to a new, highly educated Alexandrian readership that could be expected to appreciate his ironic humor, his learned allusions, and his indirection of comment on current events, ideas, and personalities. Yet the new *iambos*, like the old, is highly dramatic from the start:

> Listen to Hipponax. No, really, I have come
> from the regions where oxen are sold for nothing,
> wielding my *iambos*, that doesn't sing
> of Bupalean battle.   (*Iamb* 1.1–4)

The verses are choliambs, or "limping iambs," such as Hipponax used three centuries earlier, and the opening words may be Hipponax's own, adapted to new circumstances. The "No, really" presupposes a skeptical, laughing audience. Their laughter builds as the New Hipponax reports briefly on his return from the Underworld; he is armed like an oldtime hero—but he won't employ his *iambos* in savagely destructive invective, as Hipponax notoriously did against his enemy Bupalus. In short, Callimachus's satiric *mimesis* works both ways. He revives an ancient, strong, and highly dramatic form, but in so doing, he turns it against itself for his own artistic and critical purposes. The New Hipponax fights to make peace, to establish a world of refined aesthetic and social values in which rude, old-fashioned competition has no place. All he wants is to be the supreme arbiter of taste. It is for his "listeners"—his literally listening friends, at first, with their fine ear for learned, contrived, highly nuanced poetry, and then the spreading circles of further reader-listener-reperformers—to hear the poems' subtext, which is how far they have come, how great is the distance between the old Hipponax and the new.[23]

Lucilius's satires are analogous to the Callimachean *iambos*, though not directly, let alone exclusively, derived from it.[24] They have close affinities also to the refined literary mimes of Herodas and Theocritus, as well as to the New Comedy of Menander and his rivals.[25] Mime, pastoral, and *iambos* belong, together with elegy and epigram, to the world of Hellenistic *Kleinpoesie*, or minor poetry. They stand far below epic and tragedy in the now quasi-official hierarchy of genres, and they are play-forms (*paidiai*) like Callimachus's *iamboi*, which pose cheerfully as mere frivolity, mere after-dinner entertainment—although we are meant to notice, and to admire, the hard work of their making, and although, too, their varied mix of play and seriousness, irony and indirection, allows them sometimes to address serious human and social concerns. Lucilius's satires are clearly rooted in that same Hellenistic play-world. They are light entertainment, cheerfully informal "talks."[26] Their essence is variety and colorfulness and blurring of generic boundaries, the Greek *poikilia*, now seasoned with a new Roman liveliness, and sometimes conviction, that Callimachus might never have imagined.

Like the Hellenistic Greek poets, Lucilius collected his satires into little books (*libelli*) to be copied and circulated, first to friends and acquaintances, and then to a wider though still restricted readership that he himself describes. He writes, he says, neither for the *indoctissimi* nor for the *doctissimi*—neither for those too uncultivated to appreciate his writings nor for those overeducated people who, he is afraid, will read more into his writings than is actually there.[27] So he writes for an in-between, moderately cultivated gentleman like Laelius Decumus—what we still refer to, more or less hopefully, as the Common or Educated Reader.[28] We should not forget, however, that what we call publication was a transitional stage between one kind of performance and another:[29] between Lucilius's own dramatic readings for selected audiences of friends and their reperformance from freely circulating written copies (*libelli*), first by those same friends and supporters—who would recall Lucilius's own intonations and gestures

to a degree that we, amid our modern distractions, can scarcely imagine—
and then by widening circles of readers, and also by well-trained, highly
literate slave readers (*anagnôstai*) who knew how to restore to words inked
on papyrus rolls the breath of life.

More than any others, it was the *grammatici*, those humble or (often)
not-so-humble teachers of literature, who kept Lucilius's poetry alive in a
continuous living tradition from his own day down to Horace's. Suetonius
describes their work [after the influential Greek visitor, Crates of Mallos]:

> hactenus tamen imitati, ut carmina parum adhuc divulgata vel defunctorum
> amicorum vel si quorum aliorum probassent diligentius retractarent ac
> legendo commentandoque etiam ceteris nota facerent: . . .

> ut postea Q. Vargunteius *Annales* Enni, quos certis diebus in magna
> frequentia pronuntiabat; ut Laelius Archelaus Vettiusque Philocomus
> Lucili saturas familiaris sui, quas legisse se apud Archelaum Pompeius
> Lenaeus, apud Philocomum Valerius Cato praedicant.

> [Still, they imitated him only to the extent that they carefully reviewed
> poems that had not as yet been widely circulated—the works of dead
> friends, or of any others they approved—and by reading and comment-
> ing on them made them known to the rest of the population as well. . . .
> So Quintus Vargunteius later did in the case of Ennius's *Annals*, which
> he used to recite before a large audience on specific days; and so Laelius
> Archelaus and Vettius Philocomus did in the case of their friend Lucili-
> us's satires, which Pompeius Lenaeus and Valerius Cato boast that they
> read with Archelaus and Philocomus, respectively.][30]

These *grammatici* were scholar-teachers. They produced careful editions
and commentaries in the Alexandrian manner, and they gave exemplary
readings, practising and teaching what is still called "oral interpretation of
poetry," and republicizing their authors in the process.[31] Lucilius may not
have received great public performances like Ennius. What is encouraging,
though, is the continuity of reading from Lucilius's friends and contempo-
raries, who probably recreated and passed on something of the poet's own
manner and intonation, down through the later generation of Lenaeus,
who himself wrote partisan satire, and Valerius Cato, Catullus's friend, the
unofficial head of the Roman "Moderns," of whom it was said that "he
alone reads and makes poets" (*qui solus legit et facit poetas*). By Horace's
time, Valerius Cato represented a critical Establishment defending Old
Satire against what seemed an irreverent young pretender.[32] Yet he saw to
it that Lucilius's voice could still be heard—and Horace, when he wrote
and published his own two books of *Sermones*, could hardly have asked
for more.

Performing Satire (2): Horace

The mixed heritage of Roman satire is indicated by the contents of Horace's bookshelf as described by the busybody Damasippus in *Satires* 2.3, 11–12:

> quorsum pertinuit stipare Platona Menandro,
> Eupolin, Archilochum, comites educere tantos?

> [What was the point of packing in Plato with Menander,
> and Eupolis, and Archilochus—bringing along such
> great fellow-travelers?]

Damasippus is scolding Horace for not writing more or faster. His opening salvo reveals something of Horace's inner pressure, his struggle as a serious writer upholding standards that Damasippus and his like could never understand. It also reminds us what pleasure, understanding, and literary inspiration Horace found in his great traveling-companions, the (Greek) Classics. Plato, representing philosophy, is grouped suggestively with Menander, whose New Comedy of manners reflects philosophical depictions of character in Aristotle and Theophrastus. From Menander we move back to the Old Comedy of Eupolis (and Cratinus and Aristophanes) and, behind that, to its precursor, the *iambos* of Archilochus. These are Horace's literary and dramatic ancestors. They all contribute, in their different ways, to the "mixed dish" of Roman satire. [33]

Later on, Horace points retrospectively to a different influence, the diatribes of Bion of Borysthenes (c. 335–245 B.C.), here characterized by their casual style (*sermones*) and their biting wit (*sale nigro*).[34] These diatribes were lively informal homilies on ethical themes, combining humor and seriousness (*to spoudaiogeloion*).[35] Although we have only a few partial remains, stemming originally from published lecture notes (probably Bion's own) quoted or paraphrased by later writers and anthologizers, we can see how Bion used rhetorical and dramatic techniques to drive his arguments home.[36] He personifies abstract concepts like Poverty, who speaks in her own defense. He uses rhetorical questions, abrupt imperatives, arguments with an imagined opponent or interlocutor, popular analogies, and playful language generally. His attacks on avarice, discontent, envy, superstition, and the fear of death are good "Socratic" teaching, filtered through Cynic individualism and outspokenness (*parrhêsia*), and using the commonplaces of what we now call popular philosophy. Life is a drama, and we are actors: play the part fortune gave you as best you can. Life is a crumbling house, or a good dinner party: depart from it gratefully when the time comes. These comparisons are effective; they carry conviction still today. We find their like throughout Horace's *Satires* and *Epistles*, and before Horace, in

Lucretius's great attack on the fear of death (*DRN.* 3.830–1094). They point forward to the powerful diatribes of Epictetus in the later first century A.D. But they also belong to the Hellenistic world of entertainment literature, together with such other minor genres as iambus, mime, and pastoral; and like these, they depend on reperformance by readers and the recreation of a quasi-theatrical audience to achieve their fullest effect.

I am tempted to linger here, reading Horace's *Satires* 1.1 both as a fine performance piece in itself and, in the larger context of Book 1, as a high-water mark of Bion's influence. Let me, instead, postpone further discussion of diatribe until the next chapter (it will be important to Persius) and come to what Horace himself says about the writing and performance of satire, and about its possible and preferred audiences, in the programmatic literary satires 1.4 and 1.10.

First, the writing. In *Satires* 1.10, the epilogue to Book 1, Horace places his satire writing in relation to Lucilius and to contemporary poets and dramatists:

> turgidus Alpinus iugulat dum Memnona dumque
> defingit Rheni luteum caput, haec ego ludo,
> quae neque in aede sonent certantia iudice Tarpa,
> nec redeant iterum atque iterum spectanda theatris. . . .   (36–39)

> [While word-swollen "Alpinus" butchers Memnon and disfigures the pale-yellow source of the Rhine, I fool around with these [satires]: not stuff to resound in temple competitions with Tarpa as judge, nor to return, time and again, as theatrical spectacles. . . .]

The passage begins ironically. Horace's little, playful writings ("haec ego ludo") are sandwiched almost negligibly between Alpinus's terrible epics and the poems that, unlike Horace's, enter into public competition and display or theatrical performance. In the following catalogue of good modern poetry, however, satire finds a quasi-official place. The higher genres of tragedy and epic are sandwiched in between the lower genres of comedy and pastoral, and Horace's satire follows closely on Virgil's "tender and witty" *Eclogues*. He does not, he says, mean to displace Lucilius, the honored, if careless founder of Roman verse satire. Rather, he is bringing satire up to the highest contemporary standards of style and tone—as Lucilius himself would be doing if he lived in the post-Neoteric age. This requires painfully hard work. It also means limiting your intended audience:

> saepe stilum vertas, iterum quae digna legi sint
> scripturus, neque te ut miretur turba labores,
> contentus paucis lectoribus. an tua demens
> vilibus in ludis dictari carmina malis?   (72–75)

[You must often erase, in order to write what merits more than onetime reading; and you mustn't struggle to impress the crowd: a few readers should suffice. Or are you so crazy that you'd want your poems to be dictated in cheap low schools?]

Horace cannot worry, that is, about present popularity or future reputation, which might come down to having your poetry taught by rote in poor elementary schools. He will therefore concern himself, not with bad potential readers and reviewers (he names a few), but only with good ones. His positive list begins with Maecenas, his patron, embraced symbolically by Horace's close friends and fellow-poets,

Plotius et Varius, Maecenas Vergiliusque,   (81)

and goes on to list other representative friends and educated people who he hopes will enjoy his writings. The list emphatically crosses party lines. Horace here indicates what we might call his primary readership, though this in turn evidently stands for the further, widening circle of readers, unknown as yet, whom he might expect to reach through publication of this little book (*libellus*) of satires.[37] "Hurry, boy," he concludes, "and add these last verses to my little book."

i, puer, atque meo citus haec subscribe libello.   (92)

This ending is comical. The poet who has so much emphasized the necessity of slow, hard, careful writing seems to be dictating his verses, like Lucilius, to a scribe in a great, careless rush of words toward the finish line. But of course, his spontaneity is contrived—as we (if we are *docti*, educated in such matters) are meant to realize.

Satires 1.10 ends with the word *libello*, celebrates the completion of this little book of satires, and carefully indicates, as Lucilius had earlier, the aesthetic and critical standards to which Horace adheres and, correlative with this, the right readers he hopes to reach through publication. The artistic organization of the *libellus* is remarkable, as is its resemblance to Virgil's book of ten *Eclogues*, published three or four years earlier. Put the two books together, and you see something of the companionship, the shared Callimachean standards, of the two poet-friends.[38] At the same time, Virgil's *Eclogues* were highly dramatic pieces, like Theocritus's *Idylls*; they lent themselves to recitation and even to theatrical performance.[39] Horace's *Satires*, too, for all his disclaimers, were meant to be read aloud, to please the critical ear, not just the eye.[40]

On this point the very disclaimers are suggestive. In his earlier, very ironic *Satires* 1.4, Horace begins by emphasizing the importance of writing slowly and carefully, as Lucilius did not; he won't enter a contest to see who can turn out the most verses in an hour. Indeed, he has neither circulated his satires nor read them aloud in public (*vulgo recitare*), which is another method of circulation, common among would-be poets, hurtful to satirists' victims and dangerous for the satirists themselves. Yet this satire is full of speech: comic dialogue, everyday conversation, gossip and back-biting, and the narrator's seeming-casual chat (*sermo*). Again, Horace's dis-claimer of indiscriminate "reciting" parallels his refusal to publish for un-discriminating readers:

> nulla taberna meos habeat neque pila libellos,
> quis manus insudet vulgi Hermogenisque Tigelli.
> nec recito cuiquam nisi amicis, idque coactus,
> non ubivis coramve quibuslibet. in medio qui
> scripta foro recitent sunt multi quique lavantes;
> suave locus voci resonat conclusus.   (*Serm.* 1.4.71–76)

[I don't want some shop to display my books for sale, for every common hand to sweat over—including Tigellius Hermogenes'; I only read aloud to friends, when asked: not just anywhere, and in public, and for anyone whomsoever. Now there *are* people who give readings in the middle of the forum, or at the baths: the enclosed space makes a fine-echoing auditorium.]

Between the two pictures of undesirable things, the books put on public display and pawed over by sweaty hands, and the voices happily resounding in the forum or, better still, in the vaulted baths, Horace sets his own mod-est behavior. He reads only to friends, and upon request. His Aristotelian tact embraces time, place, and circumstance. He avoids publicity; his satires won't be circulated, prematurely and dangerously, by word of mouth (as Lucilius's satires may have been); they are carefully restricted to a limited audience; and, as Horace goes on to say, they are ultimately expressions of his own self-educational practice, derived from his good father, of holding moral conversations with himself about the good or bad ways he observes people living. It is all very innocent, and very private. Or is it? Even if Horace only reads aloud to a privileged circle of friends, his witticisms may still get out (hence his famous tact), and publication, which he has evidently planned, will bring about their general and indiscriminate circulation.

We should never focus our attention so exclusively on the mechanics of writing and publication that we forget the oral/aural dimension of Horace's satire at every stage of its emergence.[41] First, he would think up verses, at home on his couch, or walking about Rome, or traveling; then he would shape those verses slowly and carefully into first and second drafts; and when they were ready, he would test them on his friends' ears, not just their eyes. In the *Ars Poetica*, he advises young amateurs to "let anything you write enter into Maecius's ears for judgment, and your father's, and mine—and then put your manuscript away for eight or nine years" (386–89); and he recalls how severely the late Quintilius would criticize his work in progress. "If you read anything aloud (*recitares*) to Quintilius, he'd insist on changes, or tell you to start again from scratch; or, if you refused, he'd leave you to admire your own work in splendid isolation" (438–44). There is nothing like a good critical ear. What is also important, though Horace omits it pedagogically, is the encouragement and support, the positive feedback and immediate gratification that many of these private readings must have brought him—a pleasure that Persius, under harsher constraints, may have forgone.

After Horace completed his satires, he probably performed many of them for his friends in Maecenas's great house on the Esquiline. It seems likely, for example, that *Satires* 1.5, the "Journey to Brundisium," was performed not long after the event for the pleasure of Maecenas, Virgil, and Varius, Horace's fellow-travelers, taking on added dimensions of meaning and fun against their remembered, shared experience. Here Horace's ideal audience, his actual audience, and the figures in his satire would remarkably coincide. Here, too, and in other satires like 1.9 and 1.6, Maecenas or Virgil could enjoy comparing the Horace standing before them with his usual satirical persona: that simple, naïve, straightforward, trusting "Horace" who is swept along by circumstances he doesn't understand, as in *Satires* 1.5, or who speaks out, so very simply and honestly—his untutored father's own son—amid all those sophisticated friends and foes, as in *Satires* 1.3, 1.6, and 1.9. We are still taken in by that simple, confiding persona;[42] or if not, then we grow so suspicious of the ironic Horace that we look for hidden agendas everywhere. One advantage, I think, of imagining satire as performed before a not-so-hypothetical audience is that it helps us to discern a little more clearly what may be happening in and between the lines and what may not.

The last stage of Horace's writing was preparing his satire book for publication. The individual satires needed little or no revision now. What is new is their highly artistic ordering, with its groupings, its contrasts, and its strong cumulative effect, like that of Virgil's *Eclogues*. How Book 1 was received, how wide a public it reached, we can only guess. Later on, Horace says of his first lyric collection, *Odes* 1–3, that people enjoyed his poems privately but disparaged them in public. They did so, he says, because he refused to engage in literary politics and give public readings, whether at professional meetings or in the theater. Elsewhere, however, he indicates that he did take part in some public readings and mutual-admiration sessions, after all. The young Ovid, at least, once heard him read.[43]

In sum, the written and spoken word, the text of satire and the performative event, matter equally to Horace, and the one presupposes the other. If he saw himself as a professional writer, shaping and reshaping his satires toward publication with post-Lucilian care, still the life of his satires remains in the performance. Kenneth Quinn, though speaking of the *Odes*, puts it well:

> As I see the matter, performance is always implied. Even when contact with a writer takes place through a written text, the text was thought of as recording an actual performance by the writer; the published text may be the result of a series of drafts, but it is still offered as, so to speak, a transcript of a performance which the reader recreates for himself, by reading the text aloud or having it read aloud.[44]

To breathe new life into Horace's *Satires*, then, we should imitate the *grammatici* of old and see to it that reading aloud and reperformance keep pace with scholarly commentary and interpretation.

My approach so far has been mainly aesthetic, foregrounding the pleasure of the performance of satire. Now we might ask the question, deferred but not forgotten: What kinds of pleasure do these satires afford in their social and historical contexts, and for whom?

Lucilius was privileged. As a Roman knight, he needed no patron, and although he had powerful friends, including the younger Scipio, he wrote to please himself, declining, for example, to praise Scipio's military exploits in verse. Sometimes he engaged in partisan politics and feuds, attacking enemies with a violence that his successors long remembered and envied.[45] What other functions, from a sociocultural viewpoint, did his satires fulfill, besides furnishing casual entertainment for elite dinner-parties? A New Historicist might argue that as Lucilius derided outsiders, from foolish or vicious aristocrats to lower-class parasites and scoundrels, he reinforced his in-group's solidarity and self-awareness; or else, that his satires helped provide them with the "symbolic capital" (Bourdieu) of Hellenistic Greek culture, clothing a rich and powerful Roman elite with a veneer of civilized *urbanitas*.

All this Lucilius did under the ironic persona of an *elegantiae arbiter*, a self-proclaimed judge of good style in every sphere of life from food and sex to orthography, tragedy, philhellenism, friendship, and high Roman morality. We might wonder, though, with more conservative Romans, whether satire was not a two-edged sword, a threat, not just to "bad people," as Lucilius simply labeled or libeled them, but to the very mores that were now subjected, along with everything else, to the individualistic and often corrosive "criticism" of satire. For all its quasi-educational pretenses, Roman satire could never become a quite respectable genre—could never forget, or let others forget, its subversive side.

Horace's literary criticism begins differently, with limitation. He is not and cannot be Lucilius: partly from birth and social prejudice (the freedman's son), partly from changing conditions of the time, and partly because he needed Maecenas's patronage. Yet, although he could not exercise Lucilius's polemic freedom—although, indeed, he was attacked, probably as effete and un-Roman, by Lucilius's republican-minded partisans—he succeeded remarkably in making himself Lucilius's successor in satire and the critical spokesman for a new social and cultural elite, the "circle of Maecenas."[46]

Maecenas's gifts to Horace—first and foremost, the Sabine estate, with the financial independence it brought; less obviously, moral and practical support for writing, performance, and publication—were balanced by social demands and pressures at which Horace only hints obliquely.[47] What matters is that Maecenas let him write, like Lucilius, what he needed and wanted to write, and even renegotiate the terms of their "friendship" (*amicitia*) in the *Epistles*, where feelings of gratitude and obligation collide with the desire for greater independence, both outer and inner. The published *libellus* credits both parties with transcending that conflict through true generosity and loyalty. Maecenas will be remembered as the ideal patron; his poets will be envied for the (relative) freedom they enjoyed. Yet, in retrospect, Horace and Virgil provided symbolic capital and cultural legitimacy to the Principate. "Are you afraid," asked Augustus (with heavy-handed humor, requesting a poem addressed to himself), "that posterity may think you were my friend?"[48] As it turns out, Horace had reason to worry. He wrote disturbingly, sometimes, about relationships with the great and the compromises, even at best, that they invariably demand.

Although Persius, as a rich and well-connected Roman knight, had the good fortune, like Lucilius, not to need a patron, he must in his relatively private life away from Nero's court have missed the encouragement and support of a centrally influential community of poets, critics, and educated amateurs such as Lucilius and Horace had enjoyed and in part created around themselves—a community of talent that, as Persius saw it, could not be recreated in his time. His satires convey strong feelings of impotence and alienation. Remarkably, though, he made a personal and poetic virtue out of necessity, not lashing out against Nero except indirectly, but rather converting satire itself into an instrument of Stoic self-diagnosis and -reformation. If Nero, the artist-emperor, made Greece and Rome into one great theater for his narcissistic performances, Persius, turning inward, played out his psychological and spiritual struggles on the hidden stage of his little satire book (*libellus*), for himself primarily, and then for whoever, after his death, might care to read and to respond.

Two close friends, the philosopher Cornutus and the poet Caesius Bassus, prepared Persius's book for publication after his death.[49] Whether anyone heard or read the *Satires* in his lifetime is less clear. Perhaps he read them aloud to a small, trusted group of friends and relations, in some safe place like the gardens of his respected older friend, Thrasea Paetus. It may be, however, that he only read individual satires to Cornutus and Bassus, and that nobody (else?) saw the completed book before he died. Could this be what his riddle meant, "vel duo vel nemo" ("Maybe two people, maybe nobody")?

Into his hidden book Persius breathes secrets that endanger not only Nero's regime, but also the satiric tradition itself as Rome has known it. If everyone has asses' ears, what place is left for the implied audience of satire, ourselves included, to stand? And, again: whereas Lucilius and Horace advocated new, increasingly refined notions of good style in literature and life, based on Callimachean precepts of subtlety and polish, Persius can only denounce the fashionably soft, smooth, and overrefined poetry of his own time as it is practiced at court, from the (unmentioned) emperor on down; so that, in protest against this infectious degeneracy of taste, he must abandon satire's usual civilized and civilizing pretensions and appear as a redneck "half-civilized outsider" (*semipaganus*), in the prefatory *Choliambics*, or as a child who can't wait to piss, in *Satire* 1. Give him the leverage of marginalization, and he will move the satiric world—with rude guffaws.

In the remainder of this chapter, I shall follow Persius's "nonperformance" or metaperformance in *Satire* 1—his rejection of expected aims and purposes and his critique of bad contemporary literary and social performances—to its surprising, but not totally unexpected, conclusion.

Three Bad Performances

The argument proper of *Satire* 1 begins at line 13, as Persius takes us into the world of poetry writing and performance:

> scribimus inclusi, numeros ille, hic pede liber,
> grande aliquid quod pulmo animae praelargus anhelet.
> scilicet haec populo pexusque togaque recenti
> et natalicia tandem cum sardonyche albus
> sede leges celsa, liquido cum plasmate guttur
> mobile conlueris, patranti fractus ocello.
> tunc neque more probo videas nec voce serena
> ingentis trepidare Titos, cum carmina lumbum
> intrant et tremulo scalpuntur ubi intima versu.
> tun, vetule, auriculis alienis colligis escas,
> articulis quibus et dicas cute perditus "ohe"?   (1.13–23)

[We write, shut in: one in verse, another in prose, something large for overactive lungs to puff and pant over. And of course, you'll read these things to the crowd, your hair well combed, gleaming white in a new toga, and with your birthday ring: read them from your high throne, after making your throat supple with liquid modulation, the broken subject of a lustful glance. Then you might see our enormous Tituses wriggling—in no decent manner, with no vocal restraint—once the poems penetrate their parts and they are fingered intimately by the tremulous verse. Old man, are you collecting scraps for other people's ears, scraps to which you yourself, with your ruined joints and hide, would have to say, "Enough already"?]

The satire is devastating. It is also notoriously hard to interpret, especially the last two lines with their strange, intense, very mixed metaphors. I begin, though, with a different puzzle. Where are we taken by those fast-shifting first- and second-person verbs?

Imagine them now in performance; (a) the first word, "scribimus," introduces a vast literary scene: "Here we all are, writing." Persius himself is presumably included, or better, implicated in the general folly, and so are his readers unto the present day;[50] (b) with "leges" ("you will read"), we realize that Persius has started to address one particular writer whose poems will be performed before an admiring popular audience. That was presumably their aim, as it might have been Persius's own wish earlier when he was interrupted by the corrective Stoic voice; (c) with "tunc . . . videas" Persius directs his readership, taken as a single or singular individual, to step back and regard the scene critically and dispassionately, as the satirist does: "Then you might see" (or, "Then one could see . . ."); and finally, with a surprise twist, (d) he turns to attack his victim directly. This is, evidently, the bad poet-performer just described, but it could (we have a feeling) have been ourselves, for Persius's satire moves quickly. Nor does it limit itself, reassuringly, to the usual suspects.

In this first vignette, Persius reduces the *recitatio* to its lowest physical denominator. It is an exercise in lung power; still more, in self-advertisement. What does it take to be a poet nowadays? The right hair-do, the right clothes, the right accessories. The long Latin words suggest the overpowering effect of that enormous, gaudy birthday ring, so prominently displayed. We may imagine the preliminary applause. "Finally" (*tandem*, a key word, suggesting the man's dramatically slow progress, an effect that Persius's own satiric mimesis would heighten), he will give his reading—after reaching his high seat, and after clearing his throat, very slowly and deliberately, provoking the audience's expectation (and our own).

Nor is that all that is provoked. The poetry reading is eroticized to the point of pornography. It is described metaphorically as a complex and various homosexual transaction. There is, first, the sexual invitation and response of the initial eye contact between poet and audience. Then the poetry being recited makes its erotic entrance not into the ears but into the intimate lower regions, arousing great hulking hearers to a quasi-orgiastic response. The details are notoriously complex, and even untranslatable: not because Persius scholars are especially prudish nowadays, but because Persius seems deliberately ambiguous in his suggested conflation of active and passive homosexual response, and still more, in the extraordinary mix of food, sex, poetry reading, and flattery that follows—two lines that have brought strong scholars to their knees.[51] Horace had described an older man blown up by a legacy-hunter's flattery to the point where he couldn't take any more (*Satires* 2.5.96–98). In Persius it is the performer-poet who becomes exhausted, by the effort of continually feeding scraps of food/poetry/flattery to the insatiable ears of his audience, and also, varying the earlier metaphor, by the physical demands of those longtime sexual transactions. Again, the picture is ambiguous. Is the performer compared to a worn-out pathic or to an active performer who can't get it up any longer?[52] In either case, we have a sense of physical and psychological exhaustion, and perhaps of a sexual Waste Land like Eliot's, here employed to characterize the present state of poetry writing and performance at Rome.

Abruptly, an interlocutor objects:

"quo didicisse, nisi hoc fermentum et quae semel intus
innata est rupto iecore exierit caprificus?"
en pallor seniumque! o mores, usque adeone
scire tuum nihil est nisi te scire hoc sciat alter?
"at pulchrum est digito monstrari et dicier 'hic est.'
ten cirratorum centum dictata fuisse
pro nihilo pendes? "   (24–30)

["What's the point of learning, if the yeast doesn't work, if the wild fig tree, born within you, doesn't burst out through your very liver?" There's paleness for you, there's senility! The things people do! Is your knowing really so worthless if another man doesn't know that you know what you know?

"But it's splendid to be pointed at and have them say, 'That's him!' To have been the object of dictation for a hundred curly-headed kids—do you count *that* as nothing?"]

As earlier, the voices are unidentified; they need to be played out in performance. Persius is usually thought to be entering into dialogue here with one of satire's straw men, a supposed representative of the poets and their usual mentality. Probably so: but I think he is still holding converse with himself, confronting his own very natural poetic ambitions with harsh Stoic realism. The second, refuting voice insists once again on a consistent inner standard. What matters is learning, not displaying your learning to others. But the first voice has already been made to undermine its own position through rhetorical exaggeration, metaphorical confusion, and unintended obscenity. The would-be defense of poetic inspiration turns grotesque. A man's liver, the seat of passion, swells up like yeast and bursts, and out comes a wild fig tree (more sterility?).[53] After that, the poet's ambition is described in what seem more acceptable, Horatian terms: first, to be pointed out in public, as Horace was; and then, as an object of dictation in some elementary school—a fate that Horace once disdained as unworthy, but to which, in time, he seems to have become reconciled.[54] But now the finger-pointing turns ambivalent, and the poet's prospective pleasure in "having become the object of dictation of a hundred curly-haired boys" suggests, not just the debasement of poetry among the elementary school crowd to whom the teacher dictates poetry—partly for instruction in reading and grammar, and partly because multiple copies were unavailable—but a confusion of mind, as the poet savors what has already become his extended fame.

Persius's response to the interlocutor's objections is a second satiric vignette that, not coincidentally, is much concerned with life and death:

> ecce inter pocula quaerunt
> Romulidae saturi quid dia poemata narrent.
> hic aliquis, cui circum umeros hyacinthina laena est,
> rancidulum quiddam balba de nare locutus
> Phyllidas, Hypsipylas, vatum et plorabile siquid,
> eliquat ac tenero subplantat verba palato.
> adsensere viri: nunc non cinis ille poetae
> felix? non levior cippus nunc inprimit ossa?
> laudant convivae: nunc non e manibus illis,
> nunc non e tumulo fortunataque favilla
> nascentur violae?   (30–40)

[Behold Romulus's full-stuffed offspring, asking, among their cups, "What has divine Poetry to say to us?" At which, some character with a lavender cloak around his shoulders, after venting some putrid remarks from his stammering nose, strains out Phyllises, Hypsipyles, any of the old tearful Poesy, daintily tripping up the words on his tender palate. The men assent: are not the poet's ashes utterly fortunate? Does not the tombstone now press more lightly on his bones? The guests give praise: oh, now, out of those shades, out of the tomb and the oh-so-blessed cinders, will not violets spring?]

What poets want, what they have always wanted, is immortality. "Let no one grieve for me," said Ennius, "for I fly about, living, through the mouths of men." And Horace: "A great part of me will escape the death-goddess."

And Ovid, writing from exile, counts on friends back in Rome to cultivate his memory, to keep him alive through poetry recitations that will constitute virtual acts of cult worship.[55] What really happens, though? Just one more silly performance for the benefit of an after-dinner audience, "stuffed" ("saturi") and still drinking. Again a performer arises, a professional entertainer this time, wearing the latest thing in fine lavender mantles, to give them some trite love-elegy or epyllion with a preliminary critical introduction in the latest high-pathetic, narcissistic style. And the decadent Sons of Romulus applaud. They have no taste; they are "saturated" with this kind of verse, as well as with food—and they are probably not paying attention, anyway. But there is something sinister about their applause. It carries Virgilian connotations of human sacrifice: not life, but death.[56]

Indeed, this second vignette builds to a magnificent demolition, through wild comic exaggeration, of the whole received notion of literary immortality. Persius's sarcasm is noticeably strong here (as, indeed, his interlocutor will insist in the very next lines): the more so, I think, because he is outwrestling his own very human desires. His strong mockery, his antic humor (which we shall also see in *Satire* 6) springs largely from his keen awareness of death's power to frustrate human hopes and ambitions, good poets' as well as bad. No wonder it finds an echo in *Hamlet*.[57] When Laertes cries out at Ophelia's grave,

> Lay her i'the earth,
> And from her fair and unpolluted flesh
> May violets spring!   (v.i.261–63),

he is evidently deceiving himself. Hamlet knows better, especially after the gravedigger scene; he is more honest with himself and (now) with others. Yorick's skull mocks beauty, ambition, wit—and poetic creativity. What should Hamlet do, or Shakespeare—or Persius—given that dreadful awareness? Strong, mocking laughter is one way of acknowledging the fear, and perhaps of keeping it, if only momentarily, at bay.

Again the interlocutor objects:

> "rides," ait, "et nimis uncis
> naribus indulges. an erit qui velle recuset
> os populi meruisse et cedro digna locutus
> linquere nec scombros metuentia carmina nec tus? "   (40–43)

["You laugh," he says, "your nostrils curl too much. Can you show me a man who doesn't admit he wants to have earned the people's voice, to produce and leave behind poems that merit cedar, that have no fear of mackerels or incense? "]

The objection seems reasonable, Horatian. Isn't Persius being too sarcastic? Wouldn't anyone want his writings to be read, admired, and preserved? Again, the objection somewhat undermines itself, reminding us of the material and historical conditions of survival. Poems stored in cedarwood book-boxes may be honored more and live longer than poems used for fish- or incense-wrappings, and that is something, but book-boxes are still, at best, a sort of coffin.[58] Still, Persius's sarcasm quiets down, as though he has been moved by thoughts of our common human condition. This time, he starts off modestly; but his tone changes as he describes what passes for criticism nowadays, and why:

> quisquis es, o modo quem ex adverso dicere feci,
> non ego cum scribo, si forte quid aptius exit
> (quando haec rara avis est), si quid tamen aptius exit,
> laudari metuam; neque enim mihi cornea fibra est.
> sed recti finemque extremumque esse recuso
> "euge" tuum et "belle." nam "belle" hoc excute totum:
> quid non intus habet? non hic est Ilias Atti
> ebria veratro? non siqua elegidia crudi
> dictarunt proceres? non quidquid denique lectis
> scribitur in citreis? calidum scis ponere sumen,
> scis comitem horridulum trita donare lacerna,
> et "verum," inquis, "amo, verum mihi dicite de me."
> qui pote? vis dicam? nugaris, cum tibi, calve,
> pinguis aqualiculus propenso sesquipede extet.
> o Iane, a tergo quem nulla ciconia pinsit
> nec manus auriculas imitari mobilis albas
> nec linguae quantum sitiat canis Apula tantae.
> vos, o patricius sanguis, quos vivere fas est
> occipiti caeco, posticae occurrite sannae.   (44–62)

[You, whoever you are whom I just made speak against me: no, when I write, if something comes out rather well—a rare bird indeed—still, if something comes out rather well, I'll not be afraid to be praised. My fiber's not hard as horn. But I do refuse to agree that your "Great job!" and "Beautiful!" are the outer limit and scope of all that's right and good. Just shake out that "Beautiful!": what don't you find inside? Not Attius's *Iliad*, strung out on hellebore? Not the sweet little elegies tossed off by full-stuffed lordlings? Not everything, in short, that's written on citrus-wood couches? You know how to serve a pig's paunch hot, you know how to give your shivering hanger-on a worn-out coat, and you say, "I love the truth, tell me the truth about myself." How can he? Like *me* to tell you? It's no good, baldy; you're just fooling around, while your great fat paunch sticks out a foot-and-a-half before you!

O Janus [you're lucky]: no stork's bill nips you from behind; no quick hand mimics pale-white asses' ears; no tongue sticks out as far as a thirsty Apulian bitch's. As for you, gentlemen of noble blood, who are destined to live with the back of your skulls blind: you'll have to hurry to meet that backdoor sneer!]

Persius begins by unmasking his interlocutor as a Rhetorical Convention. He is teasing us, as comic poets do, and he is conversing with himself still about why one writes and for whom. As a Stoic, a rational thinker, he will dig beneath the surface of things, but his rhetorical questions convey a mounting anger and indignation at the meaninglessness of praise in a corrupt and corrupting society. This time, in what amounts to a third vignette and a third metaperformance, he shows us, first, how poetry is produced nowadays: the drug-induced epic (that wretched new *Iliad* again); the "tender little elegies" produced so incongruously by full-stuffed nobles; above all, the comfortable circumstances that make poetry writing possible. Then we see a rich man exploiting a poor dependent. After giving him a hot meal and a mangy old hand-me-down coat, he asks the man's "honest opinion" about what he's written. He can't give it, of course. So Persius gives it for him, in an explosion (his second, this time, but still building to a third) of satiric truth. The section ends, however, with images of suppression and concealment in the society at large. People are reduced to ineffective, even childish forms of protest, making rude faces and gestures behind the backs of our once respected leaders. If those great men could only turn around quickly enough, they might even catch the secret clue that Persius himself is half-withholding from us, the "asses' ears," emblem and *contrappasso* of perverse critical judgment, with which (as we shall see) the whole of society, not just King Midas, has so generously been equipped. For the fools who give and receive flattery and reject honest criticism are lowering themselves to the level of beasts in the overall scale of existence.

Persius's three vignettes help explain his initial aloofness and disdain, his withdrawal from the literary fray. In a society dominated by bad poets and flatterers, a society in which honest criticism has become impossible, why and for whom should an honest, self-critical poet write? But Persius's radical criticism goes deeper than the Horatian contrast of *we happy few*, with our good standards, *versus all of them*. The desire for literary immortality that motivates all poets to write, that motivates *us* as well as *them*, is mocked by realities of reception and performance. Not only will violets not spring from the poet's grave, but his poetry, even if it is good (and most is not), will only be what people make of it. It may survive (if it does survive) only as a form of casual entertainment, mostly unappreciated and misunderstood. Worse still, in his choliambic preface to the satire collection, Persius reduces all poetry writing to its lowest common denominator: the belly's craving for food that inspires poets, like parrots and magpies, to perform their clever vocal tricks. What once seemed a noble, independent, spiritual art, the Muses' high gift to humankind, is now revealed as a function of the material nonculture: no more, and no less.

Even granted these harsh general truths, Persius's age seems more than usually unpromising. In the following section (lines 63–106) he reveals its underlying artificiality and falseness through an Eliotic clamor of fragmented, competing voices.[59] Evidently, modern poetry is admired for its exaggerated smoothness, so easy on the ear, so lacking in any real force and substance. Persius gives us traces of an Aristophanic contest, or *agôn*, between the Old Literature and the New: between the rugged old Classical authors like Pacuvius and Accius, nostalgically misremembered and praised by grumbling elders, and the smooth, effeminate, precious, hyper-Alexandrian verse beloved by modern youth, all about orgiastic Maenads and self-castrating Attises. It is all special effects nowadays, all style and no substance. Modern poetry has no balls. And not just poetry: for rhetorical pleading in the lawcourts, once the vital center of Roman political life, has also become theatricalized; defendants give artificial performances for show, just as their prosecutors do, and both sides hope mainly for applause. Underlying the parody is a dangerous thought. As Tacitus was later to demonstrate in his *Dialogus*, oratory atrophied under the empire because the lawcourts' decision-making power had been taken over by the emperor; what was left was flattery and self-display. Take the case of Pedius. In *Satires* 1.10, written under the Triumvirate, Horace could cite Pedius (Publicola) as an example of a serious and effective pleader who wouldn't mix Greek words with Latin—a fault in which Lucilius indulged himself, and which Horace carefully avoided. But now, with fine comic intertextuality, Persius shows "Pedius" transformed into a careless defendant who doesn't live in the real world any longer, but in some never-never-land of pretentious style.

Not just Roman poetry, then, but all Roman society has become a sexual and cultural Waste Land. Its once-respected citizens have been transformed either into pathics ("Romulus, do you wag your tail?") or into Attis-like eunuchs. Bad art and bad politics reinforce one another. So, once again: what is the point of writing satire nowadays? What difference can it possibly make? Or as Persius puts it, as he begins the last, climactic section of *Satire* 1: "sed quid opus teneras mordaci radere vero / auriculas?" ("Why scrape those tender little ears with the biting truth?").

Persius's Return to the Colors

The passages just described are strong satire. They give a devastating critique of contemporary poetry, poetry-readings, and what passes for criticism. Rhetorically, they justify Persius's stubborn isolation, his refusal to look outside himself for evaluation or approval. And yet, by the satire's end, he will reverse himself and offer a new account of satiric meaning, purpose, and audience.

The ending has three parts. In the first, Persius is warned not to write satire, and he pretends to acquiesce:

> "sed quid opus teneras mordaci radere vero
> auriculas? vide sis ne maiorum tibi forte
> limina frigescant: sonat hic de nare canina
> littera." per me equidem sint omnia protinus alba;
> nil moror. euge omnes, omnes bene, mirae eritis res.
> hoc iuvat? "hic," inquis, "veto quisquam faxit oletum."
> pinge duos anguis: "pueri, sacer est locus, extra
> meiite." discedo.   (107–14)

["But why scrape tender little ears with the biting truth? Take care that great men's thresholds don't turn cold for you: one can hear the snarling sound of the dog." Well, then: so far as I'm concerned, call everything good; I make no objection. Bravo, everybody! Great job! Really wonderful! You like that? "Here," you say, "I forbid anyone to commit a nuisance." So paint two snakes: "Children, this spot is sacred; piss outside." I withdraw.]

The warning has been delayed. We expected it earlier, in connection with the adversary's " 'Quis leget haec?' "; now it is spelled out. Satire is hurtful and dangerous, and it may offend important people. Echoes of earlier charges (whether fact or fiction, or a mix of both) against Lucilius and Horace recall those poets' defenses. Lucilius (to paraphrase) put it bluntly: "I speak the truth; it needs to be spoken; but good, honest people have nothing to fear." Horace was ironic: "I only write for my own amusement and edification, and for a few close friends; and anyway, I'm a decent sort of person who wouldn't go around hurting anyone—unless, of course, someone attacks me first." (Even barking dogs have their uses.) But Persius insists that satire has to "bite," has to offend people, if it is to provide honest criticism and possibly healing in a dishonest world. The tenderness of society's so very sensitive ears, which can only bear the smoothest, most effeminate verse, is in fact a symptom of their diseased condition. To scrape those tender little ears (*auriculae*, again the vulgar diminutive, not *aures*) naturally gives offense; but again, to pursue the medical analogy, this is like what the skilled surgeon does when he scrapes or cuts away diseased flesh.[60] Similarly, in *Satire* 5, probably written earlier, Persius's mentor Cornutus reminds him that he is "skilled at scraping pale-sick habits, and nailing down faults in free-spirited play" ("pallentis radere mores / doctus et in-

genuo culpam defigere ludo" [15–16]). You can see why this surgical meta-
phor appealed so much in later times, like the Elizabethan Age. It excuses
satire's roughness, gives it an almost respectable social function. Like the
court fool, the satirist may be allowed the rare privilege—at least occasion-
ally, and within certain limits?—of telling the truth.

Although Persius feels the need to speak out as urgently as the child
needs to piss,[61] he also feels, or pretends to feel, strong constraint. So he
withdraws. "Discedo." Three long syllables. A strong, emphatic stop in
mid-verse, at the caesura. "I'm out of here." What else can a satirist do, or
a decent man, but (in Tom Stoppard's words) "withdraw in style from
the chaos"?

And yet, hardly has Persius conceded when he begins again, again takes
up arms, recalling his great predecessors and building to the satire's climac-
tic revelation:

> secuit Lucilius urbem,
> te Lupe, te Muci, et genuinum fregit in illis.
> omne vafer vitium ridenti Flaccus amico
> tangit et admissus circum praecordia ludit,
> callidus excusso populum suspendere naso.
> me muttire nefas? nec clam? nec cum scrobe? nusquam?
> hic tamen infodiam. vidi, vidi ipse, libelle:
> auriculas asini quis non habet? hoc ego opertum,
> hoc ridere meum, tam nil, nulla tibi vendo
> Iliade. (114–23)

[Lucilius lashed the city—you, Lupus, and you, Mucius—and broke his
jawbone on them. Flaccus makes his friend laugh, shrewdly touches on
his every fault, and, once let inside, plays around his heartstrings—clever,
too, at hanging the crowd from the end of his cleared-out nose; and *I'm*
not to mutter a word? Not secretly? Not in a hole? Not anywhere? Yet,
I'll dig in here. I've seen it, little book, seen it with my own eyes: *Who
doesn't have asses' ears?* This secret, this laugh of mine, this thing of
nought, I'm not selling you for any *Iliad* in the world.]

Lucilius spoke out, he attacked his enemies by name. Horace, more subtly
and ironically, infiltrated his friends' hearts; or, differently, he became
(what seemed) a confidential friend and adviser to his readers, putting his
finger on their every fault, even as he scorned the general crowd. Ideally,
perhaps, Persius will combine Lucilius's aggressiveness with Horace's play-
ful, mocking irony. By all rights, he will make a third in the grand tradition
of Roman verse satire. If he is silenced—if he can only "dig in here" and
whisper his dirty little secret into the hidden cavity of his little book—still,
this anticipates the long-delayed revelation.[62] For Persius, as it turns out,

finds himself playing the part of King Midas's barber who discovered that his master had asses' ears and could not, in the end, keep that dangerous secret to himself.

Persius's secret, that *everyone* at Rome has asses' ears, is worse. It is bad enough to offend one man if he is king, or Caesar, but if asininity is so contagious, like rhinoceritis in Ionesco's farcical play, that nobody, or almost nobody, can escape it—if everyone's literary taste and, behind it, the moral and aesthetic standards of the whole decadent society have become corrupt—what possible audience is left? The answer to Persius's first *quis*-question earlier, " 'Quis leget haec?,' " is presumably contained in the answer to the second, "nam Romae quis non?" But the syllogism is difficult to complete: (a) Persius must write satire, which requires an audience; (b) nobody today can tolerate satire, let alone appreciate it; (c) then Persius will write "for Nobody." He will whisper his great secret into his little book. If he alone, for now, knows the true value of his satirical laughter—knows how much better it is than that wretched new Latin *Iliad* that everyone is praising—then that must suffice. Again, the argument stops: over the line, after that single debased word, "Iliade."

And, irrepressibly, starts again, as, with no warning, Persius turns to address an unknown reader:

> audaci quicumque adflate Cratino
> iratum Eupolidem praegrandi cum sene palles,
> aspice et haec, si forte aliquid decoctius audis.
> inde vaporata lector mihi ferveat aure,
> non hic qui in crepidas Graiorum ludere gestit
> sordidus et lusco qui possit dicere "lusce,"
> sese aliquem credens Italo quod honore supinus
> fregerit heminas Arreti aedilis iniquas,
> nec qui abaco numeros et secto in pulvere metas
> scit risisse vafer, multum gaudere paratus
> si cynico barbam petulans nonaria vellat.
> his mane edictum, post prandia Callirhoen do.   (123–34)

[Whoever you are, who have been inspired by a blast from bold Cratinus; who grow pale over Eupolis's anger and the Great Old Man, then look at these things too, if by chance you can listen to something quite concentrated. I want a reader who, with his ear steamed open, can come to a good slow boil—not your mean-spirited type who jokes about Greek footwear, or who can say, "Hey, one-eye!" to a one-eyed man—who thinks himself somebody because, lying on his back, as a local Italian magistrate, he smashed some crooked pint-measures at Arretium; nor the type, either, who gets a great big laugh out of somebody's counting on an abacus or drawing geometric figures in the dust, and who's especially happy if a brazen hooker tugs on a Cynic's beard. Well, they can always listen to the news, and enjoy some popular stripper.]

So an acceptable reader exists, after all. It is someone who has studied the Athenian Old Comedy writers, Cratinus, Eupolis, and Aristophanes, and felt their impact, and knows what good, strong, educated laughter is about—unlike the philistines with whom *Satire* 1 mockingly ends.

In lines 123–26 Persius brings satire back to an old allegiance. Horace, in his first literary satire, began by tracing Lucilius's satiric freedom of speech (*libertas*, Greek *parrhêsia*) and wit back to the Old Comedy writers, but went on to redefine *libertas* in satire much as Menander and Terence had redefined it in comedy. The personal and social norms of friendship, tolerance, moderation, and good humor that he advocates are very much the norms of post-Aristotelian New Comedy, both Greek and Roman. But Persius goes back to where Horace began: to Lucilius, with whom he too begins, and Aristophanes, with whom he (almost) ends. The circle is complete. In the Age of Nero, not Augustus, Aristophanes, not Menander, is what you need.

As one who has, in fact, "grown pale over Aristophanes," let me respond belatedly to the challenge. For I *do* hear Aristophanes behind this last section of *Satire* 1. I hear lines from his *Frogs* where the Chorus distinguishes good people from bad, and among the good are people who appreciate Old Comedy, who "have been initiated in the [Dionysian] rites of bull-headed Cratinus." In *Frogs*, living and dead become confused; Dionysus descends into the underworld to find, and bring back, a good poet (who turns out to be Aeschylus, not Euripides); and the rich underworld where the Chorus of Initiates sings is also the place where true vitality, wisdom, and civic spirit are to be found. So, too, if I am right, Persius appeals to initiated readers and critics the other side of death. Again, I hear lines from *Wasps* where Aristophanes praises the cathartic, "purifying" power of his own Old-and-New Comedy. He has cleaned up the comic stage, or so he self-ironically professes, and if we will only listen to him, appreciate his comedy rightly, and follow his supremely good advice, he will clean up Athenian politics as well.[63]

Persius's right reader, then, will have learned from Old Comedy to appreciate the "strong distilled spirits" of his new cathartic satire. His metaphorical complexity, not least in lines 123–26, is itself a test. Cratinus impresses one like the blast of a mighty storm.[64] The reader of Aristophanes and his rivals grows pale ("palles"), partly from the effort of study, partly from awe before those great passionate creations.[65] "Decoctius aliquid" (literally "something more boiled-down") refers (a) to the highly condensed expression of good, strong poetry (Aristophanes' powerful metaphors were praised in antiquity), and (b) to the cleansing of dirty or sick ears with a stinging dose of comic or satiric truth-telling, as with vinegar. It seems likely that "audis" too has a double meaning: "if you like to hear," and "if you are in fact able to hear." If you enjoy Aristophanes, that is, you will be able to hear Persius: and not least, as I have argued, by reading him aloud, by reperforming his satires, if only in the private theater of your mind.

"So may my reader seethe," says Persius, "with steamed-open ear." There is an implicit pun here. Most writers would want the reader to "warm to their favor" (*foveat*), but Persius wants his reader to "seethe" ("ferveat"): not pleased, but changed. More important, now that they have been cleansed, the sick and tender "little ears" ("auriculae"), so all-pervasive at Rome, have given way to a single good ear ("aure")—which is where Persius wants to end, but the world won't comply with his wishes, any more than Aristophanes' world did with his. So *Satire* 1 ends with eight lines describing the reader Persius doesn't want, the average Roman philistine who laughs so mindlessly at all the usual things—at foreigners, cripples, intellectuals, and philosophers. This ending is satire in the more obvious sense of the word. It also reminds us, one last time, of Persius's isolation in present-day Rome, where everybody has asses' ears and nobody, or almost nobody, is willing or able to hear the truth that the satirist must voice.

We end with a paradox, then, and with a challenge.

The paradox, as said earlier, is that satire was made to be performed and to entertain its audience, but what Persius displays is a strange kind of nonperformance written for almost nobody in the foreseeable future: "vel duo vel nemo." A corrupt society requires strong satire, but in a corrupt society strong satire won't be tolerated or understood, or even heard. What Persius writes is condensed and difficult, and it stings. In the end, he can only whisper his secret into a little book and bury it there. I think of Eliot's *Waste Land* again:

> That corpse you planted last year in your garden,
> Has it begun to sprout? Will it bloom this year?

Persius wrote *Satire* 1 toward the end of his short life. Perhaps he was already dying. He had, as we saw, no illusions about poetic immortality. If a decent reader or two find him out, that will be their business, not his.

And this is our challenge: to dig Persius up again (so to speak), to read and reperform his satire and listen, really listen, to what it has to say. What he said of Aristophanes—that you must grow pale studying him, that you must submit yourself to the comic catharsis—shows also, I think, how he himself ideally wanted to be read, and how we should read him today: with strong laughter, yes, but also "in fear and trembling." For Persius pursues truth and integrity with a passionate self-honesty that is hard to follow. I shall say more about this in chapter 2.

Appendix

▣ ▣ ▣ ▣ ▣ ▣ ▣ ▣ ▣ ▣ ▣ ▣ ▣ ▣ ▣ ▣

THE *CHOLIAMBICS*

Nec fonte labra prolui caballino
nec in bicipiti somniasse Parnaso
memini, ut repente sic poeta prodirem.
Heliconidasque pallidamque Pirenen
illis remitto quorum imagines lambunt
hederae sequaces; ipse semipaganus
ad sacra vatum carmen adfero nostrum.
quis expedivit psittaco suum "chaire"
picamque docuit verba nostra conari?
magister artis ingenique largitor
venter, negatas artifex sequi voces.
quod si dolosi spes refulserit nummi,
corvos poetas et poetridas picas
cantare credas Pegaseium nectar.

[I haven't splashed my lips in the Nag's Spring, and I don't remember
having had a dream on twin-peaked Parnassus, that I should suddenly
emerge a poet. The girls of Helicon? Pale-faced Pirene? I'm sending
them back for the people whose portrait-busts are tongued by persistent
ivy. A half-rustic myself, to the holy rites of bards I'm contributing a
song that's all my own.

Who was it that set the parrot on to say *Bon jour* and taught the magpie
to try our human language? Master of Arts and bestower of talent,
the belly, skilled at pursuing speech that was not vouchsafed to birds.
But once that flashing coin gives its deceptive gleam, you'd think that
raven-poets and magpie-poetesses were chanting forth sheer "nectar of
Pegasus."]

I offer two working hypotheses, neither of them new. First, that Persius
intended these fourteen verses on poetry and poets to be read where editors
normally put them today, as a "nonpoetic" preface to the satire book.[66] And
second, that they are closely connected with *Satire* 1, to which they provide
a background perspective about the business of poetry making and fame,

but conversely, whose fuller satiric vignettes help us interpret the more concise and riddling pronouncements of the *Choliambics*.

Persius's choice of a sequence in choliambs, or "limping iambs," is itself significant. This was a common Hellenistic verse form, used for personal comment or criticism. Callimachus used it, as we saw, in his first *iambos*, harking back to Hipponax.[67] Catullus adapted it to express a great variety of strong feelings, from simple (reactions to bad poetry, joyful homecoming) to complex (his insoluble bond to "Lesbia"). Placed before the hexameter *Satires*, it would also recall how Lucilius moved from iambic and trochaic meters in the earlier Books 26–29 to the wonderfully flexible hexameter, which he established as the standard meter of Roman verse satire, much as Ennius had done for epic. So this is, among other things, an homage to Lucilius.

The preface falls neatly into two complementary parts. In the first, Persius sets himself comically apart from the cumulative received tradition of the Poet's Calling: from Hesiod, whom the Muses greeted on Mount Helicon and gave the gift of poetry; from Ennius, to whom Homer appeared in a dream, to tell him that in the Pythagorean sequence of reincarnations, he was his successor, indeed quite literally the new carrier of his poetic soul; and from Callimachus, whom Apollo told to walk on special paths, avoiding the trodden highways of song, and to drink from untouched springs, not from great muddied streams. Callimachus championed new, Hellenistic standards of poetic originality. He advocated poems that broke new ground, that avoided massive forms and familiar subject-matter: better the "little epic" or elegy developing a less familiar story, or a novel aspect of what had seemed familiar. Catullus, Horace, and the Augustan love-elegists, most notably Propertius, followed Callimachus's advice, transforming Latin lyric and elegy into something creative and new. The trouble, of course, was the triteness to which bright metaphors of poetic initiation and creativity were bound to succumb. By Persius's time, nothing could be less original than those "untouched springs," those by-paths of poetic subject matter (and especially what we might call the by-pathologies of love). And, ironically, it is Persius who, by making rough fun of Callimachus, now brings him up to date.

He conflates the various Initiations here with a sovereign indifference to place, manner, and circumstance that is very funny but has rather baffled the scholars—it has all gone wrong, somehow. Pegasus, the winged steed that struck the ground with its hoof, making the creative waters flow, has now become a common "nag." And Persius just can't remember what others, it seems, so easily recall: how he fell asleep on Parnassus, received an initiatory dream, and was instantly transformed into a Poet. (Could it—the point is Horatian—have taken slow, hard work?) He treats the Muses cavalierly, and the fashionable pallor of poets, and all the metaphorical apparatus of poetic fame. These things belong properly to the dead, not to the living. Whether the "ivy-tongued portrait-busts" belong to classical poets long dead or to the ghastly shades of still-living poets impatient to join that great Dead Poets Society, is left ambiguous. Should we hope that our memory, like theirs, will be "ivy-crowned," kept green after death for some indefinite time? *Satire* 1 will address that subject further.

But Persius now takes a different stance. He sets himself against all this effete poetic paraphernalia as a "semipaganus," a "half-rustic" or, more freely, a "half-uncivilized outsider"—which, indeed, the boy from Volterra might have been called when he came to school in Rome.[68] For Horace, the task of Latin poetry and drama was to shed the last vestiges of its rustic origins, so that it might become an altogether civilized and civilizing vehicle of Roman culture.[69] By contrast, Persius must return to a rougher, more honest mode of speech than Rome's tender little ears can bear. His "semipaganus" is a strikingly new and influential satiric persona. He is the outsider whose rude speech breaks through social pretensions and constraints, a simple but honest type who must speak out freely and say what he has to say. He has close affinities with the child, and also with the satyr; and despite the clearly false etymology deriving *satura* ("satire") from the Greek *satyros* ("satyr"), which Casaubon exploded in 1605, the idea of satire as a sort of "satyr play" hung on tenaciously, from Roman times through at least the early English Renaissance.

From his initial negatives, his rejection of the usual trappings and imagined significance of poetry, Persius develops a finally positive statement for this first half of his preface. He will contribute something, after all, to the sacred rites of poets (living or dead). His gift will be "something of our own" ("nostrum"): something, that is, that embraces both originality and tradition. This might sound reassuring, as though Persius had staked a claim, after all, to solid poetic achievement, if not to the traditional voice of the inspired bard. In the second group of seven verses, however, he continues to demystify poetry's more spiritual ideology and aspirations, reducing them brutally to physical necessity. Poets write to fill their bellies. Actually, this notion has an honorable lineage: in Hesiod, when the Muses address him and his fellow-shepherds teasingly as "mere bellies"; and in Homer, when Odysseus speaks, comically and humbly, of the belly's constraints. The effect is comic because he is playing the part of a helpless beggar, dependent on people's charity, and one of genuine humility and self-understanding because he is trying to express, and even to communicate to the proud young suitors (if only they could hear him) the hard truths about human limitations, and ultimately about our common mortality, that his travels, his failures and sufferings and those of his men, have taught him.[70]

Persius's comically reductionist statements about bird-poets imply a similar perspective, of human ambition and achievement set against the background of human nature and mortality. On one level, taking their cue from Horace, they mock the general run of overly imitative or even plagiaristic poets, those who miss the point of truly creative *imitatio*, of originality within a tradition. On another, they remind us comically—in ways, I think, directly reminiscent of Aristophanes' *Birds*—that our highest cultural achievements are, after all, the products of a very slow ascent from the beasts (or birds): an evolution that, in the comic or satiric view at least, may not have taken us very far. So the "*chaire*" joke, the trick played on the philhellene Albucius in Lucilius's satire, has now become a joke on all of us, Persius not least. It is a telling reminder of our beginnings and our necessary limitations. Where else should an honest satirist begin?[71]

The last three lines are ambiguous. Most obviously, they describe poets who write for a living, much as parrots imitate human speech to please their owners and be given birdseed, or as hungry parasites bring their entertaining talents to the tables of the rich. There is a hint, in "dolosi," that the parasite-poet may be deceived in his expectation of reward. But critics are hit too.[72] Flash a coin again—or give the man a dinner (as Horace warned, and as we shall be shown further in *Satire* 1)—and he'll think that a bird is a bard, that the bird-verses he hears are a sheer distillation of the Muses' own nectar. Critics are as corrupt as poets, and for the same reason. But what Persius actually says is "credas" ("you would think"). The person, finally, who is taken in—whose judgment proves erroneous, if not corrupt—is you or I. The joke is partly on Persius, insofar as he makes any poetic claims at all, but it is also, ultimately, on ourselves. We are left with a nonfoundation of critical judgment from which to read what follows, the six satirical nonperformances of our self-proclaimed nonpoet. This whole business, you might say, is for the birds.

Chapter Two

▣ ▣ ▣ ▣ ▣ ▣ ▣ ▣ ▣ ▣ ▣ ▣ ▣ ▣ ▣ ▣ ▣

SEEKING INTEGRITY

Pᴇʀsɪᴜs's *Satire* 1 marks a third, seemingly final displacement of Roman satire from the public stages, whether of theater or dinner-party, where vice would ordinarily be denounced and folly mocked. Lucilius could not be Aristophanes, Horace could not be Lucilius, and now Persius cannot be Horace. As we have seen, he makes literary virtue out of necessity, exploiting the leverage of a marginalized satirist, a "half-uncivilized outsider" (*semipaganus*), together with the explosive power of a long-suppressed truth that must somehow make itself heard. Yet, if that dangerous truth is not just political, but universal—if not just Midas (or Nero), but the whole world has asses' ears—then for what audience should an honest satirist write? And, more urgently: how should one become an honest satirist? Only, it seems, by answering the prior challenge to become—or, for a Stoic like Persius, to try to become—an honest man.

Satires 2–5, to be treated in this chapter and the next, play out ethical concerns upon an inner stage.[1] The title of chapter 2 may be misleading, for what Persius depicts is less the process of "Seeking Integrity" than the desperate urgency, in a distracted and distracting world, of taking up the search in the first place—let alone, pursuing it seriously through life. The vices and follies that Persius depicts, and by which he feels beleaguered, are the familiar stuff of satire. What is new is the intensity of his personal struggle, rendered perceptible throughout. The "different voices" of dramatic monologue are summoned to play out, in a new kind of satiric performance—though within a philosophical tradition extending from Socrates to Epictetus—the difficulties, both external and internal, by which the quest of integrity is beset almost before it can begin.

In *Satire* 2, Persius will unmask two kinds of bad performance: the scoundrel's hypocrisy that conceals vicious prayers for others' harm under a cover of ritual propriety, and the less obvious self-deceptions of people who pray ignorantly for the wrong things for themselves or others. We fashion ourselves in turn as we were fashioned, to master the world's delusive games. *Satire* 3, probing still deeper beneath the polished surfaces of people's lives to reveal the soul-sickness within, will enact a wake-up call to true (Stoic) learning and living. Its corrosive depictions of personality divided against itself, the false constructions of family and school, and the plunge downward toward disintegration and death, both physical and moral, challenge the reader to undertake the life-giving work of recon-struction. At the same time, this intellectual and moral task is adumbrated by Persius's refashioning of satire in and for a new age, as he takes up the work of Lucilius and Horace, especially the later Horace of the *Epistles*, and brings it to new completion.

Hypocrisy and Self-Deception (*Satire 2*)

After the intense inner dialogue of *Satire* 1 and the struggle to find an adequate poetic voice, readers have found *Satire* 2 easier of access, more lucid in presentation, and more focused in theme. Like Macrinus's birth-day, which it initially celebrates, it serves as a new beginning, a reintroduc-tion to satire, opening the inner group of poems (2–5) within the frame of the *libellus* (1–6). Its subject, foolish and vicious prayers, is familiar enough. What is striking, as we read and reread the satire, is how Persius probes beneath the surface of men's foolish or vicious behavior to their half-unintentional, half-willful confusion about the gods, which leads them to substitute unthinking acts of outward religiosity like ritual purifications and massive animal sacrifices for the piety and inner goodness that nature and nature's god require—a positive standard implied throughout but only becoming explicit, though as aim rather than accomplishment, at the sat-ire's close.[2]

A running literary subtext of *Satire* 2 is Persius's relation to Horace, whose spirit and language—from his *Satires* and *Epistles*, and even his *Odes*—sound through the opening sixteen lines:

> Hunc, Macrine, diem numera meliore lapillo,
> qui tibi labentis apponet candidus annos.
> funde merum genio . . .   (2.1–3)

[Mark this day's count with a finer stone, Macrinus; it will add brightly to your slipping sum of years. Pour out unmixed wine to your guardian spirit . . .]

The motif of numbering birthdays gratefully is Horatian; so, too, the con-ceit of years being added even as they slip away. Compare the birthday celebration in *Odes* 4.11, the day when "Maecenas orders the years flowing in upon him" (19–20), or, in *Odes* 2.5.13–15, the conceit that time will add to young Lalage the years it "takes from" her lover Horace (but this is wishful thinking, for the two will never meet, the one ripening, the other growing younger, in an ideal balance). The easy, humorous address to Macrinus also recalls friends addressed in Horace's (hexameter) *Epistles*. But after that grateful, contented, celebratory pause at the caesura of line 3, Persius's satire pivots on the negative contrast ("non tu . . ."), and happiness fades in the unforgiving glare of greed, folly, and malice. Yet Persius directs our gaze all the more emphatically toward Horace, conflating at least three passages from the *Satires* and *Epistles*. In (a) *Epistles* 1.16, Horace tests a friend for true inner consistency. Is he, like many, a "good man" (*vir bonus*) just for appearance's sake, one who avoids vice for fear of being found out? What would he not do, if nobody could see him?

> The "good man," object of everyone's regard in the public square and the courts, when he placates the gods by offering a pig or an ox, says "Father Janus" good and loud, and "Apollo," so everyone can hear; but under his breath, so he can't be overheard, "lovely Laverna [goddess of theft], grant me the gift of fraud; let me appear just and holy; cast a cloud of darkness over my stealing and my sin." (57–62)

Earlier, in (b) *Satires* 2.6.1–15, Horace gives thanks for his Sabine estate. He asks nothing more from Mercury, except just to confirm these gifts:

> If I haven't made my holdings greater through evildoing or lesser through neglect, and if I don't make silly prayers, either to round out my property by just adding that piece of land, or to hit upon a pot of silver, buried treasure, like the hired hand in the story who became a great landowner. . . . If I am truly grateful and content, hear my prayer: make my cattle fat for their master and everything else except my mind, and stay, as my greatest protector, by my side.

Persius surely heard the echoes of Callimachus and Virgilian pastoral in this prayer. Probably, too, he recognized the punning presence of *Maecenas*, Horace's patron, beneath that of Mercury:

> nil amplius oro,
> *Maia nate*, nisi ut propria haec mihi munera faxis.   (4–5)

> [I ask nothing more, son of Maia, except that you make
> these gifts permanent for me.]

Maecenas is, for Horace, a very present embodiment of Mercury, and the request *just* to make his gifts "propria," altogether Horace's own, conveys, together with gratitude, a considerable amount of cheek.[3]

Borrowing also from (c) *Satires* 2.5.45–50, where the wily legacy-hunter will seek a second place in a man's will after his unhealthy son, Persius has both uglified the situation and transformed ordinary greed into extraordinary malice. Uncle's funeral will be "brilliant"; the sick boy, mangy and swollen, will be "wiped out" altogether, a hotly anticipated climax to the

long, close pursuit; Nerius is doing so well—three wives buried already!
Notice how Persius has framed the "pot-of-silver" prayer with powerful
curses against anyone and everyone standing in the speaker's way. If you
indulge daydreams of magical riches, are you setting foot on the infernal
slope leading to violence, fraud, and the war of all against all? Persius's
divergent echoes of Horace unsettle our more habitual complacent read-
ings. Not only, we might now reflect, is the overall balance of *Satires* 2.6
more precarious than it first appears (unlike the Country Mouse's lifestyle
in the fable), but it is framed by darker poems: by the death-centered *Satires*
2.5, on legacy-hunting, and *Satires* 2.7, the slave Davus's quasi-Stoic dia-
tribe on freedom versus slavery, where the final charge of inconsistency, of
wavering between city and country, evidently hits home. And *Epistles* 1.16,
a Cynic-Stoic diatribe through and through, proclaims values of integrity,
resolution, and constancy with strikingly new insistence. This is not to say
that Stoicism has the last word in *Epistles* 1. Though Horace goes back to
school to relearn his moral ABCs, he will never, as he declares, "swear
fidelity to the words of any master." Yet he takes the Stoic challenge seri-
ously and gives it voice in *Epistles* 1 as never before; and Persius, as I shall
argue, takes up where Horace leaves off.

"To voice these prayers with purity" ("sancte," 15): the sarcasm is strong
and clear, but what is its object? Hypocrisy, superstition, self-delusion, or
a curious mix of the three? How, if at all, does this wretch think about
divinity? Persius pursues the inquiry, like a prosecutor pressing a reluctant
defendant in court:

> heus age, responde (minimum est quod scire laboro)
> de Iove quid sentis? estne ut praeponere cures
> hunc—cuinam? cuinam? vis Staio? an—scilicet haeres?
> quis potior iudex puerisve quis aptior orbis?
> hoc igitur quo tu Iovis aurem impellere temptas
> dic agedum Staio. "pro Iuppiter, o bone" clamet
> "Iuppiter!" at sese non clamet Iuppiter ipse?
> ignovisse putas quia, cum tonat, ocius ilex
> sulpure discutitur sacro quam tuque domusque?
> an quia non fibris ovium Ergennaque iubente
> triste iaces lucis evitandumque bidental,
> idcirco stolidam praebet tibi vellere barbam
> Iuppiter? aut quidnam est qua tu mercede deorum
> emeris auriculas? pulmone et lactibus unctis?   (2.17–30)

[Come now, reply—it's a very minor thing I want to know— what do
you think about God [lit., Jupiter]? Do you think you'd bother to
put him ahead of—"Of whom?" Of whom? Shall we say, Staius? Or—
is there a problem? Can you think of a better judge, a more suitable

protector of orphans? All right, then: take that prayer you're intent on shoving into God's ear and try it on Staius. "O God!" he'll exclaim, "Good God!" And wouldn't God exclaim, "Good *Me*!"? Do you think you're overlooked just because, when it thunders, an oak tree is split apart by the sacred lightning sooner than you and your kin? Or, just because you're not lying there in the grove as a grim and untouchable warning-object (as the sheep's entrails require, and the portent-specialist), does God therefore offer you his impassive beard to pluck? Or what *does* it cost, your special access to the gods' ears? Lungs and greasy intestines?]

The aim is Socratic, to expose contradictions in people's thought and behavior, but the method is Aristophanic, showing up confusions of old anthropomorphism and new skepticism in a distorting mirror. Already at lines 3–4 Persius imagines someone "drawing the gods aside" ("seductis divis") like a skilled lobbyist to make his unholy requests. What does the man really think about Jupiter? Is he relieved to have escaped the lightning blast from an old-fashioned angry divinity? Or does he scoff, like the Unjust Argument in Aristophanes' *Clouds*, at the simple-mindedness of such beliefs and their attendant practices of expiation? Both, perhaps; but pulling Jupiter's Stoic beard enacts unmistakable contempt: "I can insult Jupiter and get away with it." We think of the Roman senators in Livy (5.41.9) who awaited the Gauls so impassively that they were mistaken for statues (but when a Gaul pulled a senator's beard, he struck him with his staff, and all the senators were slain). Is Jupiter that unresponsive, in the skeptic's view? As helpless as —a Stoic philosopher?

Persius's last indignant question involves sacrifice. Does the man really believe that he has bought the gods' attention with his filthy lungs-and-guts offering? Later on, and more insistently, Persius will denounce the corrupting materialism of Roman religious practices; but now, at the satire's center, the scene abruptly shifts to childhood. We see a superstitious (*metuens divum*) granny or aunt warding off the evil eye from a newborn infant with obscenity and spittle, then making extravagant wishes for its future:[4]

tunc manibus quatit et spem macram supplice voto
nunc Licini in campos, nunc Crassi mittit in aedis:
"hunc optet generum rex et regina, puellae
hunc rapiant; quidquid calcaverit hic, rosa fiat."   (35–38)

[Now she swings her scrawny little hope in her arms and sends him in prayers, now into Licinius's vast fields, now into Crassus's palatial home: "May a king and queen choose him for son-in-law! May the girls run to catch him! May whatever he treads on turn to roses."]

From the world of famous Roman billionaires the child is "sent away" still further, into the realm of fairy tale, where the peasant boy marries the princess. Such stories may appear sweet and harmless, but as the strict Stoic sees it, they belong to the overall atmosphere of false thinking and wishing by which the human infant is corrupted even before it can speak. The fairy tale wishes, the childish thinking, linger not far beneath the surface of (allegedly) grown-up minds, leading not just to ingratitude for the gods' real gifts, but to murderous competition, resentment, and hatred in society.[5]

You sabotage your own wishes, says Persius, turning now to ordinary fools. You pray for health and strength, while overloading your body with rich foods; you pray for wealth, while spending your money on big animal sacrifices like a compulsive gambler, hoping that now, even now, they will pay off—until your last coin gives a lonely sigh.[6] Differently, and worse, you gild the gods' statues, as if they lusted for gold like yourself. From gilding, Persius shifts into a passionate critique of Roman so-called progress:

aurum vasa Numae Saturniaque inpulit aera
Vestalisque urnas et Tuscum fictile mutat.
o curvae in terris animae et caelestium inanis,
quid iuvat hoc, templis nostros inmittere mores
et bona dis ex hac scelerata ducere pulpa?
haec sibi corrupto casiam dissolvit olivo,
haec Calabrum coxit vitiato murice vellus,
haec bacam conchae rasisse et stringere venas
ferventis massae crudo de pulvere iussit.
peccat et haec, peccat, vitio tamen utitur. at vos
dicite, pontifices, in sancto quid facit aurum?
nempe hoc quod Veneri donatae a virgine pupae.   (59–70)

[Gold changed them all—Numa's vessels, Saturn's bronze implements, Vesta's urns, sculptures of Etruscan clay. O earthbent souls, devoid of heaven's traces, what good is this, to bring our human habits into the temples, find out the gods' likings from this accursed flesh? For flesh it was that adulterated olive oil with cinnamon, spoiled good Calabrian wool with purple shellfish-dyes, scraped out pearls from oysters, stripped fiery veins of ore from the plain dirt. Sinful stuff, all this, but it helps progress: but tell me, priests-in-charge, what good does gold effect with the sacred objects? Lots of good, sure—like the dolls girls dedicate to Venus.]

Lines 61–63 sound more Pythagorean-Platonic than Stoic.[7] Contaminated by false desires and values, overwhelmed by worldly materialism, the soul forgets its heavenly origin and destiny. We can see why these lines were quoted so often in letters and sermons by the Christian fathers, intent on how "the flesh wars against the spirit"; I take them as heartfelt, however trite the sentiment. Progress, though often useful, has its costs; conservatives and moralists regularly complain about the "sophistication" of simple olive oil or wool; but gilding the gods' statues is far worse, a defilement of the sacred ("sancto"), a horrible contradiction. If Persius compares it, finally and explosively, to the silliness of girls dedicating their dolls ("pupae") to Venus before marriage, his passionate protest—which endeared him also to sixteenth- and seventeenth-century Protestants like Isaac Casaubon—may reflect something of his own painful loss of innocence on growing up and seeing the corrupt world around him for what it was. The naïve child, nurtured on fairy tales or playing with dolls, must be left behind. There is no time for dallying with foolish daydreams when corruption and danger are everywhere, when money is everything, when the gods people worship, or pretend to worship, are reduced to gaudy, "dolled-up," ineffective statues. What *do* they really think of Jupiter?

And what, we might reasonably ask , does Persius think?

After his long catalogue of pseudo-religious idiocies and abuses, he circles back to simple, or maybe not-so-simple, piety:

quin damus id superis, de magna quod dare lance
non possit magni Messalae lippa propago?
conpositum ius fasque animo sanctosque recessus
mentis et incoctum generoso pectus honesto.
haec cedo ut admoveam templis et farre litabo.   (71–75)

[Why don't we give the gods what great Messala's bleary-eyed offspring couldn't give from his great big platter: a settled regard for laws human and divine; inmost thoughts holy and pure; a heart deep-dyed with nobility and goodness? Let me just bring these to the temples, and a plain meal-offering will be acceptable.]

True piety, first of all, lies within, as the central words "sanctosque recessus mentis" lie hidden within the rest. Earlier in the satire, inward viciousness contrasted outward pretenses and observances; now worship must be conducted in the inmost mind and heart, as in a hidden shrine, a most sacred place. Secondly, true piety requires process, like the compounding ("conpositum") of ingredients in cooking, or like the steeping ("incoctum") of woolstuffs through and through with an indelible dye.[8] But thirdly, Persius is not offering, or preparing to offer, what he has already achieved. Rather, his claim is hypothetical: "Let me bring these things to the altar." It is, indeed, like a prayer—a quiet, understated, very modest prayer to the gods, or God, or the inner spirit, to help him procure for himself what will suffice.[9] This prayer, concluding the opening satire of the inner group (2–5), helps define the goal of mental, moral, and spiritual integrity toward which Persius will represent humankind, himself not least, as struggling (or, as the case may be, not struggling) throughout the following *Satires*.

Called to Virtue (*Satire* 3)

A writer like Persius who is billed as a morally serious poet and a Stoic propagandist already has two strikes against him. Perhaps that is why many scholars have concentrated their interpretive efforts on *Satire* 1, that non-literary manifesto, rather than on *Satires* 2, 3, and 5, which are so deeply rooted in Stoic beliefs, and which reproduce many features of that largely neglected genre, the Cynic-Stoic diatribe. Yet in *Satire* 3 , a wake-up call to study philosophy, Persius turns old commonplaces of the moralizing diatribe into powerful and disturbing new poetry of lived experience. He makes us feel that it is a matter of life and death whether we respond to the call or not, whether we pursue moral and spiritual integrity or simply go on drifting through our aimless, fragmented, unexamined lives. If his satire carries conviction, that is largely because the writer is speaking, not about the achievement of healing and wholeness, but about their overriding urgency, and he is speaking first to himself. We may listen in, or perhaps join the conversation, if we so choose.

I begin with lines 66–72, where the poem shifts from inner-directed dialogue into a more outer-directed diatribe form. Persius has just introduced his key analogy between moral failure and disease: isn't it better to treat sickness in its first stages, rather than call for the doctor's help for a long-swollen body when it's much too late? With this question he strides to the podium:

> discite et, o miseri, causas cognoscite rerum:
> quid sumus et quidnam victuri gignimur, ordo
> quis datus, aut metae qua mollis flexus et unde,
> quis modus argento, quid fas optare, quid asper
> utile nummus habet, patriae carisque propinquis
> quantum elargiri deceat, quem te deus esse
> iussit et humana qua parte locatus es in re.

> [Come learn, unhappy people, what it all means: what we're made of; what life we're born to lead; where we are placed; how to make the most graceful turn around life's racecourse; what limit's set for money-making; what is the point of prayer, or of hard cash; how much it is right to spend on your country's needs, or your dear relatives; and who the god has ordered you to be; and where, in the human world, you have been stationed.]

We move out in these lines from individual wants and needs to larger obligations to family and country, and to the divine plan: a hierarchy of value familiar from Cicero and Virgil. To put it differently: our particular, often petty desires, such as the wish to accumulate wealth, are modified and reshaped as we come to see our lives in perspective, as a small though significant part of the god's plan. For, as we should come to realize ("cognoscite"), we have the privilege and the responsibility to conduct our little lives in accordance with that same power of reason, the fiery *logos*, that both burns within our hearts and keeps the great universe steady on its course.

I have, quite improperly, taken lines 66–72 out of context; yet this is how they were so often cited in late Antiquity and the Middle Ages. St. Augustine, for example, quotes them in *The City of God*, and adds, "Where do people hear these divine precepts? In the Christian churches."[10] Augustine's initial point was negative. You wouldn't have heard such things around the pagan gods. But there is also a sense that Persius *belongs* in Christian churches, that he would be at home there as a pagan prophet (that *semipaganus* again?) or, better, as an *anima naturaliter Christiana*. Elsewhere, Augustine quotes again from *Satire* 3 to illustrate the importance of conviction of sin, *cognitio vitiorum*. He honors Persius's moral contribution, although, in the end, he feels obliged to reassert the distance separating pagan from Christian: "For we are not bound to these people's authority (*horum auctoritati*) in such matters."[11] Assimilation has its limits.

Strangely enough, these seven lines, which have enjoyed such an influential afterlife on their own, are clarified and reinforced when we return them to their context. The preceding lines 63–65 introduced the dominant theme of the second half of *Satire* 3: attend to your symptoms—of moral failings, as of physical illness; call in the doctor and take his advice before it's too late. Persius also moves out from singular to plural, from personal advice to a public harangue. Then, as he turns from generally applicable human truths to the particular duties of each individual where he has been stationed, the second-person address returns to the informal, ironic style with which Part 2 began:

disce nec invideas quod multa fidelia putet
in locuplete penu, defensis pinguibus Umbris,
et piper et pernae, Marsi monumenta cluentis,
maenaque quod prima nondum defecerit orca.   (73–76)

[Learn, and don't envy all those stinking barrels in a rich man's storehouse, from fat Umbrians he defended; or pepper and hams, friendly reminders of a Marsian client; or the sprat that's not yet missing from the first big jar.]

These lines give comic relief, letting us down pleasantly from the high-soaring preacher's style and the pressure of those high ideals, back into the ordinary business of Roman life. Gratifyingly, too, this descent into the banal actually enhances our appreciation of the ideal, reminding us ("monumenta," indeed!) of the paltry everyday transactions in what my students used to call "the real world." What is the alternative to the high Stoic vision? Barrels of ham, it seems, and pepper, and anchovies, a successful lawyer's payments in kind. Success in "the real world" comes down to a mess of stinking fish. This is still satire, in case we had forgotten. It has a sting.

The injunction of *Satire* 3, to pursue the moral and spiritual healing that Stoicism provides, is reinforced by a long-elaborated medical analogy. The moral faults and passions that disturb our lives are like diseases; they grow upon us stealthily, from small to great; they have (if we happen to notice) their physical or psychosomatic symptoms; and they urgently require the attention, care, and advice of the philosopher, who is the soul's physician. Advice that must absolutely be followed, or else . . . *Satire* 3 is largely about the "or else."

All this belongs to, and reinvigorates, the Greco-Roman tradition of diatribe satire that Horace both used and mocked in his *Satires*. Whereas Horace, for example, in *Satires* 2.3 lets Damasippus, a failed businessman and a somewhat demented convert to Stoicism, preach a long-winded and ridiculous secondhand sermon on the Stoic paradox, "Only the Wise Man is Sane," so that we laugh more at Damasippus than with him, Persius deconstructs Horace's satire, unsettling familiar Horatian ironies, disorienting our perspective so that we no longer know where we should stand.[12] But I would add that Persius draws on Horace's *Epistles*, not just his *Satires*, and especially on those *Epistles* where Horace shows himself feeling sick and confused, desiring something more like the Stoic *constantia*.[13] In the end, it seems, he accepts his inconsistencies, whether temperamental or rooted in the human condition. But Persius, I shall argue, takes up the challenge where Horace (as he saw it) left off, and pursues the search for integrity not in a typical diatribe satire this time, but in a dramatic monologue like *Satire* 1 with intense inner dialogue that makes us realize in how many ways he himself is implicated in human weakness and human need. I shall develop this idea of the implicated author in the second half of this chapter. For now, let me describe the merely implied author, the gentleman and Stoic behind the scenes.

This implied author is, first, a *proficiscens*, or "advancing person," in the study and pursuit of Stoicism. Second, he is a convalescent, someone who has been seriously ill, is still a bit shaky, but has come a long way toward recovery. Let me elaborate these two notions with the help of

Seneca, who was Persius's contemporary, and whose *Moral Epistles* to his friend Lucilius may be dated between 62 A.D., when he definitively retired from Nero's court (and Persius died), and 65 A.D., when he was forced to commit suicide, one of Nero's first victims after the failed conspiracy of Piso.

First, the *proficiscens*. The Early Stoa, of Zeno and Chrysippus in Athens in the early third century B.C., held up the perfect figure of the Wise Man, the *Sophos* (Latin, *Sapiens*), as the norm for all human behavior. "Will the Wise Man do *x* or *y*? " they asked. Hence the famous Stoic paradoxes, to which Roman satire so often returns: "Only the Wise Man is Sane," "Only the Wise Man is Free," and so forth, with their corollaries, "Every fool is insane," "Every fool is a slave." By contrast, the Middle Stoa of Panaetius and Antipater in the second century, in both Athens and Rome, was less concerned with the *Sophos/Sapiens* than with that more everyday embodiment of Stoic values, the educated gentleman who carried out his various duties and responsibilities (*ta kathêkonta/officia)* and followed the law of what was fitting (*to prepon/decorum*) in his everyday behavior. The Middle Stoa also allowed for degrees of progress in virtue, as the absolutizing imagination of the early Stoa had not. Here the *proficiens*, the "advancing person," comes in.

Seneca, who represents a later third stage, combining the older Stoic drive for autonomy and moral freedom with the latitude and practical compromises of the Middle Stoa, distinguishes three subsets of *proficiscentes* in *Epistle* 75 by how easily, and into what degree of moral sickness, they can still slip back. What matters is to keep pressing forward with *studium* and *intentio*, passionate effort and straining toward the goal. So, too, in *Epistle* 71.35–36.

> They will slip back, if they haven't persevered strongly enough in the effort of going forward. For, once they have relaxed in the smallest way from that eager and constant effort (*ex studio et fideli intentione*), then they must go backward. Nobody can simply start again at the same point where he left off. So let us press on and persevere. More journeying remains than we have covered so far, but a great part of progress is *wanting to make progress*.

In short: progress in Stoic virtue, progress toward what Seneca calls right-mindedness (*bona mens*), allows of degrees, which can be measured psychologically; but what it requires most of all is *intentionality*, the constant redirecting of the human will toward its proper, rational, and divinely ordained goal.

Again, Seneca draws on the well-developed Stoic analogy between moral faults or passions and physical illnesses to proclaim the urgency of "getting well" and helping others to get well. But he describes himself, tactfully and with critical self-awareness, as a fellow-patient in the great Stoic infirmary:

> "*You're* giving *me* advice," you say? "Have you given yourself advice? Have you corrected your own faults, that you're free to attend to others'? " No, I'm not such a scoundrel as to treat others when I'm sick myself; but rather—just as if I were occupying a bed in the same hospital—I am conversing with you about our common illness and sharing with you what remedies I know. So listen to what I say as if I were talking to myself. I am letting you into my private space, and with your assistance, I am conducting a case against myself. I cry out against myself: "Count your years, man, and you'll be ashamed to indulge the same desires, work for the same frivolous goals that you had as a boy. At least make this one provision for yourself, nearing the time of death: let your vices die before you do." (*Ep.* 27.1–2)

Notice how Seneca moves back and forth between speaking to Lucilius and speaking to himself. The two, as he says, reinforce each other. This is not just a didactic ploy, a matter of rhetorical tact ("When I'm telling you this, I'm also telling myself"). Sincerity and mutuality embrace. On the one hand, writing to Lucilius gives Seneca an excuse to express what he genuinely feels about issues of the greatest importance to himself; on the other hand, Seneca's sincere desire for self-improvement motivates him to bring Lucilius into his *secretum*, into the private spaces, the backstage areas of his life. Although he is older and more experienced than Lucilius, he is not necessarily much wiser, except perhaps in humility and proven perseverance: the humility of the would-be virtuous man who has stumbled time and again, who has found himself, as we all sometimes find ourselves, carried back to Square One; and the perseverance of the would-be virtuous man who, after so many setbacks, still goes on trying.

The implied author of Persius's third satire is just such a man as Seneca describes: a Stoic *proficiscens* or *progrediens*, a graduate student in philosophy already somewhat advanced and resolutely moving forward on the path to salvation, as well as a recovering patient, a Stoic convalescent.[14] But Persius is also an implicated author, a fragile, flawed, and physically vulnerable human being like ourselves. Later on in this chapter, I shall discuss three modes of self-implication in *Satire* 3—through exchange of voices, through arguably autobiographical allusions, and through what I call "performing in the sick body"—and I shall ask what connection Persius might or might not have wished to draw between composing satire and recomposing oneself. But first, I want to situate Persius's satire more precisely within the diatribe tradition that stretches from Bion to Epictetus, and especially against Horace's twists and turns.

Where Horace Left Off

Although, as Horace himself implies, important elements of his *Sermones* were derived recognizably from Bion's *Diatribes*, most scholars today find a progressive movement away from "diatribe satire" in Book 1, as arranged for publication, and also (though differently) in Book 2. Already in *Satires* 1.1 Horace eats his diatribal cake and has it too. That is, he exploits and displays the rhetorical techniques of diatribe, transposed into a poetic idiom that he has altogether mastered; he also sets these off within a subtle framework that suggests at once his literary refinement of the Bionean genre and his social and personal elevation above the diatribe preacher.[15] It is the beginning of a personal and literary journey that will transcend satire itself as it has been known.

Many diatribe techniques, for example. are displayed in the large middle section of *Satires* 1.1, on greed (*avaritia*), as if Horace were deliberately pulling out all the stops. An imaginary interlocutor voices arguments and excuses, all carefully refuted. There are animal and slave comparisons, funny stories (with some mimicry), bits of mythology and wordplay, and through it all, the relentless argument, the appeals to reason, moderation, and plain good sense, culminating in an assertion of the Aristotelian mean. At the same time, just as the diatribe on greed is framed, somewhat confusingly for scholars, by the shorter introductory and concluding sections on discontent, the Bionean performance, though powerfully recreated, is itself transposed within the context of subtler, more refined literature meant for a more private audience. Consider just the beginning.

Horace begins with a question, addressed to his patron Maecenas, about the universality of discontent : *Qui fit, Maecenas, ut nemo . . . ?* ("How does it happen, Maecenas, that no one . . . ? ") He then proceeds to illustrate the point in theatrical fashion, first by introducing various stock types, soldier and merchant, farmer and lawyer, who express their contradictory wishes in splendid comic fashion for the ear, and with an artistic subtlety of arrangement for the reader's eye; and then, by introducing a helpful god who will enable them to change professions—which, of course, they won't. It is splendid comic mimesis, great fun still today if you read it aloud. But the contrast between the quiet, personal opening and the little dramatic mimes that follow makes us aware, first, that we are watching a performance, and second, that this performance is not public, but private: not for a street audience such as Bion ostensibly addressed, but for a select group of listeners and readers centered around Maecenas. Horace is as far from Bion as Callimachus was from Archilochus and Hipponax. He revives his diatribe effectively, but with a difference. Or, to put it in terms of persona: behind this initial cast of characters, the dramatis personae, is the quasi-

Bionean diatribe preacher; behind him, in turn, is the urbane and ironic "satirist," or presenter of the satire; and behind *him* is the author we call "Horace," an elusive person and one who is able to grow and change—not least, I suspect, with the help of these same ethical teachings that the preacher conveys, and upon which the satirist casts a suspicious eye, time and again.

Satires 1.1 by no means establishes Horace's satires, even in Book 1, as "Bionean" diatribe satires; for only the first of Horace's three triads in Book 1 (1–3, 4–6, 7–9) take the diatribe form, and these build up to the central autobiographical satires 4–6, the heart and centerpiece of Book 1. Already in *Satires* 1.2, if not before, Horace takes the persona of the diatribe satirist and makes him into a figure of fun, the *doctor ineptus*, the preacher who all too easily loses coherence and purpose. Then *Satires* 1.3 turns a corner. It begins with the diatribe satirist criticizing the extremes of inconsistency to which one human being (Tigellius) can go; but the would-be satirist is brought up short by an interruption: "Don't *you* have any faults? " In answer, Horace produces a new persona who speaks for tolerance, mutual forbearance, and friendship (*amicitia*) in human relations. The speaker attacks Stoic absolutism and especially the Stoic paradox that "all sins are equal" (*omnia peccata paria*), which he counters with Epicurean teachings out of Lucretius; but these twist in his hand, become wickedly self-parodying (thus, the "instant" account of cultural evolution at 99–112), and so discredit the speaker as somewhat *ineptus*—though less so than his dogmatic, antisocial Stoic opponent. But also, behind the speaker, there emerges still another persona, that of the simple, honest man who is Maecenas's friend:

> Say, a man is rather simple; he comes forward—the way I've often happily done with you, Maecenas—to break in, like a nuisance, on someone's resting or reading; "He's got no common sense," we say. Oh, how rashly we ratify an unfair law against ourselves! For no one is born without faults. The best man is the one weighted down by least. (*Serm.* 1.3.63–69)

"Rather simple"? Better not count on it. Yet in *Satires* 1.4–6 Horace develops this self-image with wonderful humor and irony. He is his honest father's honest son (1.4); as a loving friend and companion, he joins Maecenas on a political mission that he doesn't understand at all (1.5); at Rome, he is no match for critical, envious people, but likes being in Maecenas's circle, where even a shy, innocent freedman's son has his welcome place (1.6; see also his combat with the ambitious bore of 1.9). This is the nice, lovable Horace who, as Persius says, insinuates himself into so many readers' hearts and "plays around their heartstrings."

By *Satires* 1.4, and still more by 1.10 and 2.1, Horace has established his confident place both in Maecenas's circle and in that of Virgil, Varius, Plotius, and other poet-critic friends. He has (as he would have himself and us believe) raised himself above the low-class fools and jesters, mimes, poetasters, and con men of Rome, and he has abandoned the personal invective and aggressive spirit that characterized Lucilian satire—though not without ironic reminders that he can still wield a dangerous stylus in self-defense. And yet, as Catherine Keane has demonstrated, Horace never lets himself or us forget the primitive anger and violence beneath the civilized surface of Roman life, and of Horatian satire: the recent memory of civil war (1.7) and the threat—later realized, of course—of its recurrence (1.5); the buried cemetery, where witches work by night, beneath Maecenas's beautiful new pleasure-gardens (1.8); the wrangling of low, primitive types, in which our superior laughter is still complicit (1.5 and 1.7, again).[16] Nor may we forget the precariousness, whether of Horace's external, social advancement in the circle of Maecenas, or of the internal, self-educational and moral achievement on which his recognition (as he would have it) has been based. Even the Bore, his low antagonist in 1.9, cannot be overcome, not only because his self-assertion proves impervious to polite, civilized irony, and neither friendship (jokingly) nor law (compulsively) avail in the end, but also because this ignorant, coarse, transparent opportunist is also a shadow self who can never quite be shaken off.

The ambiguities continue in Book 2, where, after the apologia of 2.1, the satirist largely fades into the background and new personae take over: the genial countrymen of 2.2 and 2.6, the pompous gastronomic expert of 2.4, the cynical prophet-adviser of 2.3, and, most important for Persius, two thoroughly ignorant preachers of third-hand Stoic diatribe. In *Satires* 2.3, Horace falls victim to Damasippus, an ex-bankrupt and fanatical convert to Stoicism, who preaches on the Stoic paradox, "Only the Wise Man is Sane" (or, "Every Fool is Mad"). He is obviously mad himself, and his long, rambling, impetuous diatribe (in the modern sense) against avarice, ambition, luxury, love, and superstition finally cancels itself out, so that Horace can be seen both as Damasippus's helpless victim and as the behind-the-scenes writer who makes the mad satirist into the involuntary object of his own satire. Similarly, in *Satires* 2.7, Horace's slave Davus both enjoys and abuses his Saturnalian liberty to preach on another Stoic paradox, "Only the Wise Man is Free" (or, "Every Fool is a Slave"). In the end, the slave is—a slave. Which brings us to the last satire, 2.8, where Horace bids a symbolic farewell to the feast of satire or comedy, distancing himself once more, and finally, from the malice of the satirical parasite or wit (*scurra*) who is himself more properly the object of satire than its proponent. It is time to leave that wicked but enjoyable world, of which Horace, for all his protests, has been very much a part, and move on.

Persius, in turn, will be much concerned with the Damasippus and Davus diatribes. He reverses these, in ways that Daniel Hooley has well described, in his own *Satires* 3 and 5, deconstructing the easy victories of Horatian irony and unsettling the reader who was so deceptively comfortable with Horace's metasatiric demonstrations.[17] But did Horace really get off so easily? From Damasippus, perhaps, whose scattershot criticisms either miss him entirely, or glance off harmlessly, or ironically reinforce his poetic strategies; but Davus, Horace's own slave, gets in some palpable hits (as well as some ludicrously wild misses) when he accuses him of inconsistency and hypocrisy.[18] For the point is, not what Horace actually does, but what he is—and what he would do if he could get away with it. Deep down, he has the same faults as Davus, only his lust, gluttony, fascination with art, and financial extravagance are higher-class. No matter: his subservience to one desire or another still invalidates his socially assumed freedom.

In the end, Horace the victim loses his temper like a madman out of tragedy, thus proving Davus's point (and Damasippus's as well), and losing the game, even as he forces Davus back into his pre-Saturnalian place. Horace the satirist has produced yet another superb performance for Maecenas's entourage. But what of Horace the human being? Has he unfinished business to attend to? If so, he takes it up again, after a lyric interval, in the *Epistles*, poems of self-refashioning that bring us back to the Cynic-Stoic diatribe in ways that Persius, in his turn, will not so much subvert as continue and complete.

Horace's cry of pain in *Epistles* 1.8 reactivates what seemed Davus's careless probing. His life, he tells Celsus, is neither correct nor pleasant: not from external causes,

> sed quia mente minus validus quam corpore toto
> nil audire velim, nil discere, quod levet aegrum;
> fidis offendar medicis, irascar amicis,
> cur me funesto properent arcere veterno;
> quae nocuere sequar, fugiam quae profore credam;
> Romae Tibur amem ventosus, Tibure Romam.   (*Ep.* 1.8.7–12)

> [rather—my mind's less healthy than my body—I will
> not hear of any remedy at all, am shocked by honest doctors,
> cross with friends who strive to check this deadly listlessness,
> go for what harms, shun what I think would help me, at Rome
> want Tibur, and when there, veer Romewards.]   (trans. Macleod)

Rhetorically, of course, Horace uses this confession to sweeten his warning to Celsus to behave well amid success; but his pain and distress should not be ignored either here or in *Epistles* 1.1, where he complains that Maecenas worries more about his clothing and haircut than about his inconsistencies of thought, his quandaries of mind and spirit.[19] In *Epistles* 1.8, the shopworn comparison of moral fault to physical illness becomes very real. Morally and psychologically, Horace feels that he is sinking into a fatal lethargy. His restless movement back and forth between country and city is symptomatic, too, of an *akêdia*, an "uncaring" that depresses the personality, enfeebles the will. Lucretius had described this restlessness—the man who drives at full speed to the country, but, when he gets there, yawns and runs back to the city—associating it especially with the fear of death by which unenlightened people are unconsciously driven (*DRN.* 3.1053–75). Horace recognizes the symptoms well enough, sees the need for treatment, but resists it—perhaps because, unlike Lucretius, he is skeptical of the doctor-philosophers with their many conflicting "cures."

In the programmatic *Epistles* 1.1, Horace announces his retirement from poetry writing to study philosophy. There is much humor and irony here: in his self-description as a weary gladiator or aging horse; in the characterization of his painstakingly crafted poetry as just another kind of self-amusement; in the description of his philosophical wavering between strict Stoic virtue and more flexible Aristippan hedonism; and in the contrast between his declaration of independence, "not bound to take dictation from any one master," and the embarrassing need to go back to school and work on his moral ABCs. On this realization, he shifts into diatribe mode:

non possis oculo quantum contendere Lynceus,
non tamen idcirco contemnas lippus inungi; . . .   (*Ep.* 1.1.28–29)

[If your sight was no match for Lynceus's, that would
never make you refuse an ointment for your sore eyes; . . .]

The key metaphor, once again, is the well-worn analogy between physical and moral illness, healing medicine and philosophy. What is new here, and striking, is Horace's double use of the second person singular, from "possis" onward, for he is lecturing himself primarily, and another person—the usual *tu* of diatribe, the unspecified man in the audience, the Roman or later reader of this satire—only secondarily, as if we were allowed to eavesdrop on his conversation with himself in his modest little one-person classroom. Nor is this merely a rhetorical ploy. Horace's business in the *Epistles* is with himself first, and others only second. He *is* in pain, sometimes physical and often mental; he explores his condition, reports his self-diagnosis to friends who may or may not benefit from it. The old diatribe is revived, and proves highly relevant. But we hear it in a new way now: not as an alien product to be distanced and mocked, as in the Damasippus and Davus satires, but as an expression of what LaPenna has called Horace's *ricerca morale*, newly rooted in his personal life experience, and thereby acquiring renewed authority.

The reinvigorated diatribe continues in *Epistles* 1.2. While his addressee, young Lollius, has been practicing declamation at Rome in preparation for an active career, Horace has been rereading Homer, rediscovering something of the basic morality that one is taught at school. Here are negative models of passion (Paris, Agamemnon, Achilles) and a positive model of virtue (Ulysses), as well as the rabble of idle suitors and comfort-loving Phaeacians—well, that's us. Mention of these last, who revel at night and sleep until noon, provides an easy transition to the wake-up call of diatribe:

> ut iugulent hominem surgunt de nocte latrones:
> ut te ipsum serves non expergisceris? atqui
> si noles sanus, curres hydropicus; et ni
> posces ante diem librum cum lumine, si non
> intendes animum studiis et rebus honestis,
> invidia vel amore vigil torquebere.
>
> . . . .
>
> non domus et fundus, non aeris acervus et auri
> aegroto domini deduxit corpore febris,
> non animo curas . . . .
>
> . . . .
>
> sincerum est nisi vas, quodcumque infundis acescit.
>
> (*Ep.* 1.2.32–37, 47–49, 54)

[Robbers, to cut throats, rise before daybreak: will you not wake to save yourself? And yet if you will not run when sound, you will with dropsy; if you do not ask for a book and lamp by dawn, if you do not turn your thoughts to the search for goodness, you'll toss and turn on the rack of lust and envy.

. . . .

It's not his house or land, his heaps of cash and bullion that deduct the fever from the sick owner's body or the worries from his heart;

. . . .

If the jar's not clean, whatever you put in it sours.]   (trans. Macleod)

Here, as in *Epistles* 1.1, Horace and his addressee alike need to learn, to listen to the all-too-familiar lesson of diatribe. And what the diatribe tells that all-embracing second person singular is that, if you don't wake up early and study hard, you'll be tormented by one passion or another; that moral failure, like physical illness (the two share the same psychological borderland, with its psychosomatic symptomatology), must be caught early, before it becomes inveterate; that, as Lucretius said earlier in powerful verses, riches are no more proof against mental anxiety and disturbance than against physical illness; that possessions are of no benefit unless you learn to use them rightly, and pleasures are damaged as quickly for the spoiled psyche as they are when presented to the sick body. Lollius will do well to "drink in" moral lessons while he is young, impressionable, and as yet unspoiled. We shall see in *Epistles* 1.18 how much he will need the help or consolation of philosophy once he becomes embroiled in the pressures of early public life, centering around the problem of patronage. How much should one concede to the requirements, the seeming necessities, of a social-political career? Must one sell his soul—or does it just feel that way? Evidently, Lollius will lose his innocence. Perhaps Horace is struggling to regain something of his. In the end, the real business of both is to pursue goodness and knowledge, but each must do this in his own way and at his own pace. There are prizes enough for both.

The wake-up call to study philosophy, the diseased body, the faulty vessel, and the tyrant's methods of torture all recur in close proximity in Persius's *Satire* 3. They do so together with another very powerful "sick-man" image from *Epistles* 1.16, to which I now turn.[20]

Epistles 1.16 is, as Persius surely realized, the most Stoic of Horace's *Epistles*. From a deceptively casual beginning, an account of the Sabine farm with all its pleasant and healthful features, Horace proceeds to his main theme—namely, the supreme importance of being, rather than seeming, a good man:

> . . . fons etiam rivo dare nomen idoneus, ut nec
> frigidior Thracam nec purior ambiat Hebrus,
> infirmo capiti fluit utilis, utilis alvo.
> hae latebrae dulces, etiam, si credis, amoenae,
> incolumem tibi me praestant Septembribus horis.
> tu recte vivis, si curas esse quod audis.
> iactamus iampridem omnis te Roma beatum:
> sed vereor ne cui de te plus quam tibi credas,
> neve putes alium sapiente bonoque beatum,
> neu si te populus sanum recteque valentem
> dictitet, occultam febrem sub tempus edendi
> dissimules, donec manibus tremor incidat unctis.
> stultorum incurata pudor malus ulcera celat . . . .   (*Ep.* 1.16.12–24)

[There is a spring, fit for a famous river
(The Hebrus winds through Thrace no colder or purer),
Useful for healing stomach-aches and head-aches.
And here I keep myself, and the place keeps me—
A precious good, believe it, Quinctius—
In health and sweetness through September's heat.

You of course live in the way that is truly right,
If you've been careful to remain the man
That we all see in you. We hear in Rome
Talk of you, always, as "happy" . . . there is the fear,
Of course, that one might listen too much to others,
Think what they see, and strive to be that thing,
And lose by slow degrees that inward man
Others first noticed—as though, if over and over
Everyone tells you you're in marvelous health,
You might towards dinner-time, when a latent fever
Falls on you, try for a long while to disguise it,
Until the trembling rattles your food-smeared hands.
It's foolishness to camouflage our sores.]   (trans. Pinsky)[21]

The transition marked here is less casual than it appears. Horace has his illnesses, of head and stomach, and by staying in the country he eludes the greater threat of death in September: the time, as he says elsewhere, when autumn heat brings out the undertaker in his black regalia, and the hyperactive busyness of city life "brings on fevers and unseals wills" (*Epistles* 1.7, 8–9). Which is to say, that sickness and the prospect of death, whether or not eluded for the present, are very much more than a metaphor, a rhetorical ploy, for Horace.[22] If the urgency of philosophical learning and healing is powerfully enforced, once again, by the analogy of physical illness and the need of a doctor's advice and help, it is equally evident that Horace's personal sense of aging, loss, sickness, and movement toward death largely contribute to his philosophical seriousness in the *Epistles*, his resolve to put aside "playthings" and seek what is "true and fitting" (*verum atque decens*). Significantly, after he plays many variations on the theme of reality versus appearance—including a passage on honest versus dishonest prayers that will influence Persius's *Satire* 2—and comments on the supreme importance of inner disposition and intention in a manner that might recall the earlier rejected Stoic Paradox, "All Sins are Equal," he ends with an image of death. It is, however, voluntary death, in the Stoic mode, as a last-ditch assertion of moral independence in the face of tyranny.

This is not to say that Horace ever became a Stoic, or that *Epistles* 1.16 occupies a privileged place in Book 1. On the contrary: as he says self-ironically in *Epistles* 1.1, he never subscribed to any one school; he may have his high-Stoic moments, but he "backslides" quickly enough into hedonism. The artistic arrangement of *Epistles* 1 makes a similar point, for *Epistles* 1.16 is framed by the hedonistic 1.15 and the all-too-Roman 1.17, with its social dilemmas and cynical ending. And yet however inconclusive Horace's search for "the true and the fitting" may have proved, that renewed awareness of the insoluble problems and pressures of Roman life, and of human life generally, evidently reinforced the urgency of studying philosophy, giving renewed weight to what had seemed the ineffective truisms of diatribe.

I come finally to *Epistles* 2.2, where Horace eloquently, ironically, and very seriously restates his resolve to leave the poetry-writing game for the study of philosophy: ironically, because this same *Epistle* makes it abundantly clear that, for Horace, poetry writing is anything but a trivial pursuit (*ludum*); but very seriously, too, because he is deeply weary of the poets' game as it is played at Rome, and because the weariness and disillusionment that time and experience bring have driven him back to the study of philosophy that he began at Athens so many years before.[23] And philosophy, as he now describes it, is most centrally the art of enjoying life's gifts while you have them and using them well. He therefore shifts in the second half of the *Epistle* from autobiography and comments on poetry writing into diatribe mode, giving one last protreptic to the study of philosophy. What this amounts to, finally, is right preparation for death. The truism that life is a loan, not a gift, and certainly not a legal entitlement, takes on new, strong coloring against the background of mortality, recalled in powerful Lucretian phrasing. The philosophical quiz or examination of conscience, familiar from Stoic teaching and practice, here includes, in addition to the usual vices of avarice, ambition, and superstition, both anger, to which Horace elsewhere says he is prone, and fear of death, concluding thus:

> vivere si recte nescis, decede peritis.
> lusisti satis, edisti satis atque bibisti:
> tempus abire tibi est, ne potum largius aequo
> rideat et pulset lasciva decentius aetas.   (*Ep.* 2.2.213–16)

> [If you cannot live well, give way to those who can.
> You've played, eaten, and drunk enough for any man:
> it's time now to depart, unlike those drunken bores
> that young men, who more fittingly sport, kick out of doors.]

These last lines recall the harshness of Lucretius's *Natura* rebuking the old man who is unwilling to die (*DRN* 3.952–62). We have come full circle, then, from *Satires* 1.1, where Horace illustrated the prevalence of human discontent through the Bionean/Lucretian dinner-party analogy, concluding with his own play on *satis/satura*, to what might now be intended as the last line of poetry he would ever write, in preparation for that final retirement of death. It is not easy (*pace* Lucretius) to accept Nature's high impersonal laws. The old diatribe-analogy leaves a bitter aftertaste now, a hint of the ultimate meaninglessness of so much that one has given one's life to doing and creating. But it also reinforces, one last time, Horace's theme of the urgency of studying philosophy, which is finally a rehearsal for death.

We shall hear echoes of *Epistles* 2.2 in Persius, especially in *Satire* 6. My point for now is that Persius does more than deconstruct Horace's easier ironies in the *Satires*, his amusing and reassuring laughter at those inhuman Stoic paradoxes. He also continues Horace's personal and moral explorations in the *Epistles*, taking what was finally ambiguous and inconclusive there and realigning it with the Stoic teachings in which his own rebellious and passionate nature found something like salvation, though not without struggle. We see this especially in *Satire* 3, the wake-up call to philosophy, and *Satire* 5, which reinvigorates the Stoic paradox, "Only the Wise Man is Free." My further argument, reading back from Epictetus to Musonius Rufus, that the Greek diatribe was still very much alive in Persius's time and may well have influenced his satires directly, has been relegated to appendix 2.

Division Problems

The unifying theme of Persius's *Satire* 3 is clear enough. We are called to awaken from moral slumber, to study philosophy, to live attentively, and to find healing for the soul's illnesses while we yet may. The satire falls roughly into halves. In the first, a slothful youth is awakened, rebuked, and admonished to pursue philosophy; related passages describe the agonies of bad conscience and the difference between playful childhood and grown-up responsibility. In the second part, dialogue opens up into more general diatribe-preaching, summoning people to learn their place and purpose in life, and answering the philistines' scorn with the parable of the Sick Man's Progress to an ugly death. The satire ends with a quasi-medical examination, probing for moral faults, that few will pass.

In reading *Satire* 3, as in reading Epictetus (see appendix 2), we must remember that we are eavesdropping on a performance, a dramatic monologue with internal dialogue, and also that, because our text lacks stage directions and identification of speakers, we must attend closely to tonal distinctions and the interplay of characters as we reenact that performance. Dramatic repartee enlivens the satire, breathing new life into old, tired themes. But there is more. Like Epictetus, Persius implicates himself in his own preaching. He preserves the right order of honesty, first with himself, only then with others. He moves, characteristically, from dialogue to diatribe, from self-disclosure and -diagnosis to recommendations of treatment for others. The multiplication of voices, therefore, with which he begins, and through which puzzled readers must grope their way, is already the sign of his own exemplary struggle and of the human brokenness that, as the satire proclaims, only philosophy can cure.

Before giving my own version of the voices of lines 1–21, I want to pay tribute to A. E. Housman, whose brilliantly intuitive analysis of the question back in 1913 has influenced nearly a century of scholarship. Housman argued from the uses of first person plural verbs that Persius "makes division of himself" in *Satire* 3 into "the whole man," "his higher nature," and "his lower nature," and thereby "holds parley with himself."[24] Although scholars soon questioned, and largely rejected, the biographical elements in Housman's argument, I am convinced that his intuition was basically right: only that "whole man" has not yet been realized. He is, rather, the object of Persius's passionate search, as also, if we read the satire receptively, he should be of ours.

With this in mind, let me re-present Housman's three voices, giving them new names. There is, first, the *narrator* or *presenter* who sets the scene for us, introducing the action. He may also be called *the observer*, *the satirist*, or *the raconteur*. Second, there is the reluctant student: dissipated, spoilt, and lazy, who may embody something of Persius's own background and tendencies. And, third, there is the **comes, a friend or attendant or adviser**, who enters abruptly to scold the youth into taking himself and his studies more seriously, and who may later blend into the more abstract Stoic voice that preaches, especially in the satire's second half, to an unconverted world.

> **Nempe Haec Adsidue.** *iam clarum mane fenestras*
> *intrat et angustas extendit lumine rimas.*
> *stertimus, indomitum quod despumare Falernum*
> *sufficiat, quinta dum linea tangitur umbra.*
> **"en quid agis? siccas insana canicula messes**   5
> **iam dudum coquit et patula pecus omne sub ulmo est,"**
> *unus ait comitum. verumne? itan? ocius adsit*
> *huc aliquis. nemon? turgescit vitrea bilis:*
> FINDOR, *ut Arcadiae pecuaria rudere credas.*
> *iam liber et positis bicolor membrana capillis*   10
> *inque manus chartae nodosaque venit harundo.*
> *tum querimur crassus calamo quod pendeat umor.*
> *nigra sed infusa vanescit sepia lympha,*
> *dilutas querimur geminet quod fistula guttas.*
> **o miser inque dies ultra miser, hucine rerum**   15
> **venimus? a, cur non potius teneroque columbo**
> **et similis regum pueris pappare minutum**
> **poscis et iratus mammae lallare recusas?**
> **an tali studeam calamo? cui verba? quid istas**
> **succinis ambages? tibi luditur. ecfluis amens,**   20
> **contemnere. . . .**

[*Always the same thing.* *Already the windows are bright with morning, the narrow cracks are filling out with light. And WE are snoring, enough to blow the foam off last night's Falernian wine, while the shadow arrives at line five on the sundial.*

"So, what are you doing? For a long time now the mad dog-star's been baking the crops dry, and all the cattle have gone beneath the spreading elm," *says one of the companions.*

"<u>Really? You mean it? Somebody come here quick. Where is everybody?</u>" *(The glassy bile swells up.)* <u>I</u>'M SPLITTING! *(You'd think all the herds in Arcadia were braying as one.) Now the book is brought in, and the writing materials: bicolored hairless parchment, top-quality papyrus, quill pen. But then we complain because* <u>the ink's gotten much too thick</u>; *or else, when you add water, we complain because* <u>the ink's all gone</u>, *leaving multiple diluted watery drops.*

"You pathetic character, and every day more pathetic: is this what we've come to? Why don't you just go do what the little lovey-doveys do, and the little spoiled princelings: ask to have your din-din mashed up, and refuse to go ni-ni for Mom-ma? '<u>How can I study with a pen like that?</u> ' Who are you fooling? Why are you whining out all those excuses? You're leaking out, I tell you; you'll be a reject. . . ."]

It is hard to pin down these voices, which Persius himself will have distinguished in a hypothetical dramatic reading to friends, or perhaps only to himself; hard, too, to punctuate the text confidently. Even the first words, "Nempe haec adsidue," could be spoken in two very different ways: by the narrator, as a sort of title for the satire before the fuller stage setting of lines 1b--4 is introduced; or by the as yet unidentified *comes* bursting in sarcastically: "So *this* is what you've been doing [sleeping and snoring]? "[25] Sometimes, too, one voice comes through another, as when the companion imitates, with comically exaggerated pathos, the youth's lame excuses for not getting on with his homework.

The first person plural verbs in lines 1–16 that attracted Housman's attention are especially complex and fascinating with their implied or, better, implicated authorial presence.[26] Already in "*stertimus*" (3), the spoiled student is presented dramatically ("*Here we are, snoring*"), or rebuked by the companion, or possibly both; but there may be something of Persius here, too, a personal admission of weakness (such as, again, we find in Epictetus), a genuinely shared "we." So, too, with the repeated "*querimur*" of 12 and 14: "*Here we go again, complaining . . .* ," and, still more importantly, with "*venimus*" in line 16: "*Have we come to this?* " Although we read it, naturally enough, as a further sarcastic rebuke of the youth's lazy behavior by the *comes*, it may also be taken as a genuinely inclusive "we" that embraces or implicates Persius himself, the would-be self-distancing presenter of the satire. The author is thereby drawn into this intense inner dialogue to an extent that few scholars outside of Housman, that poet-scholar, may have realized—and Housman did not elaborate. Not just the satirist, but the would-be person behind him is forbidden to observe human folly from a detached, quasi-godlike position.

The point becomes clearer if we compare the opening twenty lines of Horace's *Satires* 2.3, to which Persius alludes at several points. Here a poet, evidently Horace, is being harangued by an unnamed speaker, who turns out (but only after line 16) to be Damasippus, bankrupt dealer in antiques, now turned fanatical preacher:

> "Sic raro scribis, ut toto non quater anno
> membranam poscas, scriptorum quaeque retexens,
> iratus tibi quod vini somnique benignus
> nil dignum sermone canas. quid fiet? at ipsis
> Saturnalibus huc fugisti. sobrius ergo   5
> dic aliquid dignum promissis: incipe. nil est:
> culpantur frustra calami, immeritusque laborat
> iratis natus paries dis atque poetis.
> atqui vultus erat multa et praeclara minantis,
> si vacuum tepido cepisset villula tecto.   10
> quorsum pertinuit stipare Platona Menandro,
> Eupolin, Archilochum, comites educere tantos?
> invidiam placare paras virtute relicta?
> contemnere miser; . . ."

["So rarely do you write, that you don't ask for parchment four times in the entire year—raveling and unraveling whatever you write—angry at yourself because, after giving yourself so much wine and sleep, you still can't come up with anything worth the name of satire. So, what next? You say, you ran away here on the Saturnalia. Well, then, be serious: give us some verse that's up to your potential. We're waiting. No, not a thing: the pens are blamed, but it's no use; the undeserving wall, born under the wrath of gods and poets, takes its punishment. And yet, you looked like someone of great promise, once you could just enter into the warm and peaceful shelter of your little farmhouse. What was the point, really, of packing Plato with Menander, taking Eupolis and Archilochus along, such mighty fellow-travelers? Is it your idea to abandon goodness, just deal with envy? Poor fellow, you'll be despised . . . ."]

Horace uses two voices only, two gradually identified personae, in his drama. The main speaker is Damasippus, the preacher of second-hand

Stoic diatribe, and a very good example of the *doctor ineptus* of whom Anderson, Freudenburg, and others have written; the second voice is Horace, his victim, who must endure this long harangue, and who only gets a few words in by way of reply. The ironic point of the satire will be that Damasippus, who preaches on the Stoic paradox, "Only the Wise Man is Sane," or "Every Fool is Mad," reveals himself involuntarily to be a kind of madman. "Enough is enough! " cries Horace, in the blackout line; "You are the greater madman: spare the lesser! " Damasippus does get off some good shots in his long, rambling attack on the usual vices and follies (avarice, ambition, luxury, love, superstition); and Horace, as so often, eats his cake and has it too. He deploys the resources of low diatribe and satire even as he "places" them and distances himself from them—as also from his own earlier satire, from Lucilius before that, and from those four "suitcase authors" to whom, as he so nicely indicates here, his satire is indebted. Even from the beginning, of course, Damasippus misses the point. He does not understand, any more than does the Bore (*ineptus*) of *Satires* 1.9, that a good writer is concerned with quality, not quantity.[27] He mocks Horace for "weaving and unweaving" ("retexens") his manuscript, much as Penelope, to hold off the suitors, wove her famous bier-covering for Laertes by day and secretly unraveled it by night over three long years, until she was discovered. Ironically, this satire will be Horace's longest by far, the grand centerpiece of Book 2. Ironically, too, Damasippus will turn out to be something even less than a bankrupt dealer in old bronzes, or in second-hand Stoic sermons. He will be shown up finally as a Literary Device, and an impotent one, at that.

Up to line 16, however, when Damasippus is named, Horace could have been speaking to himself. "Why aren't you getting on with the job? You've got everything you need: your snug country retreat, your peace and quiet (unlike the Saturnalian rush and confusion, all that drinking, shopping, and tumult back in Rome), your writing materials, and a few good books, just the way you like it: so what's the excuse now? " There are days when a writer succumbs to inertia, or to the more insidious temptation of *acedia*: "Why bother? It really doesn't matter in the end." Horace needed privacy; he also needed companionship and stimulation. In a very real sense, the Classics—Plato and Menander, Eupolis and Archilochus—were his *comites*, his "traveling companions." The critic he didn't need, except as a foil, was Damasippus.

For Persius, however, criticism and self-criticism are the necessary condition for moral progress. In *Satire* 3 the companion/adviser (*comes*) is not a book this time, a voice from the past: not even Horace. He is, rather, the internalized voice of reason and conscience.[28] The pens also reappear, still "blamed in vain"; but their job is different now. They are to produce, not a pleasing literary entertainment, but rather an intensely self-reflexive moral exercise addressed first to the author and only then to others. The threat of reprobation (*contemnere*) takes on new urgency in a poem that deals now, not with the loss of literary and social reputation, but with the possibility, as real to Persius as to Dante, of moral damnation.

As Hooley has shown, Horace gives us our bearings and Persius takes them away. When we read *Satires* 2.3, Horace's ironies bring us to the clear, reassuring conclusion that the Stoic preacher Damasippus is a fool, not to be taken seriously, while ordinary sensible people—like Horace, like ourselves—are really quite all right. But Persius turns Horace on his head. He reminds himself and us that without the critic's strong intervention, we might well sink into what will shortly be described as a moral coma heralding death. Laugh at the critic now, and you laugh at the doctor who might just possibly save your miserable life.

And another point: when Persius "makes division of himself," we might say that this division serves a diagnostic purpose, like Freud's ego, superego, and id, or perhaps like the Child, Parent, and Adult of "Transactional Analysis," briefly popular in the 1970s and not altogether without merit. But division may also indicate illness. When the youth, calling for writing materials, bawls out "FINDOR!" ("I'M SPLITTING! "), he means that he has a "splitting headache" from impatience, and from his hangover. This is already a psychosomatic symptom of moral faults, anger and unrestraint, to which the doctor-philosopher would pay close attention. But there is more, I think: a split or splitting personality, a surrealistic image of brokenness, anticipating the potsherds and loose clay later on.[29] Compare Dante's grisly description of the heretics and schismatics in *Inferno* 28, *seminator di scandalo e di scisma*, who suffer the same grotesque cleavage that they have inflicted on the body of Christendom. This brokenness, this pain, this lack of wholeness is where we must begin, first to understand, and then to recompose our lives. In the next sections I shall come, through reminiscence and parable, to that implied necessity of reconstruction.

Autobiographical Fragments

Twice in *Satire* 3 a screen falls down, to reveal, or appear to reveal, a portion of the writer's life. First, when the adviser, who has been telling the youth that he is a leaky or ill-made vessel, or soft clay that requires immediate shaping (20–23), meets with an objection:

> sed rure paterno
> est tibi far modicum, purum et sine labe salinum
> (quid metuas?) cultrixque foci secura patella.
> hoc satis? an deceat pulmonem rumpere ventis

stemmate quod Tusco ramum millesime ducis
censoremve tuum vel quod trabeate salutas?
ad populum phaleras! ego te intus et in cute novi. . . .   (24–30)

[You say your ancestral farm provides you with adequate food; you have a
bright, clean salt-cellar (so what could worry you?) and a carefree platter
settled beside your hearth. Is that enough? Or should you burst your
lungs boasting as how you're Number One Thousand in line from an
Old Tuscan Family? Or how you parade in full dress before your cousin
the Censor? Let the mob gape at those trappings. *I know you from within,
from beneath the skin.*] (Italics mine)

You're not ashamed, Persius continues, to live like dissolute Natta; but *he's*
so submerged in his sins that he's feeling no pain, whereas *you* know better;
you've learned moral philosophy from the Stoa, and still you waste your
energies like a silly child chasing after birds (52–62, to be discussed below).

The interjected passage (24–30) begins with an implied protest in the
Horatian mode, which is then refuted. The youth (if it is he) claims that
his life is just fine, thank you. He enjoys his ancestral property, a decent
living, and the outward signs of a simple, contented life in the Horatian
mode: the faultless salt-cellar, the carefree plate. Already we might hear a
hint of parody, recalling Horace's own self-parody in *Satires* 2.7 when the
slave Davus mocks his master's romantic but rather shaky praise of *securum
holus*, "carefree vegetables" (32). The claim of contentment is then tested
by Horace's own standard, "hoc satis?," and found wanting. Why, if the
young man is content, should he always be harping on his family connec-
tions? Something must be wrong, and that something concerns, not just
the fictional youth, but his creator. We think of the *Vita*:

"He was born in Etruria at Volterra, a Roman knight, connected by
blood with men of the senatorial class. He died near the eighth
milestone on the Via Appia, on his own property."   (4–6)

As I shall suggest later, in chapter 4, Persius probably gave much of his
short life to the economic and social responsibilities that his position re-
quired. The point for now is that he led a privileged existence, more
like the equestrian Lucilius—or, for that matter, more like Horace's
patron, Maecenas, "descended from Etruscan kings"—than like Horace
himself. Moreover, when the adviser says, "*I know you from inside, from
beneath the skin*," their dialogue is revealed as an inside joke. If the young
man's protests of moral adequacy ("No problem. It's cool.") can't fool
the adviser, that is because both personae are parts of the same person;
or, differently, because the adviser has stood where the youth now stands.
In turn, the youth should know better—really, *does* know better—than to
prop up his self-esteem with flattering thoughts of his own importance,

which merely impede his real life's work, the philosophical search for healing and wholeness.

After describing the tortures of a bad conscience, as contrasted with Natta's moral obliviousness, Persius introduces what may or may not be a second autobiographical reference, or reminiscence:

> saepe oculos, memini, tangebam parvus olivo,
> grandia si nollem morituri verba Catonis
> discere non sano multum laudanda magistro,
> quae pater adductis sudans audiret amicis.
> iure; etenim id summum, quid dexter senio ferret,
> scire erat in voto, damnosa canicula quantum
> raderet, angustae collo non fallier orcae,
> neu quis callidior buxum torquere flagello.
> haut tibi inexpertum curvos deprendere mores. . . .   (44–52)

[I remember, when I was small, I would smear ointment on my eyes when I didn't want to work on some big speech for Cato facing death, a speech that my dad might bring his friends to hear, sweating profusely. And rightly so: for my highest concern was studying double sixes and double ones, and not being fooled by the narrow neck of a jar, and whipping my wooden top with the best of them. But *you've* made yourself expert in moral issues. . . .]

Arguments about this passage have been acrimonious. How could Persius's father, who died (says the *Vita*) when Persius was only six, or even his stepfather, who died soon afterwards, still have been living when Persius trotted off to that school performance or else played hooky? The more relevant point is that, within the satire, Persius puts this reminiscence into the mouth of the *comes*, the philosophical adviser and voice of Stoic conscience. "When I was a child, I played like a child and thought like a child; but you, who have (allegedly) grown up, who have studied moral wisdom with the Stoics, should have put away childish things." The wayward youth has no excuse for fooling around any longer—nor, in this inner dialogue, has Persius, or what Housman called his "lower nature."

Because I think Persius was seriously interested in childhood and play, I want to dwell on the satiric implications of that "iure" ("rightly so"). The point is twofold: that a child who doesn't know better will naturally act like a child; and, more important, that the grown-ups who approved of these school exercises and became so excited about them were really every bit as childish in their games as the schoolboy playing hooky was in his. The point is beautifully developed in Book 1 of St.Augustine's *Confessions*, in a passage arguably influenced by Persius. Augustine describes how painfully he was punished when he didn't pay enough attention to his work: even his family, who should have pitied him, laughed at him instead. And yet, if he liked to play, so did those same grown-ups who sat in judgment on him:

> . . . but we loved playing games, and punishment was exacted by those who were generally doing the same things: only, the trifling (*nugae*) of older people is called business, but when children fool around in the same way, they are punished, and nobody feels sorry for the children in either group [that is, playful children, childish grown-ups]. Or does any good judge of the matter assert that I was rightly beaten because I played ball as a child and so, by that playing, was prevented from learning my letters as fast as possible—so I could play in a more disgraceful way when I was older? Or did the very man who beat me behave any differently when, if his fellow-teacher got the better of him in even the tiniest argument, he would be more tormented by ill temper and envy than I was when my fellow ball-player won the game? (1.9.15)

Augustine acknowledges that he was at fault: for, however silly the grown-ups were, the substance of what he learned at school could still be put to good use (and evidently was). He loved games, and especially the pride of winning; he loved to hear stories that only made his ears itch to hear more; and the same *curiositas*, as lust of the eyes now, made him passionate to see shows. Again, he spells out the irony of those *ludos maiorum* ("games, plays, shows") that were put on, or indulged in, by the grown-ups:

> The men who put on those shows are elevated to such a height of dignity that almost all parents want the same chance for their little children; yet they gladly suffer these children to be flogged if shows like this get in the way of the serious effort by which they, the parents, hope they will attain to the position of putting on the shows. (1.10.16)

Evidently, Augustine saw the same ironic pattern repeating itself, again and again, throughout his schooldays and afterward. He was given beautiful but morally seductive reading matter: Virgil's tragic love story of Dido and Aeneas; an erotically careless comedy of Terence. Although he acquired some early success in public speaking (*recitanti*, 1.17.27, the beginning of what should be a great rhetorical career), the skills he learned were technical, not moral. So he played the fool, stole food from home, and cheated at games, protesting all the more wildly if he was caught:

> Is this the innocence of childhood? No, it's not, Lord; it's not, is it, my God? For these are the very things that pass on from children's attendants and teachers, from nuts and little balls and pet birds to prefects and kings, to gold, estates, and possessions, as the later stages of life succeed to the earlier ones, and as greater punishments succeed to those

early canings. That is why, lord King, you approved of setting the sign of humility in the condition of childhood, when you said, "Of such is the Kingdom of Heaven." (1.30.19)

As Clark has shown in her excellent commentary on *Confessions* 1–4, Augustine here refutes the sentimental idea that in *Matthew* 18:2–4 Jesus was evoking childish innocence.[30] Rather, in Augustine's view, the observation of children's games, their treatment by grown-ups, and their ironic reappearance in the world of grown-up "games" constitutes a lesson in human nature, and subsequently in humility, from which we all may profit—as Augustine, in his reflections, is even now doing. If the children's behavior deserves pity, not scorn, that is, not least, because it is ours as well. At the same time, as Clark also notes, Augustine shows unusual interest in children, sympathetic awareness of their feelings, and, in the end, a strong sense of the value of childhood, as of every other stage of life.[31] If we learn humility, as against harmful pride, through honestly remembering ourselves as children, still more should we thank God for those real gifts and accomplishments of our childhood, and especially for learning, that have brought us to where we are today and, despite their common misuse (not least, by ourselves), have contributed to whatever good we have been able to achieve.

I return to Persius's schoolboy vignette, for which these passages of Augustine may offer an elaborate but very relevant gloss. Like Augustine, Persius shows unusual interest in children and childhood. Like Augustine, he does not believe in the so-called innocence of children, not even of infants: in *Satire* 2, as said earlier, he showed how babies are already being corrupted by the unrealistic and amoral fairy tale wishes of the superstitious old women who care for them. The world's stains are with us from the start; it is an easy step from pampered babyhood to the vicious prayers and ungodly behavior of grown-up men and women. So, too, in *Satire* 3. We can see it all: the packed school auditorium; the teacher showing off; the father, who brought his friends to hear this young prodigy, sweating with anxiety and pride. Will he do it well to the end? Or will he embarrass himself and, what is worse, embarrass *me* before my friends? It all matters terribly, as a harbinger of success or failure in public life.

The assignment Persius describes, to prepare a speech for Cato to give before his suicide, carries a further irony.[32] It is not clear whether the boy was meant to memorize a set speech or, more likely, to prepare and deliver a speech of his own devising. "Imagine that you are Cato," the teacher would have said, "after the defeat of the Pompeian forces at Utica. In a carefully prepared, meticulously delivered speech, explain to your friends and supporters why you have decided to commit suicide rather than to live." It is enough to give anyone sore eyes.[33] And yet, "deathbound Cato" ("morituri Catonis") will take on special importance in the early empire, as an icon of republican and Stoic *libertas*: first, because he died after fighting for the republic, which he did not choose to survive; and second, because for the Stoics (as Horace, in that very Stoic mood, said in *Epistles* 1.16) death is the last line of resistance, the final guarantee of a person's moral integrity when all else fails.[34] Moreover, we all live, like Cato, under the shadow of death, and we cannot live well unless we are also prepared to die well, or as well as possible, when the time comes.

I suggest that when Augustine read Persius, he found a confessional mode in his satires and a drive toward sincerity that seemed, in some part, to anticipate his own. Rhetorically, of course, when Persius's speaker slips back into the personal voice, he is practising *êthopoiia* ("character-depiction"), evoking the human experience that he brings to the job of preaching, or even advising. "I was young myself once"—as parents and teachers have said ever since old Phoenix came to Achilles' tent in *Iliad* 9. It may be that, in the last analysis, Persius's poetry should be taken as a privileged kind of play (*ludere*), a continuation of the children's games that he describes here. We have already met the satirist as a naughty child in *Satire* 1. What is more important in *Satire* 3 is that, of Persius's three voices or personae, not only the childishly reluctant student but also the older and wiser Stoic counselor and the satiric narrator turn out to have been implicated in the human condition in all its weakness and vulnerability. The more so, because the old, familiar analogies that the Stoic preacher uses— the broken or leaky vessel, the comatose man, the fatally untreated illness— go beyond their immediate rhetorical function, which is to illustrate the urgency of studying philosophy, and testify to a universal brokenness that even Stoicism, we might think, could hardly cure.

Images of Dissolution

The theme of *Satire* 3 is the need for moral and spiritual healing, which Stoicism uniquely provides. This theme is supported by a traditional, long-elaborated medical analogy. The moral faults and passions that disturb our lives are like diseases; they grow upon us stealthily, from small to great, and even show psychosomatic symptoms, and they require the attention, care, and advice of the philosopher-physician, advice that must absolutely be followed. Back in the 1960s, "New Critical" studies showed how Persius transformed these philosophical commonplaces into new, exciting images and scenes that gave metaphoric unity to the satire, linking the "dialogue" and "diatribe" sections. Earlier still, in my critically innocent student days, I was struck by Persius's grotesque images in *Satire* 3, his Hogarthian scenes of decay, suffering, and death. Today, more than ever, I find them horrifying. They permeate the safe walls of satire, and of the criticism of satire. They reveal the fragility, the porousness, the open-endedness of all human bodies, most emphatically including the satirist's own. All the more urgent, then, and intense is the struggle for integrity that Persius models forth in *Satire* 3, and which he first enacted in that same body, that same "leaky vessel" that we all know well enough, but generally prefer to forget.

I begin with what may seem an overkill of metaphor, at lines 20–24. Here the censor or moral tutor rebukes the dilatory student, comparing him (a) to a leaky vessel, then (b) to an unbaked one, and finally (c) to moist clay ready for the shaping:

> effluis amens,
> contemnere. sonat vitium percussa, maligne
> respondet viridi non cocta fidelia limo.
> udum et molle lutum es, nunc nunc properandus et acri
> fingendus sine fine rota.

> [You're leaking mindlessly, you'll be rejected. No good response comes from the unbaked jar with its wet clay: strike it, you hear the fault. You are soft, wet clay that needs to be taken in hand right away and shaped on the endless wheel.]

Comical and insulting, the triple comparison points up the urgency of Stoic education. Study now, not later, and you may yet pass the test of integrity. Lead a dissolute life, and it will be just that: dissolute, fragmented, flowing away. At the same time, Persius's vase-metaphors transgress their Stoic borders, the accepted and, in *Satire* 3, controlling equation of moral fault and physical sickness: for, as bodily creatures, we are all of us leaky or flawed vessels, bound to decay and death—a realization that, in this poem, must challenge, if not subvert, the moral teaching it was intended to enforce.

For his leaky jar Persius draws mainly on Lucretius's description of how morally uneducated people pour their lives' efforts into leaky vessels, where they "flow through and are lost, thanklessly" (*perfluxere atque ingrata interiere* [DRN.3.937]). The Danaids, as earlier in Plato's *Gorgias*, illustrate the point. Lucretius also compares the indulging of wrong desires, the pursuing of "impure" pleasures, with using dirty containers that spoil the taste of whatever you put into them. But other parts of his poem tell a different, less morally defined story: for often, as Segal so well showed, he depicts the human body as a frail, flawed, utterly permeable vessel that cannot easily or long protect the life-giving interconnections of mind and soul (*vitai claustra coercens*). Time and again, to prove the mortality of the soul and its interdependence with the body, Lucretius cites horrific examples of physical decay and dissolution. He is also much concerned, as males often are, with the protection or loss of precious bodily fluids. But his main point is that, body and soul together, we all *leak*, and that in the end our bodies will not "keep in a little life." Or, as Epicurus put it, every person is "an unwalled city."[35]

At the end of the first half of *Satire* 3, Persius's *vas* metaphor takes on a comic literalness:

> stertis adhuc laxumque caput conpage soluta
> oscitat hesternum dissutis undique malis.
> est aliquid quo tendis et in quod derigis arcum?
> an passim sequeris corvos testaque lutoque,
> securus quo pes ferat, atque ex tempore vivis?   (58–62)

[You are still snoring. Your head falls loose with its neck-joints unhinged; it yawns off yesterday from unsewn jaws. Have you a goal, a place to direct your shot? Or do you just run after the crows, in all directions, throwing sherds or clay, not caring where your feet may take you, but living off the moment?]

The reluctant student has relapsed, it seems, into physical and moral somnolence. He is so relaxed, indeed, that his head almost falls off; he snores so violently that his jaws almost become unhinged—images that will recur in the death-scene later on. But there is a further, horrendous suggestion. The youth has quite regressed, "gone to pieces." When, like a careless child, he throws sherds and clay at the crows, it is as though he were throwing away parts of his unformed self.[36] So much for dissolute living. "Clay thou art, and unto clay thou shalt return."

The second, diatribal half of *Satire* 3 introduces the central comparison of philosopher and doctor:

> elleborum frustra, cum iam cutis aegra tumebit,
> poscentis videas; venienti occurrite morbo,
> et quid opus Cratero magnos promittere montis?   (63–65)

[You can see people clamoring in vain for hellebore when their sick hide is already swollen. Hurry and fight the disease at its onset—or would you rather promise great mountains of money to Doctor Craterus?]

The powerful lines on human life and purpose, "discite et, o miseri . . ." (cited earlier), follow, but now a brawny centurion intervenes, ridiculing philosophers. They are, in his caricature, stooped and bent, intent on their thoughts, muttering to themselves, weighing their words, and concentrated on "the crazy dreams of some old invalid."—"And that's what you're pale about? That's why a man shouldn't eat? " To classical scholars, whose business it is to distinguish, say, between Pythagoras and Epicurus, the joke is on the confused, know-nothing centurion. We are also, with reason, sensitive to his attacks. But they are still, we must admit, very funny, and we might imagine the speaker of the dramatic monologue, who was once Persius himself, playing the centurion's part with a comic mimesis that might have come straight from Aristophanes' *Clouds*. We laugh with him, not just at him. I emphasize this laughter because Persius gives us, here, a good old comic *agôn*—one in which, to be sure, the Stoic rebuttalist will have the last big laugh.

In the climactic parable of the Sick Man's Death, the invalid disregards his doctor's orders, disregards his friend's warning (he's looking pale), eats, drinks, and bathes, and suddenly dies. What is striking is the ugliness, the grotesqueness of the description, especially against the background of Horace's *Epistles* 1.16.[37] There, in his most Stoic poem, Horace urged the need of self-knowledge and strong moral standards, using the analogy of disease. It is as foolish to go by public opinion in moral questions as in matters of health:

> . . . neu si te populus sanum recteque valentem
> dictitet, occultam febrem sub tempus edendi
> dissimules, donec manibus tremor incidat unctis.   (21–23)

[(and I am afraid) that, if the crowd should assert, time and again, that you are fine and healthy, you might keep your fever concealed until, when dinner comes, your greasy hands are taken with a fit of trembling.]

The deluded man shakes with a fever that may prove mortal. Horace doesn't spell out the results, but Persius does. For him, the punishment is deserved, and it comes with sudden obscene violence:

> turgidus hic epulis atque albo ventre lavatur,
> gutture sulpureas lente exhalante mephites.
> sed tremor inter vina subit calidumque trientem
> excutit e manibus, dentes crepuere retecti,
> uncta cadunt laxis tunc pulmentaria labris.   (98–102)

[Swollen with food, with pale white belly, he goes to the bath, his throat slowly exhaling sulphurous fumes. But a trembling seizes him even as he drinks, shaking the warm winecup out of his hand; his teeth are bared and they chatter; and now the greasy tidbits drop from his unresisting lips.]

The man shakes violently all over; his hands lose their grip; his teeth chatter, as his lips part in a loose grimace that will become, directly, the mocking grimace of death. The last laugh is quite literally *on him*. As the food falls from his now loosened lips ("uncta cadunt laxis tunc pulmentaria labris," one of the ugliest lines in all Latin poetry), we are reminded of the reluctant, easy-living student earlier, relaxed and almost drowned in spiritual torpor, or else yawning with weariness and boredom to the point of becoming almost literally unhinged.[38]

And there is more. Though we may live sluggishly, things move fast enough after death: horns and tapers ready; prepare the corpse; feet first, out the door; and "he" is carried away by his newly freed slaves (and presumably forgotten). Juvenal will take the story further in *Satire* 1. His selfish, solitary glutton will be mocked, after a sudden death, at other people's dinner tables; the angry clients (*amici*) will applaud the funeral procession as it passes (142-46). We are on the way to Scrooge and the Ghost of Christmas yet to come. But I return to two quietly sarcastic points in Persius. First, the dead man is "tandem[que] . . . conpositus" ("finally gotten together"; 103–4) after his loose, fragmented life. Should we say that, in the end, his life achieved closure? But differently, the corpse is "lutatus" (104): not just "smeared" with unguents, but also, more literally, "turned to mud," or clay. In bodily matters, closure is a brief pretense. Dissolution is real, and forever.

Recomposing a Life

The images of decay and death in *Satire* 3 are strikingly original. They show Persius at his strongest, as a master of "uglification and derision." We find a similar mix of the horrible and grotesque elsewhere in contemporary poetry: in Seneca's *Phaedra*, for example, when Hippolytus's body must be reassembled like a jigsaw puzzle; or in Lucan's *Bellum Civile*, as he describes dismemberment and sudden death in battle, or the results of snakebite in the African desert—horrific moments of decomposition, metamorphosis, and loss of human identity that Dante recycles to great effect in the *Inferno*, and which make us reflect on what it is to be human, and how easily and terribly that humanity is lost.[39] What Lucan is conveying goes beyond the wretchedness of civil war. It is, still more, the meaninglessness of things in a world dominated by human passions and by Fortune, and where the Stoic Providence is nowhere to be found, except perhaps in the intransigent heart of the defeated Cato. What Persius is conveying, as he reuses Horace's images and metaphors, changing and intensifying them—much as, again, Lucan intensifies those of Virgil—is more the ordinary terror, which we mostly repress, of living in bodies that are always so unprotected, and are bound to decay and dissolution in the end.

Consider again that scornful "tandemque . . . conpositus." The dead man is "finally gotten together"—fixed up, that is, for the funeral ceremonies— but of course, his body will suffer decay and decomposure in the natural order of things. At the same time, the phrase "tandemque . . . conpositus" recalls precisely what the dead man neglected in life, the urgent need to "get himself together," to impose order on his scattered life before death could take him by surprise and turn him back into clay ("lutatus"). Such "composure" belongs to the Stoic ideal as Seneca, for example, describes it in *De Vita Beata*. A man, he proclaims, should prove superior to externals, prepared for good fortune or bad, firm in resolution; such a man, it is understood, will be *compositum ordinatumque*, which Costa translates as "calm and disciplined." But the Latin says more. It suggests a process, now completed, by which a person is "gotten together." The mind, says Seneca, must exercise a godlike self-control. Inner concord, self-agreement in every word and action without any dissension or hesitation, will follow.[40]

Persius "came to know Seneca late," says the *Vita*, "but not so that he was taken by his *ingenium* ("temperament, character, talent," 24–25). As we read *De Vita Beata*, we may easily imagine his mental reservations about Seneca's verbal expansiveness, his courtly compromises, and the enormous riches about which, here and elsewhere, he protests too much. All the same, Persius would probably have concurred with the Stoic ideals as Seneca describes them, and also with Seneca's (perhaps) heartfelt self-defense as one "advancing" (*proficiens*) toward an ideal that he has not yet attained, an eager striver (*studiosus*) whose trying might adhere to that splendid Stoic sequence, *qui haec facere proponet, volet, temptabit, ad deos iter faciet*. That is: you set your goal clearly before your mind (*proponet*); you fix your will accordingly (*volet*: what I earlier called intentionality); and you make the attempt (*temptabit*). Even if you fail, Seneca concludes, you will fall praiseworthily "from mighty aspirations."

Positively viewed, *Satire* 3 is a wake-up call to virtue. In the old familiar analogy, as a seriously sick man must follow the doctor's advice, or else . . . , so only philosophy can diagnose our moral sickness and confusion and teach us how these should be healed. What is new, I argue—what we could not find in Seneca—is the passionate intensity of Persius's response, his self-awareness as one deeply implicated in the struggle (moral, and physical too?) against decay and death, and his vision of the living hell to which non- or regressive Stoics surrender their lives—the deadly fall into moral and spiritual oblivion, personal disintegration. Before we decide how to read the deceptively simple ending of *Satire* 3, we should review those horrific vignettes earlier: the careless, profligate Natta, "going under" so obliviously with his hardened arteries and his hardened soul; the man who awakens to the still-living nightmare of a bad conscience, plunging downwards into the void; the man who yawns off yesterday's debauch with a loosened head and unhinged jaws that anticipate his body's dissolution back into loose clay; and then, climactically, the fool's sudden, very ugly death after ignoring the many warnings of his doctor and friends. This is the darkest of Persius's *Satires*, and the most memorable. Taking it in, emotionally as well as intellectually, requires time and attention. We must not hurry past the more common human fears about the body's death and dissolution—fears which, however vain they prove, even Stoic *proficientes* must still acknowledge and combat—in our rush to complete the body/mind analogy and point the (for Persius, for ourselves?) reassuringly familiar moral.[41]

It is not, indeed, just an implied author whom we should imagine standing before us, like one of Homer's ghosts drinking the blood that lets him speak, but an implicated author, implicated in the physicality of the very body in which he first performed his satires (if only for himself). This was a body, after all, that may have been frailer than most—that may already have given its tenant notice of his impending eviction. After his father's death and his stepfather's, according to the *Vita*, he found new father-figures: Cornutus, first of all, but also "two learned, upright men who keenly pursued philosophy, Claudius Agathinus, a Spartan doctor, and Petronius Aristocrates Magnes, older men whom he uniquely admired and imitated" (25–29). Role models matter enormously. Should we think of that Stoic doctor, concerned with body and soul together, and of Persius's early death, *vitio stomachi*? Was it cancer? Did that disease cast a backward shadow on his later years, and on his poetry?

As a good Stoic and a good student-teacher, Persius practices a *meditatio mortis*, a regular confrontation with decay and death. Rightly performed, such a meditation reinforces resolutions and habits of right living, though there is always the danger of falling back into a rebellious, unphilosophical grasping at life, the negative pole of Horace's *carpe diem*. It also tests the sincerity of the author's convictions and their power to overcome false notions about death, along with accompanying impulses of horror and protest. Lucretius did much the same thing in Book 3 of his *De Rerum Natura*. In Persius's satire, as in Lucretius's epic, the emotional urgencies evoked by images of bodily vulnerability, decay, and death may challenge and test the philosophical argument, but they do not finally refute it. Poetry and philosophy, feeling and thought, self-searching and education of others, still keep pace one with another.

Only now, after we acknowledge their elemental force and challenge, can those horrific images of death and dissolution be felt to reflect the still greater horror of moral corruption, even as they constitute a wake-up call from the dissolute dreams of ordinary nonliving. It is the passions and vices, after all, that are truly repulsive. We might compare Lucretius, again, on the alleged pains of Tartarus, which he treats as an allegory of the inner torments that fools and criminals suffer in this life, and also Dante's *Inferno*, where horrific images of punishment in Hell mirror the increasingly debased and wretched states of soul into which sinners fall (the *contrapasso*); for, in the end, Persius writes not about the decaying body, but about the struggling soul.

With these warnings—for we may even now be misled—I come to the ending of *Satire* 3, the diagnostic test in which the body-mind analogy is spelled out most clearly:

> "tange, miser, venas et pone in pectore dextram;
> nil calet hic. summosque pedes attinge manusque;
> non frigent." visa est si forte pecunia, sive
> candida vicini subrisit molle puella,
> cor tibi rite salit? positum est algente catino
> durum holus et populi cribro decussa farina:
> temptemus fauces; tenero latet ulcus in ore
> putre quod haut deceat plebeia radere beta.
> alges, cum excussit membris timor albus aristas;
> nunc face supposita fervescit sanguis et ira
> scintillant oculi, dicisque facisque quod ipse
> non sani esse hominis non sanus iuret Orestes.   (107–18)

["Feel my veins, wretched man. Put your right hand on my chest: nothing's overheated here. Feel my fingers and toes: they are not cold." If you catch sight of money; if the neighbor's light-skinned slavegirl sends a smile your way, does your heart beat normally? Rough veggies are served on a cold plate, and coarsegrained cereal: let's examine your throat. Yes, there's an ulcerated place in that tender mouth that it wouldn't at all do to scrape with a plebeian beet. You get cold when pale fear has shaken out harvests from your limbs [that is, made your hair stand on end]; and now your blood boils like water over the flames, your eyes blaze with anger, and you say and do things that even the mad Orestes would swear were the mark of a man who wasn't sane.]

The philistine interlocutor objects that the Sick Man Parable doesn't apply to him since he's in perfectly good health. The philosophical adviser, here playing doctor, responds by testing him for moral weaknesses, which are betrayed by their psychosomatic manifestations: the speeded-up heartbeat of lust; the tender sensitivity of an overdelicate palate; the cold shiver of fear; and, climatically and half-jokingly, the hot flush of anger, the blazing eyes, and the rush of senseless, angry words provoked by this very procedure.

Scholarly discussions of this ending have focused, appropriately, on Persius's allusions to Horace: to *Satires* 2.3, the mad Damasippus's long and muddled diatribe on the Stoic paradox, "Only the Wise Man is sane" (or healthy); to the farcical ending of *Satires* 2.7, where Horace finally loses his temper and tells his slave Davus to stop lecturing him (on true slavery), or else . . . ; and to *Epistles* 2.2, which ended with a similar diagnostic quiz, addressed not least to himself. Most strikingly, Persius turns diatribe satire on its head, deconstructing the Horatian ironies, and giving the (now serious) philosophical adviser the last word. But equally, as said earlier, he revives Horace's work of moral self-examination, especially in *Epistles* 1.1, 1.2, 1.16, and 2.2, where familiar old clichés acquire new life and force from rehearsals of mortality. Indeed, the quiz in *Epistles* 2.2 includes, though unemphatically, the fear of death, and ends with a hard-won affirmation of satisfaction and gratitude.

And Persius's ending? After the horrors earlier it seems surprisingly mild, like a return to Horace's gentler, more ironic mode of humor. Money, a pretty girl: not much danger here; untreated sore in delicate mouth: a comic exaggeration of sensibilities; then quickly on to fear, anger, and the Horatian blackout. But is Persius putting us on? Is he inviting us, not just to enjoy some relief after all that emotional intensity, but also to relax into an easier state of mind, a more superficially Horatian mode, in which we might laugh off our symptoms and ignore the philosopher's healing advice? We have that choice—though we may not have it for long.

Horatian questions about poetry and philosophy remain. We might ask, for example: could the discipline of writing honestly and well, in the "little world" of art, serve as a useful focus, an easily perceived model for the effective discipline and reforming of our lives—the writer's first, then others'—so that we might become whole people at last? That is evidently what the *studiosus* should be doing. In *Satire* 3, however, we never get beyond the splitting self. Rather, Persius's emphatic cry, "FINDOR!" ("I'M SPLITTING?"), applies, on the one hand, to the satiric technique of "different voices" about which Housman and his successors were so perceptive, and, on the other, to a fatal self-division in life, a "going to pieces" completely in life and death. The point is that literary composition cannot "put us together" in any finally meaningful way, any more than arranging a dead man's burial coverings. As yet, Persius's new satire offers no saving reassurances. As we proceed through the *libellus*, things will get worse for the satirist—he will hit bottom in *Satire* 4—before they get better (if indeed they do) in *Satire* 5.

Appendix

▣ ▣ ▣ ▣ ▣ ▣ ▣ ▣ ▣ ▣ ▣ ▣ ▣ ▣ ▣ ▣ ▣

EPICTETUS, DIATRIBE, AND PERSIUS

WHEN SCHOLARS of Roman satire retrace the influence of "Bionean diatribe" on Lucilius, Horace, and (indirectly) Persius, they miss that other opportunity of reading backward from the *Discourses* of Epictetus reconstructed from notes and memory by his former student, Arrian of Nicomedia. Epictetus was himself the student of Musonius Rufus, "the Roman Socrates," who was Persius's contemporary.[42] The continuity of their teaching appears from passages like the following, where Epictetus stresses the necessity of training in strict logical reasoning:

> Why are we still lazy, easygoing, and sluggish? Why do we keep finding excuses for not toiling and staying awake as we construct and develop our power of reason? "So I make a mistake in these matters. I haven't killed my father, have I? " Slave, what's killing your father got to do with it? You're asking what you did? You committed just the one fault you were able to commit in the circumstances. Look, I said the same thing to Rufus when he criticized me for not discovering what was left out in a certain syllogism. "It's not," said I, "as if I'd burned down the Capitol." And he: "Slave," he said, "in this matter the thing left out *is* the Capitol." (1.7.31–32, trans. Oldfather)

Like Socrates in Plato's *Symposium*, Epictetus mitigates the harshness of his criticism by telling this story on himself: only, unlike the fictional Diotima, Rufus was real enough, especially in the remembered rough humor of his teaching. Something of the master's voice can surely be heard in Epictetus's own teaching, as when he in turn addresses his student as "Slave." Having internalized Musonius's Socratic/Cynic/Stoic teaching, he will rebuke himself in the same way whenever he catches himself thinking or behaving slavishly. Because he, too, though constantly pressing on, never forgets the danger of slipping back, the "we" of his first person plurals is more than merely pedagogical or condescending. It is, rather, the more genuinely inclusive, since self-implicating, "we" of shared human experience, aspiration, and at least potential relapse into error and folly.

In his prefatory letter to Lucius Gellius, Arrian argues that these *Discourses* of Epictetus represent a faithful, unadorned version of the lectures he once attended:

But whatever I heard him say I used to write down, word for word, as best I could, endeavouring to preserve it as a memorial, for my own future use, of his way of thinking and the frankness of his speech (*dianoias kai parrhêsias*).

[Epictetus aimed] at nothing else but to incite the minds of his hearers to the best things. If, now, these words of his should produce this same effect, they would have, I think, just that success which the words of the philosophers ought to have; but if not, let those who read them be assured of this, that when Epictetus himself spoke them, the hearer could not help but feel exactly what Epictetus wanted him to feel. If, however, the words by themselves do not produce this effect, perhaps I am at fault, or else, perhaps, it cannot well be otherwise. Farewell.

Scholars argue at length about how faithfully Arrian recalls Epictetus's sayings.[43] Had he used shorthand? Was he carried away by imitating Xenophon on Socrates? No definitive answer is possible. What is more important, I think, is to follow Arrian's guidance, to realize the inevitable discrepancy between the spoken word and its written record, and to reimagine the power of the original performance—and its pleasure, too, for the blend of play and seriousness (*to spoudaiogeloion*) is essential to diatribe. We see it especially in Epictetus's uses of dialogue: to enliven discussions of Stoic dogma, to make points memorable, and to bring conflicting viewpoints to life, often satirizing wrong ideas and attitudes, with comic mimesis, so as to inculcate and reinforce right ones.

Much that Anthony Long, then, says about the complexities of Epictetus's style and the other reasons we find him difficult to read may be applied, mutatis mutandis, to Persius:

He may be addressing or referring to an actual or imaginary layman, a rival philosopher, beginning or mature students, or voicing thoughts that apply to anyone, including himself. We also need to make constant allowance for his exaggeration, irony, and self-deprecation—all marks of his deliberate imitation of Socrates.

On the surface Epictetus may seem thoroughly accessible. His conversational idiom clamors for attention, and his rhetorical devices—repetition, imperatives, homely examples, anecdotes, and caustic injunctions—keep us engaged. Actually, however, the discourses are often complex and sometimes obscure. When they use dialogue, it can be difficult to assign the parts between the authorial persona and the imaginary interlocutor. Epictetus may alternate rapidly, as we have seen, between the protreptic, elenctic, and doctrinal styles. . . . His more technical arguments can be far from straightforward. Above all, we need to be constantly alert to his shifts of tone and to remember that the discourses in their delivered form would have been accompanied by pauses, gestures, changes of facial expression, and vocal modulation. All of these performative actions would have given his audience perspectives on his teaching that we can scarcely replicate, though we may get some sense of them by dwelling on certain expressions and by reading between the lines. We need also to remember that Arrian's record, largely accurate though I take it to be, probably involves more compression than Epictetus himself used.[44]

Long's account is invaluable. For accuracy, fullness of detail, and balance of ideas, it should be read in its entirety. For now, let me dwell briefly on three intertwined aspects of Epictetus's teaching that come close to Persius: (a) comic and satiric elements of performance; (b) the play of voices, sometimes internalized, in dialogue; and (c) the teacher's own shared involvement in the struggle toward moral perfection.

With regard to the first, when we read the *Discourses*, mentally noting their rhetorical techniques, we should realize to what extent they were originally dramatic performances with a strong mimetic bent. To appreciate them fully, we would need what Arrian cannot give us, but what we remember of our own best teachers: bodily movements and gestures, facial expressions, changes of intonation, and so forth. Occasionally, we get a hint. In 1.27.18, after discussing how humans attain knowledge of things, Epictetus remarks sarcastically, "How do I know? Well, when I want to swallow a bit of food, I don't put it *there*, I put it *here*." Two gestures: to the backside, then the mouth?[45] Elsewhere, too, the diatribe speaker indulges in moments of clowning familiar from comedy or mime but out of place in respectable oratory.

Second, and closer to Persius's *Satires*, is the dramatic play of voices in dialogue. For the reader, they are often hard to distinguish, not least when they come out of the blue; performance "in different voices" would have made things clearer.[46] Sometimes, as Barbara Wehner has shown in her thoroughgoing study, Epictetus's students interrupt, or are imagined to interrupt, with serious questions or objections to be answered; more often, a fictive interlocutor raises objections or complaints that are made to sound foolish, even childish, and are easily refuted and set right; sometimes an inner voice, even from within Epictetus himself, makes itself heard, again to be ridiculed and/or refuted in a dialogue with himself that can be remembered, internalized by his students, and reproduced at times of temptation, uncertainty, or distress.[47]

In 1.12.24, for example, after Epictetus has been discussing the importance of accepting things as they are, living in accordance with nature, and not complaining (as Socrates didn't complain, even in prison), a voice breaks in: "That I should have gotten a crippled leg!" And a second voice answers: "Slave, are you going to lay a complaint against the universe on account of one wretched little leg? Won't you let it go—make a donation of it to the Sum of Things? " We may imagine the comic mimesis here, the tonal contrast of childish whining and harsh grown-up rebuke. Not a straw man, this time, but Epictetus himself, an ex-slave with a crippled leg, is wonderfully implicated in this demonstration of right-versus-wrong thinking.[48] He rubs his poor leg (it really does hurt); the ordinary, childish person within him, closely tied to the body's vicissitudes and pains, gives a comically exaggerated groan, amusing the students, perhaps relieving the teacher, and illustrating our general tendency to feel sorry for ourselves for all kinds of reasons—but then, an abrupt, harsh rebuke cuts through emotional self-indulgence like a knife. The rebuking voice that, as we saw, might once have belonged to Musonius Rufus has now become Epictetus's own inner conscience (or superego), the introjected voice of Stoic reason, or what he elsewhere calls the *daimôn* assigned by Zeus to supervise each one of us individually.[49]

Long, again, has written well about the importance of "internalizing Stoicism," not just elucidating or justifying it (47); about Socratic self-examination, "dialogue with the self," elenctic and protreptic, which students learn to practice on themselves (85–86); about self-examination and self-discovery (90). Thus, in 4.9, after being "as caustic as any ancient satirist in his representation of the vanity of human wishes" (138), and after directly admonishing a man to reclaim his lost decency, integrity, and freedom,

> Epictetus shifts from the admonitory tone of 71 to a more mentoring and genial voice. He offers the lapsed Stoic a lesson in selfhood by drawing a vivid contrast between external compulsion, which may require a third party's intervention, and the self as a locus of internal dialogue and persuasion. The recommendation to engage oneself in conversation is not simply the injunction to pull oneself together. Rather, it reflects Epictetus' tireless insistence that internal dialogue, self-address, and self-examination are our essential resources for monitoring experience and shaping one's life in accordance with the normative principles of human nature. (139)

Passages like the above help us retrospectively to appreciate difficult aspects of style and thought in Persius's satires, especially the first and third. One striking example: I believe that, in the compressed interchange of *Satire* 1. 2–3,

> "*quis leget haec?*" *min tu* istud ais? Nemo hercule. "nemo? "
> vel duo vel nemo. . . .

> ["*Who'll read this stuff?*" *You're* asking *me* that? No one, by Hercules. "No one? " Maybe two people, maybe no one. . . .]

Persius gives voice to his own very real (if momentary) impulse or tempta-
tion, to desire poetic fame; he identifies this desire as an example of the
vanity of human wishes (line 1); and he rejects it—indeed, has rejected it,
with admirable decisiveness and self-irony, before we know it. In Stoic
terms (if we read between the lines) he does what we all should be doing
constantly: examines a misleading impression, refuses to give assent to it,
and reminds himself that, in the proper scheme of values, literary achieve-
ment is just one more "preferred indifferent" like health or riches. The
process, for Persius's readers as for Epictetus's students, will be exemplary.
For the poet, too, as for the teacher, it also gives cathartic expression to
many strong impulses and reactions of the imperfect heart. As *emotional
self-recognizance*, it reinforces the moral and spiritual education of a still
weak and vulnerable individual who is striving to live more wholeheartedly
in obedience to God and Destiny.

Thirdly, the goal of philosophical study and effort can be described as
integrity, autonomy, and fixity of purpose (or, loosely, free will). As Long,
again, well argues, Epictetus's usual focus is on progress rather than
achievement (225, 230); he treats all people, himself most of all, as progres-
sives (112); and he insists most strongly on the importance of making
progress here and now (272, from the *Manual*, 51):

> What kind of teacher, then, are you still waiting for in order to refer
> your self-improvement to him? You are no longer a boy but a full-grown
> man. If you are careless and lazy now and keep putting things off and
> always deferring the day after which you will attend to yourself, you will
> not notice that you are making no progress but you will live and die as
> someone quite ordinary. From now on, resolve to live as a grown-up
> who is making progress [and see that every day matters].

Significantly, too, Epictetus undercuts any reliance on diatribe as such. He
regularly reminds his students, and by extension his future readers, of the
vast difference between academic performance and genuine moral achieve-
ment. He is critical of people whose main concern is to display their rhetor-
ical talent and their philosophical learning—people who, we might say, had
taken their Ph.D. in Stoic philosophy and written several highly regarded
monographs on the more difficult works of Chrysippus. In 2.1.29–35, after
the master has been holding forth on the nature of true inner freedom as
against social convention (much like Persius in *Satire* 5), a graduate student
protests—he has been writing the most polished philosophical essays at the
master's direction—and is rebuked:

> Even now, when the crisis demands an answer, what will you do? Go
> and read from your writings and boast, "See how well I compose dia-
> logues"? Don't do it, fellow. Say, rather: "See how my desires don't

miscarry . . ." Display your knowledge of one thing only: how not to miss the right goal, fall into the wrong. (35)

Here, as often in Plato's *Dialogues*, there is a powerful tension between rhetoric and philosophy. Epictetus himself has no problem: he makes fun of the very genre he is using, the moral lecture or diatribe, and he can deal quite well, thank you, with any morally subversive tendencies that arise within himself. But he has to be firm, time and again, in warning his students not to put the rhetorical cart before the philosophical horse. Plato showed in his brilliant writings that the written word, his own included, was not to be trusted, that it was an inadequate substitute for the personal cut-and-thrust of Socratic dialogue. Epictetus shows, in his powerful diatribes, that the spoken word cannot be trusted either. The proof of philosophical study lies in the power, progressively demonstrated throughout one's life, to make right choices and avoid wrong ones. There, and there alone—for student and teacher alike—is that insignificant *summa cum laude* to be found. Indeed, the teacher's own final business is to make himself dispensable,[50] to become, at best, part of that inner voice of reason and conscience by which his students may guide themselves to lead genuinely valuable lives.

Chapter Three

EXPLORING FREEDOM

IT IS HARD, for many reasons, to talk about Persius and Roman politics. Although allusions to Nero and his court have often and easily been suspected in the *Satires*, starting with King Midas (allegedly removed from *Satire* 1 by Cornutus, lest Nero think the satire was aimed at him—as of course, on one level, it was)—still, Nero and Neronian politics are mainly conspicuous by their absence from Persius's writings. So we are left to reconstruct the story as best we can.

When Persius thought about Nero (37–68 A.D.), three years his junior, he could well have judged him in terms of performance. Ideally, realizing his youthful, god-given promise, Nero was expected to usher in a new Golden Age for Rome. In the more realistic view, under Seneca's tutelage, he would be a second Augustus, moderating the uses of power, showing respect for constitutional forms and Roman traditions, and working with the senate: a program, at least, of decent simulation. Instead (though more obviously after 62 A.D., when Persius died), he ruled autocratically, adopting outward features of Hellenistic monarchy, and the performances for which he chose to be applauded in Greece, where he felt most comfortable, and in Italy, were in lyre-playing and singing. Augustus on his deathbed had asked, "Have I played my part well?" Posterity, except for a few die-hard republicans, largely assented. But when Nero, before his enforced suicide, exclaimed, "What an artist dies with me!" (*Qualis artifex pereo*), the imperial achievements he boasted of were hardly those that many thoughtful Romans, let alone Augustus, would have applauded.[1]

Persius, too, fails to give the expected performance. Rather than attack Nero directly or decry the hollowness of contemporary political life, he apparently limits his criticism to stylistic matters—though corruption of style and taste, spreading outward from Midas/Nero and his court, implies social and political degeneration as well. But he gives another strong hint in *Satire* 1 of the kind of satire that, for many reasons, he can't and won't write. As he describes the usual uncritical and flattering response to pretentious modern oratory that is all hyper-euphonious style and no substance, his exclamation, *an Romule ceves?* ("Romulus, do you take up the rear?"), recalls how Catullus had spoken out, with old republican *libertas*, against

Pompey and Caesar and their henchmen: *cinaede Romule, haec videbis et feres*? ("Romulus, you queer, will you see these things and *submit* to them?").[2] Catullus's social position and connections still allowed him to get away, like Lucilius two generations earlier, with such performances of aggression, but that older satiric *libertas*, already more mocked than mourned by Horace, was long dead when Persius began to write.

The present chapter, *Exploring Freedom*, follows Persius through *Satires* 4 and 5. *Satire* 4 begins with the failure of philosophy (Socrates) to guide the youthful energy of politics (Alcibiades); the reader quickly thinks of Seneca and Nero, but then satire itself becomes compromised in what seems an endless regress, a universal failure of self-knowledge. By contrast, *Satire* 5 depicts a double movement of regeneration for Persius: first, as a student, under the moral guidance of his teacher and friend, Cornutus; and then as a satirist, denouncing vice and folly via the Stoic paradox, "Only the Wise Man is Free." The satire is both old and new. The vices and follies of humankind—avarice and luxury, lust, ambition, superstition—are still invincibly there, as they were for Lucilius and Horace. But the diatribe against them evinces new authority, whether from the firmness of Stoic judgment informing it, or from the poet's readiness to move outward now from his acknowledged self-limitations and laugh at the world's vanities as a proper satirist should.

The chapter concludes with a speculative reconstruction of what Persius does not tell us, but what we can read between the lines: his experience as "another dissident under Nero." I shall give a further, more extensive but still hypothetical picture of his life and work, based largely on the *Vita*, in Chapter 4.

Shadows of Falsehood (*Satire* 4)

Although this chapter is mainly about Persius's long *Satire* 5, I shall begin with *Satire* 4 for two reasons. First, because Persius placed this, his shortest satire, as a foil and curtain-raiser to *Satire* 5, his longest, and second, because *Satire* 4, as savage as it is short, declares the bankruptcy not only of politics—its ostensible subject—and of social intercourse, but also, by implication, of satire itself.[3] Its plea for self-knowledge emerges from a harsh, ugly depiction of moral and social failure. But satire, which might bring healing, or at least salutary correction, seems to be caught up irrevocably into that same Waste Land, and is marked with the sign of impotence. How, then, we shall have to ask, with Persius, might we reascend into a world of sanity and creative strength?

He begins abruptly:

"rem populi tractas?" (barbatum haec crede magistrum
dicere, sorbitio tollit quem dira cicutae)
"quo fretus?" Dic hoc, magni pupille Pericli.
scilicet ingenium et rerum prudentia velox
ante pilos venit, dicenda tacendave calles.
ergo ubi commota fervet plebecula bile,
fert animus calidae fecisse silentia turbae
maiestate manus. quid deinde loquere? "Quirites,
hoc puta non iustum est, illud male, rectius illud."
scis etenim iustum gemina suspendere lance
ancipitis librae, rectum discernis ubi inter
curva subit vel cum fallit pede regula varo,
et potis es nigrum vitio praefigere theta.
quin tu igitur summa nequiquam pelle decorus
ante diem blando caudam iactare popello
desinis, Anticyras melior sorbere meracas? . . .'   (4.1–16)

["Handling the people's affairs?" Imagine the bearded teacher is
speaking, the one who was carried off by swallowing hemlock. "With
what assurance?" Explain, great Pericles' ward. No doubt about it: brains
and good sense came quick, before your facial hair; you're skilled at
knowing what and what not to say. So, then: when the mob's anger is
roused to the boiling point, your mind prompts you to quiet the hot
crowd with a hand's majestic gesture. And then? What will you say?
"People, I think, this course of action's unjust; that one is wrong; that
other's more correct." For you know well how to evaluate justice, adjust
the scales of the tricky balance, discern the straight path amid crooked
bends and diversity of rules, and fix upon vice the black Delete of death.
No, it's not enough, that fine-looking outward hide of yours. Stop show-
ing off your tail at the people's asking. Better to swallow whole cities of
hemlock."]

The scene is evidently taken from Plato's *First Alcibiades*, where Socrates
convicts the brash young aristocrat of his moral and personal unreadiness
to enter into serious political life and, as he imagines, take control of Athens
by means of his brilliance, his riches and connections, his personal cha-
risma, and his mastery, presumably inherited from Pericles, of demagogic
skills. Here, as in Plato's *Symposium*, Alcibiades' tragedy is one of ignorance
and refusal. He will not submit himself to the Socratic discipline of moral
reform based on philosophical self-interrogation and study of true values,
shaping an inward standard for himself against which political aspirations
can and should be measured.[4] Socrates' comments here (10–13) are phrased
in Stoic-sounding terms of virtue and vice, right and wrong, and the ratio-

nal evaluation of human actions. And they are delivered with strong sarcasm, for Alcibiades does not really "know" these things. If he did, he wouldn't engage in the politics of flattery and charm, as a dog fawns on people, or as a peacock displays its beautiful tail (a sexualizing of politics, in keeping with the mixed metaphors of perverted sexuality throughout *Satire* 4).[5] But the truth is that this youth's ultimate desires are sensual: to eat luxurious meals, to tan his pretty little body in the sun. A person so immature can have no real effectiveness in politics, because he has no real standards, convictions, or goals for himself or others.

Even as Persius endorses Socrates' criticism of Alcibiades he also subverts it, for the scene where the youth rises to proclaim serious philosophical sentiments before a popular audience is patently ridiculous. This goes beyond sarcasm. It suggests that even if the speaker were genuinely grounded in philosophy, as Alcibiades is not, he might still make a fool of himself in public, like a schoolboy repeating his lesson unthinkingly before a derisive audience. Persius may be glancing here at Seneca, who tried to instill moral and philosophical ideas in the young prince, his charge.[6] (The "five good years" of Nero's tutelage under Seneca and Burrus were probably over.) Whether or not Persius respected Seneca (and it seems unlikely), he can hardly have joined in the perhaps widespread hope that the musical, cultured young prince would become a philosopher-king. But there is more. How should Seneca succeed where Socrates himself had failed? How can any philosopher, however gifted, hope to influence the mess and corruption of political life, whether it takes the form of the uncontrollable Athenian democracy or the absolute rule, at Rome, of one unbridled youth?

Abruptly, as if disillusioned, the "Socratic" section breaks off, and the satire moves into public scenes of criticizing and backbiting that suggest the impotence, not of philosophy now, but of satire itself. A transitional statement (23–24) continues the theme of the need for self-knowledge via the truism that we see our neighbor's faults (the pack on our neighbor's back) but not our own; the advice to "live with yourself" and know your own inadequacies will be repeated at the poem's end. The satiric vignettes that follow, illustrating the universal lack of self-knowledge, will, however, also reveal a universal backbiting that comes disturbingly close to satire, at least in a rudimentary form. Two people are talking. *X*: "Do you know Vettius, the rich guy with the vast estates?" And *Y*: "You mean, the fellow who . . ."; and, with telling details and probably some comic mimesis, he describes a man so miserly that he only eats and drinks the most wretched fare. But then, if "you" take your ease in the sun, as Alcibiades was depicted as doing earlier—the luxurious life, opposite to the miser's—a stranger nearby will denounce you as a sexual hypocrite:

"hi mores! penem arcanaque lumbi
runcantem populo marcentis pandere vulvas.
tum, cum maxillis balanatum gausape pectas,
inguinibus quare detonsus gurgulio extat?
quinque palaestritae licet haec plantaria vellant
elixasque nates labefactent forcipe adunca,
non tamen ista filix ullo mansuescit aratro." (35–41)

["Such goings-on! Weeding your lower parts, displaying your withered old portals to the people. Given the woolly, scented beard you comb, why does your little weevil stick out bare from your groin? No: not even if five handlers pulled and tugged at the new growth with curved pincers after they boiled your buttocks to make them soft: no amount of plowing can make wild vegetation tame."]

As Kissel noted, the image of rank vegetation ("filix") growing uncontrolled recalls a passage in Horace's *Satires* 1.3 about the need for mutual tolerance and forbearance, based on genuine self-knowledge. Before you criticize another, says Horace, you should scrutinize yourself for any bad habits that nature or custom may have sown in you: "wild vegetation that needs burning springs up in neglected fields" (34–37). But Persius turns Horace's corrective advice into a second example of character assassination, so that the Horatian satirist (and Persius after him?) becomes implicated in his own criticism.[7] The satirist satirized: is the process endless? All this might simply have reinforced the Socratic/Stoic injunction of acquiring self-knowledge, but there is more. What Persius shows us finally is a Waste Land vision in which sexual perversion, impotence, and sterility are, as in Eliot's poem, remarkably combined.

Of these, the homosexual metaphors have been pressed hardest by critics, at least for the last third of *Satire* 4. The second man attacked is an aging queen; his self-exposed nudity, his laughably unsuccessful efforts at depilation, give the lie to his philosophic beard (a contrast that Juvenal will develop in his second satire).[8] Less obviously, this passage links up with obscene hints earlier. I suggest—and I have a dirty mind, but one trained, as Persius thought proper, by "growing pale over Aristophanes"— that the satire's titular first words, "rem populi tractas?" ("Handling the city's affairs?"),[9] closely followed by "sorbitio" ("swallowing" or "sucking"; cf. "sorbere," 16), introduce the would-be politician as a sexual pervert and flatterer; a play, very likely, on Greek *dêmagôgein*, right out of Aristophanes' *Knights*.[10]

Politics sucks, and so does (everyday) satire, but that is not the worst:

caedimus inque vicem praebemus crura sagittis.
vivitur hoc pacto, sic novimus. ilia subter

caecum vulnus habes, sed lato balteus auro
praetegit. ut mavis, da verba et decipe nervos,
si potes. (42–46)

[By turns we strike and offer our shins to arrows. Life is like that, or so
we were taught. Beneath your groin you've got an unseen wound, but a
wide gold belt covers it safely. Have it your own way: do your fooling,
and cheat your own muscles—if you can.]

The man here addressed is impotent. He may fool others, but he cannot
fool his own "nerves," any more than the fool in *Satire* 3 could forever
disregard his fatal illness. To ignore your faults is not just foolish, antisocial
behavior, as in Horace: it is downright dangerous. At the same time, the
sexual wound translates self-ignorance into a more widespread impotence,
a generalized failure of nerve in an unfruitful world.[11]

The similarities with Eliot's *The Waste Land* are striking. Eliot built his
poem, as Dame Helen Gardner said,

upon the myth of the mysterious sickness of the Fisher King in the Grail
stories and the blight of infertility which has fallen upon his lands, which
can only be lifted when the destined Deliverer asks the magic question
or performs the magic act. . .

. . . *The Waste Land* moves, if it moves at all, toward some moment which
is outside the poem and may never come, which we are still waiting for
at the close. It does not so much move towards a solution as make clearer
and clearer that a solution is not within our power. We can only wait for
the rain to fall.[12]

Eliot's images of sterility and barrenness—dried-up landscapes in Parts 1
and 5, marital stalemate and abortion in 2, emptily casual sex in 3—are at
least juxtaposed, whether satirically or wistfully, with memories of beautiful
landscapes and richly meaningful (though often tragic) emotional experi-
ences in poetry, drama, and art. And near the end there is "a damp gust /
bringing rain," and then thunder over the Himalayas, the hint, if not prom-
ise, of a mighty fructifying storm. In Persius's satire, too, the dried-up
vegetation and sexual wound indicate deep-set wounds in modern society,
but even the memory of rain is withheld; there is only the Socratic/Stoic
call to self-knowledge, rejected at the poem's start by Alcibiades, yet re-
sumed in an abrupt last appeal:

respue quod non es; tollat sua munera cerdo.
tecum habita; noris quam sit tibi curta supellex. (51–52)

[Spit out what's not you; away with the leather-maker's
wares. Live with yourself; you'll realize how much your
furnishings fall short.][13]

This is no longer just Socrates speaking to Alcibiades. It is an inter-nalized Socratic/Stoic voice convicting us all, Persius included, of moral inadequacy.

The unifying theme of *Satire* 4 is the need for self-knowledge, whether in Athens or in Rome. A secondary theme is impotence: not just moral and physical impotence in the Age of Nero, but a failure of nerve at the core of people's lives. But where can healing be found? Following Plato, we might look for an honest man to tell the truth to whoever will listen. Yet the satirist, who might have been such a man, only exacerbates the problem, for while satire regularly proclaims its intention to improve society by showing up its faults, the satirist as an individual—or, better, the implicated author concealed behind the persona of "the satirist"—cannot be absolved of the vices of pride, envy, and especially malice that make themselves heard through satire.[14] How could any of them—of us—escape complicity in these messy human emotions?

Satire 4 ends, then, where *Satire* 3 began, with a call to wakefulness, yet it is not just the youthful Alcibiades who is called: it is the satirist, and Persius, and the reader. Nor is self-knowledge merely a question of hearing or reading philosophy. You might live close to Socrates himself and still fail the test. You might know all the Stoic answers like Seneca and still fail to adequately educate yourself, let alone your savage princely charge. Or you might be a Stoic satirist like Persius. For him especially the road to salvation goes through the valley of humiliation. In order to make any real progress, we must realize our sheer ignorance about things that matter, the power and extent of our self-delusions, the gap between our public persona and our deep-down impotence to accomplish anything truly creative and worthwhile. The still Socratic irony is that here and only here, in convic-tion of ignorance, can we start again. When Persius, in the next *Satire*, returns in grateful memory to his Stoic tutelage under Cornutus, he will take up where Alcibiades (and perhaps Nero) left off. He will also submit his sincerity to the test: a sincerity founded, if not in sure self-knowledge, yet in the will to self-education and intellectual and moral progress on which, for an honest Stoic, any real accomplishment must be based.

Modes of Disclosure (*Satire* 5)

Satire 5 starts with redirection. After a first speaker begins in bombastic, mock-epic style, "Poets always say they'd like to have a hundred voices, a hundred mouths and tongues," another voice intervenes—an internal monitor, perhaps the internalized voice of Cornutus—advising Persius to abandon such self-parodying, high-poetic themes and style and do what he's learned to do: namely, write satire. For Persius (the praise is directive) doesn't huff and puff at the bellows of pretentious verse. Rather,

> verba togae sequeris iunctura callidus acri,
> ore teres modico, pallentis radere mores
> doctus et ingenuo culpam defigere ludo. (5.14–16)

[You go for ordinary words, keenly and shrewdly combined in a moderate style; you are skilled at scraping pale-sick habits, nailing down faults in free-spirited play.]

Persius's satire writing is both described here and reauthorized. Why not proceed directly to the theme of freedom ("libertate opus est," 73)? One simple answer is that Persius wants to pay tribute to Cornutus, responding to his teacher's confidence in him. Another, less simple answer is that he wants to redefine the satirist's "personal voice," placing himself in the confessional tradition of Lucilius and Horace before preaching in diatribe mode to an unconverted world. But this also means acknowledging the shadows of falsehood and hypocrisy in which, as *Satire* 4 showed, all satirists are implicated. How escape from that endless regress, of insincerity rebuked by insincerity?

A critical voice in *Satire* 4 posed the challenge:

> ut nemo in sese temptat descendere, nemo,
> sed praecedenti spectatur mantica tergo! (23–24)

[How no one risks descending into himself;
all gaze on the pack [of faults] on the back of the man ahead.]

In *Satire* 4 Persius descended into a hell of human viciousness—albeit, perhaps, with a faint hope of reascent into the light of Stoic reason. In *Satire* 5 he moves inward and outward again, in a quasi-Platonic pattern: inward, to memories of personal experience, which make up the most autobiographical section of the *Satires*; and then outward, in a renewal of Stoic diatribe, to the great universal theme of human freedom. The unusual seriousness and intensity (though not without humor) of his self-disclosure early on facilitates the wild comic laughter with which, while deconstructing Horace's ironies, he reconstructs and revindicates the old Stoic paradox that "Only the Wise Man is Free," or "Every Fool is a Slave." At the same time, he demonstrates his poetic originality by playing new, critical variations on the "personal voice" with which Lucilius and then Horace had experimented. How does Persius read Horace reading Lucilius?

Horace identifies Lucilius's satire principally with its Old Comic *libertas*, its savage attacks on individuals. He himself inherits but redefines that freedom. His satires, as he quite reasonably claims, are aesthetically refined and morally and socially responsible. Rooted in a more inward freedom than Lucilius knew, they celebrate and promote honest friendship, *amicitia*, both within Maecenas's circle and, by extension, within the larger world of Roman society and politics in the turbulent Thirties. Whether Horace genuinely admired Lucilius's oldtime satiric outspokenness, or even envied it, we cannot say, but about his alleged sincerity he evidently has doubts:

> me pedibus delectat claudere verba
> Lucili ritu nostrum melioris utroque.
> ille velut fidis arcana sodalibus olim
> credebat libris, neque si male cesserat olim
> decurrens alio, neque si bene; quo fit ut omnis
> votiva pateat veluti descripta tabella
> vita senis.   (*Serm.* 2.1.28–33)

[What gives *me* pleasure is putting words into [metrical] feet in Lucilius's mode, a better man than either of us. He'd confide his inmost secrets to his books, as to trusted friends. Whether things went badly for him or well, he never ran off anywhere else: so the old man's entire life is exposed, as though on a votive tablet. I follow him.]

The more obvious criticism is aesthetic. Lucilius was always in a hurry, running, not walking. (Those metrical feet are not always under control.) As William Anderson observed, the artistic standard of Roman votive tablets—a picture of yourself, say, escaping shipwreck—is not the highest.[15] But there is more. Lucilius wrote openly about things not discussed in public, like his sexual adventures and misadventures. Confiding in books as in trusted friends sounds nice but is really absurd. To publish secrets is to publish secrets—and Horace lets us know, time and again (and often to the scholar's irritation), that *he* can keep a secret.

Was Lucilius more honest than Horace? We would say today that his satiric *libertas* had its own rhetoric, its own artistic conventions, as Archilochus's *iambos* had, or the "personal" comments in a parabasis of Aristophanes. Neither authorial assertion nor generic convention establishes honesty as such. Compare what Henry Adams, in the preface to his *Education of Henry Adams*, says of Rousseau:

> Jean Jacques Rousseau began his famous "Confessions" by a vehement appeal to the Deity: "I have shown myself as I was; contemptible and vile when I was so; good, generous, sublime when I was so; I have unveiled my interior such as Thou thyself hast seen it, Eternal Father! Collect about me the innumerable swarm of my fellows; let them hear my confessions; let them groan at my unworthiness; let them blush at my meannesses! Let each of them discover his heart in his turn at the foot of thy throne with the same sincerity; and then let any one of them tell thee if he dares: 'I was a better man!' "

Jean Jacques was a very great educator in the manner of the eighteenth century, and has been commonly thought to have had more influence than any other teacher of his time; but his peculiar method of improving human nature has not been universally admired. Most educators of the nineteenth century have declined to show themselves before their scholars as objects more vile or contemptible than necessary, and even the humblest teacher hides, if possible, the faults with which nature has generously embellished us all, as it did Jean Jacques, thinking, as most religious minds are apt to do, that the Eternal Father himself may not feel unmixed pleasure at our thrusting under his eyes chiefly the least agreeable details of his creation.

Adams is very cutting. His heavy irony, with all that Puritan New England snobbery, grates on us today. He makes us realize, though, that there is something self-serving and fraudulent about Rousseau's claim to utter and complete self-disclosure. Rousseau admits his faults, to be sure, and some of them are pretty bad, but he tries overall to put his actions in the best possible light, so that we shall like him, appreciate his inner goodness, and forgive him his lapses, which are only human. (Augustine did rather better in his *Confessions* when he let God be the independent prosecutor, the counsel for the defense, and the final judge of all these things.)

Horace criticizes Lucilius as Adams will criticize Rousseau, albeit with less savage irony and, I think, more genuine admiration. He knows that Lucilius revealed much of himself; he may also suspect, as we do, that those candid self-revelations followed their own social/satiric agenda. But we have learned to be suspicious of Horace, too, and our modern wariness was anticipated by Persius, who contrasts Horace's subtle ironic fencing with Lucilius's more obvious "lashing of the city":

> secuit Lucilius urbem,
> te Lupe, te Muci, et genuinum fregit in illis.
> omne vafer vitium ridenti Flaccus amico
> tangit et admissus circum praecordia ludit,
> callidus excusso populum suspendere naso.   (*Sat.* 1.114–18)

[Lucilius lashed the city—you, Lupus, and you, Mucius— and broke his jawbone on them. Flaccus makes his friend laugh, shrewdly touches on his every fault, and, once let inside, plays around his heartstrings—clever too, at hanging the crowd from the end of his cleared-out nose.]

Even, that is, while Horace lets us feel that we are insiders, like his friends, and unlike the great unwashed mob outside, he is playing with us ("ludit"), tricking us into a false sense of intimacy: maybe to our benefit, but then it is he who becomes intimate with us, who reads our failings, not the reverse. So we should exercise caution in giving him, as it seems, our confidence.

Scholars talk today about Horace's "self-fashioning." To some, like Armstrong and Lyne, this means that he knew how to get ahead in the world by making the right impression, projecting the right ethos, taking on the right persona—and there is much truth in this. Horace succeeded remarkably in making a place for himself in Maecenas's circle, then in Roman society generally. He made friends, influenced people, left a lasting impression on his age. But his self-fashioning, I think, had another side. As he tried on different personae and different attitudes, I think that Horace came to know himself better, to grow as a person, through his special mix of humor and seriousness. And I think (following Persius) that he tricks us, as a friend might, through his art into growing a little ourselves into self-awareness and personhood. Certainly, his satire needs a warning label, such as Persius puts on it. It is mocking and self-mocking; it carries no guarantee of sincerity. But even if Horace only taught us to trade in worse masks for better, we might be grateful.

Consider his evolving treatment of the issue of patronage. Throughout his first collection of *Odes* Horace pays tribute to Maecenas, thanks him for his benefits, dedicates his poetry to him, assures him of his lasting loyalty, devotion, and companionship even in the face of death. In the *Epistles*, however, as the attraction of retreat, philosophical reflection, and self-recognizance becomes stronger, Horace subjects his relation to Maecenas to new, sometimes painful scrutiny. In *Epistles* 1.7, he insists on the supreme value of independence, even if this requires the breaking of a close relationship (but, of course, it won't—Maecenas is too generous for that, and Horace too grateful). In *Epistles* 1.1, Horace says (humorously, but with a painful edge of complaint) that Maecenas cares more about a frayed sleeve than about his whole unraveling state of soul. Even the best kind of patronage, it seems, has its limits.

As Persius makes his confession to Cornutus in *Satire* 5, he deliberately evokes several "personal" passages in which Horace speaks of his father and his patron.[16] Not only, it seems, will Cornutus combine these two offices: he will be the spiritual patron that Horace never had, the one who attends seriously to his friend's uncertainties, his inconsistencies, his disturbances of soul. And Persius, in turn, rather than assert his own sincerity, like Lucilius, or ironize it, like Horace, will offer it up for testing, so that whatever in it is false, exaggerated, or merely derivative may be rejected, leaving a residue (or so he hopes) of originality, honesty, and truth.

He turns to Cornutus, then, focusing his speech on that single person as audience, and disregarding the likelihood of eavesdroppers:[17]

secrete loquimur. tibi nunc hortante Camena
excutienda damus praecordia, quantaque nostrae
pars tua sit, Cornute, animae, tibi, dulcis amice,

ostendisse iuvat. pulsa, dinoscere cautus
quid solidum crepet et pictae tectoria linguae.
hic ego centenas ausim deposcere fauces,
ut quantum mihi te sinuoso in pectore fixi
voce traham pura, totumque hoc verba resignent
quod latet arcana non enarrabile fibra.   (*Sat.* 5.21–29)

[We're talking in private. Now, at the Muse's bidding, I give you my heartstrings to shake out. And it gives me pleasure to have shown you, Cornutus, dear friend, how great a part of my soul belongs to you. Try me, and knock. You're careful to distinguish what rings solid from the plastered-over concealments of a coated tongue. And here I myself would demand a hundred jaws, to draw out in clear speech how entirely I've fixed you within my winding heart, and so my words may unseal and reveal the entire unspeakable truth that's hidden within my entrails.]

Show is better than tell. Rather than protest too much, or too tritely, or put on any kind of performance, he will leave it to Cornutus to "sound his heartstrings," to test how sincere his affection is, and his loyalty.[18] Horace spoke of Virgil as "half of my soul" (*animae dimidium meae*) in *Odes* 1.3, and again, of Maecenas as "part of my soul" (*meae . . . partem animae*) in *Odes* 2.17. Persius leaves the proportions open. Cornutus must discover for himself, by testing, just "how great a part of my soul belongs to you." The grotesque images and complex mixed metaphors in the following lines suggest Persius's struggle for sincerity, his anxiety to avoid triteness of response. Cornutus can and will distinguish "what rings solid" (like an unforged coin) from "the plastered-over concealments of a painted tongue." The philosopher-friend probing for hypocrisy fuses here with the doctor who observes symptoms such as the coated tongue, who probes deeply into the folds and recesses of one's vitals. What Cornutus should find, deeply implanted in Persius's heart, is . . . himself.

The culminating metaphor is "resignent" ("unseal and reveal").[19] On one level, it suggests the reverse hypocrisy of the man who offers his inner thoughts and feelings to be unfolded. On another, it suggests the ultimate sincerity of a last will and testament, unsealed and read (like Persius's satire book?) only after one is dead—after the disease probed or unprobed by the doctor has done its worst. But what gives the word its special force and meaning is Persius's dialogue with Horace. In *Odes* 3.29, his grand tribute to Maecenas, where their two lives are juxtaposed, Horace speaks of his attitude toward Fortune's gifts:

laudo manentem; si celeris quatit
pennas, resigno quae dedit et mea
    virtute me involvo. . .   (53–55)

[If she stays, I give thanks; if she shakes her swift
wings (to fly away), I resign her gifts and wrap myself
in my virtue. . .]

. . . a humorous picture, but with undertones of serious resolve. In *Epistles*
1.7, Horace tells Maecenas of his settled intention to remain in the country
through the heavy season of autumn, when public busyness "brings on
fevers and unseals wills" (*et testamenta resignat*, 9); and then, after telling
the fable of the weasel who got stuck in the corn-bin, he concludes,

hac ego si compellor imagine, cuncta resigno; . . .
inspice si possum donata reponere laetus.   (*Ep.* 1.7.34, 39)

[If I'm forced, indeed, by this parable, then I resign everything; . . .
See if I'm able to return my gifts, and gladly.]

Horace's declaration of independence, his offer to return all of Maecenas's
gifts (including, most notably, the Sabine estate), both recalls his earlier
assertion of independence of fortune in *Odes* 3.29, also to Maecenas, and
anticipates the Mena-Philippus parable later in *Epistles* 1.7, where the cli-
ent, abused by an uncaring patron, must finally relinquish the gift of a
country life that has caused him so much grief. The parable, presumably,
does not fit. Maecenas's generosity is real, and Horace's loyalty and grati-
tude likewise. The shadow selves may be acknowledged and rejected; the
gifts of Maecenas, and of fortune, may remain for the time being, until that
last fearful "resignation" of death.

The subtext, then, of Persius's "revelation" to Cornutus is the difference
between their philosophically grounded friendship and the patron-client
relationship of Maecenas and Horace, which, albeit exemplary, still re-
mained rather shaky. For Cornutus is the spiritual patron that Horace
never had. The Stoic philosopher is the soul's doctor—hardly a trite meta-
phor now, considering Persius's constant awareness of the body's suscepti-
bility to disease and death. Cornutus can probe attitudes, "inspect" the
heart's secret places as Maecenas never would or could.

It seems as though these first tortured lines that delve so paradoxically
into the problem of sincerity and its expression in words give Persius
the freedom subsequently to speak more simply and directly about his
debt to Cornutus. I almost said, to speak like Horace, but the differences
remain crucial.

cum primum pavido custos mihi purpura cessit
bullaque subcinctis Laribus donata pependit,
cum blandi comites totaque impune Subura
permisit sparsisse oculos iam candidus umbo,
cumque iter ambiguum est et vitae nescius error

diducit trepidas ramosa in compita mentes,
me tibi supposui. teneros tu suscipis annos
Socratico, Cornute, sinu. tum fallere sollers
adposita intortos extendit regula mores
et premitur ratione animus vincique laborat
artificemque tuo ducit sub pollice voltum.   (30–40)

[When my protective purple left me, frightened,
and my amulet hung up, a gift to the boyish Lares;
when friends are seductive; when my new white toga
let me scatter my eyes over the whole Subura;
when the way is doubtful; when, ignorant and fearful,
minds draw diversely toward the branching crossroads,
I put myself under your protection. You take up
our tender years in your Socratic bosom.
The tricky rule straightens out twisted habits;
impressed by reason, the mind struggles to surrender,
producing an artful face beneath your thumb.]

Persius begins by describing a time of spiritual crisis in his life, when he left the safety of childhood, represented by the *toga praetexta* and the protective *bulla*, or magical amulet, and entered into the turbulent period of adolescence. What might normally seem a heady experience of sudden new freedom for the growing boy is seen, instead, as a dangerous and confusing time of liminality whose destructive possibilities appear in the seductions, here suggestively juxtaposed, of flattering companions and the red-light district.[20] Here again Persius transforms an Horatian subtext. The stammering "cum primum pavido custos mihi purpura cessit bullaque" recalls and somewhat parodies Horace's description of his first meeting with Maecenas:

ut veni coram, singultim pauca locutus,
infans namque pudor prohibebat plura profari,
non ego me claro natum patre, non ego circum
me Satureiano vectari rura caballo,
sed quod eram narro. responcdes, ut tuus est mos,
pauca: abeo; et revocas nono post mense iubesque
esse in amicorum numero.   (*Serm.* 1.6.56–62)

[When I came before you, stammering a few words— for a childish modesty kept me from saying more— I told you, not that my father was noble, not that a Satureian nag conveyed me around the countryside, but only what I was. You answered, as is your way, just a few words; I went; then you recalled me eight months later, told me to count myself in your friends' company.]

Horace's childish shyness before the great man (almost literally "infans," "speechless" like a babe) is exaggerated here for comic effect. We may imagine the laughter of Maecenas and his friends as *Satires* 1.6 is performed before them. They know better than to take Horace at his disingenuous word! The hints of pain even in the budding relationship, with Maecenas's intimidating brevity of speech and then the long period of waiting, or gestation, are almost forgotten in Horace's newfound satisfaction in Maecenas's circle. Later, toward the end of the satire, he describes the leisurely life that his renunciation of political ambition, which Maecenas will appreciate, has made possible. Among other things, he "wanders about [*pererro*] through the deceptive Circus and the forum by evening." We think of sheep safely grazing in Virgilian pastoral. It is a safe and happy world, an urban idyll in which Horace has been allowed to participate.

For young Persius things are different. Horace's casual sightseeing in lowlife districts of Rome now becomes a gruesome "scattering of eyes," suggesting distraction, dissipation, loss of vision. Horace's careless browsing becomes a dangerously confusing "wandering" on dark paths, amid bewildering choices of direction. And now, rather than go forward, Persius begins again. He gives himself into the protective care of Cornutus, who reparents him like a foster-mother giving a little child the breast, or maybe like Zeus when he sewed the infant Dionysus into his thigh and gave him a second birth. (So much for Horace's period of gestation!) The picture has been called homoerotic--a playful hint, perhaps, but it should not distract us from the main point: that Persius found a second father in Cornutus, made a new and right beginning of a life that threatened to go dangerously wrong.

Next he describes his reeducation metaphorically, in sometimes paradoxical conceits. As his mind submits to the tricky rule of reason (the Stoic *logos*), his will, as yet imperfect, "labors to be overcome," to cooperate in that enforced submission. He takes on new features much as clay is shaped by the potter—the very operation that the muddy/unformed/half-baked/leaky student of *Satire* 3 resisted.[21] In a further, paradoxical union of active effort and passive submission, Persius "takes on an artful countenance," a face artistically created, but also the face of an artist who will be creative in his turn: an artistic persona, to be sure, and potentially deceptive (as said earlier), and very much in the satiric tradition of all those splendid Lucilian and Horatian personae, but also, perhaps, as real a face as a youth may hope to attain.

In the final section of this confession, Persius leaps forward again from impressionable childhood and emotional/spiritual dependency to a newfound maturity of mind and spirit, now expressed in terms of balance and equality:

tecum etenim longos memini consumere soles
et tecum primas epulis decerpere noctes.
unum opus et requiem pariter disponimus ambo
atque verecunda laxamus seria mensa.
non equidem hoc dubites, amborum foedere certo
consentire dies et ab uno sidere duci.
nostra vel aequali suspendit tempora Libra
Parca tenax veri, seu nata fidelibus hora
dividit in Geminos concordia fata duorum
Saturnumque gravem nostro Iove frangimus una,
nescio quod certe est quod me tibi temperat astrum.   (41–51)

[With you I remember spending long days and evenings wrested away from feasting. Together we arranged our work and our rest, relaxing serious study with modest suppers. Never doubt it: your days and mine are joined in a fixed bond, guided by a single constellation. Whether a true and reliable Fate holds both our lives in an equal Balance [*Libra*], or an hour created for loyalty divides our likeminded fates between the Twins and, together, we break heavy Saturn with our Jove— certainly, some star harmonizes me with you.]

Although Cornutus remains Persius's teacher and mentor, they associate together on a basis of true Stoic equality. They spend long days together, share an almost monastic balance of study and relaxation, and enjoy simple meals together, always in satire an emblem of the good life. Their harmony is so great, it must have been written in the stars. This points us back again to Horace, this time to *Odes* 2.17, where he reassures the hypochondriacal Maecenas of his enduring affection and loyalty. He will follow him in death, when the day comes, as in life; their governing stars are aligned (some astrological conceits here), and their lives follow a similar pattern—for example, Maecenas just recently recovered from serious illness, and Horace escaped being killed by that wretched tree.[22] Persius takes several details from Horace and reorganizes them. He has the same light touch, the same enjoyment of poetic conceits, although as a Stoic he may take more seriously the movement of heavenly bodies in their connectedness with human lives than did Horace.[23] Evidently, his life is aligned with Cornutus's, as Horace's was with Maecenas's. There is a cheerful continuity between the two relationships, as between the two masters of satirical self-presentation. But even as Persius outstrips Horace in emphasizing the impact of the Scales with their equality and balance ("aequali . . . Libra"), and of the Twins ("Gemini"), on the two friends, he also prompts us to think, inevitably, about differences between the two sets of relationships. Horace was never Maecenas's equal. Their friendship was threatened, especially toward the end, by serious imbalances—even if these were outweighed, ideally, by good humor and generous affection. But the high equality between Persius and Cornutus, achieved through good Stoic education and well-ordered living, succeeded so very well, so far beyond that between Horace and Maecenas, that it might really have seemed to have been written in the stars.

"Every Fool a Slave"

After his confession Persius moves outward again, into a three-part philosophical diatribe: first (a), a general section on the diversity of human pursuits and passions, and the urgency of studying philosophy (52–72); then (b) a lively argument about what constitutes true freedom (73–131), beginning "libertate opus est" ("Liberty is wanted! "). True *libertas*, the Stoic preacher argues, differs from legal emancipation. To be free, you must know and practice the right use of things, whereas most people are enslaved to their own desires and fears. In (c) the climactic section (132–88), the great ruling passions are reviewed, from avarice and prodigality to love, ambition, and superstition. The satire ends with a quick reversal, as a Roman centurion, representing the philistine public, laughs at all these foolish Greeks.

After beginning section (a), Persius unexpectedly reverts to his teacher Cornutus: partly, it seems, as a focus of direction in life, as against the bewildering diversity of ordinary human compulsions, from moneymaking (the trader) to feasting, athletics, gambling, and sex. But he does so also to touch base again with his own personal education and values:

> at te nocturnis iuvat impallescere chartis;
> cultor enim iuvenum purgatas inseris aures
> fruge Cleanthea. petite hinc, puerique senesque,
> finem animo certum miserisque viatica canis.   (62–65)

[But *you* like growing pale over nightly papers; you cultivate young men, you cleanse their ears and sow them with Cleanthean fruit. From here, children and elders, direct your lives, provide for your old age.]

The cleansed-ears metaphor, here grotesquely conjoined with farming, later characterizes the enlightened Stoic speaker:

> "mendose colligis," inquit
> Stoicus hic aurem mordaci lotus aceto.   (85–86)

["Your conclusion is faulty," says this Stoic, whose ear has been washed with stinging vinegar.]

The unnamed speaker could be Cornutus or his internalized voice. More likely, I think, Persius points to himself with "Stoicus hic" as a recent graduate turned teacher, offering public instruction now, or perhaps rehearsing his Stoic diatribe under Cornutus's approving eye; yet his cold, impersonal language in this section suggests how completely he has been absorbed into the Stoic ranks. All the more striking, by contrast, is the exuberant playfulness of the long concluding section (c), which comes very close to Roman comedy.

In the first scene (132–56), abbreviated and paraphrased below, two personified Addictions clash. Imagine the satirist's one-man mimetic performance:

> You're lying in bed, snoring. "Get up," says *Avaritia*. "Hey, get up."
> You don't. "Get up."—"I can't."—"Get up! "—"And do
> what?"—"*He's* asking? Bring in some merchandise." [A silly list
> follows.] "Trade something. Swear an oath, any oath. . . " And he's off
> to the boat—

> except that *Luxuria* [the enjoyment of comfort and ease] gets to him
> first, draws him aside. "Where are you off to in such a hurry? What do
> you really want—to sit on deck, on some old coil of rope, drinking rotten
> old wine? What are you looking for? Twelve percent interest? Relax and
> enjoy yourself, while you still may. . . "

The speaker's summary recalls a favorite stage device of Roman comedy:

> So what are you to do? You're torn by two hooks, pulled in two different
> directions at once. Will you follow this master or that one?
> You'll have to come up and do what each of them wants by turns,
> wandering back and forth from one to the other.   (154–56)

This is like Tranio, the comic slave, in a lively scene from Plautus's *Mostellaria* (532–654). On one side, Stage Left, is the moneylender Misargyrides; on the other, Stage Right, the old father Theopropides. "I want my money," cries the one. "Where is my interest?" And the other: "Who is this man, Tranio? Why is he screaming at you?" And poor Tranio goes back and forth, practicing his own special brand of shuttle diplomacy, holding off his young master's ruin and his own—for just a little while longer. For the comic staging, compare the scene in Shakespeare's *Henry IV, Part 1*, where Hal and Poins tease Francis, the drawer. "Anon, anon, Sir," calls Francis, pulled in two directions. We all have days like that.

Again, Persius's version of *amor* (161–75) is taken, though not quite directly, from the famous opening scene of Terence's *Eunuchus* (1–18). "So what should I do now! " asks the distracted lover Phaedria. "Shouldn't I go, not even now, when she summons me of her own accord? Or rather, should I prepare myself not to bear a paid woman's insults any longer?" In his mind, and probably in his stage movements, Phaedria wanders back and forth between his desire to get free of Thais and his obviously stronger desire to return to her, however badly she treats him. For love, as his slave Parmeno points out, is an irrational business; there's no order or logic to it at all, and if you try to make sense of it, that's "like going crazy in a rational way" (*ut cum ratione insanias* [16–18]).

Persius conflates Terence with Horace, who took Terence's lines earlier (some literally, some paraphrased), put them neatly into hexameters, and made them part of Damasippus's long, raving diatribe against vice and folly in *Satires* 2.3.259–71. Persius takes the same scene and practices literary one-upmanship, going back to the original Greek *Eunouchos* of Menander that Terence had turned into Latin.[24] He also coarsens Phaedria's soliloquy with obscene double entendres, more Plautine than Terentian, and suggesting, if not fear of castration, at least strong concern with the damage that sexual indulgence can cause.[25] In the end (in the slave's prediction), Persius's helpless lover comes around to the lines with which his predecessors in Menander (?), Terence, and Horace had begun, a rearrangement that, together with the intertextual play, gives us a weird sense of déjà vu. Love's script just keeps on restaging itself. If we are slaves to the passion of love, then we, too, are reduced to those recurrent personae, foolish comic lovers in the endlessly mirrored succession of foolish comic lovers. Will we ever learn? And, differently: will the satirist who speaks for reason be any more effective than Davus or Parmeno, the would-be clever slaves of New Comedy—or, for that matter, more effective than the slave Davus in Horace's *Satires* 2.7, who expounded (very crudely, though sometimes hitting home) the Stoic paradox, "Every fool a slave?"[26]

Davus, we remember, preaches to his master with Saturnalian license. His scattershot criticisms often miss the mark; surely Horace is not the humiliated would-be adulterer of comedy and mime. Yet other lines hit home, enraging him: "Get out, and fast, or I'll send you off to hard labor on the farm! " The threatened punishment, the sudden abrogation of the Saturnalian game and reassertion of the master's real-life authority, evoke familiar conventions of Roman comedy, especially in the farcical mode beloved by Plautus. In *Satires* 2.7, "Horace" loses the game by losing his temper, thus somewhat proving Davus's point (and Damasippus's too), even as he puts him in his place. His creator is left to face the challenges of inner freedom and self-consistency in his own time, especially in the *Epistles*, and in his own way.

Persius's review of slavish addictions in *Satire* 5 takes up where Davus (and Damasippus, and Horace) left off.[27] On the one hand, it derives new moral authority from Persius's Stoic confession earlier, and from Cornutus's express approval of what he has become and what he is writing, for he has been "progressing" both in his personal quest for integrity and freedom and in his special gift of acknowledging obstacles to that freedom, both outer and inner, through his satire. On the other hand, his laughter is wonderfully subversive, like the comic slave's in Plautus, as it indicates the artificiality and arbitrariness of social institutions like manumission. The praetor's wand (*vindicta*) cannot confer genuine freedom; Dama remains, will always remain, a slave at heart. Only Stoic learning and discipline bring genuine freedom. Yet, curiously, that freedom was adumbrated by Plautus's clever slaves, as Kathleen McCarthy has argued:

> This freedom from another's viewpoint inside our own heads is the miraculous freedom with which the clever slave is endowed. What makes this freedom so powerful and so attractive is that it goes far beyond the juridical freedom that we might think of as the opposite of slavery. It embodies rather the illusion that anyone can be free from others' subjectivity (in Bakhtin's terms, that anyone can be truly monologic).[28]

In Plautus's farcical comedies, the clever slave's subversive expressions of freedom are cut short—reassuringly, for a conservative Roman audience—by the ending of holiday play, the reimposition of law and order. So, too, in Horace, but in Persius, as I see it, rebellion is ongoing. If the responsible Stoic life is marked by the discipline of constant acceptance, of following willingly along the path laid down by Fate, yet Persius's satire, however sanctioned it may be as licensed play (*ingenuo ludo*, 5.16), is emotionally fueled by protest. Faced, that is, with the childishness of allegedly grown-up pursuits, the satirist recovers—still more, and programmatically, in *Satire* 1—the enormous comic energy of the rebellious child.

Persius's overall rejection of contemporary Roman society is conveyed, oddly enough, through the following curtailment of satire. *Avaritia* and *Luxuria* shared twenty-nine lines of diatribe, *Amor* was allotted fifteen, but *Ambitio* is dismissed in less than four. Horace's Damasippus had told a funny story about a father who made his sons swear not to run for public office (*Sat.* 2.3.179–81). The cost is prohibitive—all those chickpeas, beans, and lupines (to be thrown to the crowd, during the electioneering)—and the rewards are trivial: official dress, then [becoming] a bronze statue. A long, meandering section follows, in which King Agamemnon is convicted of madness for sacrificing his daughter Iphigenia. Persius's vignette recalls Horace's, but with a difference. Three foodstuffs are reduced to one, just chickpeas now, *cicer* (recalling Cicero's famous career?). The crowd now quarrels over the food thrown to them, and the ambitious man's culminating hope is that his springtime Games will still be remembered by old men sunning themselves. This comes close to Juvenal's "bread and circuses." Under the old Republic, competition for power was fierce and expensive. Now, under the Empire, elections have been reduced to popularity contests. If Persius gives *Ambitio* only four hurried lines, that shows how negligible she has become.

Superstition gets more space, and more intensity. Horace's Damasippus, in his fifteen lines, had developed two memorable vignettes: first, the freedman's son who runs around all the crossroad shrines, sober, in early morning, praying to all the gods to make an exception of him, save him from dying; and then the mother who vows to stand her son naked in the cold Tiber if his deadly fever leaves him—a sure way of bringing it back (*Sat.* 2.3.281–95). The passage ends with *timore deorum* ("fear of the gods," Greek *deisidaimonia*). Persius, by contrast, flashes a succession of ugly images before our minds:

> at cum
> Herodis venere dies unctaque fenestra
> dispositae pinguem nebulam vomuere lucernae
> portantes violas rubrumque amplexa catinum
> cauda natat thynni, tumet alba fidelia vino,
> labra moves tacitus recutitaque sabbata palles.
> tum nigri lemures ovoque pericula rupto,
> tum grandes galli et cum sistro lusca sacerdos
> incussere deos inflantis corpora, si non
> praedictum ter mane caput gustaveris ali.   (179–88)

[But when Herod's days have come; when the violet- wreathed lamps set out on greasy windowsills vomit out their fat fog; when the tunny's end, swimming in sauce, overfills the red platter, and the winecask swells to the brim, you mutter silent prayers, palesick with fear at the circumcised Sabbath. And then: black ghosts; danger from broken eggs; swollen eunuchs of Cybele, and Isis's one-eyed priestess with her magic rattle—all striking the fear of gods into you, gods who swell up your body—unless you taste your clove of garlic three times per morning.]

Superficially read, the passage trivializes "religious" procedures, dismissing them as foreign and grotesque, but Persius carefully evokes their underlying fear and dread. The Jewish observances are no longer the joke that Horace makes them in *Satires* 1.9.67–72, when his friend, the joker Aristius Fuscus, fails to rescue him from the Bore:

Horace:	"You said you wanted to tell me something in private?"
Fuscus:	"Yes, I remember, but I'll tell you at a better time. Today's the Thirtieth-and-Sabbath: do you want to fart in the face of the docked Jews [*curtis Iudaeis*]? "
Horace:	"I have no religious scruples [*religio*]."
Fuscus:	"But I have. I'm a weaker type, one of the many. Pardon me: another time."

Horace's little drama implies a mix of prejudice and careless contempt for Jewish practices that right-minded Romans would share. Persius, by contrast, carefully develops what he conceives as the murky, oppressive atmosphere of the Sabbath meal: first the smoking lamps, which may cloud people's minds, not just their rooms; then the heavy, heavy meal; and finally, the weird muttering of prayers in which "you" join, palesick with fear ("palles," here in the bad sense). The sense of fear continues in lines 185–87, with the black, ghostly "lemures" who stalk you by night and the weirdly deformed servants of Cybele and Isis, who frighten you with demonic possession unless you take the prescribed three bites of garlic every morning. So fear, at last, dissolves in laughter.[29]

Differently, Persius recalls Horace's final quiz in *Epistles* 2.2, which tested his reader and himself for symptoms of ambition, fear of death, anger, and especially superstition:

> somnia, terrores magicos, miracula, sagas,
> nocturnos lemures portentaque Thessala rides?   (*Ep.* 2.2.208–9)

> [Dreams, magical terrors, miracles, witches, ghosts by
> night, Thessalian portents—do you laugh at all of these?]

Six subtypes of scare: quickly evoked, and as quickly dismissed. But Persius's laughter is no light mockery. It carries strong indignation at the power and danger of superstition; at the worldwide corruption of genuine religious feeling and practice; at the misdirection of *pallor* away from the hard philosophical study that alone can instill true reverence for Divinity. *Satire* 2, we remember, opened the inner group of satires by denouncing religious hypocrisy, ignorance, and self-deception. Innocence had become delusion; habits were everywhere corrupted; holiness and integrity retreated into the inner sanctum of the rightly disciplined heart. Does *Satire* 5 close the inner group by reinforcing—in the *superstitio* passage, and in the last three lines where a philistine centurion laughs at all these "Greeks"—a sense of universal and inevitable moral decay? How should we hear that final laughter?

> dixeris haec inter varicosos centuriones,
> continuo crassum ridet Pulfenius ingens
> et centum Graecos curto centusse licetur.   (189–91)

> [When you say these things amid the varicose-veined
> centurions, big Pulfenius laughs loud and coarsely:
> he'll give a plugged nickel for a hundred Greeks.]

Most obviously, Persius takes Horace's laughter at Damasippus, the third-hand Stoic street-preacher of *Satires* 2.3, and turns it against the scoffers. His centurion is cousin to Petronius's invincibly and wonderfully ignorant

Trimalchio, whose will proclaims that he "left thirty millions and never listened to a philosopher." The coarse guffaw, the scattershot abuse, even the varicose veins reinforce, not weaken, the Stoic paradox under attack; for, in the words of Alexander Pope,

> To Vice and Folly to confine the jest,
> sets half the World, God knows, against the rest;
> did not the Sneer of more impartial men
> at Sense and Virtue, balance all again.[30]

Yet Persius plays both sides. He writes the centurion's lines, too, and performs them with gusto, joining heartily in that final explosion of coarse laughter. Maybe this laughter is cathartic, releasing long-suppressed feelings of inhibition and constraint, and even dislike, after all that physical and psychological self-denial? Or maybe it is a reaction to overwhelming feelings of futility in the face of so much ignorance, confusion, and folly? Wouldn't it be nice to desert from the weary, embattled little camp of Stoic philosophers?

Persius's laughter is explosive and childlike, but never simple. It is not the detached, ironic laughter of rational superiority that we find in Horace, nor is it the detached, scornful, and finally cynical laughter that we find in Juvenal. It is wild, passionate, caring, and *involved*—somewhere undefined, then, on the satiric continuum between idealism and despair. In short— before Plautus and Terence (cited above) and Menander—it is Aristophanic.

Another Dissident under Nero

"Libertate opus est," says the diatribe speaker—"Liberty is wanted." In the private, interior world to which Persius so often and so insistently returns, the proclamation becomes, first of all, a summons to moral integrity and self-awareness, and a call to throw off the domination of avarice, luxury, love, ambition, superstition—all the usual passions and addictions. Yet in the public world, these words assume other, dangerous meanings. They evoke, if not a program of political reform, let alone some hopelessly impractical plan to restore the Republic, still the stirring of a desire, at least, to recover a more meaningful political life, and an at least symbolic protest against the emperor and his court. But might Persius's words have counted for anything in what my students used to call "the real world"? Might they have come, or been brought, to Nero's attention?

It depends on the timing. If we follow Tacitus, the years 59–62 A.D., when Persius probably wrote (but did not circulate) his *Satires*, belonged to a middle period of Nero's rule, no longer very hopeful, but not yet the worst. Earlier, in the so-called "good years," 54–59, when the young Nero was guided by Seneca and Burrus, people could hope at least for a decent, restrained monarchy, one that observed traditional mores, valued senatorial advice, and showed a decent regard for public opinion. It is hard to say, even reading Tacitus, just how and when the situation changed.[31] One notable turning-point was Nero's murder of his mother, Agrippina, in 59, after which the senate gave official thanks for the emperor's safety, and only one honest man, Thrasea Paetus, walked out of the gathering in disgust. After 60, Nero increasingly assumes the persona of the Greek musician and play-actor, together with that of the orientalizing Hellenistic monarch. Around 61 Seneca begins, as he says, to "sound the retreat," withdrawing into a more private world—and writing tragedies about the losing struggle of reason and decency against passion, violence, cruelty, and revenge. In 62 Burrus dies and is replaced by the horrible Tigellinus. Also in 62 a certain Antistius is tried under the dangerous *maiestas* law for writing scurrilous verses against Nero. He gets off with exile, thanks partly to Thrasea's intervention—with which Nero was not pleased.[32]

Antistius's trial suggests how Persius might have fared, had time and circumstance been different: still more, the fall of Lucan, who broke with Nero probably in 63, was alienated from the court, and eventually was caught up, like so many others, in Piso's failed conspiracy of 65.[33] Lucan, Seneca, and Petronius were forced to commit suicide. Thrasea died in 66. Helvidius Priscus, another Stoic martyr in the making, was exiled. Later, Cornutus went into exile. Is it hard to imagine how Persius might have been slandered, had he lived into 65 and published his *Satires*? In *Satire* 1 (the informer might have alleged, though not without some danger to himself), King Midas means Nero.[34] In *Satire* 4, Alcibiades and Socrates are Nero and Seneca. In *Satire* 6, Caligula's fake triumphs point to Nero's. I have argued, to be sure, that Persius's satires are much more than barely veiled political lampoons or allegories: that, in fact, Persius turns the satirical impulse against itself as he probes more deeply into the realities of human nature, starting from his own. The essential point, for him, is that everyone has asses' ears, not just King Midas (or Nero). Yet Midas, though unmentioned, is—like the elephant in the room—inescapably and memorably there.[35] Had Persius lived and his writings become known, he might easily have been exiled or driven to suicide. He might even have been broken like Lucan, who betrayed his mother before the end. Without ignoring these painful might-have-beens, let us consider what part Persius might in fact have played as a member of the Stoic opposition. Was he a Dissident? If so, could it have made a difference?

There was no organized Stoic Opposition to Nero, though Stoics like Musonius Rufus and Cornutus were sometimes exiled, and Stoic demeanor could be adduced for purposes of slander.[36] In principle, Stoics liked monarchy; they just wanted conscientious, responsible rulers. As for whether one should enter into public life or not, that was a personal decision, dependent on character and circumstance. Some people remained in, or withdrew into, private life, where integrity was easier to maintain. Some became involved in public life, receiving rewards, compromising to a lesser or greater extent with the regime, and trying to do some good: as Seneca evidently did, though he was badly compromised before his final retirement. The great question was how to draw a line past which one wouldn't assent, flatter, "dissimulate," or compromise any longer. We see Thrasea Paetus, more than once, drawing such a line.[37] We also catch moments when a philosopher, like a director of conscience, gives particular advice: thus Musonius Rufus deters Thrasea from a thoughtless, premature suicide.[38] More usually, we may imagine, Stoicism stiffened people's resolve in the face of probable disgrace, exile, or death. "What must I do," they will have asked—people like Thrasea, Rubellius Plautus, Borea Soranus, Helvidius Priscus—"to live and die with integrity?"

What practical good does it do, to draw such moral lines? Idealistic protest, as an historian like Tacitus sees it, may actually do harm, and a failed revolt like Piso's conspiracy, followed by terrible reprisals, may in retrospect seem worse than no revolt at all.[39] Yet there remains the beauty and inspiration of visible moral choice like Thrasea's, what Epictetus calls "the purple thread" against its colorless background. In a dishonest, perverse, badly compromised world it is good to be reminded of what honesty means. Before speculating further about Persius's behavior and its possible meaning, let me clarify some relevant issues with the help of a wise and moving essay, "The Power of the Powerless" (October 1978), by Václav Havel, a gifted writer and, after the fall of communism, the much-admired president of the Czech Republic, but in earlier decades a notable "dissident" and prisoner of conscience. The following quotations and paraphrases are taken from a 1989 collection of Havel's essays entitled *Living in Truth*.

What matters, Havel argues over and over again, is to be honest, to serve the truth, which may be done in many ways. He cites "writers who write as they wish without regard for censorship or official demands and who issue their work—when official publishers refuse to print it—as *samizdat*." Other heartening examples follow, of freethinking scholars, teachers, artists, protesters against injustice, young people, "everyone who shares this independent culture" (86–87). The good, decent people of and for whom Havel writes may do only "small-scale work," like Masaryk, concrete actions on behalf of individual rights (99). They struggle as need and opportunity present themselves: to renew the human order; to rehabilitate "values like openness, responsibility, solidarity, love" (118). They participate in "the everyday, thankless and never ending struggle of human beings to live more fully, truthfully and in quiet dignity" (113). They help awaken "conscience and the will to truth" within what Havel calls "the hidden sphere," within "structures that are open, dynamic and small; [for] beyond a certain point, human ties like personal trust and personal responsibility cannot work." (118). Yet these private acts may affect the larger society and change it in unforeseen ways. By creating genuine, though small-scale, communities, they provide a "human and social alternative" (106) to the inhuman and oppressive structures of what Havel calls a post-totalitarian society (to which, he would surely add, our own technology- and market-driven structures bear many resemblances), and they may play a part in the partial reformation or in the eventual collapse of the existing structures. But we should not, Havel argues, become caught up in political abstractions or counterprograms. Rather, we should do our work, stick to concrete things, like the signing of Charter 77, and not worry too much about the results.[40]

These last recommendations may fit Persius, who wrote deeply honest satires without worrying too much about the results, and who may also have fulfilled familial and social obligations very well indeed (see section 4.1, below). But he was not as isolated as his satires suggest. The *Vita* tells us that "from the age of ten he was very greatly cherished by Thrasea Paetus, to the point of traveling abroad with him sometimes. His relative, Arria, was Thrasea's wife" (30–32).[41] That was a dangerous relationship. Isn't it likely that, when they traveled together, Thrasea discussed political and imperial matters with Persius—and that Persius kept his mouth closed more successfully than Midas's barber? Horace, too, kept quiet about his conversations with Maecenas, which he tells us were only about trivia. The hint is teasing, indeed insulting. In Persius's satires, not even the hint remains.

Now, if I may "narrativize" a little: imagine Persius reading aloud from his *Satires* to a small, trusted gathering of relations and close friends, perhaps in the gardens of Thrasea.[42] In his unique way, he would be proclaiming and reinforcing the same values of honesty and truth about which Havel speaks, and in the same quiet, effective way. He was, then, in his lifetime a small-*d* dissident, though not as well known as if his poems had been circulated as *samizdat*. And after his death, when the *libellus* was published and people "marveled at it and snatched it up" (*Vita* 49–50), he must have been welcomed into the company of those men and women who somehow lived the truth, like Havel's "poets, painters, musicians, or simply ordinary citizens who were able to maintain their human dignity" (60). His poems made, and continued to make, a difference.

Havel uses the story of "The Emperor's New Clothes" to illustrate what an ordinary person can accomplish by acting independently, disregarding officially endorsed rituals even in small ways:

By breaking the rules of the game, he has disrupted the game as such. He has exposed it as a mere game. He has shattered the world of appearances, the fundamental pillar of the system. . . He has demonstrated that living a lie is living a lie. He has broken through the exalted facade of the system and exposed the real, base foundations of power. *He has said that the emperor is naked.* (56; italics mine)

Here, like a widely circulated political cartoon, the story of "The Emperor's New Clothes" points the way to defy repression, liberate rebellious instincts, maybe even bring down an unpopular regime. That is why, again, the Midas story is so dangerous to tyrants: especially as Persius presents it in his prologue satire, where the energy required to suppress it in the name of civility, restraint, and safety only makes it burst out finally with unstoppable explosive force. During Persius's lifetime, the explosion may only have been experienced within safe walls, but after his death, when the *Satires* were quickly and widely circulated, the Midas story must have evoked strong, rebellious laughter, building resistance to Nero, weakening his control.[43]

To fast forward, briefly, it is no accident that Persius's last great appearance in English literature, in Pope's *Epistle to Dr. Arbuthnot* (1731–1735), refurbishes the Midas story:

'Tis sung, when *Midas'* Ears began to spring,
(*Midas*, a sacred person and a King)
His very Minister who spy'd them first
(Some say his Queen) was forc'd to speak, or burst.
And is not mine, my Friend, a sorer case,
When ev'ry Coxcomb perks them in my face?
"Good friend forbear! you deal in dang'rous things,
I'd never name Queens, Ministers, or Kings;
Keep close to Ears, and those let asses prick,
'Tis nothing."—Nothing? if they bite and kick?
Out with it, *Dunciad*! let the secret pass,
That Secret to each Fool, that he's an ass:
The truth once told, (and wherefore shou'd we lie?)
The Queen of *Midas* slept, and so may I.   (69–82)

Following the scholiastic tradition according to which Persius muted his attack on Nero, changing "auriculas asini Mida rex habet" to "auriculas asini quis non habet," Pope recreates, as he believes, the spirit of true independence with which Persius should ideally have written his satire. He attacks King George II as a foolish animal-ruler who not only has asses' ears, but bites and kicks like a donkey as well, and he extends the attack to Queen Caroline and Prime Minister Walpole, who were thought to act in collusion. But Pope has it both ways. As Howard Weinbrot says: "Pope also adopts part of Persius's printed, not censored, version by generalizing onto the literary world: each London and Roman fool is an ass, for in literary, moral, and asinine matters the principle of *ad exemplum regis* extends down the social scale."[44]

Pope may be Persius's last, best reader among major British poets, but essentially his Persius has been assimilated to Juvenal in style and spirit. Nor is this anything new. Dryden, in his *Discourse on Satire*, had given Persius high points for content but objected strongly to the density and opacity of his style; and he, more than anyone, made Persius the "odd man out" that he has been ever since, leaving the contest of satiric excellence to be fought out between Horace and Juvenal.[45] So, too, with Pope. Although he imitates some gentler, more personal passages from Horace (the good-natured old mother, for example, in place of Horace's father), his overall tendency in *Arbuthnot*, as elsewhere, is toward Juvenal; indeed, the *Dunciad* reference points to Pope's greatest, most Juvenalian satire. He reads Persius, too, through Juvenal, giving his Midas story new directness and power: but what is missing? The explosive violence, certainly, but more important, the author's implicit self-inclusion in the company of ass-eared fools, and the incipient call to honesty, beginning with self-honesty. That everyone has asses' ears is not just a (transparent) veil over political reality. It is *the* reality—political, social, literary, even spiritual—with which every one of us, not least the satirist, must begin.

In describing the attraction of Juvenalian satire, especially in harsh periods, Weinbrot says, "Surely one is more moved by matters of personal, national, and spiritual life and death than by whether one should agree with the Stoic view of the world, or with the need to polish one's verse."[46] The dig, of course, is at Persius. Yet I contend that, for Persius, whether one assented to the Stoic view of the world and lived by it or not *was* a matter of "personal, national, and spiritual life and death" more than one finds in Juvenal—not to add, the only sane response to a world full of contagiously braying asses, from kings down to poets. The way to freedom is philosophy—to inner freedom, first and foremost—but this freedom is contagious, it breeds a spirit of honest independence and resistance to tyranny that makes Pope's partisan posing and literary-rhetorical self-praise seem unconvincing, even self-serving, by contrast. Might Persius not be, after all, a better "reception fit" than Juvenal (or Horace) for our own fearfully overcast days?[47]

Chapter Four

LIFE, DEATH, AND ART

"Aulus Persius Flaccus was born the day before the Nones of
December, in the consulship of Fabius Persicus and Lucius Vitellius
[December 4, 34 A.D.], and died the eighth day before the Kalends
of December, in the consulship of Publius Marius and Afinius Gallus
[November 24, 62 A.D.]."

"He died near the eighth milestone on the Appian Way, on his
own property."

"His father Flaccus died when he was about six. Later, Fulvia Sisennia
married Fusius, a Roman knight, and buried him too within a few
years."

"He left sums of money to his mother and sister, but requested
his mother in codicils to leave money [the numbers are confused],
silver, and seven hundred books of Chrysippus [the Stoic philosopher:
an extremely valuable gift] to Cornutus, who returned the money
and silver but kept the books."

"[He] died of a stomach ailment in his thirtieth year
[more confusion here]."
—*Vita*, 1–9, 35–40, 50

B<small>IRTH</small>, death, and wills: the hard facts available to the biographer help
us ground the author as a real and vulnerable human being like ourselves.
Chapter 4, accordingly, deals largely with life and death issues, both within
the satire book and without. How do the *Satires* fit into the larger picture
of Persius's life, with its social privileges and responsibilities? Did he some-
times rebel, as *Satire* 6 may suggest, against the laws of life, death, and
reason? How did he deal with all those distracting thoughts and sensations
evoked by imaginings of death—the terror of falling into nothingness, the
longing for enduring fame, the worry that our little struggles and achieve-
ments are ultimately futile? "O curas hominum! o quantum est in rebus
inane!" Do the grotesque visions of the *Satires* belie Persius's Stoic beliefs

and intentions? Or do the *Satires* exorcize tempting voices by laughing them down? Did they help their author, in the end, to "make his will"?

In my ongoing investigation, section 4.1 sets the scene for Persius's life and work. I begin with the ash-chests in the Museo Guarnacci in Volterra, which make that later Etrusco-Roman culture in both life and death so real to us, and move on to speculate about the duties and responsibilities (*officia*) that must have occupied the greater part of Persius's time and attention. Section 4.2 follows him as he moves in *Satire* 6 from late Horatian acceptance and calm into expressions of wild rebellion. Section 4.3 traces the theme of the Ages of Man in the completed *libellus*: first, the implied orderly progression from infancy, through childhood and adolescence, to mature adulthood in *Satires* 2–5, the inner group; but then, in the framing *Satires* 6 and 1, the follies and failures of the generations, youths and graybeards alike—and the correspondingly powerful new call for satire.

Section 4.4 returns to speculation, this time psychological, about the emotional recognizance that satire writing may have afforded Persius, helping him expose those disturbing "impressions" (*phantasiai*) of fear and desire that the mature Stoic must finally delete. I conclude with a plea for "recognizing" Persius, both in the ordinary sense of the word, so he may take his place once more in the canon between Horace and Juvenal as a first-rate satirist, and in the extraordinary self-scrutinizing and -refashioning sense that his *Satires* exemplify—and which the reader is challenged, in his or her turn, to follow.

Between Volterra and Rome

What most surprises us in the *Vita* , as we emerge from the literary-critical shelter of the *Satires* text, is the easy conjunction of private and public. After the dates of Persius's birth and death, we read:

> natus in Etruria Volaterris, eques Romanus, sanguine et affinitate primi ordinis viris coniunctus, decessit ad octavum militarium via Appia in praediis suis.

> [He was born in Etruria at Volaterrae, a Roman knight, with blood and family connections to men of the first rank. He died at the eighth milestone on the Via Appia, on his own property.]

Persius is sometimes dismissed as helplessly neurotic. "Did brooding about death affect your psychosexual development?" a modern reader might wonder. "Were you emotionally dominated by all those female relatives? Did you, for compensation, throw yourself into all those intense male friendships?" Such questions seem natural in this psychologically saturated age. But then, *in praediis suis*: there are more public questions too. What position(s) did Persius occupy in Etrusco-Roman society? What different worlds did he inhabit? What privileges had he? What responsibilities? What was he doing most of the time, when he wasn't writing satire?

Let me start with Volterra and its ash-chests—that is, with life and death—and then make my speculative way to Persius's lifestyle and business duties. In what follows, I am heavily indebted to my former colleague Nicola Terrenato, who works with Etrusco-Roman sites, knows Volterra and the Cecina Valley as well as anybody, and took us there on a cold early-November day in 1998.

Volterra is remote and impressive. It is a hill town in northwest Etruria about 250 kilometers from Rome, difficult of access, easily fortified, and held against invaders for most of its existence. Unlike Etruscan towns further south, it was never destroyed and colonized by the Romans. Its leaders, most notably the Caecina family, and its communal structures came through the civil wars largely unchanged, though "decades-long negotiation" was required; see Cicero's speech *Pro Caecina* and a related letter to a commissioner in charge of potential land redistribution. Most remarkably, the Volterran elite into which Persius was born were able to maintain their traditional, feudal way of life over many centuries, almost as if the great changes of Roman political, social, and economic history had never happened.[1]

D. H. Lawrence, that gifted writer, introduces us to Volterra with a thoughtful, deliberate pace:

> Volterra is the most northerly of the great Etruscan cities of the west. It lies back some thirty miles from the sea, on a towering great bluff of rock that gets all the winds and sees all the world, looking out down the valley of the Cecina to the sea, south over vale and high land to the tips of Elba, north to the imminent mountains of Carrara, inward over the wide hills of the Pre-Appenines, to the heart of Tuscany.

> You leave the Rome-Pisa train at Cecina, and slowly wind up the valley of the stream of that name, a green, romantic, forgotten sort of valley, in spite of all the come-and-go of ancient Etruscans and Romans, medieval Volterrans and Pisans, and modern traffic. But the traffic is not heavy. Volterra is a sort of inland island, still curiously isolated, and grim.[2]

Lawrence then describes his visit to the alabaster workshops. Volterra was always famous for its alabaster, and in 1927 the shops were mainly full of junk for tourists to buy. (Not much has changed.) But the tone changes—he visits the Museo Guarnacci:

> But it is the old alabaster jars we want to see, not the new. As we hurry down the stony street the rain, icy cold, begins to fall. We flee through

the glass doors of the museum, which has just opened, and which seems as if the alabaster inside had to be kept at a low temperature, for the place is dead-cold as a refrigerator. . . .

We pay our tickets, and start in. It is really a very attractive and pleasant museum, but we had struck such a bitter cold April morning, with icy rain falling in the courtyard, that I felt as near to being in the tomb as I have ever done. Yet very soon, in the rooms with all those hundreds of little sarcophagi, ash-coffins, or urns, as they are called, the strength of the old life began to warm one up.[3]

Let me follow, briefly, in Lawrence's footsteps—though the Museo is warmer now and better managed during business hours, and our professional scholarly attention insulates us somewhat from feelings and thoughts that might not always warm the human heart.

In their conservative, traditionalist way, the people of Volterra stuck to cremation long after other Etruscan peoples were practicing inhumation. The dead person's body was burned on the funeral pyre, and the ashes (Latin *cineres*) were collected and placed in one of those "little sarcophagi," what Italian scholars today call *ciste*, or "chests." These in turn were placed in family tombs: on ledges, perhaps, around the sides of a big underground chamber honoring some principal ancestor.

In the Museo Guarnacci, as Lawrence said, you can see hundreds of these *ciste*: a crazy disorganized jumble of mismatched bottoms and lids from all different periods. The bottoms are roughly rectangular. Their sculptured designs seem to be generic. Some show mythological creatures like centaurs or sea monsters. Others show the dead man or woman, or both together, setting forth in a carriage for the land of the dead, where they will be greeted by the demonic figures who have charge of these matters. In one especially moving scene, the dead man's wife clings to the horses, holding them back from the inevitable journey.

The lids, on the other hand, show the dead man or woman in sculptured relief. The heads are nearly life-sized, the bodies are squashed flat, but some of these, at least, may give us realistic portraits of the dead. There is a powerful Etruscan nobleman, making a libation from his *patara*. There is a good-looking boy, Aulus Caecina, who died at twelve. And there is my favorite relief, on the *Urna Degli Sposi*, where an older couple recline together affectionately. They have wonderful craggy faces. The man holds a *patara* from which he has just poured a libation. Is he thanking the gods for their good life together under the lengthening shadow of death?[4]

I think of the beautiful but very different sixth-century B.C. sarcophagus of the "Married Couple" now in the Villa Giulia museum in Rome. That, too, shows affection and intimacy. (Charlotte Orth, my wife, wrote a sketch about it in which the dead observe their living visitors with amusement.)

It was a woman's world as well as a man's. Etruscan women joined their husbands at feasts—which shocked the Romans. But our older couple at Volterra are beautiful too in their rugged way. They are very strong, very much alive. I think of Persius's older relatives, Arria the Elder and her husband, Caecina Paetus, who died together after the failed conspiracy of Scribonianus in 42 A.D.. As the story goes, Paetus was going to stab himself first, but he hesitated, so Arria went ahead, saying, "Paetus, it doesn't hurt!" (*Paete, non dolet*).[5] I'd like to believe that it happened, just so. And while I'm in a fanciful mood, I'd rather like to believe that the old married couple on the *Urna degli Sposi* were in fact Persius's great-grandparents, and that he inherited some of that enduring strength of character that we've been looking at.

Let me waive thoughts of ashes, death, and burial for now (they will inevitably return) in order to place Persius's life and work in a more public context, between Volterra and Rome, than students of his poetry have usually imagined.

The Persii were evidently a leading family of Volterra, related to the Caecinae.[6] Like other members of the Etrusco-Roman elite, they moved between the different worlds of country and town, between the farms of the Cecina Valley, "a rural society still regulated by traditional, pre-Roman relationships," where they were old-style feudal landlords, and the more Romanized styles of city life. In Persius's time, Volterra was completing its second great period of rebuilding and Romanization. Yet it, too, kept its distance, spiritual as well as physical, from great Rome, so that even within the town borders families like the Persii must have felt themselves moving between different worlds. As Terrenato describes it:

> On the one hand is their massive adoption of Roman culture, especially in the sphere of prestige goods. Urban and rural residences, language, artistic tastes were modeled on the prevailing fashions in the Roman world. On the other, funerary customs, and probably some private religious practices, retained strong Etruscan elements. . . . If nothing else, this traditional heritage was essential in keeping open a communication channel with the lower rural classes.[7]

Let me now, again with Terrenato's help, make a few guesses about how Persius lived, how he spent his time, and how he moved, physically and imaginatively, between the different worlds of Volterra and Rome.

When he assumed the *toga virilis* at fifteen or sixteen—a challenging transition, as he represents it in *Satire* 5—Persius took on new adult responsibilities together with new privileges and liberties. He was now the man of the family, in charge (at least formally) of his family's business affairs, which must have been extensive.[8] Probably he had at least four residences to go with his different responsibilities: (a) his family home in Volterra, where he supervised the business affairs of his mother, his sister, his aunt, and himself; (b) a villa in the countryside where, like a feudal lord, he would watch over the lives of his dependents, taking an interest in their day-to-day affairs, their needs, and their farms' productivity, and settling disputes among them; (c) a house in Rome, for a mix of pleasure and business; and (d) a larger villa outside of Rome, where one could do official entertaining—presumably near that "eighth milestone on the Via Appia" where Persius was buried. Against such a background, what should we conclude about his life and work?

To put it simply: he probably spent most of his time not writing poetry, but performing personal, familial, and communal duties. If he was praised posthumously, as in the *Vita*, for his unusual *pietas* in caring for his mother, his sister, and his aunt, it seems likely that, as a serious Stoic, he extended this diligence to larger circles of family, friends, acquaintances, and dependents.[9] Recall the anonymous preacher's call to instruction in *Satire 3*:

> discite et, o miseri, causas cognoscite rerum:
> quid sumus et quidnam victuri gignimur, ordo
> quis datus, aut metae qua mollis flexus et unde,
> quis modus argento, quid fas optare, quid asper
> utile nummus habet, patriae carisque propinquis
> quantum elargiri deceat, quem te deus esse
> iussit et humana qua parte locatus es in re.   (3.66–72)

> [Come learn, unhappy people, what it all means:
> what we're made of; what life we're born to lead;
> where we are placed; how to make the most graceful
> turn around life's racecourse; what limit's set for
> money-making; what is the point of prayer, or of hard cash;
> how much it is right to spend on your country's needs,
> or your dear relatives; and who the god has ordered you to be;
> and where, in the human world, you have been stationed.]

From a high overview of human life, seen as a question, an arrangement, and a racecourse, these verses move to the right and generous uses of money, and from there to the need to discover our proper, god-given roles in life. Persius probably followed these Stoic precepts, starting from his "dear relatives." He seems, from the scant evidence (both positive and negative), to have been a good man, one who tried to live congruently with his principles. If he wrote poetry "rarely and slowly," as the *Vita* says, this was not only because he was a literary perfectionist like Horace, in the Hellenistic manner (though of course, he was), but because he spent most of his time enacting the various interrelated roles or personae—son, brother, nephew, friend, landlord, citizen, as well as poet—that had been assigned by the god, and in terms of which his self-definition had to be constructed. Which is, ironically, where Persius's deceptive and dialectical satiric personae may finally point. Do the two sets of roles complement and reinforce each other? Or is art, finally, a stalking-horse for life?

I shall return to this question in section 4.4, where I ask why Persius wrote satire. More immediately, let me return to those Volterran ash-chests, and to how thoughts of death and burial challenge all our constructed personae, even the noblest and best. Poets and satirists know this well. So Lucretius, of a general faced with drowning: *eripitur persona, manet res* (*DRN*. 3.58: "Mask is ripped away, reality remains.") So, too, Persius, in *Satire* 1, marking not just the idiocy of dilettantism and false flattery,

> adsensere viri: nunc non cinis ille poetae
> felix? non levior cippus nunc inprimit ossa?
> laudant convivae: nunc non e manibus illis,
> nunc non e tumulo fortunataque favilla
> nascentur violae?　　　　　　　　　　　　　　　　(1. 36–40)

> [The men assent: are not the poet's ashes utterly fortunate?
> Does not the tombstone now press lighter on his bones?
> The guests give praise: oh, now, out of those shades, out
> of the tomb and the oh-so-blessed cinders, will not violets spring?]

but also the folly of all poetic ambition, including the writer's own. This is a bitter pill for even a Stoic to swallow. In *Satire* 6, where Persius returns insistently to the right and wrong uses of money, the dramatic irruption of anger and indignation into what might have remained a peaceful Horatian setting conveys a passionate, very human protest against the inevitability of death, which philosophers teach us, as best they can, to accept with equanimity.

The Land, the Sea, and the Heir (*Satire* 6)

Satire 6 begins like one of Horace's *Epistles*, addressing a friend, establishing both writer and recipient in time and place:

> Admovit iam bruma foco te, Basse, Sabino?

> [Has winter moved you, Bassus, to your Sabine hearth?]

It is the winter solstice, the shortest, darkest day of the year. Caesius Bassus, who wrote lyric poetry like Horace, is staying, also like Horace, in Sabine country. Persius praises him for his strong, masculine verse and the vigorous, playful spirit he carries into old age. By contrast, Persius describes

himself as wintering at Portus Lunae (the modern Gulf of Spezia). The
gentle humor with which he describes his protective surroundings is again
Horatian. The Ligurian shore warms "for me," the wintry sea is "mine."[10]
Ennius, too, had praised the harbor—which brings Persius, by a curious
leap of thought, to Ennius's foolish fantasy (also derided by Lucretius) of
the transmigration of souls, which will be a foil in *Satire* 6 to the strong
reality of death.[11]

The two contrasting but complementary scenes imply different sides and
uses of the Horatian inheritance. Bassus now wears the lyric mantle; Per-
sius continues the *Satires* and, especially now, the *Epistles*. He will be like
Horace and unlike; his originality will appear in divergence. First, however,
he voices familiar Horatian sentiments in such an unexpectedly Horatian
voice that we might well suspect parody. Like Horace, he refuses to covet
other people's property and riches. Like Horace, he chooses moderate en-
joyment of things, an Aristotelian mean between avarice and prodigality,
between the comic miser who grudgingly gives himself a pathetic little
birthday treat and the prodigal youth who devours his substance "in great-
hearted fashion." Are the two extremes, we might wonder, related? Has
the miserly father, in good Hogarthian fashion, produced a prodigal heir?
The great inside joke—the literary subtext of *Satire* 6—is that *Persius is
Horace's prodigal heir.*[12]

Horace's typical method is coincidence, then divergence: after Alcaeus,
in the Soracte or Cleopatra Odes; or, earlier, after Lucilius, in *Satires* 1.5,
the "Journey to Brundisium," where the coincidence, then divergence of
the ways taken is a compelling metaphor of Horace's creative originality
within the tradition of Latin verse satire. So, here, Persius's initial Horatian
mood of calm assurance and contentment is interrupted by a sudden call
for help:

> messe tenus propria vive et granaria (fas est)
> emole. quid metuas? occa et seges altera in herba est.
> at vocat officium, trabe rupta Bruttia saxa
> prendit amicus inops remque omnem surdaque vota
> condidit Ionio, iacet ipse in litore et una
> ingentes de puppe dei iamque obvia mergis
> costa ratis lacerae; nunc et de caespite vivo
> frange aliquid, largire inopi, ne pictus oberret
> caerulea in tabula.   (6.25–33)

[Live to the limits of your own harvest, grind out your stores. No fear:
just harrow, another crop is on the blade. But duty calls: a ship is
wrecked, a ruined friend clings to the Bruttian rocks; all his wealth, his
unheard prayers, he has left buried in the Ionian Sea; he himself lies (like

dead) on the shore, along with the great gods from the stern and the ribs of the torn vessel, exposed to seagulls. Break off something now, even from the living turf; give lavishly to the poor man, so he won't wander around pictured on a sea-blue painted plank.]

The shipwreck, described with ironic pathos, recalls the wreck of Aeneas's ships off Carthage. If the poor man isn't helped, if "you" don't break off some of your safe, landed wealth to help him, he will become a beggar, displaying the usual picture of his disaster. Worse still, "pictus" suggests, he will be reduced to a mere image of himself.[13]

Persius introduces the shipwreck, then, (with ironic echoes of Horace) as an image of human need and obligation that subverts the old precept of using, but not going beyond, your landed income; for sometimes duty calls us to act recklessly, to spend some of that sacred capital. At the same time, he contrasts the sea's unpredictability and danger to the felt security of land, and of landed wealth. The quiet sea, "my sea," beside which Persius winters has become, in less than twenty lines, the stormy sea that smashes up ships, tossing travelers' helpless bodies onto the beach. Another poet, Horace perhaps, might have moralized about how merchants, in their unbounded greed, expose themselves so rashly to sudden death. But the point is universal. Lucretius, refuting the notion of divine providence, compares the helpless newborn human babe to a shipwrecked sailor cast up "upon the shores of light" (*in luminis oras*).[14] It is not just that human life is difficult and sad. It is that we come out of the great sea of darkness and the unknown when we are born, and we go back into that same great sea—into darkness and the unknown—when we die. Lucretius would say, not to worry. Our atoms are recycled in death, which is "nothing to us," for "we" aren't there any more. Yet the image of life's bright coastline is memorable, and Housman might have echoed something of Persius's feeling when he wrote,

> Here, on the level sand,
> Between the sea and land,
> What shall I build or write
> Against the fall of night? (*More Poems*, 45)

The call for help, then, recalls the needs and obligations of our common humanity. It is interrupted in turn by a counterobjection: your heir won't be pleased by your invading capital; he'll skimp on your funeral rites. Let me backtrack here, before discussing Persius's reply, for the association of land and the heir with life-and-death issues brings this satire into a profound dialogue with Horace's very personal, even valedictory reflections on human life, most notably his own, in *Epistles* 2.2.[15]

In the first half of that *Epistle*, Horace describes his reasons for abandoning lyric poetry. Poetry writing, if you take it seriously (and most people don't), is difficult, painful work, and Horace claims—half-seriously, half-ironically—that he is no longer fitted for it by circumstances or temperament. More than that: it is a young people's game, whereas he himself is aging and so must turn to philosophy, to learn the measures and rhythms not now of verse but of right living before it is too late. Here the subject shifts to philosophy, its value and its urgency. Among other benefits, it teaches us about property. People are greedy for riches, greedy to amass estates and hold on to them; but nature laughs at property laws and boundaries. Things are ours for the using, but in the end nothing really belongs to us:

> sed vocat usque suum, qua populus adsita certis
> limitibus vicina refugit iurgia; tamquam
> sit proprium quicquam, puncto quod mobilis horae
> nunc prece, nunc pretio, nunc vi, nunc morte suprema
> permutet dominos et cedat in altera iura.
> sic quia perpetuus nulli datur usus, et heres
> heredem alterius velut unda supervenit undam,
> quid vici prosunt aut horrea? quidve Calabris
> saltibus adiecti Lucani, si metit Orcus
> grandia cum parvis, non exorabilis auro?   (*Ep*.2.2.170–79)

> [Yet he calls it his to where the firm line of poplars
> has fled from litigation—as if anything were owned that,
> a pin-point in time's moving pattern, by gift, sale, force,
> or at last by death, can pass into the hands of a new master.
> Since, then, nothing is held in perpetuity, and heir climbs over
> heir like wave on wave, what good are manors, barns and
> pastures stretching through Lucania and Calabria, if Death,
> the incorruptible, reaps great and small?] (trans. Macleod)

The prospect of that "wave on wave" of heirs—a hint of sea, here too, amid the seemingly solid reassurances of landed property—reminds us yet again of the inevitability of Death, that great harvester and leveler, who puts finish to our foolish ambitions and yearnings. Horace draws his own not very philosophical conclusions. He rejects the common desire for so many possessions, so many *things*. He wonders, bemusedly, why two brothers go to opposite extremes, one given to utter relaxation and play, the other a compulsive, workaholic farmer. As for himself, he will make use of things (*utar*, very emphatic) and spend freely, not worrying about what his future heir will think:

> utar et ex modico quantum res poscet acervo
> tollam, nec metuam quid de me iudicet heres,
> quod non plura datis invenerit: . . .   (191–93)

[I'll take from my modest fortune what I need,
not caring what my heir will think of me
when he gets no more than I did; . . .] (trans. Macleod)

And yet, Horace asserts, he will walk a careful mean between the spend-
thrift and the miser. The main thing is to enjoy what you have while you
have it, like a schoolboy on his brief holidays. Is this something new that
Horace has learned from studying philosophy? Or is it his old, hard-won
sense of contentment and gratitude, together with that half-rebellious *carpe
diem*, the desire to grasp life's pleasures now, because life is short? The
Epistle's ending, the advice to depart from life like a satisfied dinner-guest,
circles back to Greek diatribe, Lucretius, and the ending of Horace's own
Satires 1.1, but with new and bitter self-irony, for the dinner-guest advised
or rebuked by Nature is now the poet-teacher-satirist himself.

The figure of the heir, then, in Horace's *Epistle*, as in earlier *Satires* and
Odes, serves not only as a rebuke to greed and possessiveness and an induce-
ment to live well in the present, but also as a more dangerous, less ethically
controllable reminder of the apparent futility of all human effort in the
face of death.[16] The challenge he poses is all the stronger if Horace wrote
Epistles 2.2 as a last will and testament, giving an often ironic, yet deeply
serious and personal account of his life and work for posterity. Persius, in
turn, reads and responds to the challenge with a remarkable mix of philo-
sophic composure, heartfelt indignation, and a wild antic humor that
strangely and powerfully unites the two.

Your heir will be angry if you curtail the principal, warns an unnamed
speaker; he'll neglect the funeral feast and burial ointments. *Tun bona inco-
lumis minuas?* ("What makes you think you can get away with reducing
the estate?") Persius responds coolly, contemptuously. How does the heir
presume to instruct him, anyway? Why should he "fear these things the
other side of the ashes" (*cinere ulterior*), once he is dead? Now he takes the
offensive. In a parody of Virgil's great passage in *Aeneid 6* where Anchises
shows Aeneas the grand procession of his Italic and Roman descendants to
come, including Julius Caesar, whom he urgently begs to reject civil war,
and the younger Marcellus, for whose untimely death he grieves, Persius
calls his unknown heir out of the throng and teases him by proposing lavish
expenditures to which he dare not object:

>   at tu, meus heres,
> quisquis eris, paulum a turba seductior audi.
> o bone, num ignoras? missa est a Caesare laurus
> insignem ob cladem Germanae pubis et aris
> frigidus excutitur cinis ac iam postibus arma,
> iam chlamidas regum, iam lutea gausapa captis
> essedaque ingentesque locat Caesonia Rhenos.

dis igitur genioque ducis centum paria ob res
egregie gestas induco. quis vetat? aude.
vae, nisi conives. oleum artocreasque popello
largior. an prohibes? dic clare. . . .   (41–51)

[But you, my heir—whoever you are, who will be my heir— draw aside
a little from the crowd and pay attention. Dear Sir, You don't know? A
laurel wreath has arrived from Caesar, honoring an impressive slaughter
of German youth: altars are being swept clean of cold ashes; and, right
now, captured weapons for display, royal cloaks, blond-bearded captives,
war chariots, and great River Rhines—all these Caesonia is now renting.
To the gods, then, and our Leader's genius I vow a hundred pairs of
gladiators to celebrate such fine success. Who says me nay? Just you try.
Woe to you, if you don't close an eye! I'm throwing pizza to the mob.
Are you stopping me? Speak out clearly. . . .]

This is, first, comedy of role reversal. Ordinarily, the strict father restrains
and disciplines his extravagant son; but here, the son (for his own selfish
reasons) behaves like a spoilsport parent. We might think of old Demea at
the end of Terence's *Adelphi*, teasing his permissive and self-superior
brother Micio with a frenzy of put-on extravagance—or better, of the old
reprobate Philocleon at the end of Aristophanes' *Wasps*, confounding the
spoilsport son who presumed to re-educate him earlier. At the same time,
the emperor's triumph brings us into the "real world" of history, which in
fact has very little reality about it. Caligula (the scene is taken from earlier
history) wants to celebrate a triumph for a great victory in Germany that
never really happened. Altars are relit, weapons and royal cloaks are dis-
played, and prisoners in greasy cloaks, chariots, and huge River Rhines are
rented by the empress Caesonia. It is all staging: not just history theatrical-
ized, but theater reinventing history as it should have happened. And of
course, the enforced, theatrical celebration brings us back to the contem-
porary world of Nero, the actor-impresario, where you can't absent your-
self from political or artistic performances, or abstain from applause, let
alone object openly to anything. Rome has become a world of play-acting.
Indeed, when Persius refers to Caligula instead of Nero, he may himself
be practicing an obvious kind of dissimulation.[17] It is the formula later
adopted by Juvenal, to attack vice under the names of people now dead: a
safety net for the satirist, except that a single malicious whisper, "He means
Nero," could easily cut through the net, letting him fall to his death.

    The argument proceeds, bringing us back to earth. The heir talks back;
he can always refuse an inheritance, together with its concomitant respon-
sibilities, but Persius, for his part, can always find another heir, if not in
the direct line or near family, then some unknown "Manius" (a beggar)
out there somewhere. "What, that son of earth (*filius terrae*)?" The heir is

shocked, but Persius presses the point. Push your lineage far enough back and you reach a "son of earth." Snobbery is silly; from earth we all come, and to earth (or dust and ashes, *cineres*) we all return. But this thought leads, not to philosophical equanimity or resignation, but to a violent intensification of the argument with the unknown heir:

> qui prior es, cur me in decursu lampada poscis?
> sum tibi Mercurius; venio deus huc ego ut ille
> pingitur. an renuis? vis tu gaudere relictis?
> "dest aliquid summae." minui mihi, sed tibi totum est
> quidquid id est. ubi sit, fuge quaerere, quod mihi quondam
> legarat Tadius, neu dicta, "pone paterna,
> fenoris accedat merces, hinc exime sumptus,
> quid relicum est?" relicum? nunc nunc impensius ungue,
> ungue, puer, caules. mihi festa luce coquatur
> urtica et fissa fumosum sinciput aure,
> ut tuus iste nepos, olim satur anseris extis,
> cum morosa vago singultiet inguine vena,
> patriciae inmeiat volvae? mihi trama figurae
> sit reliqua, ast illi tremat omento popa venter?   (61–74)

[You there, in front: why ask for my torch while I'm still running? For your purposes, I'm Mercury—just like that god in a picture. Are you refusing? Won't you kindly enjoy what's left? "Something's missing from the total." That's my business, if there's less; but you get it all, whatever it comes to. Don't ask where Tadius's legacy has gone; don't read me a schoolmaster's lesson: "Set down what your father left, add the accumulated interest, subtract the expenses: what's the remainder?" Remainder? Soak the cabbages, boy— soak them (with dressing) right now. Do you want me to fast on nettles and chopped pig's brains over the holidays so that someday that spendthrift offspring of yours, stuffed with *pâté de foie gras*, when his fastidiously wandering vein throbs with desire, may piss into a patrician womb? Leave me lean and hungry, while his great belly palpitates with excess fat?]

In what we must imagine, following Lucretius, as the long torchrace of human life over the generations, Persius's heir bursts forward impatiently to grab the torch before his time; that is, he treats his father as somebody already dead. But Persius is alive and kicking. When the heir, in a still more pronounced role reversal, lectures him like an old-fashioned Roman father about income, expenses, and the bottom line, he builds to a little explosion of quite ordinary self-indulgence, and then to a larger explosion against that future spendthrift heir who will squander whatever money has been saved over the generations on gluttony, sex, and social ambition (the last two neatly telescoped in that "patrician womb"). Here the satire proper, or improper, climaxes. The quieter ending, starting *vende animam lucro* ("Sell your soul for gain"), is like an afterthought. How and when can greed, the desire to make your "pile" (*acervus*) grow and grow and grow, ever find a limit? When that moment arrives (that is, never), Chrysippus's grain-of-wheat puzzle will be solved.

How should we read this ending? Here again, more than ever, it helps to keep Horace in mind. Thematically, *Satire* 6 brings us back to Horace's very first *Satire* (1.1), mainly a humorous diatribe against greed, in which the speaker contrasts men's excessive desire for gain with the limits of use and enjoyment imposed by nature. The ant, for example, builds her little pile (*acervus*) of grain, but draws on it later; it is folly to want to "draw from a great big pile" for its own sake. But nobody is content ; everyone fixes his eyes competitively on the chariot ahead, not the many chariots behind, which is why no one is prepared and willing to depart from life like a full (*satur*) dinner guest. Symbolically, however, Horace knows how to say "That's enough, now" (*iam satis est*) when it comes to finishing this satire.[18] His acceptance of aesthetic limits, here and elsewhere, implies a corresponding, very Epicurean acceptance of moral limits in his life and work. Yet, even for him—and more clearly in such later satires as 1.5, the "Journey to Brundisium," and 1.10, which closes Book 1 of the *Satires*—closure still seems arbitrary, like a comic blackout.

Persius's ending, too, seems both right and arbitrary. How should one end a satire, or indeed, a collection of satires, when the stuff of satire increases exponentially together with greed itself?[19] His circling back to Horace's first *Satire*, written about a century earlier, suggests that the satirist's work is futile: we are back exactly where we started. Differently viewed, the persistence of human vice and folly requires the persistence of satire. Persius follows Horace, who followed Lucilius, in the satire-race (and Juvenal will follow Persius, denouncing excesses, pretensions, and crimes that have never been so vast, or so blatant). The literary continuity, the passing on of the satiric torch, seems appropriate. The unending greed of humankind, the same old *avaritia* under ever-new guises, together with the monstrously conspicuous consumption (*luxuria*) that is its counterpart, may be aesthetically and morally appalling, but for the satirist it is a never-failing source of inspiration.

We have come far from the tranquil beginning of *Satire* 6, so very different from the preceding *Satires*, so very close to Horace's first book of *Epistles* in style and thought. Were we, then, tricked? Were we tempted to believe that, once Persius, as Horace's literary heir in satire, had so clearly demonstrated his independence and new creativity in *Satires* 1–5, he felt free to backtrack, to pay his master the belated tribute of close, grateful imitation, and to acquiesce in that typically Horatian mood of gratitude and contentment within the limits imposed by nature—limits that greedy fools will never understand? The ethical and psychological contrast between moderation and excess, satisfaction with what we have and self-exacerbating greed for more, was a Horatian leitmotif. Persius endorses it strongly, giving it first and last place in *Satire* 6. But he departs from it too, as the sea turns stormy and passionate thoughts of death challenge his tentative equanimity: departs, with Horatian originality, from the Horatian model (coincidence, then divergence), but also returns to take up another part of his literary and psychological inheritance—the uncompleted personal struggles of *Epistles* 1 and 2.2, struggles with inconsistency and indecision, with anxiety and discontent, and especially with those attacks of bitterness that inevitably come with contemplating age and death. As Persius reread *Epistles* 2.2, the moments of intense bitterness—Horace's pivotal, self-ironic *nimirum* (141), his final turning against himself of the Lucretian and early-Horatian injunction to leave life's feast in a grateful, timely manner (213–16)—must have struck his imagination powerfully, the more so if, as I suspect, he was already composing himself to die a good Stoic death.

Persius's wild laughter about the heir in *Satire* 6, echoing earlier Horatian passages from the *Satires* and *Odes* as well as the *Epistles*, surely relieved the poet's overcharged heart. I am reminded of a passage in Boswell's *Life* where Samuel Johnson, who feared death as strongly as anyone has before or since, breaks out into a fit of wild, uncontrolled laughter at the thought of a friend's proudly and ostentatiously making his will.[20] Persius's laughter, too, is cathartic. Passing beyond the familiar ethical implications, which remain valid, about the getting and spending of money, it plays out strong feelings of rebellion against nature's law, reluctance to "go gentle into that good night." In this way, satire clears the way for philosophy—eclectic for Horace; the Stoicism of Chrysippus, significantly cited in the last line, for Persius—to finish the job as best it can. Still, the very extravagance of *Satire* 6 as it goes, once more, beyond accepted Horatian bounds is a beautiful last tribute to Horace, an acknowledgment by his prodigal heir of the rich inheritance that he has used so passionately and well, and even increased in a way that must have left him, on the aesthetic level at least, greatly content.

Reading the *Libellus*: Children and Grown-ups

If Persius's *Satires*, taken individually, are notoriously hard to read, the reading of the collection has been inhibited by scholarly uncertainties. We don't know in what order the *Satires* were composed. Very likely, *Satire* 1 was written late; but what about the (initially) so mellow and Horatian *Satire* 6? And then: was the *libellus* actually finished by Persius? According to the *Vita*, "he wrote both rarely and slowly; this very book was left incomplete. Some verses were taken away from the end, so that it appeared as though finished. Cornutus went over it lightly and gave it to Caesius Bassus to edit, at his request" (42–45). We know so little. Shouldn't we save our questions for the individual *Satires*?

I maintain that, waiving (though not forgetting) these and other uncertainties, we should read the *libellus* as a whole and in its present order.[21] I am assuming, first, that Persius himself prepared the collection to be read as we have it, and second, that Cornutus and Bassus, prominently honored in *Satires* 5 and 6, were familiar with the *libellus*, and with something of its anticipated posthumous effect, through private reading and performance.[22]

There are many ways of reading the *libellus*. I choose to follow the theme of "children and grown-ups." Persius, I shall argue, is vitally interested in the different stages of human growth from childhood to old age, in rites of passage, and in the different ways that people pass or fail the test of maturity. For him, as a convinced Stoic, the human body and mind follow an ordered, providential pattern in their natural development, while the mediating soul maintains a continuity of selfhood amid the mysterious changes of human life. As Seneca puts it

> Alia est aetas infantis, pueri, adulescentis, senis; ego tamen idem sum, qui et infans fui et puer et adulescens. Sic, quamvis atque alia cuique constitutio sit, conciliatio constitutionis suae eadem est. Non enim puerum mihi aut iuvenem aut senem, sed me natura commendat. (*Ep.* 121.16)

> [The ages of infant, child, youth, and old man are distinct, yet I am one and the same, who have been infant, child, and youth. Thus, although the organization of each stage differs, the unifying sense of that organization remains constant. For what nature entrusts to me is not the child, youth, or old man, but myself.]

"This belief," as Reydams-Schils says, "must be essential to a sense of self, and to the meaningfulness of human resolutions and commitments over time, hence to any genuine moral progress. These would be reinforced by memory, by practices of mindfulness, by the keeping of journals and the like. But Seneca's lines also suggest the mystery of our lives, of ourselves over time. How we are/are not the same."[23]

Persius's *libellus* is permeated from beginning to end with his feeling for "the mystery of our lives, of ourselves over time." As a satirist, he unmasks the childish attitudes of grown-ups, however much disguised by their hypocritical pretenses to virtue, the trite old precepts they love to mouth. At the same time, satire writing helps Persius rediscover his own childlike power of creativity and play, which empowers his attack on vice and folly, yet saves him from succumbing to *senium*, that weary, boring, premature old-aging of the spirit.

Although Persius's literary treatment of games and play brings him into close dialogue, once again, with the Horace of the *Epistles*, the distinction between childish and childlike behavior owes much to Greek philosophy and diatribe, and may best be illustrated by the preserved discourses of Epictetus. For example: "If circumstances don't suit you, don't be less brave than the children who say, 'I'm not playing any more'—or, if you stay, then don't complain." The comparison is paradoxical and funny. We all know, and scarcely want to imitate, the child who throws a tantrum, throws the board over, stalks away from the game. That is childish in the extreme, yet it may teach us how to see our life with detachment as a play or game we participate in, but whose tokens we should never take too seriously. Elsewhere, Epictetus compares his recommended behavior to Saturnalian play. You join in the fun; you play your assigned role; you humor the other players, the way we humor children in their pastimes. But when this crosses a certain line (of basic human decency, of right behavior), you stop playing. In other words: don't spoil the (social or political) game unless you must, but always remember that it's only a game, from which you should depart when the right moment comes—or again, what a beautiful game Socrates played, like a skilled ball-player, when confronted with imprisonment and death![24]

It seems likely that Persius maintained, or tried to maintain, this play perspective, which extends from Socrates and Plato, through Bion of Borysthenes, to Musonius Rufus and Epictetus. But his most important source was Horace's *Epistles*, especially as they ring changes on the ambiguous notion of *ludus* ("play" or "game"). In his programmatic *Epistles* 1.1, Horace portrays himself as a retired gladiator, unwilling to rejoin the fray. For him, now, it is no longer worth the effort. Here, and in the long valedictory *Epistles* 2.2, he satirizes the "games people play" in the competitive world of literary production and performance, even as he justifies, more positively, his turn from play to seriousness, from poetry writing to philosophy. Ironically, of course, his satire reflects the seriousness with which he himself has always taken poetry writing, his own or others'. Differently, in *Epistles* 1.1, 52–64, the playful children (*pueri ludentes*) with their sing-song moral verses—*rex eris si recte facies, si non facies non eris* ("Do right, and you will be a king; do wrong, you'll not be anything")—are more serious, more in touch with ultimate reality, than their childish elders, who like schoolboys take dictation from Wall Street: "Make money, always make money. Virtue after Cash!" As Horace himself reviews the ABCs of right living, his idiosyncratic return to school joins *senex* with *puer* in a shared, rejuvenating folly that might still redeem his later years from weariness and failure. It is a return to play in the deepest sense: play that precedes and underlies all those different games, whether of businessmen or poets, and of which the playful "nonpoetry" of the *Epistles* themselves may be, in the end, a successful and healing manifestation.[25]

Persius, in his turn, adapts Horace's satiric perspective on children and grown-ups. He describes his own satire writing as a "free man's play" (*ingenuo . . . ludo*, 5.16), authorized by Cornutus in the name of philosophy. He admires his friend Bassus as "an older man outstanding in [literary?] play" (*egregius lusisse senex*, 6.6). It all sounds very much like Horace and his world, but there are differences, and these are crucial. *Satires* 2–5—the inner portion of the *libellus*—focus largely on the continuing childishness, the large-scale refusal of maturity, found at all stages of human life. (Persius's own right growth, thanks to Cornutus, is the rare exception.) We might expect the satirist to react, like Horace, with bemused tolerance of human folly, or else (reading back from Juvenal), with anger and indignation. Instead, in *Satires* 1 and 6 (the outer frame), he takes on the persona, first, of a naughty child who must scream out his insults, and then, of a naughty old man who will not submit to his spoilsport son's control. Which brings us back, finally, not to philosophy but to high comedy.

Persius begins *Satire* 2 with birthday wishes for his friend Macrinus, and he places a newborn child at the poem's center.[26] This is a real baby, a scrawny little unidealized creature like Shakespeare's "infant / mewling and puking in the nurse's arms."[27] Female relatives (grandmother, aunt, nurse) lift it from the cradle; they add to its natural wetness with their superstitious spittle; and, swinging it in their arms, they imprint it with fanciful, ultimately dangerous wishes for fame and fortune. Spiritually speaking, human beings are unmade from the start. What seems like pristine innocence is corrupted, sooner than we realize, by the world. It will not be so easy, later on, to get birthday wishes right—as Macrinus, presumably, manages to do.

Persius reminds us, too, of childhood vulnerability. One of the malicious sotto voce prayers he describes is for the death of a sickly *pupillus*, a fatherless boy standing in the way of an inheritance, "for he is mangy and acutely swollen with bile" (13–14). Shortly afterward, Persius mentions Staius, a notoriously corrupt judge: "Who could be better (he asks sarcastically), more suitable for fatherless children?" (20). Momentarily, we might envision Persius, who lost his father and stepfather young, as just such a vulnerable *pupillus*, growing up against the odds in a threatening world.

Satire 2, then, opens the inner group of satires (2–5) with an illusion of innocence that is quickly dispelled. It ends with the implied, closely related question: In this altogether materialistic world, greedy at best, murderous at worst, how can we grow up well? Superficial rites of passage—when girls, for example, dedicate their dolls to Venus before marriage (70)—are meaningless. What is needed, rather (the last three lines balance the first), is to reorder our minds and reimprint the inner places of our hearts with genuine goodness and piety. Only then will the gods listen to our prayers.

Satire 3 begins with the childish behavior of a youth who might, in one aspect, be Persius himself; who needs to study his philosophy lesson, but is too hung-over, lazy, and full of superficial complaints to get down to work. What the companion/tutor/adviser stresses, with his playful mockery, is the regressiveness of such behavior:

> O miser, inque dies ultra miser, hucine rerum
> venimus? a, cur non potius teneroque columbo
> et similis regum pueris pappare minutim
> poscis et iratus mammae lallare recusas?   (3.15–18)

> [You pathetic character, and every day more pathetic: is this what we've come to? Why don't you just go do what the little lovey-doveys do, and the little spoiled princelings: ask to have your din-din mashed up, and refuse to go ni-ni for Mom-ma?]

Regression is always tempting. The beginning student who doesn't press forward may easily be swept backward; even an advanced *progrediens* like Persius must be aware that he has not entirely and forever overcome that pull backward, the promptings and refusals of the not-quite-regenerate mind and heart. Dramatically, again, it is a short step from the babyish behavior at the satire's beginning to the fool's death at the end from ignoring the philosopher-doctor's advice. Life is a gift, like that early morning light coming through the shutters (1–2), but we waste it, and all too quickly it is gone.

So much for childishness, but a later passage (44–51) suggests a different perspective. Persius's (inner?) adviser tells how he used to play hooky from school, and rightly so (*iure*, 48). We expect him to give the obvious reason, that he was only a child then, caught up in fun and games, whereas the youth addressed at 52–62 has received a good Stoic education, so has no excuse for wasting his life like a boy throwing potsherds at crows. On a different reading, the schoolboy reacted correctly when he refused to play the declamation game, which was ostensibly about Cato and (Stoic) virtue, but more truly, for those sweating fathers, indicated their sons' promise of success in business, law, and Caesarian politics. Isn't it better to retain, and to nurture, the heart of a rebellious child?

Satire 4 presents failure of maturity in the person of Alcibiades, who embarks on public life before his beard comes, or his good judgment. A reader of Persius (if such yet existed) would inevitably think of Nero, still a youth, yet eagerly outgrowing the constraint of his would-be tutors. (Even Socrates had failed—and Seneca was no Socrates.) But the satire points to a more universal failure of self-knowledge. "How nobody dares descend into his own depths, but all gaze on the pack [of faults] on their neighbor's back" (23–24). The satirist is emphatically not exempted from this self-ignorant, mutually backbiting world. Indeed, the last line, the call to "know how far your [sexual and moral] furnishings fall short," could be addressed, first and foremost, to himself.

But Persius, in *Satire* 5, emerges strong and resolute from adolescent crisis, as Alcibiades (and Nero) had not. Unlike Horace, he describes the onset of adolescence as a confusing, dangerous time when childhood protections are withdrawn and sexual and other temptations are strong: when, in short, life can become terribly "scattered." But now he takes the saving step, entrusting himself to Cornutus's tutelage like a newborn babe:

> me tibi supposui. teneros tu suscipis annos
> Socratico, Cornute, sinu. (5. 36–37)

[I put myself under your care; you took up my tender years in your Socratic bosom.]

The language is playfully erotic, too, recalling Plato. But what it more seriously conveys is a sense of recommencing life properly, which leaves Persius both free to pursue philosophy, the one necessary pursuit, as Horace had insisted, for children and elders alike (*puerique senesque*, 5.64), and authorized, in his longest, most accessible satire, to indulge his "free man's play" (*ingenuo . . . ludo*, 5.16).[28]

Yet the outer frame of the *libellus* tells a harsher, less Horatian story. In *Satire* 1, what seemed adult seriousness is unmasked, early on, as hypocrisy and fraud:

> Nam Romae quis non—a, si fas dicere—sed fas
> tum cum ad canitiem et nostrum istud vivere triste
> aspexi ac nucibus facimus quaecumque relictis,
> cum sapimus patruos. tunc tunc—ignoscite (nolo,
> quid faciam?) sed sum petulanti splene—cachinno. (1.8–12)

[For, at Rome, who is/does not—ah, if it's right to speak—but of course it's right, when I look at those gray hairs and that grim, "grown-up" front we display, though living in any way whatsoever—it's then, it's then (sorry, can't help it, my spleen compels me), I have to— roar with laughter.]

We are supposed, normally, to put childhood toys aside and grow up. Instead, the alleged grown-ups in Roman society have assumed the trappings and poses of age without acquiring the necessary discipline. Despite their grey hairs and "Dutch uncle" frowns, they lack conviction and they lack purpose.[29] But all this tedious and fake "old-age conduct" (*canities*, 9; *senium*, 26) only conjures up its reverse, the screamed-out insults and mocking gestures of the naughty child. The patron, usually flattered, becomes an obscenely fat baldhead. Only Janus, who has two faces, can escape the mockery—the stork's bill, the asses' ears, the stuck-out tongue—directed at our noble litterateurs behind their backs. And similarly, the satirist who must speak out, if only (for now) into his little book, is like the boy who has to "commit a nuisance" in the sacred place. His satire is one enormous guffaw, one great, irrepressible outburst of truthtelling mockery in a hypocritical world.

Satire 6 begins with an Horatian image of true maturity in the figure of Bassus, the older friend whose poetry symbolically ranges from masculine Roman lyric to deliberate, controlled playfulness (of light verse):

mox iuvenes agitare iocos et pollice honesto
egregius lusisse senex.   (5–6)

[And shortly, though old, you set youthful fun in motion, sporting uncommonly with your upright thumb.]

This fusion, as we saw, of play and seriousness evokes, and pays tribute to, the older Horace's achievement in *Epistles* 1 and 2.2. Persius is grateful always, like Horace before him, for moments of peace and tranquility, as well as for his literary inheritance, but reminders of suffering (the shipwrecked man) and sudden death disrupt any too facile, borrowed mood of contentment. Finally, the grasping heir reawakens his indignation—and his more simply satiric voice. In *Satire* 1, the world's hypocrisy and foolishness drove him to assume the strong, unabashed persona of the naughty child. Now, in *Satire* 6, he becomes a naughty old man right out of Aristophanes, like Philocleon in *The Wasps* unashamedly confronting, and finally routing, his pretentious son. He won't give in to *senium*, that widespread "old-age spirit" of worry and moralizing.[30] From beginning to end, his *Satires* voice a neo-Aristophanic protest against any and all spoilsport attitudes, not least within himself, that might diminish his zest for life.

How, then, should we read the *libellus*? As a call to maturity in the face of a misguided and misdirecting world (*Satires* 2–5)? Or a Quixotic protest against the grown-up silliness everywhere to be seen (*Satires* 1 and 6)? Persius is clearly fascinated by life's different stages and the challenges they raise. He invites us to imagine his own hard-won maturity, with its strong Stoic scaffolding, first provided by Cornutus (*Satire* 5), but his first and last words in the *libellus* imply life's rebuke to the moralist, together with its ever-renewed stimulus to the satirist. The result is a brilliant fusion of seriousness and play. Why, really, Persius wrote satire—how, in the end, it might have contributed to his own right growth as a person—I shall ask in the following, valedictory pages.

Recognizing Persius

> It is Stalinist Russia; a little Jew requests permission to emigrate. "Why do you want to leave?" asks the official. "Don't we feed you well?" "I can't complain." "And your housing?" "I can't complain." "And the medical care? " "I can't complain." After many such questions: "So why do you want to leave our wonderful country? "
> —"I can't complain."

In Persius's first *Satire* truth and wild laughter explode out of repression. We think first and most naturally of the social-political dimension suggested by the King Midas allusion, the powerful inhibition of speaking out the truth about Nero, his court, and the Roman society that tolerates them. Why does Persius (or his satiric persona) write satire? Because he must speak out, must guffaw—though only into the (temporary) silence of his little book, and even there extending the dangerous Midas cartoon to a generality of fools: "Who doesn't have asses' ears?" But now, looking back at Persius's work, I want to suggest a second, equally weighty source of repression from which his rebellious laughter bursts forth. There are many things in life about which a Stoic and a gentleman "can't complain," many dangerously subversive feelings, such as anger, or grief, or fear of death, that cannot be acknowledged freely and fully, even to oneself. How shall they find a voice?

The official Stoic line is clear, especially in Cicero and Seneca. Ordinary emotions (*affectus*) are harmful because they are based on false notions of good and bad to which the mind wrongly assents. Preliminary impulses—of grief at a friend's death, or anger at an insult, or fear when sailing and a bad storm blows up—are natural and not blameworthy, but we must never give assent to the false notion that death, in general or particular, is an evil, or that insults harm us, and so forth—assent that finds expression in wrongful grief, anger, and fear.[31] We must always be on our guard against such emotions. Like soldiers on campaign, we must maintain self-discipline at all times, which will carry into our bodily demeanor, facial expression, and language. Not for one moment—not even at home, in bed—are we off duty.[32]

But this Stoic vigilance carries new dangers. Our strictness of life might cause us to become inhumane, *stolidi* (as the joke went), not *Stoici*.[33] Or we might lose the creative power and enthusiasm traditionally associated with Eros, Dionysus, and the Muses.[34] Or we might fall into moral and emotional lethargy, *accidia*.[35] Or we might fail to express proper indignation, even outrage, at the right time.[36] Or the feelings we have denied might cause psychological distress, even physical illness.[37] Or they might resurface in powerful new forms—as repressed grief, for example, can turn into terrible anger. Think of Aeneas, Virgil's Stoic hero and Augustan role model, who becomes another Achilles in the end:

> Talia voce refert curisque ingentibus aeger
> spem vultu simulat, premit altum corde dolorem.   (*Aen.* 1.208–9)

> [So goes his speech. Though sick with enormous cares,
> he counterfeits hope in his face, presses grief down deep in his heart.]

I suggest that, in addition to the reasons usually adduced for writing satire—to fool around in idle moments, to fill a vacancy, to speak out (somehow), to say something new and important, "because it's what [literarily and personally] I can do"—Persius wrote satire *as a means of emotional self-recognizance*, a playful way to let "minority voices" be heard, to purge-and-clarify subversive inner complaints in a satiric yet Stoic catharsis.[38] What is remarkable, what most distinguishes him from Horace before and Juvenal after, is the poetic and personal intensity of his Socratic/Stoic drive to know himself. If *Satire* 2 unmasks hypocrisy and attacks folly and vice with pre-Juvenalian *indignatio*, *Satires* 3 and 4 trace a journey into the interior, into a heart of darkness that is—or would be, but for the grace of reason and Stoic teaching—his own.

His explosive laughter, then, is more than conventionally scornful. It joins the relief of emotional self-expression and the pleasure of enhanced wholemindedness and wholeheartedness with something of *fou rire*, the antic laughter of one who has confronted not just men's follies ("O curas hominum! o quantum est in rebus inane!"), but the Void itself. At its deepest level, his emotional self-recognizance through satire reveals and overcomes fears of nonbeing, together with the concomitant desire to evade mortality somehow through personal achievement—maybe through poetic fame? Which is where *Satire* 1 begins.

The Stoics valued poetry, not least for its power to illustrate emotion.[39] Chrysippus, it was said, copied out almost Euripides' entire *Medea* in his (lost) study of anger and its effects; and Cicero, in his largely Stoic *Tusculan Disputations*, quotes beautiful arias from Ennius to convey feelings of intense grief (though what we have, of course, is libretto fragments without music and song—*O patria mia, quando ti rivedró?*). Poetry, to the philosopher, is always suspect; it can seduce untutored minds into false beliefs, strengthening the very emotions that should be kept under control. But, at the same time, it can help us understand—at a safe aesthetic distance—the challenge of the enemy without and within. Philosophically, Persius follows Chrysippus, but poetically, where the passions are concerned, he comes closest to Lucretius. Hence the following digression.

Lucretius in Book 3 says he must "clarify" (*claranda*) the nature of mind and soul, so as to dispel the fear of death:

et metus ille foras praeceps Acheruntis agendus,
funditus humanam qui vitam turbat ab imo
omnia suffundens mortis nigrore neque ullam
esse voluptatem liquidam puramque relinquit.   (*DRN.* 3.37–40)

[And that fear of Hell must be driven out headlong,
the fear that muddies human life from its depths, staining
everything with death's blackness, and leaves no pleasure
to be clear and pure.]

Notice his emphasis here, as always, on the subconscious (*suffundens*) nature of the psychological disturbances that infect our lives. Even though (he continues) people assert their intellectual unconcern with death, their behavior under extreme circumstances betrays them; for, even exiled and miserable, they cling to the old religious rituals and beliefs:

quo magis in dubiis hominem spectare periclis
convenit adversisque in rebus noscere qui sit;
nam verae voces tum demum pectore ab imo
eliciuntur et eripitur persona, manet res.   (3.55–58)

[All the more, then, should one observe a man closely under stress of danger and ascertain what he is when things go badly; for then true voices are drawn out from the heart's depths: mask is torn away, reality remains.]

In ordinary life, most people conceal their deeper fears from themselves, let alone from others. But their blind impulses (*caeca cupido*, 59) to amass wealth and power—impulses that are never satisfied, yet destroy communal life—"are nurtured in large part by the fear of death" (3.64).

Lucretius declaims powerfully and rhetorically, in the diatribe tradition, against wrongheaded ideas and emotions; he ridicules them logically and dismissively, yet his scornful, indignant laughter is surprisingly revelatory. Thus we are made to feel how religion "looms over us" (a play on *superstitio*), weighing down our spirits, or how lovers wander, uncertain and confused about what they want, in the very act of intercourse.[40] So too, when his tremendous attack on the fear of death in Book 3 supplements logical analysis and argument (our life-giving atomic configurations are dissolved in death, so "we" are no longer there) with playful, yet evocative demythologizing (the fabled tortures of Hell are what fools suffer in this life—unsatisfied greed, ambition, lust, and so forth) and satirical diatribe preaching (if you've enjoyed life, you should depart from it gratefully, as from a good dinner-party; if you haven't, then you never will, no matter how long you might live). In the end, I agree with Kenney that Lucretius fails to acknowledge our deepest fears: of death as extinction, of loss of self, of nothingness, of the end of human experience as we know it. But he does bring out, if only to ridicule their irrationality, some nightmarish images of death and dying that haunt our unconscious.[41]

Here is an example (but the whole passage, 3.870–93, should be read in Latin):

> Proinde ubi se videas hominem indignarier ipsum,
> post mortem fore ut aut putescat corpore posto
> aut flammis interfiat malisve ferarum,
> scire licet non sincerum sonere atque subesse
> caecum aliquem cordi stimulum, quamvis neget ipse
> credere se quemquam sibi sensum in morte futurum. . . .   (3.870–75)

[So therefore, when you see a man complain that it isn't fair that he will rot away after his body is buried, or that he will perish in flames or by the jaws of wild beasts, you may know that he doesn't ring true, and that some blind prodding force works beneath his heart, no matter how much he may deny that he thinks he will feel anything after death. . . .]

Our fears, Lucretius continues, are illogical. When we imagine ourselves burning on the funeral pyre, or torn by animals, or buried under a heavy weight of earth, we are conflating our subjective, perceiving self, which will no longer be present, with the unfeeling corpse. Yet this delusive "contamination" resembles the ordinary experience of nightmares, like those described later in Book 4: of being killed in war, or being mangled by panthers or lions, or dying, or falling headlong from a great height (the image will reappear in Persius):

> multi, de montibus altis
> ut qui praecipitent ad terram corpore toto,
> exterrentur et ex somno quasi mentibu' capti
> vix ad se redeunt permoti corporis aestu.   (4. 1020–23)

[Many, as though from high mountain peaks they are falling headlong to the ground, are terrified out of their right minds; and coming out of sleep, their minds are still prisoners of illusion, and just barely, their bodies drenched in sweat, do they return to their own selves.]

The implied comparison works two ways. On the one hand, it suggests the unreality of our habitual, unthinking images of death and dying. On the other, it acknowledges precisely the nightmarish power of those unconscious terrors that, without our realizing it, haunt our waking lives, spoiling our pleasure in life, fueling our futile and destructive drives for wealth, power, and false security.[42] Lucretius would have appreciated how Shakespeare, in *Measure for Measure*, strips away Claudio's moral façade as he pleads ignobly with Isabella to save his life:

Claudio: Death is a fearful thing.
Isabella: And shamed life, a hateful.
Claudio: Ay, but to die, and go we know not where,
            To lie in cold obstruction, and to rot,
            This sensible warm motion, to become
            A kneaded clod. . . .[43]

Shamed by his sister, Claudio repents—and we, the audience, may be brought with him to a better state of mind ("I am so out of love with life, that I will sue to be rid of it."); the ending will be happy, but for a moment, *eripitur persona, manet res*. Psychological, even spiritual healing begins by stripping away the mask, the habitual face we show to others and also to ourselves. But poetry, dramatic or satiric, gives voice to powerful fears and desires, acknowledging them first, then reordering them, as best it can, in the overall scheme of things.

Of all Lucretius's images, the leaky vessel (*vas*) seems to have impressed Persius most with its moral but also existential implications. In Book 3, 1003–10, the mythic punishment of the Danaids, doomed forever to carry water in leaky jars, is read as an allegory of our insatiability and ingratitude for all the good things of life. Again, in the proem of Book 6, Epicurus is praised for realizing that people's dissatisfactions and complaints were due to the bad state of the *vas*, which was both leaky (*pertusum fluxumque*), so it could never be filled, and filthy, so it contaminated whatever was put within. So he "cleansed hearts (*purgavit pectora*) with truthful sayings," setting forth the limits of desire and fear, and showing how the goal of happiness might be achieved. The metaphor of cleansing, *purgare*, like the Greek *kathairein*, joins notions of religious "purification," moral and psychological "purgation," and intellectual "clarification." For the philosopher, the healing process begins in the mind, with right understanding, and works downward, but for the poet, it begins with the heart, with the exposure and acknowledgment of those powerful, deep-lying fears and desires crying out for help. For the leaky *vas* is more than allegorical. It conveys the fearful reality of our constitution: a transient, briefly life-giving configuration of atoms (body, mind, and soul), including much emptiness (*inane*) within itself, hence always more or less vulnerable to dissolution. It is not, in the end—despite what moralists may say, or diatribe speakers, or philosophers in satiric mode—a comforting picture.

I return to Persius, to a tormented passage in *Satire* 3. What tyrant, asks the speaker, ever induced greater pain and fear

"imus,
imus praecipites" quam si sibi dicat et intus
palleat infelix quod proxima nesciat uxor?   (41–43)

[. . . than if one should say to himself, "We're falling, falling headlong! "
and turn pale within, poor wretch, at what his wife, lying beside him,
can never know.]

Persius may be parodying a passage from Seneca here:

> What, then, is more beautiful than this habit of carefully reviewing [*excu-
> tiendi*] the entire day? And how delightful the sleep that follows this self-
> examination [*post recognitionem sui*]—how tranquil it is, how deep and
> untroubled, when the soul has either praised or admonished itself, and
> when this secret examiner and critic of self has given report [*cognovit*] of
> its own character! I avail myself of this privilege, and every day I plead
> my cause before the bar of self. When the light has been removed from
> sight and my wife, long aware of my habit, has become silent, I scan the
> whole of my day and retrace all my deeds and words. I conceal nothing
> from myself, I omit nothing. For why should I shrink from any of my
> mistakes, when I may commune thus with myself?

> "See that you never do that again; I will pardon you this time." (*De Ira*
> 3.36.3–4; trans. Basore)[44]

Did Persius sense a touch of special pleading here (though qualified by
self-humor), an all too complacent settling into sleep, the moral checkbook
neatly balanced for the day? What he especially parodies, then, would
be Seneca's treatment of his wife. She is well-trained; she knows better
than to interrupt his meditation before he goes to his well-earned rest. But
in Persius's satire, where things are less clearly defined—where we can't
help wondering, what *has* the man been doing? Has he murdered some-
one, or pursued some sexual by-path to a scary end?—the man emerges
from nightmare to a lonely waking terror that his wife's physical presence
cannot allay.[45] The ostensible moral is that it is worse to be aware of one's
failings without taking steps to remedy them than simply to be oblivious,
like Natta:

sed stupet hic vitio et fibris increvit opimum
pingue, caret culpa, nescit quid perdat, et alto
demersus summa rursus non bullit in unda.   (32–34)

[But this fellow is torpid with vice; his liver is overgrown with rich fat;
he can't be blamed, he doesn't know what he's losing, he's sunk so very
deep that he never bubbles up again above the waves.]

Death and dying are everywhere in *Satire* 3. Overtly, they enforce the moral: study philosophy as you would consult a doctor, before it is too late. But nightmare cannot be allegorized away. Natta may slip away unconsciously, with a moral heart attack from all that excess fat (anticipating the fool's sudden death in the culminating parable, 88–106), but Persius gives us a compelling image of going down for the third time in the sea of death. Similarly, "imus, imus praecipites" (42–43) recalls the dream of falling that Lucretius associated with unconscious fears of death and dying. It is the ordinary nightmare that haunts us all.[46]

Persius's *recognitio sui*, then, in *Satire* 3 is more complex than Seneca's, and less reassuring. Metaphorically, it is medical diagnosis, not judicial procedure. Even as its images of sickness and sudden death function as shock treatment, rousing us from our habitual lethargy to seek our philosophical salvation in fear and trembling, these same images insist powerfully on our bodily weakness, our Lucretian vulnerability to the forces of death and dissolution (although, in the Stoic view, our spirit may eventually be reintegrated into the rational, world-ordering fire that is God).[47] Reading *Satire* 3, then, we descend into the abyss. We take recognizance, not just of intellectual and moral truths, but of the deeper, existential anxieties of nonbeing.

Which is why, before moving on with Persius, we might listen again to the centurion's guffaws at lines 77–87. Yes, we laugh at his philistinism, his wonderfully ignorant mish-mash of ideas about philosophers. But we also laugh *with* him. We laugh at the pretensions of intellectuals who claim to be better than we, who disregard ordinary human feelings and experience, who would reorganize our lives under reason's unrelenting rule. We laugh as naughty schoolchildren laugh at their teachers, and as Aristophanes, the great–great-grandfather of Roman satire, laughed—so very wickedly—at Socrates. And Persius, I am sure, laughed uproariously too as he performed the centurion's part: not just with scorn, but with the *fou rire*, the antic laughter of one who has looked into the abyss, and with the explosive relief of one who has found, in satire, a way of recognizing his inmost feelings and letting their voices be heard, really heard, even as they are reassumed into the ordered structures of poetry and the philosophic life.

Most genuinely creative poets, indeed, resemble the little child who said, "How can I know what I think 'til I see what I say?" Consider again Persius's indignant outburst against the greedy heir in *Satire* 6. The quiet, Horatian beginning misleads the reader into expecting a quiet, reasonable, Horatian satire—an expectation subverted before we know it—but for Persius, the writing process must have been heuristic too, revealing his own unexpectedly strong feelings of anger and indignation at the whole business of death, about which he "can't complain": feelings which are not only purged through release but clarified through recognition, completing, with a last unexpected twist, the satiric catharsis heralded in *Satire* 1. To which I finally return.

Persius's great opening line, "O curas hominum! O quantum est in rebus inane!" conflates Lucilius with Lucretius, recalling not only such Lucretian phrases as *curae inanes*, but also the physical reality behind them, the infinity of empty space within and without our little lives, and thus giving new force and meaning to the tired metaphor of moral vacuity. We should especially remember Lucretius's depiction of avarice and ambition as *curae inanes*, nurtured in no small part by the fear of death.[48] Similarly, when Cicero, in his Stoicizing preface to Book 3 of the *Tusculans* describes how people are led astray from birth—by nurses and parents, poets and teachers, and the entire apparatus of society's beliefs and expectations, so that their sickness of mind and soul requires the medicine of philosophy—he represents this universal corruption of nature as a triumph of *vanitas* ("emptiness, unreality") over *veritas* ("reality, truth"): for example, the *inanitas* with which men pursue a false image of fame and glory.

> These things [public office, military commands, popularity] attract the noblest among us, so that, even as they pursue that genuine distinction which is the one chief aim of their nature, they spend their lives in great emptiness (*in summa inanitate*) , chasing not a solid figure of virtue but only a shadow-shape of glory.
>
> For real glory is a solid thing, clearly modeled and not shadowy at all: it is the unanimous praise of good persons, approval sounded without bias by those who know how to judge excellence of character. It is, as it were, the reflection or echo of such excellence, and there is no need for good men to disown it, since it is the regular accompaniment to right actions. But there is another sort of glory, which pretends to imitate the first, and which is rash and ill-considered, frequently praising misdeeds and faults. This is popular acclaim. (*Tusc.* 3.1.3–4; trans. Graver)

So too, in *Satire* 1, Persius turns the spotlight of satiric honesty not just upon the falsity and deception of the fashionable literary and literary-critical world, but upon a more specific vanity in which the poet himself is implicated. " '*Quis leget haec?*' " (" '*Who will read these things?*' "). As said earlier, the interlocutor who interrupts Persius's grand opening with this abrupt question is usually taken as a voice of caution and restraint (whether friend, adviser, or *adversarius*) in the tradition of Lucilius and Horace. "What audience, really, are you aiming at? How will they receive these great *Satires* of yours? Will they be pleased? Or offended? And why, for that matter, should anyone read them in the first place?" All this is there, and will be spelled out further at lines 107–10. But in another, still more significant reading the question " '*Quis leget haec?*' " indicates the specific vanity of Persius's own poetic ambition, with all its shadowy concerns. There is so much latent anxiety in those three words. "Will I be read, and appreciated? Will I compete successfully with Lucilius and Horace, and be admitted to the pantheon of Roman satirists? Will I be remembered through my poetry, so that my voice, or something of my voice, will still be heard long after my death?" Or simply, in another three words: "*Will I survive?*"

Together with its devastating critique of fashionable poetry and criticism, *Satire* 1 explores the vanity of poetic ambition. What does it come down to, in the end? The perverse gratifications of performance; being pointed at in the street, or dictated to a hundred curly-haired school-children; and then, after you're dead, becoming the object of some stylish, affected recitation—what difference, except in vain fancy, will it make to the poet's ashes in his tomb?

The interlocutor persists, like an inner voice that will not be silenced. Is there anyone living who could deny the wish for poetic fame? But the wish's very expression—to "have earned the people's mouth," to "leave behind poems unafraid of [being used as wrappings for] mackerels and incense"—subverts itself, suggesting the material and temporal limitations of our hopes at best, as well as the deep fear of oblivion that drives them on. (Juvenal will take these images of futility further in his *Satire* 7.) But the interlocutor's challenge elicits a serious response. Persius "wouldn't be afraid to be praised if something in fact comes out rather decently." (We smile at the understatement.) The problem, he continues, is that the coinage of praise has become debased, whether in the socioeconomic exchanges of flattery for food or in the tired, thoughtless, self-satirizing common-places of the old Ancients-versus-Moderns debate. So Persius's desire for poetic fame implicates him, at least potentially, in the triumph of Vanity that his satire is, or started to be, all about.

As a Stoic, of course, Persius would distinguish the passing impulse, "I'd like to be remembered," from the settled emotion and wrongheaded belief, "Poetic fame is truly desirable and worthwhile." Technically, fame is only a "preferred indifferent," like health or long life.[49] In this sense, modest conditionality ("I wouldn't mind . . .") is entirely realistic. Cicero argued that most people pursue, not true nobility and virtue, as nature intends, but false images of glory. Fame should be a by-product of virtuous public activity, not a meretricious substitute for it. And so (if I may read between his closing lines) for Persius: his business is to write honestly and well, for himself primarily, and then for whatever readers can and will appreciate honest satire—people who can listen, and understand, and maybe in some measure be healed by the further catharsis that this satire, like the Old Comedy long before it, has to offer.[50]

I wanted, when I began this book, to help Persius be "recognized" in the simpler sense once again, to reconfirm at least his traditional place between Horace and Juvenal (and I wouldn't have minded—I'm only human—receiving a little credit myself for his rehabilitation). Even while writing, however, I found myself being drawn into Persius's *recognitio sui*, his challenge, first to himself, then to his reader, to take on a genuinely human face. What I have come to admire in Persius, through his *Satires*, is not anything like completion of the Stoic journey toward sainthood, but rather a clear vision of what that journey entails: unblinking awareness of the human condition, one's own especially, and the will to keep striving in the face of innumerable obstacles, both without and within. It is the cumulative sense of this awareness and this striving that helps us see Persius as more than the satiric persona "Persius," and as more than the sum of the different voices in the *Satires*. We see that he knows his, and our, limitations better than most, but that he is resolved, all the same, to become a real person, a genuine human being.

Although our search for Persius remains largely incomplete, because we know so little about his life and work, after all, and what little we know raises other important but unanswerable questions; although we mourn the incompleteness of his life and his "play" when we compare it, especially, to Horace's (recall that perfect-tense "lusisse" of his tribute to Bassus, and indirectly to Horace, in *Satire* 6): still, the poetry he bequeathed to posterity has enough finish about it to suggest that its maker must have felt, on one level at least, satisfied with his achievement, even as, on another, he entrusted himself and his life's meaning to the judgment of fate. So if we, who still search for Persius, can recognize him a little through his art, that is, as he might say, *our* affair.[51]

Epilogue

🅕 🅕 🅕 🅕 🅕 🅕 🅕 🅕 🅕 🅕 🅕 🅕 🅕 🅕 🅕 🅕

FROM PERSIUS TO JUVENAL

WHEN you move on from Persius to Juvenal, with whom he is bound up in your Oxford Classical Text (as he has been in so many different texts since 1470); when you work your way through these five books of *Satires*, averaging 767 lines each (and *Satire* 6, on women, only three lines short of Persius's entire work if you include the *Choliambics*), and imagine Juvenal writing, as Persius could not, from around age forty to age seventy (and he would have written more, but death cuts aspirations short); when you follow the changes in subject-matter and style that his longer life allowed; when you abandon your critical reserve and give yourself over to the rhetorical flow of his verse, building, building, rising to climax, and falling back into anticlimax and surprise; when you are swept along by such a torrent of anger and indignation at the social inequities and abuses that are always with us (another thieving CEO in this morning's paper, who despoiled his company and ruined his workers and may never get sent to prison [there is always a well-paid lawyer and a new appeal; I had a student once who talked about the "criminal overworld"]); when the chasm between rich and poor widens daily, and Classics professors are inadequately paid—aren't you so overwhelmed by all this that you think of Juvenal as the runaway supreme Roman satirist and quite forget about Horace, let alone Persius?

I do not intend, in what follows, to weigh Persius's merits against Juvenal's. What interests me, rather, is his seminal though unobtrusive presence in these later Satires. If my examples, taken from *Satires* 1 and 7 especially, help us appreciate Juvenal against the background of Persius, they also help us to see, in retrospect, what Persius was doing and (just as important) what he was *not* doing with the same or similar material. Here, then, is Juvenal reading Persius—and being read by him.

Satire 1

Juvenal's programmatic first satire, an *apologia* (account, not apology) of why he must write satire, places him in the obvious line of Lucilius, Horace,

and Persius. All three, in their different ways, justify their choice and pro-
claim, against unfriendly or friendly warnings, their intention to persist,
Lucilius (as it seems) more directly, Horace more ironically, and Persius
with a not-quite muted explosiveness that much influenced the rhetorical
build-up of Juvenal's *Satire* 1. If Horace imposed new moral and stylistic
standards on Lucilian satire and Persius, in turn, transformed it into a more
inward exploration of human life, his own not least, Juvenal redirects it
outwardly into the sweeping attack on vice and folly that we usually expect
from satire, reclaiming Lucilius's aggressiveness and wild playfulness, while
admitting a single (apparent) compromise: he will not attack the living,
only the dead.

"Though nature refuse," says Juvenal, concluding the first half, "indigna-
tion creates verse." This *indignatio*, literally the feeling or expression of an
"undeservedness" in things, is a passionate response to what the speaker
sees as life's unfairness: vile people getting ahead in life (and ahead of *me*—
some self-undercutting here); the social order disrupted; the moral order
ignored; vice and folly everywhere; the patron-client relation horribly de-
based. He takes us with him into Rome's streets to witness the horrible
scene. But who is the speaker, and how should he be judged? We call him
"Juvenal" or "the satirist" to remind ourselves that the speaker is a persona,
not the author himself—though he may voice many of the author's own
feelings, prejudices, and concerns.[1] Also Juvenal makes it clear from the
start that his satire is a performance, or better (this comes close to Persius's
Satire 1) an antiperformance, a creative "revenge" on the long and tedious
public recitations of mediocre epic, lyric, and drama to which he has been
subjected. For he, too, as he says, learned declamatory techniques at school:

> et nos ergo manum ferulae subduximus, et nos
> consilium dedimus Sullae, privatus ut altum
> dormiret. (1.15–17)

> [I, too, have snatched my hand from under the cane; I, too,
> have tendered advice to Sulla to retire from public life
> and sleep the sleep of the just.][2] (trans. Rudd)

These neatly turned lines convey an ironic continuity, together with in-
tense weariness and boredom, from the schoolboy's remembered struggle
to write and recite half-decent compositions on tired old themes ("Should
George Washington, having beaten the British, make himself a king?") to
all those uninspired modern productions of poetry, with their trite subject-
matter and pseudo-modernistic style, to which Juvenal has been forced to
listen again and again and again. By contrast, he himself is compelled, sim-
ply compelled to write by the never-before-witnessed superabundance of
folly and triumph of vice: not only to write satire, but to write it in the

grand style of oratory, returning it to its old, grandiloquent, epic heights. Spread wide the sails, drive the (Lucilian) war-chariot over the plains!

It is hard to judge this speaker, to differentiate this persona from the author who may even now be giving a *recitatio* or performance. Are we meant to laugh at how he is carried away by his own passion, leaping impetuously from one idea or prejudice to another? Listening to his harangue, should we be learning (as from Horace and Persius) to become more reasonable, honest, and charitable human beings? That is not clear. Reading Juvenal might actually make us more cynical than before, less inclined to struggle for decency and justice in public life. What does seem clear is that appreciation of Juvenal begins in pleasure. Thus Dryden, in 1693:

> *Juvenal* [as against Horace; Persius has become third man out] is of a more Vigorous and Masculine Wit, he gives me as much Pleasure as I can bear: He fully satisfies my Expectation, he Treats his Subject home: His Spleen is raised, and he raises mine: I have the Pleasure of Concernment in all he says; He drives his Reader along with him. . . . When he gives over, 'tis a sign the Subject is exhausted, and the Wit of Man can carry it no further.[3]

It almost sounds pornographic (at least, to a reader of Persius or Juvenal); it raises questions of the reader's complicity, even today, in the emotional release of prejudice, anger, and hostility, however vicariously expressed or tempered by humor; yet this delight in Juvenal's artistic imagination and skill, with all its expansiveness and force of emotional persuasion, is still where criticism must begin, if not end. It will be hard, in retrospect, for Persius to compete.

In *Satire* 1, Juvenal provokes *indignatio* most powerfully through a series of running contrasts between the self-indulgent yet miserly rich and the needy, forgotten poor. Although *avaritia* and *luxuria* are usually treated as opposites, as in Persius's *Satire* 5, Juvenal pictures an unholy alliance of the two:

> When did the pocket of greed gape wider? When was our dicing
> ever so reckless?. . . .
>   Is it just simple madness to lose a hundred
> thousand, and then refuse a shirt to a shivering slave?
> Which of our grandfathers built so many villas, or dined off
> seven courses, alone?   (1.87–95)

This is not just wastefulness, not just extravagance of building or (as in Lucilius) dining, but something new: the solitary glutton.

Juvenal then takes us through a poor man's long, frustrating day. It begins with the *sportula*, once a real "basket" of food, part of the old system of reciprocal exchange of care by the rich and respectful attendance by the poor, but now debased into a small hand-out of money at the gate—but, even there, the needy poor are crowded out by the old nobility, whose birth and social rank, they loudly proclaim, entitles them to be first in line, and by the even greedier *nouveaux riches*, whose enormous wealth entitles them, as also by welfare frauds. At the day's end the poor clients, old and tired, depart the rich man's house without any supper, to buy a meager bit of cabbage and firewood, while their nonpatron dines extravagantly on all the good things of land and sea, and dines—contrary to all custom and decency—entirely alone. "Who could bear this *stinginess of luxury*? " Juvenal asks. "How enormous that gullet has to be, that serves itself entire boars— an animal born for dinner-parties! " But there is a twist, recalling Persius (and, behind him, Horace):[4]

poena tamen praesens, cum tu deponis amictus
turgidus et crudum pavonem in balnea portas.
hinc subitae mortes atque intestata senectus.
it nova nec tristis per cunctas fabula cenas;
ducitur iratis plaudendum funus amicis.   (1.142–46)

[But a reckoning is nigh. When you strip and, within that bloated
body, carry an undigested peacock into the bath-house,
death steps in, too quick for a will; old age is cancelled.
At once the joyful news goes dancing around the dinners.
The funeral cortege departs to the cheers of indignant friends.]

In Persius's *Satire* 3, the sick man's apoplexy crowned a warning parable. Disregarding the Stoic philosopher's teaching is quite as dangerous as ignoring the advice of a doctor who descries the symptoms of a deadly fever. Unusually, Juvenal here omits, not augments, Persius's ugliest details. After the funny peacock business—an extravagant host might have a peacock borne showily into the dining-room, but this man dines alone, then carries that whole "undigested peacock" in his belly into the baths—there is an ellipse between life and the aftermath of death. In Persius, "yesterday's freedmen," newly emancipated by their master's sudden death, carry out his bier. Juvenal adds further strokes of irony. First, the dead man becomes a "fabula," a topic of dinner-party conversation. Second, the little funeral procession is "applauded" ("plaudendum") instead of "lamented" ("plangendum"), by angry "amicis," a word literally meaning "friends" and traditionally used of both patron and client.[5] Had the rich man treated his dependents decently—had he shared his food with others—he might have had real friends to weep at his death. I think of Scrooge's vision in *A Christmas Carol*:

"It's likely to be a very cheap funeral," said the same speaker; "for upon my life I don't know anybody to go to it. Suppose we make up a party and volunteer? "

"I don't mind going if a lunch is provided," observed the gentleman with the excrescence on his nose. "But I must be fed, if I make one."

Another laugh.[6]

But Dickens, unlike Juvenal, allows the wretched old miser to repent before it is really too late.

Persius concludes *Satire* 3 with a philosophical test, probing for weaknesses of soul. He ends with cold and heat: briefly, the chill of fear, then the blood boiling, the eyes blazing with anger, the examinee (as in Horace) turning madman. Juvenal then picks up this fire imagery in the climactic passage of *Satire* 1 following the "sudden-death" vignette.. Earlier people, says the would-be satirist (meaning Lucilius), "wrote simply and honestly whatever they wanted with their blazing mind" (*animo flagrante*). "Set down Tigellinus," says his would-be adviser or more cautious self, "and you'll be made a living torch." Even earlier, "Whenever burning Lucilius raged," that fierce warrior, listeners went cold and hot with guilty feelings. So Juvenal compromises: "I'll try and see what may be permitted against those whose ashes are buried along the Flaminian and Latin Ways." He'll speak ill only of the dead, like Tigellinus (above), prefect under Nero. At the same time, he ends his prospectus with death and burial. The hot ashes— of angry satirists, together with their victims—have grown cold. A reminder, often repeated in Juvenal, of the "Vanity of Human Wishes."

Satire 2

Persius's presence is especially noticeable in Juvenal's *Satire* 1 and also in *Satire* 7, on the unhappy condition of poets and other intellectual workers, especially teachers. Before *Satire* 7, however, I want to look at *Satire* 2, on gender inversion and (in part) hypocrisy, which helps us read Persius's *Satire* 4 with greater confidence, yet brings us back to moral ambiguities in that poem which Juvenal may have chosen to simplify or ignore.

Look again at lines 33–41, quoted and discussed earlier, of which Dryden says:

> As for the Chastity of his Thoughts, *Casaubon* denies not, but that one particular passage, in the Fourth Satire, *At, si unctus cesses*, &c. is not only the most obscure, but the most obscene of all his Works: I understood it, but for that Reason turn'd it over.[7]

(Has anyone suspected a joke here?) Certainly, we feel relief when we turn from this intense passage to Juvenal's more lucid and extensive portrayal of Roman pathics in *Satire* 2, beginning with an attack on hypocritical preachers of old-time morality, whose houses are filled with busts of Greek philosophers:

frontis nulla fides; quis enim non vicus abundat
tristibus obscenis? castigas turpia, cum sis
inter Socraticos notissima fossa cinaedos?
hispida membra quidem et durae per bracchia saetae
promittunt atrocem animum, sed podice levi
caeduntur tumidae medico ridente mariscae. . . .   (2.8–13)

[Faces are not to be trusted. Why, every street is just full
of stern-faced sodomites. How can you lash corruption when *you*
are the most notorious furrow among our Socratic fairies?
Hirsute limbs, it is true, and arms that are stiff with bristles,
bespeak "a soul of adamant"; but your anus is smooth, as the surgeon
notes with a grin when he takes a knife to your swollen piles.]

And again, after stating his preference for the simpler, more obvious pathic
whose facial expression and effeminate gait give him away, he resumes:

sed peiores, qui talia verbis
Herculis invadunt et de virtute locuti
clunem agitant.   (2. 19–21)

[Far worse are those who condemn perversion
in Hercules' style, and having held forth about manly virtue,
wiggle their rumps.]

It is great fun: the pithy summary ("frontis nulla fides"); the forcible juxta-
position of opposites; the contrast of high language and low; the syntactic
and metrical build-up before the highlighted fall into obscene revelation;
the seeming-spontaneous yet highly structured restatements of the same
basic point or contrast. We are carried along easily by the flow, laughing
at the punch-lines, proclaiming (a little too loudly?) our complete assent.

Again, the outward movement of *Satire* 2 is reassuringly easy to follow.
Juvenal takes us by well-marked transitions and easy escalation from hy-
pocrisy to shamelessness, which is even worse; to Creticus, who prosecutes
adulteresses while exhibiting himself in thin, diaphanous clothing; from
private orgies to Gracchus's public marriage ceremony—and, to top that,
his masochistic, totally degrading self-spectacle in the arena. Geographi-
cally, too, the spread of corruption is easily traced: not, as usual, from
the provinces inward to Rome (in *Satire* 3, it will be the influx of all
those demoralizing Greeks), but from Rome now outward to the hitherto
innocent frontiers.

The speakers, too, are clearly delineated. The main speaker, though un-
named, "is immediately established as the raging, indignant, narrow-
minded, chauvinistic bigot of Satire 1, who sees Rome as a city seething
with corruption."[8] A second speaker, Laronia, intervenes at lines 36–63,

responding to moralistic invocations of the adultery law with her own out-
spoken attack on hypocritical pathics. This is not, of course, a genuine
female voice. But it anticipates further experiments with persona, from the
disgruntled "Umbricius" of *Satire* 3, who assumes the main body of Juve-
nal's complaint against the City, allowing the author to remain largely de-
tached, to Naevolus, the unhappy bisexual stud of *Satire* 9, who shows
himself just as small-minded, greedy, petulant, and ridiculous as the rich
pathic Virro whom he has serviced for so long, with so little reward. We
have come a long way from the hapless dependents of *Satire* 1, with whom
Juvenal seems to have felt genuine sympathy. Perhaps long years of living
and writing satire have brought him Democritean detachment. Or perhaps
he is just tired of hearing, or even voicing, complaints.

Back, then, to Persius: may we read his sunbather more confidently now
as a hypocrite whose depilated nether parts belie the promise of his Stoic
beard?[9] That would seem reasonable; yet Persius's abrupt transitions and
shifts of speaker leave us uncertain about the accuracy and relevance of this
particular moral judgment. Is Persius suggesting that those who avoid the
one extreme, of *avaritia*, succumb all too easily to the other extreme, of
self-indulgence, *luxuria*? Is the judgment deserved or merely slanderous?
And, if deserved, is it fair retribution (much as in *Juvenal* 2) for the hypo-
critical moralist who has just raised laughter against the miser? Maybe so,
but Persius abruptly and confusingly shifts direction. First, with *populo mar-
centis pandere vulvas* ("spread open your withered portals for the people"):
a suggestion of male prostitution, recalling the treatment of Alcibiades ear-
lier—but this pathetic old deviant is no Alcibiades. And second, with the
metaphor of sterility, commonly associated with pathics who cannot bear
children (see, again, *Juvenal* 2 and 9), but which Persius develops into his
larger "Waste Land" vision of moral and social breakdown.

In the end, Persius is less interested in homosexuality or even hypocrisy
than in failure of self-knowledge, which includes projection of faults upon
others. As you and I enjoy and play out for ourselves those satiric vignettes
of the miser and the sunbather, recreating the malicious voices of Roman
gossip, we become complicit in self-ignorance, distracted from self-
knowledge, caught up in the malicious war of all against all. "That's how
we live, that's all we 'know' " (*vivitur hoc pacto, sic novimus*). When Persius
ends, "Live with yourself; know how much your furnishings fall short," he
is offering a satiric version of the Socratic watchword, "Know Thyself."
The satirist is implicated, with all the rest of us, in the pleasures of malice,
slander, and projection. Morally speaking, he has reached a dead end.

And Juvenal? Does he, unlike Laronia, convict himself of hypocritical
moralizing? Does he make us realize our voyeuristic complicity in those
impressive denunciations of vice? That is not clear. Perhaps his satiric per-
formance is cathartic, clearing our minds and hearts by the strong expres-

sion of anger and indignation, then bringing us to finer, postmoralistic judgments? Or does he train us to be satirists ourselves, so that when we hear, for example, "Christian" preachers denouncing gays and lesbians, we may find an appropriate retort?

Satire 7

Persius's influence is especially noticeable in *Satire* 7, on the material dependency of intellectual workers, especially poets, and their need of patronage (usually lacking nowadays, despite an emperor's generosity). It is remarkable how much of Juvenal's material, however expanded and clarified, with many memorable effects, is already present in Persius's *Satire* 1. Recall his three *recitatio* scenes, rendered now in Brooks's fine translation:[10]

> We write shut up like sages, verse or prose,
> Some spacious thing, to exercise the soul
> And stretch the lungs. Now for the public pose;
> Coiffure, clean toga with the birthday stone
> (Sardonychal splendor): up to the speaker's station:
> Recite: the throat is syrupy: the eyes
> Languish duly, hinting at copulation.
> Then see, in no strict mode or quiet tone,
> Our high patricians palpitate, as song
> Enters their loins trilling, to scrape the bone.
> (Old pimp, collecting scraps for others' ears,
> Till, stripped, you beg them to be left alone.)
>
> "Why learn, unless the germinal, the wild fig-tree
> Once inborn, splits the heart's case to appear?"
> Look at your pallor and old age. Lord, must it be
> Nothing at all for you to know, unless
> Another comes to know your knowingness?
>
> "But think of fame: to draw the indication
> Of tongues and fingers pointing, to provide
> Legions of schoolboys with their recitation,
> Is it all nothing?"
>
>   Discovered, dining well
> And well drunk, the sons of Romulus. They seek
> What tales celestial poetry has to tell.
> Enter one appareled in a violet cape,
> Droning some mouldy morsel through his nose;

All Phyllises, Hypsipyles, the bards'
Drippings he redistills, and shuffles woes
Over his lisping palate.

                        Our heroes cheer,
The poet's dust receives the accolade;
The headstone presses lighter on his bones.
The banqueters applaud; now from the shade,
Now from the mound and beatific ash
Let violets spring. "Mocking," you say, "denotes
A loftiness in the nose. Will any man deny
Wanting the people's well-deserved votes,
His words entrusted to archival store,
Encedared poems which fear no second use
As haddock-wrappings or excelsior? "

Opponent, or whoever you may be
I've made to contradict, by no means, when
I write, if something turns out decently,
Do I fear praise; my bowels are not of bone.
But the end and term of right I will refuse
To be your "excellent" and "nicely done."
Shake out this "nicely"; what do you find
That's not inside? Look, Attius' Iliad
Blind drunk on hellebore, see, elegy
Dictated belching by some Aenead,
And at the bottom, all that's written from
The citron couches of celebrity.
You serve hot tripe, donate an ancient coat
To your gooseflesh retainer, and "Honesty,
Please, honesty" you ask; "say what you think
Of me." How can he? Let me speak his piece.
You and your poetic trifles, baldhead, . . .

And now, *Juvenal* 7.36–47:

Here are his tricks. To avoid giving *you* any money, that patron, for
whose service you have left the temple of the Muses and Apollo,
composes verses himself, and is second only to Homer (well, *he's* a
thousand years older). If the heady prospect of fame leads you to give a
recital, he lends you a damp-mottled building, a house pressed into
service although it has been locked for years, with a door which makes
a noise like a herd of frightened pigs. He's good at supplying freedmen
to sit at the end of each row, and at placing his attendants' booming

voices around the hall; but none of your lordships will ever provide the cost of the benches, or the tiers of seats which are raised aloft on a rented framework, or the front-row chairs which must be returned when the show is over.

The contrast is powerful, between what the patron is skilled at providing—all that tumult of flattering applause (usually, one imagines, for his wonderful self)—and what he grudgingly provides, and mostly does *not* provide, for his needy poet-dependent.[11] Note also the escalation of material requirements since Persius's time. For what has become a big theatrical production, albeit in a disgusting, old, rented house, all these *things* are needed, from benches for the lesser folk to comfortable chairs for the elite: things that students today must struggle to visualize, and scholars to explicate, but which already in Juvenal suggest the overwhelming mass of material needs by which the poor aspiring poet is overwhelmed.

And always was. Only a spirit free from daily anxiety can produce great poetry, roaming freely through the Muses' woods and streams; "Horace's belly is full" when he writes his Bacchic odes (*satur est cum dicit Horatius "euhoe"*), and without servants and decent household arrangements, Virgil could never have sung of battles, trumpets, war-chariots, and Furies. The contrasts, between inspired song and lowdown ordinary needs, are very funny. They also reflect inwardly, on satire writing: first, because *satura* originally meant "a miscellany" (as Juvenal recalls in *Satire* 1.85–86, proclaiming that all the actions, desires, fears, and other passions of humankind will constitute the *farrago* ["mish-mash," "medley"] of his book); and second, because Horace played programmatically on *satis, satur,* and *satura* at the end of his first satire:

> inde fit ut raro qui se vixisse beatum
> dicat, et exacto contentus tempore vita
> cedat uti conviva satur, reperire queamus.
> iam satis est. ne me Crispini scrinia lippi
> compilasse putes, verbum non amplius addam.   (1.117–21)

> [Which is why we rarely can find a person who can say
> his life's been happy, who can depart content, like a full-fed
> dinner-guest, when his span of life is done. Now, that's enough.
> So you won't think I've ransacked Crispinus's desk, I won't
> add a word more.]

Unlike the greedy misers of *Satire* 1 who pile up riches they can never enjoy, Horace urges Epicurean contentment, which will culminate in a grateful departure from life; similarly, he knows in satire writing (as perhaps Lucilius did not) when enough is enough. The literary ideal is Callimachean, closely paralleled in Virgil's *Eclogues*: "Keep my goats fat but my spirit thin." But Maecenas, Juvenal implies, was a generous patron who kept his poets well fed—unlike "Numitor" today:

> [Impoverished Numitor has nothing to give his client; he does
> have enough for gifts to Quintilla; nor did he lack the funds
> to buy a lion (already tamed), who had to be fed
> with masses of meat. I suppose a beast is less expensive,
> and it takes so very much more to fill a poet's guts.]   (7.74–78)

Juvenal never alludes obviously to Persius's *Choliambics*, which refer all production of poetry (not to add, what passes for criticism) to the belly's imperious needs.[12] But after mocking Lucan, who could be "content with fame in his marble gardens," he describes Statius's poetry and performances in erotic terms reminiscent of Persius's *Satire* 1:

> curritur ad vocem iucundam et carmen amicae
> Thebaidos, laetam cum fecit Statius urbem
> promisitque diem: tanta dulcedine captos
> adficit ille animos tantaque libidine volgi
> auditur. sed cum fregit subsellia versu
> esurit, intactam Paridi nisi vendit Agaven.   (7.82–87)

> [When Statius has made the city happy by fixing a day,
> there's a rush to hear his attractive voice and the strains of his darling
> *Thebaid*. He duly holds their hearts enthralled by his sweetness;
> and the people listen in total rapture. But when, with his verses,
> he has caused them all to break the benches in their wild excitement,
> he starves—unless he can sell his virgin *Agave* to Paris.]

Statius's charming epic, *The Thebaid*, is portrayed here as a prostitute, with Statius as the pimp who arranges her assignations. His recitations "break up" the audience with orgiastic delight (recalling, but simplifying, the complex homoerotic transactions between poet and audience in Persius's *Satire* 1.15–23), but it all comes to nothing unless he can sell his virgin tragedy *Agave* to the producer/dancer Paris. The stage is everything now. The stage grants riches, grants nobility. But there is no Maecenas, no adequate or even semiadequate patron to justify a poet's pallor and self-discipline today.

After reviewing the (mostly) unrewarded and unrewarding efforts of historians, lawyers, and professors of rhetoric, Juvenal comes at last to the lowly schoolmaster who teaches poetry, including Horace and Virgil, to unruly schoolboys. The poets' fate here completes and further ironizes the earlier section on poetry, with creative allusions both to Horace and to Persius using Horace. In *Satires* 1.10, Horace says that a good writer must be satisfied, as he is, with a few good readers; "Or [he asks scornfully] are you so crazy as to want your poems to be dictated in cheap schools? "

Differently, in *Epistles* 1.20, he envisions his poetry book after publication as an ambitious young male prostitute, well-treated at first, but then coming down in the world until finally he becomes an aged schoolmaster teaching children their ABCs. Persius draws on the earlier passage, and on Horace's expression of pleasure in *Odes* 4.3 at being "pointed out by the fingers of passers-by" (*quod monstror digito praetereuntium*, 22), for his interlocutor's protest that poetic fame is desirable:

> "at pulchrum est digito monstrari et dicier 'hic est.'
> ten cirratorum centum dictata fuisse
> pro nihilo pendes? "　　　　　　　　　　　　　　　(1.28–30)

Not only is finger-pointing ambiguous, suggesting (in a context replete with obscene metaphors) that universally obscene gesture, but the schoolchildren become a curly-headed mob, and the poet has been transformed, as though dead (in the interlocutor's confused imagining), into an object of dictation. It is as though he were dreaming, looking back at himself from the other side of the grave.

Persius's interlocutor, again, wants to live (following an old poetic tradition) on people's lips, and to leave writings worthy of preservation with cedar oil, unafraid of (being used as scrap paper to wrap) mackerels and incense. The whole point is to survive. But Juvenal's schoolmaster endures inadequate pay, long hours, and inhuman teaching conditions in the modest hope that not all his efforts will perish:

> dummodo non pereat totidem olfecisse lucernas
> quot stabant pueri, cum totus decolor esset
> Flaccus et haereret nigro fuligo Maroni.　　　　　(7.225–27)

> [provided there's *some* return for smelling all those lamps
> (one for every boy in the class) while Flaccus went dark
> all over, and Maro was covered by a layer of filthy soot.]

Poets are preserved at a cost. Quintus Horatius Flaccus (one of those apotropaic Roman *cognomina*, meaning "weary" or "limp"—so too, in the satiric succession, Aulus Persius Flaccus) has become what he humorously predicted, or worse: a begrimed, smoke-blackened schoolbook.[13] ("Take out your *Flaccus* and read from the top of page four, being mindful of ictus and word-accent! ") So too with [P. Vergilius] "Maro." By contrast, the teacher is expected to possess encyclopedic, even impossible knowledge, so that he can answer the most absurd and trivial Virgil questions, such as: "What was the name of Anchises' nurse? " "Precisely how many jars of wine did the Sicilians give to the Trojans? " Literary understanding has been reduced to a game of Trivial Pursuit.

We may, still, in our own rebelliousness, enjoy seeing the examiner examined, but the gap between parental expectations and school performance becomes fully absurd, if not tragic, toward the satire's end. In an earlier passage on the *rhetor*, Juvenal invoked blessings on the ancestors who "wanted the teacher to be in the place of a revered parent" (*sancti . . . parentis . . . loco*, 209–10). Similarly, the *grammaticus* is expected to shape the children's morals:

> exigite ut mores teneros ceu pollice ducat,
> ut si quis cera vultum facit; exigite ut sit
> is pater ipsius coetus, ne turpia ludant,
> ne faciant vicibus. Non est leve tot puerorum
> observare manus oculosque in fine trementis.   (7.237–41)

[Make sure that he moulds the children's characters, just as a sculptor
models a face from wax with his thumb. Make sure that in fact
he's a father to the group, to stop them playing indecent tricks
and doing it to each other. With so many pupils, it's hard
to watch the hurried movements of hand and eye at a climax.]

The passage carries ironic echoes, from Horace's defense of the value of poetry, in *Epistles* 2.1, to Augustus,

> os tenerum pueri balbumque poeta figurat,
> torquet ab obscenis iam nunc sermonibus aurem,
> mox etiam pectus praeceptis format amicis,
> asperitatis et invidiae corrector et irae; . . .   (126–29)

[The poet shapes the tender lips of youth
and turns its ear to decency and truth;
his soft instruction so informs the mind
that malice fades and roughness is refined. . . .]

and from Persius's tribute to Cornutus in *Satire* 5.39–40:

> et premitur ratione animus vincique laborat
> artificemque tuo ducit sub pollice voltum.

[and impressed by reason, the mind struggles to surrender,
producing an artful face beneath your thumb.]

If poets shape our humanity, then teachers of poetry have a noble calling. Unfortunately, Juvenal's schoolmaster must give most of his attention to seeing, or trying to see, that the older boys don't masturbate each other at the back of the classroom. So much for teaching, and for poetry.

Does Juvenal, we might ask, reflect like Persius on the value and meaning of his own satire writing? He does so only once, perhaps, and fleetingly, right after those rented benches, chairs, and other recitation-furnishings:

> nos tamen hoc agimus tenuique in pulvere sulcos
> ducimus et litus sterili versamus aratro.
> nam si discedas, tenet insanabile multos
> scribendi cacoethes et aegro in corde senescit.   (7.48–52)

> [We still keep at it, however, driving furrows along
> the powdery dust, and turning the shore with our barren plow.
> For if you try to break free, you are held in a noose by the craving
> to excel as a writer, which becomes a chronic disease in your heart.]

Is the first person plural, "nos . . . agimus," more than rhetorically tactful self-inclusion in the ranks of unrewarded poets? Or does Juvenal give way momentarily to a personal sense of futility and discouragement? We write still, as in *Satire* 1, because we must—because the compulsion to write, like any other neurosis, must be obeyed. Yet satire writing, like all poetry writing, is finally unproductive: not only because generous patrons and adequate rewards for good writing are lacking nowadays, but because we ourselves and our best efforts, themselves contingent on circumstance, come to dust in the end. Persius would have pursued the "writer's itch" to its psychological roots, diagnosed the illness in himself, as in others, and handed it over to the philosopher-surgeon for healing. Juvenal, more fatalistic, moves toward his "Vanity of Human Wishes" in *Satire* 10. Had he written a book about his own satire writing, he might well have called it *The Sterile Plough*.

Satire 10

My own early teachers dictated poems to us, steeped our minds and imaginations in poetry while stressing English grammar. We had, for example, Gray's *Elegy in a Country Churchyard*:

> The boast of heraldry, the pomp of power,
> And all that beauty, all that wealth e'er gave
> Awaits alike the inevitable hour:
> The paths of glory lead but to the grave.

Awaits, Mr. Edwards insisted, not *Await*: *boast* as object, *hour* as subject. And we had Shelley's *Ozymandias*:

> I met a traveler in an antique land
> Who said, a vast and trunkless head of stone
> Stands in the desert. . . .

Juvenal would have liked this little sonnet about the vanity of human pre-
tensions and dreams of grandeur, giving reader reception bonus points
when some boy inevitably said, "stands in the *dessert*," driving poor Mr.
Edwards wild.

Juvenal's *Satire* 10, often called "The Vanity of Human Wishes" after
Johnson's great *Imitation*, develops a familiar theme with familiar subhead-
ings: wealth, power, eloquence, military glory, long life, and beauty. Horace
reworked this traditional diatribe material in *Satires* 2.3 and *Epistles* 1.6; so
too Persius, in *Satire* 5. His *Satire* 2, on vicious, foolish, and deluded prayers
(*vota*), sometimes negated by people's self-defeating practices, surely in-
fluenced *Juvenal* 10. More significantly, Juvenal has taken the opening line
of Persius's *Satire* 1, "O curas hominum! o quantum est in rebus inane! ",
and run with it, but without letting himself be distracted like Persius by an
interlocutor who would turn the question against the poet-satirist himself.
Yet Persius, I think, is never quite forgotten, as two passages on military
glory will show.

First, on Hannibal. In a few lines Juvenal describes his swift campaign,
his remarkable ambitions and achievements—but always humorously
undercut ("Nothing's been accomplished, if I don't . . . set down my stan-
dard in the middle of the Subura" [Rome's low-life district]; "What a photo
opportunity: the one-eyed general on the Gaetulian beast"). Then a fast
cut, to Hannibal's flight into exile—that amazing new client at a barbarian
court, waiting for the local kinglet to wake up—and his death:

finem animae, quae res humanas miscuit olim,
non gladii, non saxa dabut nec tela, sed ille
Cannarum vindex et tanti sanguinis ultor
anulus. i, demens, et saevas curre per Alpes
ut pueris placeas et declamatio fias.   (10.163–67)

[That soul which once convulsed the world will meet its end,
not from a sword, or stones, or spears, but from an object
which, avenging Cannae, will take reprisal for all that bloodshed—
a ring. Go on, you maniac; charge through the Alpine wastes
to entertain a class of boys and become an oration!]

A doubly anticlimactic end: first, death (by poison) from such a little ring;
but then, life turned into story, to entertain schoolchildren, and into a set
theme for composition and recitation, *declamatio*.

This last anticlimax takes us back to the section on teachers of rhetoric
in *Satire* 7, beginning *declamare doces*? (150, "Do you teach declamation? ").
Here Juvenal conveys the unutterable weariness, boredom, and frustration
of having to listen to all those trite compositions—and each one twice, read
sitting and recited standing, about the Athenian tyrant-slayers—but it is

the poor teacher who is really being slain by all this "repeated garbage." And then there is the struggle to get your pay when, after you've taught them to argue like lawyers, they claim they've learned nothing (an old joke and controversy):

"culpa docentis
scilicet arguitur, quod laevae parte mamillae
nil salit Arcadico iuveni, cuius mihi sexta
quaque die miserum dirus caput Hannibal implet,
quidquid id est de quo deliberat, an petat urbem
a Cannis, an post nimbos et fulmina cautus
circumagat madidas a tempestate cohortes.
quantum vis stipulare et protinus accipe: quid do
ut totiens illum pater audiat?"   (7.158–66)

["No doubt it's the teacher's
fault that our young Arcadian bumpkin feels not a spark
of intellectual power in his skull, when at five-day intervals
he pounds his 'Hannibal the Terrible' into my aching head,
no matter what the question at issue (should he strike at the city
straight from Cannae, or after the thunderstorm should he play safe
and order his rain-soaked cohorts to do an about turn?).
State your price, and I'll pay on the nail, whatever it costs,
if only his father could hear him as often as I do."]

Hannibal is still "dirus," wickedly dangerous for the exhausted teacher now who must listen to repeated "suasoriae," exhortations to Hannibal either to march directly on Rome or to take warning from portents and avoid the city. For his climax, Juvenal inverts a passage from Persius's *Satire* 3, on playing hooky from school:

saepe oculos, memini, tangebam parvus olivo,
grandia si nollem morituri verba Catonis
discere non sano multum laudanda magistro,
quae pater adductis sudans audiret amicis.   (3.44–47)

[I remember, when I was small, I would smear ointment
on my eyes when I didn't want to work on some big speech
for Cato facing death, a speech my dad might bring his friends
to hear, sweating profusely.]

Note, again, the contradiction between the moral beauty of Cato's suicide and the practical use to which it is here subjected. For Persius, the sweating fathers represent the misguided values of the so-called grown-up world. For Juvenal's weary teacher, the best revenge would be to make the father listen to all, yes *all*, of this accumulated rubbish himself.

Returning to *Juvenal* 10, an earlier, introductory passage describes that wished-for military glory in terms of spoils displayed—all those *things*, again, and most of them broken—and triumphal arches with sculptured reliefs.[14] It's all about rewards and reputation, not virtue:

> patriam tamen obruit olim
> gloria paucorum et laudis titulique cupido
> haesuri saxis cinerum custodibus, ad quae
> discutienda valent sterilis mala robora fici,
> quandoquidem data sunt ipsis quoque fata sepulchris.   (10.142–46)

> [Often states have been ruined by a few men's
> greed for fame, by their passion for praise and for titles inscribed
> in the stones protecting their ashes—stones which the boorish
> strength of the barren fig-tree succeeds in splitting apart;
> for even funeral monuments have their allotted life-span.]

Juvenal draws here on two passages in Persius's *Satire* 1: the sardonic lines (translated above) about how happy the dead poet must be in his tomb, now that he is praised at fashionable dinner-parties:

> adsensere viri: nunc non cinis ille poetae
> felix? Non levior cippus nunc inprimit ossa?
> laudant convivae: nunc non e manibus illis,
> nunc non e tumulo fortunataque favilla
> nascentur violae?   (1.36–40)

The lines play on the traditional pious wish, *sit tibi terra levis* ("May the earth rest lightly on your bones"), as well as the grotesque metaphorical expression of poetic inspiration that Persius gives to his interlocutor earlier,

> "quo didicisse, nisi hoc fermentum et quae semel intus
> innata est rupto iecore exierit caprificus?"   (1.24–25)

Here the violent demand of inner feeling to burst out, to find expression somehow—a demand closely bound up with the satirist's own dominant theme of speaking out—culminates in a grotesque image of sterility (with homosexual associations), disease, and self-destruction. What Juvenal has intuitively grasped is that the two passages are imaginatively connected, that the wild fig-tree bursting the liver anticipates (elided in Persius, spelled out in Juvenal) the wild fig-tree bursting through the tomb. In Persius, it is the poet's honesty that must somehow break through all those literary/social pretenses and disguises. In Juvenal, death and decay have the last words, mocking our Ozymandian efforts—"Look on my works, ye mighty, and despair!"—to commemorate ourselves through monuments that will last.

Juvenal ends *Satire* 1 by asking what, if anything, we should pray for, when so many human hopes and aspirations end in failure. Let me compare three endings, piling Juvenal on Horace and Persius on Juvenal.

In *Epistles* 1.18, after warning young Lollius about the difficulties and dangers of serving a powerful patron, Horace describes his own happiness and relief at returning, once more, to his beloved countryside, watered by the cold Digentia that restores him to himself (*me quotiens reficit . . .*). How does he feel, then? What are his prayers?

> sit mihi, quod nunc est, etiam minus, et mihi vivam
> quod superest aevi, si quid superesse volunt di;
> sit bona librorum et provisae frugis in annum
> copia, nec fluitem dubiae spe pendulus horae.
> sed satis est orare Iovem qui ponit et aufert,
> det vitam, det opes: aequum mi animum ipse parabo.   (107–12)

> [May I have what I have now, or less. May I live out my remaining
> time, if the gods wish me to have more time. May I have a good
> supply of books and food provisions for the coming year, and
> not hang in suspense before each uncertain hour. But it's enough
> to ask Jupiter, who gives and takes, for life and means; a good,
> balanced mind I'll provide for myself.]

His syntax illustrates the intended balance. He asks for longer life, but only as the gods see fit; asks for books and food, the mind's need right up there with the body's; asks for the security, the life and means, that only the gods can give, but will do his part too, by contributing a proper and sane disposition—by which all these good things can be used rightly and enjoyed.

Juvenal's ending is ironic, skeptical, and funny. "If you'll take my advice," he says, "you'll allow the gods to measure out what best suits us, what will serve us best, instead of asking for great things that may not turn out well. Still, if you *must* pray for something—if you *must* sacrifice those divine little porker sausages—then you'd best pray for a healthy mind in a healthy body (*mens sana in corpore sano*), and good attitudes toward length of life, hard work, and so forth:

> monstro quod ipse tibi possis dare; semita certe
> tranquillae per virtutem patet unica vitae.
> nullum numen habes, si sit prudentia; nos te,
> nos facimus, Fortuna, deam caeloque locamus.   (10.363–66)

> [The things that I recommend you can grant to yourself; it is certain
> that the tranquil life can only be reached by the path of goodness.
> Lady Luck, if the truth were known, you possess no power;
> it is we who make you a goddess and give you a place in heaven.]

A strong ending, but we have moved far from Horace's thoughtful, carefully balanced wishes, and from prayer.

Compare now the ending of Persius's *Satire 2*:

quin damus id superis, de magna quod dare lance
non possit magni Messalae lippa propago?
conpositum ius fasque animo sanctosque recessus
mentis et incoctum generoso pectus honesto.
haec cedo ut admoveam templis et farre litabo.   (2.71–75)

[Why don't we give the gods what great Messala's bleary- eyed
offspring couldn't give from his great big platter: a settled regard
for laws human and divine; inmost thoughts holy and pure; a heart
deep-dyed with nobility and goodness. Let me just bring these
to the temples, and a plain meal-offering will be acceptable.]

Throughout this satire Persius has denounced evildoing, folly, and superstition in religious matters; he has contrasted inner viciousness with outward shows of observance; he has ridiculed superstitious prayers, self-defeating animal sacrifices, and the gilding of statues, the projecting of perverted human values upon the gods. In the end, like Horace and Juvenal, he lists what he himself will provide, in terms that suggest the hard-won effects ("conpositum," "incoctum") of moral training and practice. Holiness lies not in outward rituals but in a deep-set integrity of mind and soul, deserving of true reverence ("sanctosque recessus mentis"). Yet all this is set in a humbly hypothetical frame, from "quin damus" (a modest proposal, "Why don't we give . . . ? ") to "haec cedo [a modest condition, 'Just let me bring these gifts'] . . . et farre litabo."[15]

It is, though hard-won as always, a touchingly simple ending.

NOTES

PROLOGUE
IN SEARCH OF PERSIUS

1. Donne's debt to Persius: Baumlin 1986, 104; Wheeler 1992, 77, quotes Thomas Freeman's 1614 verses: "Thy *Satyres* short, too soone we them o'erlooke, / I prethee *Persius* write a bigger booke." Cf. also Sullivan 1984, 7 and 49: "The so-called 'crabbedness' in Donne's Satires is sometimes attributed to his imitating the verbal complexity of Persius."

2. "Renaissance self-fashioning": from Greenblatt 1980; see Edwards 1997 on "self-scrutiny and self-transformation" as described or modeled in Seneca's letters. She notes the ambiguity of *fingere*, "to mould or fashion" (29–30), and her reflections on Thomas More (35), after Greenblatt, are highly suggestive for Seneca. Cf. also Porter 2006, 169: "Self-fashioning is the contemporary attractive idea, most recently promoted by Foucault, that subjects are not found in the world but are invented, that they can take possession of their fabricated lives by becoming their own authors." Foucault often cites Seneca's ascetic precepts; cf. *De Brev. Vit.* 24.1–3 on *se formare*, etc.

3. I quote these lines, with the older spelling from Milgate's 1967 edition, to enhance their strange intensity still today.

4. Baumlin 1986, 71; what Hester 1982, 29, says about Donne's position "as a man seeking salvation, and an artist seeking definition" fits Persius nicely. Cf. also Hutchison 1970.

5. Hester, 17.

6. For satiric personae generally, cf. Braund 1996. To modern critics' questions about person and persona, add the further confusion in which recent authors have delighted; cf. Halpern 1995, citing Borges, who begins, "It is to my other self, to Borges, that things happen," and ends, "I cannot tell which one person is writing this page." And, in the middle: [apart from language] "I am doomed to oblivion, utterly doomed, and no more than certain flashes of my existence can survive in the work of my other." Philip Roth's *The Counterlife* is a masterpiece of confusion along similar lines. Differently, Wray 2001, 164, cites Frank Bidart's criticism of the common modern idea of a protected "I," separate from the author. I would argue myself for a continuing interplay, effecting change both ways, between the author and the persona that she creates.

7. The four-person theory: Gill 1988.

8. Reydams-Schils 1998, 35.

9. Epictetus gives typical Stoic advice (1.29.41–44; 4.7.12–18): assume different roles as needed; act your part well, but do not confuse your mask and costume with yourself. Cf. also Epict. 1.2.7, 14, 28, with Dobbin's commentary, 82. Note Inwood's warning (2005) that the concept of the "self" was not yet realized in

Seneca's time; but also Sorabji 2000, 250: "The idea of acting in accordance with one's persona is the closest ancient analogue I know to the modern notion of authenticity."

10. See my discussion in 4.1 below, with notes.

11. Rostagni 1944, 167, argued for attribution (as in the mss.) to M. Valerius Probus, the famous *grammaticus* working a decade or two after Persius's death, with precise information on facts, persons, and environs. Kaster 1995, 247–48, finding no evidence that Probus ever wrote a commentary on Persius, argues rather that the *Vita* "preserves a Suetonian core, deriving from the *De Poetis.*" Could both be possible?

12. My use of [Stoic] "intentionality" follows Colish 1985, 170 and 195; cf. the Stoic emphasis on maintaining a healthy *tonos* in life, but also the emotional strain of constant attention-and-effort (*contentio, intentio*: Cic. *Tusc.* 2.23.54, 24.58).

13. Kernan 1959, 60, quotes Guy Davenport for the Elizabethan belief that a genuine satire was obscure: "The obscurity arising from the difficult and glancing allusions, the sudden and abrupt transitions of thought, the unexpected insertion of conversation not clearly divided between the speakers, and the highly-coloured rhetoric in the satires of Juvenal and Persius, was taken as characteristic of the form itself." (*Collected Poems of Joseph Hall*, xxv.) He also quotes John Marston (61): "Persius is crabby, because antient, and his ierks . . . dusky. . . . *Chaucer* is hard even to our understandings: who knowes not the reason? How much more these old Satyres which expresse themselves in terms, that breathed not long even in theyr dayes. But had we then lived, the understanding of them had been nothing hard." If, as Wheeler argues (1992, 113), Elizabethan verse satirists practiced deliberate obscurity partly for self-protection, they may also have read this motive back to their Roman predecessors.

On Persius's "obscurity," cf. also Powell 1992, 152–53: "There is no difficulty in supposing that Persius may have been clearly intelligible in his own generation, but less so thereafter; and yet the fact that his satires were preserved at all must indicate that later generations had at least some perception of his meaning and literary merits."

14. From Casaubon's introduction to his 1605 commentary on Persius (Medine, 285); he goes on to cite other difficult authors, including Thucydides, Plato, Pindar, Aristophanes, and Theocritus. Among the causes of obscurity he lists time, changes of custom, and a difficult, cultivated genre, one with frequent changes of persona, as in drama.

15. Thus, Sullivan 1984, 7: "the age that has learned to appreciate John Donne and produced the poetry of Ezra Pound, T. S.Eliot, and Wallace Stevens should not have had any difficulty with the poetry of Persius."

16. The best critical reevaluations of the older Persius criticism are in Italian: LaPenna 1981, Pasoli 1985, Squillante Saccone 1985. For our excitement but also our early reservations about the New Criticism, cf. Reckford 1991, 209–11 (with some self-satire); Putnam 2001, 329–30.

17. Author, text, reader: cf. the unusually clear and sensible review in Woodman and Powell's Epilogue (1992, 208–15). Death of the author: Barthes 1975, 45 ("As institution, the author is dead . . ."); but Barthes 1991, 165–66, reconsiders the figure of the author ("the writing subject") and toys with "the amicable return of the author." On renewed interest in the author, see now Whitmarsh 2006, 108

and n. 14 ("particularly in feminist, postcolonial, and Marxist theory"), and 107–8, quoting Bakhtin 1986a, 106: "The event of the life of the text, that is its true essence, always develops on the boundary between two consciousnesses, two subjects. The author is thus as vital a subjectivity as the reader." Whitmarsh adds, "Among his final jottings, Bakhtin distinguished 'primary' authors from 'secondary' authors: the primary author is the real human being who consciously and physically composes the work, while the secondary is the controlling consciousness within the text. The primary author is inaccessible, except insofar as the secondary author is a reflex of the primary. As readers, we engage with the secondary. Nevertheless, the interpretative process depends fundamentally upon the desire to reanimate authors in all their fullness."

18. Fish 1980; cf. 28: "Essentially what the method does is *slow down* the reading experience, so that "events" one does not notice in normal time, but which do occur, are brought before our analytical attentions." Reading is creative, criticism playful and provisional, "an interim report" (174–75). Iser 1978, 26–27: "We can say that literary texts initiate 'performances' of meaning rather than actually formulating meanings themselves." Similarly, Iser 1978 (but note his preference, ix–x, for the German term *Wirkungstheorie*, comprising both effect and response). Barthes 1991, 189: "To read a text is to discover—on a corporeal, not a conscious level—how it was written; to invest oneself in the production, not the product." Slater on Petronius: 1990, 21–22. After Jauss: Edmunds 1992, on Horace, C. 1.22, with Nauta's critique (1994, 221–24). Steiner 1989, 47: "[I]deals of immediacy, of personal engagement and answerability"; also 179, "that which comes to call on us" (visitation and summons together). Steiner argues the need of a "metaphysics of presence" to undergird the "reciprocal freedoms" of the artist's call and our response (198).

19. Fowler 2000.

20. According to Marmorale 1956, 77 and n. 3, about two-fifths of Persius's verses had Horace in them. The best introduction to his Horatian borrowings is Rudd 1976, 55–83 ("Imitations"), especially for *Satire* 1 (53–64) and Persius's possible trains of association in various places. "In Persius's case," he argues [as against Keats or Coleridge], "the reminiscences are in the main deliberate allusions and are expected to be recognized and appreciated as such. Clearly at some time he committed most of the *Sermones* [and, I would add, the *Epistles*] to memory, and he had them constantly within call when composing his Satires," although "the process leading to it [the allusion] may often have been only partly conscious" (82–83). As Hooley says (1984, 82), "Here (just as in translation) one is permitted a privileged glimpse into the adaptive and recreative workings of a poet's mind." But Edmunds's caveat (1992, 43) should also be remembered: "For philology, allusion is material that is objectively there in the text. For aesthetic reading, allusion is something that requires the participation of the reader and, if noticed, is integrated into the developing meaning of the text being read."

For the theoretical controversy regarding "Allusion and Intertext," cf. Hinds 1997, especially 47–51, on "the limits of intertextualism." If critics moved away from "allusion" because of "the ultimate unknowability of the poet's intention" (47–48), not to mention the many reductionist simplifications, whether historicizing or psychologizing, committed by "biographical intentionalists," to focus instead on the text as experienced at its multiple and democratically unprivileged points of reception, Hinds also sees a countermovement today away from both extremes, old and new: "Just as there is a philological fundamentalism which occludes broader discursive dynamics in its privileging of tight authorial control [cf. section 1], so there is an opposite kind of fundamentalism—an intertextualist fundamentalism—which privileges reader reception so single-mindedly as to wish the alluding author out of existence altogether" (48).

My own preference for "allusion" over "intertextuality" may be justified in part by the play element in *ad + ludere* ("to play with reference toward" something). Not only is this an apt term for the creative play by which human beings consciously adapt words, phrases, and lines that the unconscious, or poetic memory, supplies, but it suits the *ingenuo . . . ludo*, described above, of Persius's satire, in which two authorial intentions collide, or better, *collude*: literarily, the will to reshape and redefine Roman verse satire, after Horace, in a new, highly creative manner; and philosophically, the will to use satire as a vehicle for moral and spiritual exploration, not least of oneself.

21. For a fine account of this process, cf. Kallendorf 2006, 68–70, proposing "a . . . model that focuses on the relationship between the modern critic and the alluding author as two different but interconnected readers" (68).

22. Cf. Barthes's development (1991, 165) of the psychoanalytic notion that the reader is "in a transferential relation of self-analysis with the text." Henderson (1999, 231) uses transference and countertransference, after Lacan, in a theory of reading: "Readers do not only work on texts, but texts work on readers, and this involves a complex double dialectic of two bodies inscribed in language. . . . The writer as much as the reader is in transference with that intersubjective existent, the text." Cf. also Slater 1990, 251, on Petronius's *Satyricon*: "Like the other, canonical classical texts, it is an abiding presence, of which we are the ephemeral readings. It is their concreteness which allows us to ask whether we wish to be what the Classics read in us—and if not, to change ourselves until we read and are read aright."

23. Thus, one of my readers urged further consideration of "the larger political and social dynamics of ancient performance settings. . . . Pleasure is never innocent; it always entails the politics of our values." Fair enough; I have complied with the request (in section 1.4), but cf. Barthes 1975, 57: "No sooner has a word been said, somewhere, about the pleasure of the text, than two policemen are ready to jump on you: the political policeman and the psychoanalytic policeman: futility and/or guilt, pleasure is either idle or vain, a class notion or an illusion."

24. Bourdieu 1987.

25. Martindale 2005a, esp. 10–12, "a plea . . . to give aesthetics a turn" (10), and 119–29, a revindication of Kant's claim in his Third Critique that we can form disinterested judgments of beauty. Beauty is here "an umbrella term to describe anything in nature or art that evokes a delight-inducing play of our mental faculties in our response" (16).

26. T. S. Eliot, "Little Gidding" (1942).

CHAPTER ONE
PERFORMING PRIVATELY

1. The different views about *Satire* 1.1–2 are well summarized by Kissel, 109–12. I basically follow Pasoli 1982, 100–102n45, who argues that line 1 is a whole line from Lucilius, probably Book 10, but greatly enriched by Lucretian allusions

(and Lucretius may have borrowed from Lucilius), and that the half-line 2a is also from Lucilius, probably Book 26. The phrase *in rebus inane* occurs ten times in Lucretius, and *est in rebus inane*, four times. I do not believe, *pace* Zetzel 1977, that the scholiast on *Pers.* 1.2 wrote *Lucilii* mistakenly for *Lucretii*; cf. Scholz 1986, 338–39; but I agree with Zetzel that "the whole verse may not be from Lucilius either" (42). Ferri 1993, 158, hits the mark: "Persio ha trovato proprio quello più ambiguamente simile in Lucrezio." Sosin's account (1999, 284–87) of Lucretian references, especially Lucr. 2.14 in a satiric context, is valuable even if one rejects his main argument.

2. Puelma Piwonka 1978, 28–29, suggests that the god begins his complaint with this cry out of concern for the Roman people. A god's-eye view, then, which Persius first assumes, then rejects?

3. Cf. Lucilius 651–52M, discussed by Christes 1971, 104–5, on satiric freedom of speech. Lucilius defends his right to be indiscreet in a satire in Book 26 that, Christes argues, is not identical with the introductory satire.

4. Lucilius 591–94M ; for further discussion, see section 1.3, below. The famous line, *Persium non curo legere, Laelium Decumum volo*, must have tickled *our* Persius's funnybone; also Cic. *De Fin.* 1.3.7: *Nec vero ut noster Lucilius recusabo, quominus omnes mea legant. Utinam esset ille Persius.*

5. Possibly the duo were Cornutus and Caesius Bassus, who acted as Persius's literary executors (*Vita*, 44–45).

6. Marsyas or Pan? See the discussion of lines 120–21 in Kissel 1990. Pan would be familiar from Ovid, *Met.* l.146–93, but the satyr Marsyas might fit Persius's thought better; cf. Horace, *Sat.* 1.6.120–21.

7. The reading of the *Vita*, 58, and *scholia* to 1.120–21, *Mida rex habet*, was accepted by a minority of scholars, from Casaubon to Bo. Allegedly, Cornutus changed the verse because Nero could have seen it as referring to himself (without Persius having so intended it?—which makes him unusually foolish); the earlier statement in the *Vita*, that Persius intended this against Nero, may have grown secondarily out of the Nero story (Kissel 1990, 269).

8. See Coffey 1976, 98–99, on the danger under the early empire of what was perceived as innuendo. Nero, though, may have been comparatively tolerant before the Pisonian Conspiracy of 65 A.D.

9. Cf. Hooley 1998, 26 (offered as one of two alternatives): "Is the interlocutor a hypostasized inner self, the conventional 'reasonable' poet, set over against the radical iconoclasm of the satiric 'Persius?'" See also Relihan 1989, 154, on the imaginary interlocutor as "the literary presentation of the split personality, as the *adversarius* becomes the author's own second thoughts or other half' [but with a difference, I think, in *Satire* 1, where the poet's own first thoughts are corrected by his Stoic conscience]; and 157–58: "For Persius more than other satirists reveals his doubts and his errors." Cf. also Relihan's important argument (145–46) that "the language of Persius' *Satires* is a private language, a language of self-communion; that his Satires are in the main constructed as dialogues within the author's self; that the *Satires* are not primarily directed toward an external audience."

10. Cf. Johnson 1992, 202, on "the carnal pleasure [still today] in reading poems aloud, the heard voices evoking images and sounds and meanings."

11. So already Hendrickson 1928a, 103: "But in fact P. nowhere in the first satire employs dialogue. His utterance is lively mimetic monologue throughout, re-

flecting always in his own words the objections of hostile criticism or friendly advice. . . . We should recognize . . . skill and vivacity in the construction of a literary form which incorporates dialogue in monologue with a flavor of irony and mocking criticism far more pungent than a regular dialogue affords."

12. Cf. Ehlers 1990, 179, on the importance of oral performance (*recitatio*) for clarity and understanding when negotiating the medley of voices and shifts of speaker that confuse the reader: "Ich bin überzeugt, dass sich auch Stellen, die wir heute für unklar oder unverständlich halten, mit Hilfe der Mimik, der Gestik und der Sprachmittel eines Rezitators dem Publikum eindeutig mitteilen liessen." On the dramatic nature of satire generally, see Muecke 1990, 35; Braund 1996, vi, 1, 52–59; of Persius's satire, Keane 2006, 17; on orality throughout the writing process, Cavallo 1989, 333–34 ("Voce e gesto davanno alla lettura il carattere di un *performance*") (334).

13. Most early reactions to *The Waste Land* were hostile: cf. Clarke 1990, vol. 2; Rainey 2005; for example, "The mingling of willful obscurity and weak vaudeville" (Louis Untermeyer, in Clarke 2:82); "It is a reasonable conjecture to say that Mr. Eliot does not want to communicate his suffering to the general reader. To such he desires [it] to be incomprehensible" (Gorham Munson, in Clarke 2:126.) Harold Monro, who "observed that in England it [the poem] was treated chiefly with indignation or contempt" (Clarke 2:87), adds further comments in an imagined dialogue that might well recall Persius (88):

> May I direct some criticism upon your poem? But first I should mention that I know it was not written for me. You never thought of me as among your potential appreciative audience. You thought of nobody, and you were true to yourself. Yet, in a sense, you did think of me. You wanted to irritate me, because I belong to the beastly age in which you are doomed to live.

Among more positive impressions, we hear Virginia Woolf: "Eliot dined last Sunday to read his poem. He sang it and chanted it rhythmed it. It has great beauty and force of phrase: symmetry; & tensity. What connects it together, I'm not so sure" (North 2001, 137). And Edmund Wilson comments on the power and brilliance of the poetry: "That is also why, for all its complicated correspondences and its recondite references and quotations, 'The Waste Land' is intelligible at first reading. . . . In Eliot the very images and the sound of the words—even when we do not know precisely why he has chosen them—are charged with a strange poignancy which seems to bring us into the heart of the singer" (Clarke 2:75).

14. The title, taken from Dickens's *Our Mutual Friend* (bk. 1, chap. 16), heads parts 1 and 2 in the typescript drafts in *WLFT* (Eliot 1971). Gardner (2001, 79) comments, "I suppose this is another and unpoetical way of saying, 'I Tiresias have foresuffered all.' The poem was to be an exercise in ventriloquism. The poet, like Sloppy reading to Betty Higden in *Our Mutual Friend*, is behind all the voices of men and women we are asked to listen to." Thormählen (1978, 28–29) reminds us that Dickens is "the London satirist *par excellence* in English fiction" (30); he was famous, too, for his dramatic readings. The "different voices" in *The Waste Land* are especially problematic where punctuation is omitted or withdrawn (cf. the Lil scene, 45) and in the absence of stage directions (83). Paraphrasing Langbaum, she

cites the former's argument that "the dramatic monologue in The Waste Land . . . is that of a modern consciousness speaking through a collage of voices" (84–85).

15. For Pound's excisions, to which Eliot assented quickly and submissively, see *WLFT* (Eliot 1971). As Donahue (2000, 111) says, "The first drafts show that the poet's original sense of his poem made it, even more than the final version, a medley of dissociated voices. . . . It still strikes me as a poem of different voices, heard, overheard, voices off, voices on." Cf. also Kenner 1973, 27, 36, on the earlier *Waste Land* as more evidently "urban satire," with many more lines in the styles of Dryden and Pope; but urban satire is transferred to the "urban apocalypse" and the journey through the waste land (46). Lines 135–72, from "A Game of Chess," play closely with music-hall comedy.

16. Cf. Hooley 1997, 61, on Persius: "It is the intentionally contrived disorder of the poet rewriting his tradition that is able to contrive the right response to poetry's broken past and present. We have in this 'Persius,' then, not the singular man of virtue walking disappointedly from the mess of the world into some fastness of misanthropic loneliness, but an artist explicitly setting about the project of re-fashioning the nature of the poetic, thinking it through before our eyes, declaring it to be at once the stuff of that tradition itself and necessarily and radically 'other.' "

17. Forster 1936, 112–13.

18. Eliot 1950, 248.

19. Paratore 1968, 3–4, offers two possible interpretations: (a) the public fighting over copies; and (b, the less likely) criticisms alternating with praise. Pasoli 1985, 1813n1, chooses (a), "*contendersene le coppie.*" Cf. also Marmorale's reminder (1956, 97f.) that Persius was once loved and understood, the evidence of Martial (4.29.7–8) and Quintilian (*Inst.* 10.1.94), and the confused tradition, reflected in the *Vita*, 20–22, of Lucan's enthusiasm for Persius's poetry. (I would keep *recitantem*: Lucan reciting Persius [after P's death] and almost interrupting his own reading from sheer excitement. But the story may be apocryphal; cf. Morford 1984, 4).

20. Gruen 1992, 290–91.

21. On the "dramatic *satura*" (Livy 7.2.4–17) and its problematic influence on the literary satires of Ennius and his successors, see the discussion and bibliography in LaFleur 1981, 1809n51; see also Citroni 1989, 318–19. Hendrickson 1894 denounced the whole idea of the "dramatic *satura*" as a spurious invention of Varro and others in their attempt to follow closely the Aristotelian and post-Aristotelian analysis of the development of Greek drama, especially comedy (an analysis that Horace also follows in *Ep.* 2.1.145–55). Yet a recent commentator (Oakley 1998) denies that Livy was following Aristotle all that closely and reopens the question— very likely, there existed a form of drama known as *satura*. Was it a kind of vaudeville entertainment, consisting of organized skits and song-and-dance numbers? Or, just possibly, a kind of satyr drama that survived in Italy? In Ullman's view (1914, 17–18), the term *satura* denoted a "miscellaneous performance," but he concludes, "Even if it were true that *satura* was an ancient term, it would be entirely wrong . . . to claim any relation between these *saturae* and those of Ennius and Lucilius" (18). I disagree: there is an affinity, if not a close connection, between these two varied, playful, and highly dramatic forms.

22. On Naevius, cf. Aulus Gellius's report (3.3.15) that he was thrown into prison *ob assiduam maledicentiam et probra in principes civitatis de Graecorum poetarum*

more dicta, a clear reference, I think, to Athenian Old Comedy; cf. Diomedes' mainline definition, which can be traced back to Varro (cf. Scholz 1986a, 359–60): *satura dicitur carmen apud Romanos nunc quidem maledicum et ad carpendum hominum vitia archaeae comoediae charactere compositum, quale scripserunt Lucilius et Horatius et Persius . . . at olim carmen quod ex variis poematibus constabat satura vocabatur, quale scripserunt Pacuvius et Ennius*. Oakley (1998, 57) suggests the possible influence also of Greek satyr plays, which had become satirical by the later fourth century. Did Lucilius revive something of that oldtime comic aggressiveness in his satires for more private stages? Gratwick (1982, 164) comments ironically, "In view of this explicitness, it is amusing to read that Lucilius himself lost a case which he brought against an unknown comedian (*auctor ad Her*, 2.19; cf. 1.24), who had named him from the stage." Cf. also Edwards 1993, 131, on later personal attacks in mime, and (116–17) on how "the text of a drama could be given a contemporary political meaning, through the interaction of players and audience."

23. Differently, Rosen (2007, 183–84) argues for "the notion that Callimachus's program in *Iambus* 1 was to promote and defend his own *iamboi* as deeply Hipponactean rather than to distance himself from that archaic form."

24. For Lucilius and Callimachus, see Puelma Piwonka 1978: on mimetic and performative elements in Callimachus's *iamboi*, 299–300, 312–13; on the "mimic and dialogic element" in Lucilius, close to sketches of "ethical" types in New Comedy, 59–61.

25. Cf. Richard Thomas's fine account (1999, 44–52) of how Demeas's soliloquy in Menander, *Samia* 325–56, is adapted by Catullus (8) to his own amatory situation—an excellent example of how "traditional elements can be transformed to suit a new context" (52). I would add that much of Menander's dramatic power will carry over into Catullus's poem, insofar as it will be read aloud and performed.

26. On *sermo* as "casual talk," used by Lucilius and Horace to designate their satires, giving the impression of "the improvised and spontaneous," cf. Puelma Piwonka 1978, 84, 89; Scholz 1986a, 335–36.

27. Lucilius 592M, *Persium non curo legere, Laelium Decumum volo*, with Crassus's comment, *Nam ut C. Lucilius . . . dicere solebat neque se ab indoctissimis neque a doctissimis legi velle, quod alteri nihil intellegerent, alteri plus fortasse quam ipse* (Cic., *De Or.* 2.6.25); also 595M, a Ciceronian variation.

28. Cf. Citroni 1990, 92, on the significance of Lucilius's choice [at 592, 595–96M] of a *pubblico medio*—not a *pubblico popolare*—including political and cultural leaders. I wonder whether Cicero's comment at *De Fin.* 1.3.7 may not have become an inside joke for *our* Persius: *Nec vero ut noster Lucilius recusabo quominus omnes mea legant. Utinam esset ille Persius!*

29. On the processes of circulation, always difficult to control, and publication, see Fedeli 1989, Citroni 1990.

30. See *Kaster 1995, 43, for how the grammatici* "set about making the poetry of Naevius, Ennius, and Lucilius better known to their fellows" (ca. 160–100 B.C.). Archelaus and Philocomus will have taught Lucilius's satires after his death; Cato and Lenaeus will have read Lucilius with them not before the 80s (62–63); indeed, Lenaeus, a freedman of Lucilius's great-nephew Pompey, wrote a kind of Lucilian satire himself (77, comparing other political invective of the later republic, 179–80).

Exploiting his Dionysian name, Lenaeus may have exemplified the excessive *libertas* of satire that Horace criticizes and works to modify in *Satires* 1.4 and elsewhere.

31. On the work of the *grammatici*, see Quinn 1982, 93–115. It included reading aloud/performance of literature (*anagnôsis/praelegere*) and critical interpretation (*krisis poêmatôn/interpretari*). "Reading is . . . the authoritative performance of a scholar-critic, the enactment of his understanding of the text" (104). Quinn cites the *Technê* of Dionysius Thrax: "The reader must assume the appropriate persona, take account of the metre, and adopt the appropriate speaking voice."

32. Persius's own teacher, Remmius Palaemon (Kaster, 228–42), preferred Virgil and Horace to older writers; contrast Horace's teacher Orbilius, who flogged his pupils into appreciating ancient authors like Livius Andronicus in the face of modern prejudice (*Ep.* 2.1.69–72, *Sat.*1.10. *c–h*; Hendrickson 1916 argues for the latter "as the original beginning of our satire—subsequently deleted by the poet himself"). Valerius Cato edited and taught Lucilius, but without the flogging (*a–d*).

33. Freudenburg (1993, 96–108) emphasizes Horace's eclecticism: rather than "dismiss one tradition in favor of another . . . he has, rather, created a dramatic world that draws upon the best features of Greek Comedy, both Old and New, the iambographic and the Aristotelian." (100). "He is determined to have it all" (108). But the Aristotelian-Ciceronian tradition of liberal humor seems dominant in the *Satires*, with Lucilius and Archilochus as secondary voices, more evident in the *Epodes*.

34. *Ep.*2.2.60 suggests that some people enjoyed the rough, biting wit that Bion contributed to the *Satires*; the unspecified "ille" may be putting a one-sided, even wrongheaded, emphasis on this one aspect of Horace's satires, or again, his misunderstanding may have some basis in truth. Kindstrand (1976, 156) suggests a likely reference to Bion's father's (alleged) business as a seller of spices (*tarichopôlês*).

35. On diatribe, see J. L. Moles in *OCD*, 3 ed., 463–64; see also Oltramare 1926. We only have scattered remains of Bion's so-called diatribes, stemming from lecture notes (probably his own), quotations, and paraphrases: well collected and annotated by Kindstrand (1976). As Kindstrand suggests (23), "The word *diatribê* refers to some sort of occupation and later to the actual teaching. It also became transferred to the written form of the given teaching. The name *diatribê* tells us nothing of the literary form but refers exclusively to the circumstances under which this literary work was originally delivered." Essentially a monologue (43), it shows little influence of Socratic dialogue, despite much "Socratic" influence via the Cynic tradition (44–45). The surviving fragments probably come from Bion's public lectures (13). As Kindstrand also says, "The possible influence of Bion on Lucilius has been discussed by Fiske, pp. 178 ff. and grossly exaggerated. . . . The similarities we find are of a very commonplace character and do not prove a closer relationship."

36. Bion was called *theatrikos*, much given to humorous distortion and uglification (Diog. Laert. 7.52–53), and variously indebted to Old Comedy, New Comedy, and mime (Kindstrand 1976, 45–47). Freudenburg 1993, 39n86, concludes, "It is quite possible that Bion, like his contemporary Menippus, . . . was more interested in self-parody and vivid performance than he was in serious moralizing."

37. Citroni (1990, 104) puts it well: "Questa cerchia privata rappresenta la concretizzazione attuale, sperimentale del poeta stesso, di quello pubblico ideale, colto

e raffinato, cui egli aspira e che spera in realtà di trovare anche in altri ambienti, in altri luoghi, e nel futuro."

38. Cf. Leach 1978.

39. Cf. Donatus's tribute to Virgil's vocal and bodily expressiveness in reading from his own work: *Iulium Montanum poetam solitum dicere, involaturum se Vergilio quaedam, si et vocem posset et os et hypocrisin; eosdem enim versus ipso pronuntiante bene sonare, sine illo inanes esse mutosque* (Vita Verg. 28–29).

40. Importance of the critical ear: *Horace, Ep.* 2.3.386–88, 438; Cavallo 1989, 314–15. Although Edmunds (2001, 84) emphasizes Horace's contribution to "a new literary culture, which is a reading culture," and argues (112) that reading, not performance, is always primary, he still reminds us (116) that "[t]he bookroll is tantamount to a script."

41. For the stages of writing, cf. Reckford 1999a (on *Satires* 1.5); Quinn 1982, 169–71. For the continuing importance of performance at all stages, see Cavallo 1989, 334; Fedeli 1989, 349.

42. Cf. Schlegel 2001 for a fine account of Horace's persona, "constructed to reassure the reader by undermining the threat of satiric speech and by revising the genre he has inherited from Lucilius" (13), and also for some ways that dangerous, old-fashioned satire reemerges in Book 1.

43. Rejection of public readings, *Ep.*1.19.35–49; sometimes taking part, *Ep.* 2.2.91–105; Ovid heard him read, *Tr.* 4.10.49–50.

44. Quinn (1982), 156–57.

45. Raschke (1987) depicts Lucilius as an independent but partisan writer, generally conservative in his views, allied to the younger Scipio and opposed to the Gracchan reforms. On Lucilius and Scipio, cf. Gârtner 2001, 97–98; Lefèvre 2001, 140–42; on friends and enemies, Gârtner 2001; Lefèvre, 144–47.

46. Schlegel (2001, 67–68) argues that Horace deploys the nonthreatening satiric stance of the low-status outsider who is almost a clown (as in *Satires* 1.5), yet enjoys an insider's high privileges in Maecenas's circle.

47. Cf. DuQuesnay 1984, 25: "Above all, he received access to scribes and papyrus, books, audiences for his recitations, and, presumably as an extension of this, the 'publication' of his poems." Similarly, White 1993, 35–63, esp. 52–53.

48. *Vita Horati* (Klingner): *an vereris ne apud posteros infame tibi sit, quod videaris familiaris nobis esse?*

49. *Vita Persi*, 43–44: *leviter contraxit Cornutus et Caesio Basso, petenti ut ipse ederet, tradidit edendum.*

50. Cf. Bramble 1974, 73: *scribimus inclusi*, from Horace's *scribimus indocti* (*Ep.* 2.1.117), "reprimands those who shut themselves away from the real world, to indulge their sickly inclinations." Does Persius include himself among these?

51. A few brave efforts: Reckford 1962, 476–83; Bramble 1974, 78–99; Pasoli 1982, 234–37 (reviewing Bramble); Miller 1998, 266–68 (" . . . a kind of impossible sexual monstrosity in Roman ideology's normative zero-sum game" [267]). Reckford's defense of a repeated *auriculis* at 23 has not generally found acceptance, despite Pasoli 1982, 331, and Freudenburg 2001, 172; but it gains strength from the play on *auri-culis* noted by Bramble, 80n1, 82n2: cf. the punning title of John [not Bert] Lahr's biography of Joe Orton, "Prick Up Your Ears," cited by Fitzgerald 1995a, 51, for Catullus.

52. I use "active/passive homosexual" as conventional descriptive shorthand for the distinction that Persius himself here blurs, though it comes out more clearly in *Satire* 4; however, the normal Greco-Roman contrast is between queer "pathic" sexuality, as represented by the *cinaedus*, and the supposedly normal male sexual aggressiveness that fucks anyone and anything in its path—male or female, young or old, whatever. For a more nuanced discussion, cf. Williams 1999, esp. 1–14 ("Introduction") and 160–224 ("Sexual Roles and Identities").

53. Bramble 1974, 92, thinks any connection of *caprificus* with a tomb would be secondary and emphasizes rather the image of "sterility, both literary and sexual" (93), but I see this as anticipating thoughts of death and burial in the next section, esp. 39–40, and the vanity of poetic ambition in the face of mortality (cf. later, Juvenal, *Sat.* 10.144–46).

54. *Digito monstrari*: from Horace, *C.* 4.3.22, *quod monstror digito praetereuntium*—but in Persius, suggesting an obscene gesture? Dictation in schools: from Horace, *Ep.* 1.18.13–14, *Ep.* 1.20.17–18, *Ep.* 2.1.70–71, but probably returning more in spirit to the contemptuous *Serm.* 1.10.74–75, *an tua demens / vilibus in ludis dictari carmina malis?*

55. *Ennius, Epigrammata* 2 (Vahlen); Horace, *C.* 3.30.6–7; Ovid, *Tr.* 4.10; cf. King 1998 for an incisive account of Ovid's expression of his wish to be "cultivated" through readings after his exile-death and physical death by a community of readers. The reading of Ovid's poetry is assimilated "to a commemorative act performed at a memorial banquet" (117).

56. Cf. Virgil, *Aen.* 2.130, from Sinon's false story, hence with strong overtones of deception and danger.

57. Cf. Highet 1949, 216, with remarks on how Shakespeare might have read and remembered this passage from Persius; also now [I find] Kissel, 164n177.

58. Fish and incense: Persius here conflates Catullus 95.7, Horace, *Ep.* 2.1.267–70, and *Ep.* 2.3.331–32. For the association of fish and funerals, see Kilpatrick 1990, 11: "[to Catullus's fish market] Horace here adds funeral imagery, in which the covered bookcase becomes the coffin of the wretch whose reputation could not survive association with incompetents." I agree: this helps build Persius's metaphorical train of thought at 1.36–43.

59. The arrangement of speakers in the first part, 63–91, is the more difficult. My own tentative reading follows. Lines 63–65a: "Persius," summarizing the current talk of modern poetic smoothness. Lines 65a–66: Voice A, an example of that *populi sermo*, on technical expertise. Lines 67–68: Voice B, a development: matter for high poetry. Lines 69–75ab: Voice C, very conservative, with unwitting self-parody, to be applauded sarcastically by Persius at 76c. Lines 76–78: Voice D, of "bleary-eyed fathers" expressing nostalgic but unwittingly self-parodying regret for the old Classical authors, Accius and Pacuvius. Lines 79–91: the section closes with Persius commenting on modern stylistic perversity—a reaction against Voice D— as it makes its way into the public realm, becoming ludicrously all-pervasive.

In the second part, 92–106, the sequence of speakers is delineated more clearly. Lines 92–95: Voice E, defending the Moderns, with involuntary self-parody. Lines 96–97: Voice F, or perhaps a continuation of Voice E, attacking Virgil's *Aeneid* as ridiculously old-fashioned now. Line 98: Persius, requesting a sample of the New. Lines 99–102: Voice G, or F continuing, gives self-parodying modern examples.

Lines 103–106: Persius gives judgment against the New. All of the preceding makes best sense when seen against the background of the Aeschylus-Euripides *agôn* in Aristophanes' *Frogs*, 830–1413, where Aeschylus is strong and moral but old-fashioned and incomprehensible, whereas Euripides is modern, clever, and innovative, but immoral, decadent, and stylistically perverse. The *agôn* covers both subject-matter and style, with parody exercised on both sides. So, too, in Persius: the parodic presentation of the Old, whether intentional or not, in 76–78, looks forward to the self-parodying presentation of modern poetry in 93–95 and 99–102. Persius also, like Aristophanes, joins aesthetic and moral concerns, and plays with metaphors of critical "weighing and measuring." Like Dionysus, too, he will be the final judge.

60. Cleansing of tender or diseased ears: Reckford 1962, 478–81, with notes; anticipated by Persius 5.86 and several Horatian passages earlier; perhaps anticipated too by *excusso naso* (118), partly for *emuncto* (cf. Hor., *Serm.* 1.4.8, *emunctae naris*, used of Lucilius), but also a favorite metaphor for inner examination, "shaking things out," and "getting under the skin."

61. Hooley 1997, 58–59, sees Persius using Horace, *Ars P.* 470–72, so that "the action [of pissing] places him directly in the role of the mad poet" (59).

62. Cf. Lucilius 652M, from the once-introductory Book 26: *neu muttires quicquam, neu misteria ecferres foras* (a fine Plautine expansion of meaning, recalled by Persius with a strong sense of déjà vu); also 957–58M, *mihi necesse est eloqui, / nam scio Amyclas tacendo periisse.*

63. Cf. *Frogs*, 830–1413 (see n. 59, above); *Frogs*, 354–58, and 368 on Aristophanes' comic rites of purification (catharsis) and initiation, as against more vulgar jokes (358); cf. Reckford 1987, 413–17, and Dover's note on 355; possible echoes also of *Knights*, 1373–81 and *Wasps*, 1043–45. Cucchiarelli (2001, 200–201) argues for the influence of *Thesmophoriazusae*, esp. 130–33; he also (203n60) compares Persius, *Sat.* 4.35–41 with *Acharnians* 119 and *Frogs* 1070–71. As Fiske (1971, 31) said, Persius adopts "a far more favorable attitude than either Aristotle or Horace to the Old Comedy."

64. Meanings of "adflate" range from "inspired" to "blasted" (Bramble 1974, 192, "blasted by its emotional force"; cf. Virgil, *Aen.* 2.648–49).

65. "Palles" here combines at least two ideas: the scholarly effort that looks "sick" to the outside world but is truly salutary, and the effect of a shattering literary experience (Kissel, 275, admits only the latter); cf. also *Sat.* 3.42–43, 85, 94, 96, and 5.62. Very likely, Persius is also playing here with Aristophanes' *Clouds*, 103, where students of philosophy are ridiculed as pale from their life indoors, and scoring a reversal-point against the Master.

APPENDIX ONE
THE *CHOLIAMBICS*

66. Most editors have rightly placed the *Choliambics* at the beginning, despite the majority of mss.: cf. Paratore 1968, 171–82; Pasoli 1982, 131–41.

67. Pasoli 1982, 98n24, argues for the influence of Callimachus's *iamboi* rather than Phoenix of Colophon's choliambs; also for the influence of Lucilius, compar-

ing Petronius, *Satyr.* 5 and Agamemnon's comments at the end of *Satyr.* 4 (*sed ne me putes improbasse schedium Lucilianae humilitatis, quod sentio, et ipse carmine effingam*). Cf. also Cucchiarelli 2001, 189–94, emphasizing *iambos* 1 in the Hipponax-Callimachus-Lucilius line and *iambos* 13 (fr. 203, 15f.) on the opposition of spirit and belly. Persius's parrot should also be seen against the background of *iambos* 2, where Zeus takes human speech away from the beasts and gives various animal noises to different human groups; cf. Puelma Piwonka 1978, 218–27.

68. See Pasoli's fine discussion (1982, 401–13) of "polisemia e ambiguità": *semipaganus* = (1) *semipoeta* (scholia), only half a poet; (2) *semirusticus* [the reverse side of *semipoeta*]: so half-uneducated, half-rustic, half a poet; and add (3) a macaronic play on *pêgê*, "spring" (*fonte caballino*,1; *Pegaseium nectar*, 14). Cf. D'Anna 1964: Persius pictures himself as a boorish outsider, easily rejected as such by the official poet's club; he sets himself against the "Roman Callimacheanism" of Propertius, while yet following in the same *recusatio* tradition; and he uses that "roughness" as a device to affirm his own sincerity. Cf. also Ferri 1993, 149 (Persius as "poeta emarginato"); Whitehead 1996, 20 (it may refer "to Persius' sense of his own ethnic, and perhaps also linguistic marginalization—his awareness of his Etruscan origins"); Plaza 2006, 182 (Persius may be both halfway in and halfway out). In any event, he is playing with, and exploiting, his liminality.

69. Comedy (*kômôidia, comoedia*) came, in one old etymologizing variant (probably adopted by Varro) from the villages, *kômai*; in Latin, then, from the *ludi compitalicii*: cf. Virgil, *G.* 2.382, *pagos et compita circum*, and 386, *versibus incomptis ludunt*. Horace (*Ep.* 2.1.159–60) wants to flush away the remains of that rusticity, *vestigia ruris*, from modern drama; he has tried to reform Roman satire in an analogous fashion. But Persius in his *Choliambics* reverses the movement, returning—or better, half-returning—to satire's vigorous roots in the countryside.

70. Homer, *Od.* 7.215–21; Hesiod, *Theog.* 26–28.

71. Horace, *Ep.*1.3.15–20, uses the crow fable as a warning against plagiarism; cf. Macleod 1977, 362. But Persius takes it further: *all* poets are frauds!

72. Cf. Relihan 1989, 151: "The poem would assert: I am not a poet, and my motivation is my stomach; yet an audience of sycophants would readily believe I am a poet. It is a point made throughout *Satire* 1, that the audience of a poet is utterly indifferent to the truth, and that a poet's interest in the approval of his audience is wholly misplaced." Cf. also Reckford 1962, 503, on the critic "whose belly forces him, like the stuffed clients in *Satire* 1, to praise his patron's bad efforts."

CHAPTER TWO
SEEKING INTEGRITY

1. My anonymous first reader gave the following critical advice, which I have gratefully adopted:

The performance theme drops after analysis of *Sat.* 1, and there is no good reason it should not, for other poems clearly have other priorities. But transition from the failure of public performance examined in the first satire to other emphases in the rest of the poetry book might be afforded by noting that in 2–6 P. seems to re-stage the stoic/ethical dramas of these later poems on an inner stage or mindscape: if public performance is corrupted, non-public introspective performance may be the satirist's best resort. . . . Certainly, all the dramatic elements of the first satire are here too: characters, dialogues, different voices, vignettes, spectacle, language intended to unsettle a hypothetical viewer. So, for instance, *Sat.* 2 might be seen as the succession of roles one plays with the script of secret desire before (an audience of) the gods. *Sat.* 3 is another kind of performance, as noted. . . . And so on.

2. See Hooley's fine account (1997, 175–201, esp. 178–82) of how Persius develops possibilities he finds in Horace to "show a physical progression" and trace "a course of characteristic moral devolution. . . . While Horace attends to the hypocrisies of self-interested prayer incidentally and in the course of other discussions, Persius focuses on corrupted prayer and through it illustrates a process of moral regression" (181). I would add that Persius also recalls Horace's movement from the gentle beginning of *Serm.* 2.6 to the more Stoicizing and harshly realistic *Ep.* 1.16.

3. Cf. Reckford 1997, 595 and n. 22.

4. Cf. Malamud 1996, 47, on the word-play, *Macrinus . . . spem macram*, and on the *dies lustricus*, "the ninth day after birth on which Roman infants were purified and named." Hence the special ugliness of the impurification rites at 31–34. Macrinus, like Persius, has been lucky to survive.

5. Corruption of the young, from birth, in Stoic thinking: *Diog. Laert.* 7.89 (*diastrephesthai*); Cicero, *Tusc.* 3.1.2 (*ut paene cum lacte nutricis errorem suxisse videamur*); Musonius 6, 17ff. (Henss, and cf. Lutz 1947, 52–54). Posidonius, differently, may have argued for a natural human tendency to good, despite a seed of evil within humans, not yet working from without (Laurenti 1989). Nussbaum 389n68 clarifies the Stoic position on how children, though born innocent, come to passion and error: (a) through "the conversation of those around them"; and (b) through "the persuasiveness of appearances," as children become habituated to seeking pleasurable sensations and avoiding painful ones.

6. Cf. Flintoff 1982 for food images in *Satire* 2, the ways Persius depicts human impiety toward the gods together with self-delusion and self-harm, extravagance and waste together with meanness and stupidity; thus especially on *pulpa* (2.63): "In a manner almost worthy of science fiction it seems that the being which has been so obsessed with tendering the insides of animals to the gods has now turned into meat himself" (351). Similarly, Keane 2006, 59–60: "Persius shows the vital boundary between human and offering collapsing; his exposing satire undoes the cultural work of sacrifice." (60).

7. Cf. Henss 1955, 288, on *Satire* 2.61, which adds a new sense of moral and spiritual torpor to Horace's humorous *Serm.* 2.2.77–79.

8. Cf. Rudd 1986, 103–4: "Even the spiritual qualities at the end of the satire, which recall those of Macrinus at the beginning, are presented in culinary terms: *ius* and *fas* (human and divine commands) are blended in the soul, and, still more astonishing, the heart is to be cooked in high-quality honour (*incoctum generoso honesto*). Such spiritual food-offerings *are* acceptable to the gods."

9. Good prayer: Rutherford 1989, 200–205 (with 202–3 on Persius); Newman 1989, 1501, on dialogue with god or address by god in Epictetus: "Such dialogues are not so much prayers as meditations on how best to conform one's judgments with the divine judgments." Cf. Cleanthes' *Hymn to Zeus*; Brunt 1974, 14–17, on the religion of Marcus Aurelius, close to Epictetus's teachings, emphasizing praise and thanksgiving: "At the least the cults symbolized that reverence for the divine that he certainly felt." (10). Cf. also Asmis 1989, 2236, on Marcus's later notion: "The intellect is a deity, *daimon*, that has emanated from the universal deity; as such, it must be worshipped and kept pure by the individual, acting as a priest." "For Marcus, the personal divinity is not a visitor or guardian spirit that watches over a person from outside, but one's true self" (2243).

Persius's Stoic notions of the decline of religion from early piety probably owed much to Cornutus's teaching and his *Epidromê*, a critical handbook of mythology; cf. Nock's comment (1931, col. 1003) on Persius's attack on superstition at 5.179–88 and the damage done by money to cult-simplicity at 2.59: "Dies sind Topoi der Satire, sie hatten aber für einen Schüler des K. besondere Bedeutung." So also, Most 1989, 2052: "The discussion of what to pray for and what not to pray for to the gods and the attacks on superstition in the second satire can be viewed as an application of the concluding words of the '*Epidromê*' [now quoted in their own succinct and powerful Greek]."

10. Augustine, *Civ.* 2.6.59, cited by Hagendahl 1967, 217.

11. Augustine, *a mag.* 9.28 (also cited by Hagendahl). Although Augustine cuts off discussion abruptly, being "anxious to mark his distance from pagan authors" (Hagendahl, 474), he has used Persius to clarify a moral issue, the importance of our coming to understand how sin operates in our lives and those of others. This presupposes a good critical reading of Persius's lines.

12. On Persius's *Satire* 3 as a "responsive countercreation" to Horace, *Satires* 2.3, see Hooley 1997, 206–29. In Hooley's view, Persius effects "not so much a shift away from irony as an unsettling of customary Horatian indicators of that irony" (211), so that diatribe becomes "functional" again and can be taken seriously, though not "simply" seriously (216).

13. Thus Ferri 1993, 59–143, sees Horace's *Epistles* as a move away from satire as entertainment, toward "raccogliamento" ("recollection" facilitated by the self-distancing of retirement to the country), and so as a transition to Persius—who, however, returns to the Lucilian aggressiveness that Horace abandoned. I argue, somewhat differently, that Persius saw himself as completing the literary-philosophical work that Horace left incomplete, even in the *Epistles*.

14. Cf. also Seneca, *de vita beata* 24.4, on what the *studiosissimus sapientiae* will say, as against the one who has attained wisdom: "Don't hold me to the letter. I'm still in process of formation" (*cum maxime facio me et formo et ad exemplar ingens attollo; si processero quantumque proposui, exige ut dictis facta respondeant . . .*).

15. Cf. Freudenburg 1993, 3–51, on Horace's parodying of diatribe (whose tradition already included much exaggeration and self-parody) and its close affinity to comedy.

16. Keane 2006, esp. chap. 2 (42–72).

17. Hooley 1997, chaps. 2 and 5.

18. Cf. Bernstein 1986–87 for a "more painful and more politically unsettling" reading of *Satires* 2.7 than usual (452).

19. In his self-ironic way, Horace is challenging the reader, too, to take his problems seriously. Macleod (1979), Labate (1981, 35), Citroni (1991, 283–84), LaPenna (1993), and Johnson (1993) respond strongly and sensitively to the challenge. Differently, Bowditch (2001) highlights Horace's struggle with problems of patronage, his need "to recover, or poetically negotiate for himself, a compromised autonomy" (21), and the tensions and ambiguities found throughout the *Epistles* (164–70 and *passim*).

20. For the wake-up call, cf. *Ep*. 1.2.32–37; the diseased body, 48, 52–53 (including dirty ears; *auriculas* again); the faulty *vas*, 48, and the *testa* that will preserve the fresh scent it was first imbued with (like good education), 69–70; the tyrant's method of torture, 68–69.

21. Pinsky's *An Explanation of America* (1979), addressed to his young daughter, includes both a fine poetic translation of *Ep*. 1.16 and a poetic commentary on this Epistle, with reflections on Horace's life and work (Part 2, III–IV); cf. also Bowditch's comments (1996). I am grateful to have heard first Bowditch, then Pinsky, at a conference on "The Horatian Bimillennium: The Reception of Horace's Poetry Since the Seventeenth Century," organized by Bernard Frischer and held at the Clark Library, UCLA, on November 6, 1993.

22. We underestimate, because we cannot prove, the reality of Horace's physical ailments, but cf. *Epp*. 1.7.2–9, 1.15.3–9, 1.16.4 (if not only general), 1.18.104–5 (if not only metaphorical), and Horace's rejection of Augustus's invitation to become his private secretary (*Vita Horat.*, in Klingner 1970) on grounds of ill health, which was probably not (*pace* Fraenkel 1915, 18) just a thin excuse.

23. Play and seriousness: cf. (a) Macleod 1979, esp. 286: Horace "renounces" poetry writing once again, and "finally," as childish play, compared to the serious pursuit of wisdom and truth. Yet the seriousness and care that he puts into poetry writing are analogous to the serious pursuit of philosophy, the fashioning of good verse to the fashioning of a genuine self. Macleod's incisive discussion should be read in its entirety. (b) Moles 2002, 140: "The complex and intricate 'play' element does not erase the Epistles' philosophical seriousness, but there is an implicit challenge to penetrate the 'play' to that underlying seriousness." (c) Reckford 2002, 6–7: "It [poetry] may, to be sure, distract one from life's most urgent obligation, the business of living well, and dying well; but it may also provide, as in Horace's *Epistles*, a means of exploring the conflicting demands of human life and our usually inconsistent response to those demands."

24. Housman 1913, 16–18; cf. the discussions of Reckford 1962, 494–95 (and, with renewed appreciation, Reckford 2001, 141–44); Rudd 1970; Jenkinson 1973, 521–34; Kissel 1990, 368–73 and nn.; Hooley 1997, 202–7. By using the first person plural *stertimus*, Persius establishes his role *"als die eines beteiligten* [!] *und damit bereits mittelbar in das Geschehen involvierten Beobachters"* (Kissel 1990, 376). *Satire* 1.1–12 presents a comparably intense inner dialogue; also *Satire* 5.1–18, if Witke (1970, 89–90) is right in thinking that Cornutus does not speak lines 5–18 (except as an internalized voice?). On the inwardness of dialogue in Persius's satires generally, see the perceptive comments of Relihan 1989, 152–54, with special reference to Menippean satire such as Varro's *Bimarcus* (154, and cf. n. 36 on Bakhtin).

25. For the latter, cf. Rudd 1970, 187. My own tentative arrangement of voices follows. Let PC represent Persius-as-*comes*; PN, Persius-as-narrator; PA, Persius as *adulescens*; and PS, Persius as generalized diatribe speaker: then 1a (PC), 1b–4 (PN), 5–6 (PC), 7 (PN/PA), 8–9 (PA/PN), 10–14 (PN, with some mimesis of PA); 15–34 (PC and/or PN joining in, with mimesis of PA at 19a, 25–26); similarly, 35–43 and (more directed at PA) 44–62. Then PS from 63 to 76ff., with dramatic confrontations and insets at 77–87, 88–106. Does 107–18 return us to PC and PA, somewhat as Jenkinson 1973, 547–49, argues? That is not so clear.

26. Among Horace's varied uses of the first person plural, Ferri (1993, 83–84) describes "un plurale sociativo," encouraging progress through knowledge, but more often, he says, it takes the form of a *pluralis in culpa*: cf. *Ep.* 1.2.27–29, *nos numeri sumus*; 1.11.28–29, *strenua nos exercet inertia*. All this, taken together, "l'appello ad un' interiorità che dovrebbe commuovere e coinvolgere tutti gli uomini," looks forward to Seneca and Persius. Differently, I would note Horace's shift from the satiric second person singular in *Ep.* 1.6.17–20 and *passim* to the first person plurals of 50 (*mercemur servum*) and 56–61 (*eamus, piscemur, venemur . . . crudi tumidique lavemur*), injunctions that are partly sarcastic encouragement but partly also a shared dramatic experiment, playing out possible scenarios.

27. Persius draws on Horace's *Ep.* 1.2.34–27, as said, but also on *Ep.* 2.1.111–13, *ipse ego . . . et prius orto sole vigil calamum et chartas et scrinia posco*. Cf. also 104, *mane domo vigilare*, and Brink's note (3.151) on 112–13. Beneath the self-irony, Horace's writing, not dictating here, implies serious self-critical effort; he's a professional, playing at being an amateur. Persius makes the desired self-criticism philosophically, not (or not just) literarily instrumental.

28. Cf. Dobbin, 149 (on *Epict.* 1.14.11–17): "A consequence of pantheism drawn: god is present in each of us, in the fragment called the *daimon*. This functions as the human conscience; and so assists in the process of moral surveillance."

29. I part company with Clausen and several other editors, though not with Bo, when I put "*FINDOR*!" in quotation marks as a loud exclamation. The more usual term would be *rumpor*, "burst with emotion": cf. Kissel, 381–82. Gowers (1994, 142) shares my view, which we came to independently, of the significance of "findor": "There, in the word *findor* (literally, 'I am split in two') is the first intimation of the poet's split personality." Cf. also Hooley 2004, 226: "But this funny, surprising little verb *findor* does at least pick up and reaffirm the idea of fragmentation, the broken, unresolved, unfinished self. Multiplicity and irresolution stand in opposition to unity, either formal or thematic, and as such are characteristic (of) middles." And Plaza 2006, 221–35: "Once the thesis of a split 'Persius' is accepted, it may form the basis for a closer investigation of how the satirist mocks his disintegrating persona here."

30. Clark (1995) 115: "The most common interpretation of this saying was in terms of the innocence of children, in particular their freedom from the desires which beset older people. A. sees a continuity from childish to adult desires and a change only in their objects, not their nature. He interprets the saying in terms of the humility—literally the low standing—of children."

31. Clark, 100 (on *Conf.* 1.9.15, *nemo misereatur pueros vel illos vel utrosque*): "The adults are pitiable . . . because they are concerned with trivialities. The theme of false adult values appears in moral philosophy as a reproach to adults, but A. is

exceptional both in showing intense awareness of the child's perspective and in being prepared to think it important instead of dismissing it as childish."

32. In defense of the reading, "morituri verba Catonis / discere" (AB), as against "morituro verba Catoni / dicere" (P, suggesting a *suasoria*), see Tandoi 1965, 315–22. Most likely, as Tandoi argues, the schoolmaster (*grammaticus*) assigned a theme—a version of Cato's last words, a soliloquy before dying—to be embellished according to stylistic norms, gotten by heart (hence "discere"), and declaimed to an audience of fellow pupils and visiting relations and friends (327). A further irony (330–31) is the distance between the heroic solitude of Cato's last words and the new, degraded social uses, the "infernal publicity," to which they are now put.

33. Cucchiarelli 2001, 76, suggests that the young Persius, playing at being *lippus*, was following in the poetic footsteps of Horace, *Sat.* 1.5.30–31 (the bleary-eyed poet who couldn't see what was actually going on in the larger political world; cf. Reckford 1999, 525–26).

34. Cato became a Stoic hero, *acerrimus sui vindex* (Seneca, *De Prov.* 2.11; cf. Inwood 2005, 306–7). To anyone with republican sympathies, most notably Lucan, "Caesar" must anticipate the line of emperor-tyrants; cf., indeed, Persius's not-so-innocent truism about the self-laceration of "cruel tyrants" ("saevos punire tyrannos," 35, only ten lines before "morituri verba Catonis"). Thrasea wrote a dangerous biography of the younger Cato (Plut., *Cato Minor* 25, 36); years later, in his *Dialogus* (dramatic date, 74–75 A.D.), Tacitus indicates the dangers of gossip, slander, and willful misinterpretation that Curiatus Maternus might incur through his *Cato*.

35. For the leaky or fragile vessel, cf. Reckford 1998, 341–42, nn. 7–16 on *effluo*; Pl. *Gorg.* 493a5–b3 and *Symp.* 186c5–7; Epicurus, fr. 62 (Usener); Lucr. 3.434–41, 551–57, 935–37, 1008–10, 6.17–25; Segal 1990, 140 and *passim*.

36. My teacher, Robert Brooks, made this suggestion in March 1951. *Lutum*, like the Greek *pêlos*, can refer both to the clay or earth used by masons and potters from which, in the creation myth and elsewhere, humans were first fashioned, and to the mud or mire that we usually avoid. Henss 1955, 280, refers us to Horace, *Ep.* 2.2.8, *argilla quidvis imitabere uda*. Cf. Pasoli 1982, 215, on *lutatus* (3.104), "muddied," used mockingly for the more usual *illitus*, "smeared," and n. 10, on *lutea pellis* (3.95): the differing quantities of *luteus* and *lutatus* are not a problem. "Probabilmente v'è anche un'allusione al 'fango' di cui è formato il corpo, ormai senza vita." Persius may be bringing a largely dead metaphor, *dissolutus*, back to life; cf. Nussbaum 1994, 394: "Distress, *lupê*, Chrysippus etymologizes, gets its name from the verb *luo*, "dissolve": it is a dissolution of the entire person (Cic. *TD* 3.61; cf. Plato *Crat.* 419c)."

37. Persius conflates *Ep.* 1.16.19–23 with *Ep.* 1.6.61 (*crudi tumidique lavemur*), where Horace ironically suggests different goals in life. He may also be using Lucilius's "sickness satire," discussed by Christes 1971, 61–71.

38. Other foreshadowings of death are Natta's moral coma, and maybe heart attack (31–34), the tyrant's torture and threat of death (39–41), and the guilty man's dream of falling headlong from a great height (41–43). I shall discuss these images further in section 4.4, below.

39. Most 1992 discusses the fascination with dismemberment seen throughout Seneca's tragedies and also in Lucan's *Pharsalia*; he also notes the disturbing questions about human identity thereby raised for Stoics. Cf. also Tarrant on *Thyestes* 432–33, *et lacerae domus / componit artus*; "*legere . . . artus*: a densely-packed and ominous phrase: *componere* here has a medical sense of "setting" broken bones (cf. Celsus 8.10.2), but it both looks back to the Chorus's belief that the brothers have "composed" their differences (338) and forward to the moment when Atreus carefully "arranges" the children before killing them (694); *lacerae domus* is also bitterly ironic, foreshadowing the dismemberment of Thyestes' sons (cf. 60–61) and their "rending" by their father (cf. 277–78)."

40. Cf. Seneca, *ad Helv.* 171–72, contrasting false appearance, *per ipsum tamen compositum fictumque vultum*, with the man who, submitting to reason's rule, *in perpetuum componitur*; also *Ep.* 4.1: seek to enjoy *emendato animo et composito*; you'll find the process enjoyable too, *dum emendas, etiam dum componis*. Cf. also Hadot 1998, 195–97, on the idea, here exemplified by Marcus Aurelius, of "composing" one's life through a series of harmonious right actions.

41. Cf. Marcus Aurelius (*Med.* 9.36; Hadot 1998, 166) for a proper Stoic approach to death and decomposition: look at them realistically, don't attribute false values to them. Persius's poetry, by contrast, expresses the natural sensations of horror and revulsion that we all feel, and Persius surely felt, toward these human realities. See my discussion of Persius's "emotional recognizance" in section 4.4, below.

APPENDIX TWO
EPICTETUS, DIATRIBE, AND PERSIUS

42. For a good summary of Gaius Musonius Rufus's life and work, see Lutz 1947, 14–18. A Roman *eques*, born of an Etruscan family in Volsinii probably before 30 A.D., he may well have been known to Persius. Epictetus cites his teaching at 1.1.26–27, 1.7.30–32, 1.9.29–30, 3.6.10, and especially 3.23.2: "Rufus used to say, 'If you have nothing better to do than to praise me, then I am speaking to no purpose.' Wherefore he spoke in such a way that each of us as we sat there fancied someone had gone to Rufus and told him of our faults; so effective was his grasp of what men actually do, so vividly did he set before each man's eyes his particular weaknesses." Their styles appear different because Musonius mostly survives through his pupil "Lucius"; as Long says (1983, 996), "This man quite clearly has not attempted to retain the manner of oral delivery. So Musonius may have influenced Epictetus more directly than the present form of both their works suggests." For continuity from Epictetus to Marcus Aurelius, cf. Rutherford 1989 and Hadot 1998. Laurenti 1989 convincingly reconstructs the arrangement of Musonius's diatribe from our scant remains. Another admirable figure recalled by Epictetus is Demetrius the Cynic, who responded fearlessly to Nero's threats. (For an overview of the neo-Cynic movement, see Reale 1989, 145–63).

43. For discussion of the problems, see Stadter 1980, 26–27; Long 1982, 989–90; Hershbell 1989, 2152–53; Dobbin 1998, xxii–xxiii; Wehner 2004, 27–53. What

we have might best be called "Arrian's Discourses of Epictetus" (Stadter), for it is neither a literal transcription of Epictetus's lectures nor "the voice of Arrian" (Long). What is striking, though, is how clearly and consistently what I take to be Epictetus's own voice comes through—much more reliably than Socrates' voice in Plato's writings, let alone in Xenophon's. Note also that Arrian was probably connected through marriage or adoption with the *gens Arria* (Stadter, 2 and n. 10), so may have been a distant relative of Persius!

44. Long 2000, 107, 128.

45. As Oldfather (1925, 176n1) puts it, with old-fashioned caution: "The accompanying gesture explained the allusion, which was probably to the eye and the mouth, as in II.20.28. A Cynic like Diogenes would very likely have illustrated his point in somewhat coarser fashion; and this is not impossible in the present instance." Wehner 2004 cites other examples of humor, ridicule, and caricature: 101, 112 (babyish behavior; cf. Pers. 3.16–18), and 142, a satiric anecdote about flattering the great man who has been put in charge of the Emperor's chamber pot (Epict. 1.19.16–19).

46. In Epict. 2.6.6–10, for example, a voice of ambition begins without introduction, "Go salute X!"; a philosophical voice replies, quite unconcerned with impressing anybody; then Chrysippus is quoted. Cf. Long 1983, 991: "Arrian has four ways of beginning a discourse: an imperative in the second person singular (as here [in Epict. 4.3]), a question raised by or put to Epictetus, a narrative generally introducing discussion between Epictetus and the pupil or visitor, and a moral statement that is to be proved or examined. . . . The 'you' whom he addresses, even when identified with an individual or type of person, is everyman, so to speak, and does not exclude himself. Epictetus uses dialogue as a teaching device, not as a way of indicating that he is holier than thou."

47. Wehner 2004 is especially good on "die Bedeutung der dialogische Elemente im Dienste der Willenserziehung" (16), the use of pronouns (55–65), and talking with oneself (79–105). Newman 1989, 1479–80, sees dialogue in the literary productions of Seneca or "Epictetus" as belonging to the act of *meditatio*, which he claims was a Stoic innovation (1482).

48. Another passage with strong personal implications is Epict. 1.10.7–13. The teacher is weary (7–8) and tempted to *accidia*; he'd rather go back to sleep than prepare the day's lesson; when young people fool around, he feels like joining them—though it would be better to join them if they behaved like serious students (12–13). The humor gives comic relief but also reinforces the importance of studying, and teaching, seriously.

49. On the *daimôn* assigned by Zeus to each of us to be our guardian, cf. Epict. 1.14.11–12; "This functions as the human conscience, and so assists in the process of moral surveillance" (Dobbin, 149). Cf. also Hadot 1998, 122–24, citing Chrysippus (123) and borrowing nicely from Claudel: "Someone within me, more myself than myself" (124 and n. 18).

50. A joke on myself: winding up a grand last lecture in a big undergraduate course, I once proclaimed, "In the end, it is the teacher's business to make himself indispensable!" A Freudian slip: I meant, of course, to say "dispensable"—my tongue knew better.

CHAPTER THREE
EXPLORING FREEDOM

1. For Nero's performances, expected and actual, cf. now Griffin 2008. (I thank Miriam Griffin for letting me see corrected proofs of this essay before publication.) Note that Nero received the *toga virilis* early, by special dispensation, at the age of thirteen, and acceded to the throne before he was seventeen.

2. Catullus 29, 5 and 9; cf. also Cat. 93, and Wray 2001, 58–59, on the later loss of "the relatively free exchange of spoken and written invective." Wray, 59n17, cites the story about Asinius Pollio, three decades after Catullus's death: "When asked why a man of his reputation for wit had failed to respond in kind to a satiric invective poem directed at him by Augustus, Pollio responded, 'It's hard to write a poem against a man who can write your death warrant' " (*Non est facile in eum scribere qui potest proscribere*, Macrob. *Sat.* 2.4.21).

3. Hooley (1997) reads *Satire* 4 well as a disorienting poem, one that takes the reader from the relative clarity of the initial Socrates-Alcibiades dialogue into a confusing interchange of critical voices. There is a "progressive lack of guideposts"; satire itself is thrown into question as one more link in the chain of mutual criticism and attack; the satirist, the author and the reader are all challenged to "descend into yourself," into the darkness of the unknown, sinful self. Peterson 1972–1973 and Littlewood 2002 are also valuable. For Peterson, "The investigation [in *Satire* 4] undermines confidence and the introspection fragments personal identity. . . . The very language he uses—scarcely controlled images of death, lust, and disorder—suggest the truth about the meaning of his poem—not the luminous self-knowledge of the venerable GNÔTHI SEAUTON, but the terror of discovering in oneself a fatal wound." For Littlewood, *Satire* 4 reveals a failure of nerve, a bankruptcy of satire, with degeneration too of Socratic dialectic as Persius moves "from Socrates' noble hemlock-drinking to the miser's sour vinegar, and from Platonic eroticism (even failed, as in the *First Alcibiades*) to ordinary sexual posturing and impotence." Cf. also Connor 1987, 56–62, on the ambiguity of voices at 4.23–41 and the satirist's involvement in the destructive processes here described.

4. The story remained exemplary after Plato, especially among Stoics: how Socrates brought Alcibiades to an awareness of his own worthlessness, with painful feelings of shame and distress (Cicero, *Tusc.* 3.77–78; Epict. 3.25–30, 37). This may have occasioned an "Alcibiades problem": were such negative emotions ever valuable? As Sorabji (2000, 52) points out, "Socrates and Epictetus alike think that self-dissatisfaction is a vital spur to improvement, and Epictetus says that the novice's reaction to his lecture should be one of agony." (The sage, of course, feels no such emotions.) But Alcibiades' repentance was abortive; he didn't persist in the hard work of healing, so his bad feelings proved worthless after all. What, we might ask, would this imply for the reader of satire? Or the writer?

For Persius's use of Plato's *First Alcibiades* and other Socratic works, mostly lost, cf. Dessen [1968] 1996, 58–70, 97–105, with important differences (62–63). Plato's Alcibiades stands up to advise the Athenians, but needs self-knowledge first (130) and a protective antidote against becoming a *dêmerastês* and being corrupted (132a). Interestingly, Persius may also have used Plato's *Second Alcibiades*, which recommends "reverent reserve" (*euphêmia*, 149b) as against dangerous, risky prayers, in *Satire* 2.

5. Flattery and prostitution merge. Kissel rightly explains "caudam iactare" (15) as "spread your tail" (the peacock, hence flattery), not "wag your tail" (the dog); cf. Horace, *Serm.* 2.2.26, *et picta pandat spectacula cauda*; I would add that *Pers.* 4.36, "populo marcentis pandere vulvas," confirms the metaphorical meaning of political prostitution. (I still read *vulvas*, "wombs" [suggestive also of *valvas*, "portals"], though Kissel, 548–49, argues well for *bulbos*, like withered flowers or vegetables, which would have the advantage of reintroducing the agricultural metaphor.)

6. Cf. Griffin 1976, 47: "Perhaps the *De Clementia* is a pretence to convince the public that Seneca was training their ruler to be a philosopher-king," with some defense of the Stoics who were thought "unlikely to furnish good advice to *principes* or *reges*." Is Persius showing up that ideal as sheer folly? Or criticizing Seneca's failure to speak the truth to Nero (72)?

7. For the positive Stoic norm of moral judgment, see Inwood 2005, 201–23, "Moral Judgment in Seneca." The nonsage, aware of his own personal limitations, should "temper or avoid passing moral judgments" (215; cf. also 218). Note that "caedimus" (42), indicating mutual criticism, also carries on the homosexual motif from the preceding lines. Cf. Connor 1987, 61: "The imagery mixes sex and war." What Walters (1998, 355–56) says about Juvenal 2 goes further, and may be read back into Persius: "More covertly, it [focusing on bodies] enables the readership to implicate themselves pleasantly in the spectacle of deviancy while at the same time reaffirming their own non-deviant status."

8. On the *cinaedus* as "gender deviant" rather than "homosexual," cf. Williams 1999, 161, 175–78, 210-ll; on exploitative mockery of the *cinaedus* that maintains "the sacrosanctity of masculinity," 181; on *cinaedi* concealing their identity, 188–89, 191. Williams's comments on Martial 7.10 come close to Persius: "Olus represents a type that must have been instantly recognizable to Martial's readers: someone who maliciously gossips about other people's lives (especially their sexual and financial situations), while himself hardly being unimpeachable in either area" (191). He also cites Juvenal 4.106, *improbior saturam scribente cinaedo*; if this was proverbial, as Williams suggests (179), we might read it back into Persius's satire.

9. Cf. Richlin 1983, 188, on Persius's mixed metaphors beginning with foreplay in line 1: ". . . do you fondle the people's thing?" (We arrived independently at the same indecent view.)

10. In Aristophanes' *Knights*, the politician is caricatured as a market-seller, a low, shameless type, flattering the people in order to control them (*dêmagôgein*); cf. 423–26, 1242. Cf. also Tartari Chersoni (2005) on Aristophanic echoes, many from *Ecclesiazusae*, in *Sat.* 4.33–41.

11. On sterility at 4.41, contrasted with agricultural fertility, cf. Pasoli 1985, 1823–24; differently, Miller 1998, 265–71, emphasizing Persius's negativity here as against the fuller "grotesque" of Bakhtinian comedy. At 21–22 Baucis peddles *ocima*, a supposed remedy for impotence. Although Kissel (1990) doubts a sexual reference at 44–46 ("caecum vulnus . . . decipe nervos"), Pasoli (1972, 152) was surely correct in seeing a sexual wound, with implications of impotence. Cf. also 51, *cerdo* (n. 13, below); *Sat.* 2.41, *poscis opem nervis . . .* ; and in *Satire* 1, probably written later, sexual failure and exhaustion (22–23), the barren *caprificus* (25), *pallor seniumque* (26), and

the total disappearance of old Roman masculinity (103–6).I have wondered whether Persius plays implicitly, here or elsewhere, with his cognomen *Flaccus*, as his predecessor Horace does at *Epod.* 15.12; cf. Harrison 2007, 129: "The pun on Horace's name (*si quid in Flacco viri est*, evoking *flaccus*, 'floppy') implies that he will not be up to Archilochean standards of firmness, in invective style or phallic performance, a quasi-literal display of the theme of impotence so central to the Horatian *Epode 1.*" Cf. Watson 1995, 188–202.

12. Cf. Gardner 1959, esp. 78–98 ("The Dry Season"; quotations here from 85, 87), and Eliot's own famous note on his debt to Jessie Fisher's book, *From Ritual to Romance*, on the Grail legend. His earlier sexual vignettes, especially in Part 3 ("The Fire Sermon"), both hetero- and homosexual (Mr. Eugenides), thus add up to more than a falling away from high patterns of love and lovemaking (Virgil, Spenser, Shakespeare, et cetera): they point toward a generalized state of impotence in contemporary society, a lack of true creativity (physical, spiritual, artistic), with sterility replacing potency and fertility.

13. In addition to the obscene hint in *respue* (4.51), there is a clear indication of impotence in *cerdo*; cf. Herodas, *Mimiambos* 6 (Loeb), 48f: Cerdo, a cobbler (who reappears in *Mim.* 7), has made a wonderfully large and comfortable dildo—evidently, an improvement on the male sexuality currently available to the excited women. Cf. again the failed *nervi* at *Sat.* 4.45–46 that give the man away.

14. Relihan 1989 puts it well: Persius's recognition of his own faults . . . provides the basis for criticism of others (158–59); Persius looks inside himself, feels the horror (160–61). "He is a critic of himself first, trying to discover his own moral motivations; and trying simultaneously to decide to what extent this self-definition creates a satirist, and to what extent an autonomous human being" (158). "From the point of view of Stoic doctrine, the Stoic satirist is as surprising and paradoxical a creation as is the Cynic satirist: the Stoic is as guilty as those whose sins he describes."

15. Cf. Pope's imaginative version of Horace, *Serm.* 2.1. 28–34: "I love to pour out all myself, as plain / As downright *Shippen*, or as old *Montagne.* / In them, as certain to be loved as seen, / The Soul stood forth, nor kept a Thought within" (*Imitation*, 51–54); for that matter, cf. Nehamas 1998, 101–27, on problems of the artificial and the natural in Montaigne's Socratic effort. On Lucilius and the crude votive tablet, cf. Anderson [1963] 1982, 30–32; on sincerity and its necessarily and artistically artificial expression, Rudd 1976, 148–49; on Lucilius's rhetoric of sincerity, Harrison 1987; Citroni 1989, 314—but Lucilius also opened up, in satire, a new space for private feeling and experience (327). For the high Stoic standard of sincerity, cf. Asmis 1989, 2237–38, on Marcus Aurelius's emphasis on *alêtheia* ("truth," "truthfulness,") with "related qualities of sincerity, simplicity, freedom from deception, and absence of pride and pretense."

16. *Sat.* 5.30–40 should be read against the Horatian background of "fathers" (Lucilius, Maecenas, Horace's blood father) discussed by Schlegel 2000.

17. I agree with Witke 1970, 89–90, that Cornutus does not speak lines 5–18; "secrete loquimur" suggests both Persius's private inwardness and his paradoxical sharing of that privacy with Cornutus in a tentative outward movement of satire.

18. The word *praecordia* recalls both Lucilius's profession of satiric honesty (*ego ubi quem ex praecordiis / ecfero versum*, 590–91M) and Horace's implicit reduction of

that "honesty" to a drunken vomiting of abuse (*Serm.* 1.4.86–89). In Persius, these same *praecordia* are subjected to the philosopher-doctor's examination.

19. To simplify an argument that I hope to develop elsewhere: Horace uses *resigno* primarily in the sense of "repay" (*OLD* 2), with transfer of ownership, and Persius in the sense of "disclose fully" (*OLD* 1), but with some idea of repayment of benefits, after Horace, and also some idea of the ultimate disclosure when the will is unsealed and read. Bowditch 2001, 185–90, sees duplicity of thought, a "counterfeit gesture" in Horace's offer to Maecenas; to surrender the Sabine estate would be a kind of death. Is that what Persius saw, or thought he saw, in Horace? Note, in any case, his modest shift from Horace's present indicative, *cuncta resigno*, to his own more tentative subjunctive, "verba resignent." His offer to Maecenas also reworks Horace, *Ep.* 1.7.39, *inspice si possum donata reponere laetus*, along with his own medical "inspection" at *Sat.* 3.88–90.

20. At the crossroads: cf. also *Sat.* 3.56–57, *et tibi quae Samios diduxit littera ramos / surgentem dextro monstravit litore callem*; and Lutz 1979, 38, on "the Y of Pythagoras, which was Greek in origin and became associated with Neopythagoreanism in the East, but was introduced into [medieval] Western literature by the Roman satirist, Persius." For a more normal, easygoing view of adolescence (with a dig at the Stoics), contrast Cicero, *Pro Caelio* 42, cited by Williams 1999, 46: *detur aliqui ludus aetati; sit adulescentia liberior; non omnia voluptatibus denegentur; non semper superet vera illa et derecta ratio; vincat aliquando cupiditas voluptasque rationem, dum modo illa in hoc genere praescriptio moderatioque teneatur*. Cf. also Williams, 67, on *pudicitia* as "sexual integrity" of the freeborn of both sexes.

21. The metaphor of fashioning with clay recalls the warning of *Pers.* 3.23–24, *udum et molle lutum es, nunc nunc properandus at acri / fingendus sine fine rota* (a lifelong process, then). Contrast Horace, *Ars P.* 161–63, where the youth's happiness in his newfound freedom (*tandem custode remoto*) is balanced by his moral instability (*cereus in vitium flecti*).

22. Nisbet-Hubbard, discussing this passage (281–87, with bibliography, 271), conclude that "Horace did not himself take astrology seriously," but that Maecenas probably "was interested in the subject and knew his own horoscope." In contrast with Persius later, he "says simply that the two men's signs are in a sympathetic relationship" (283). Similarly, McDermott 1982, 226: "In effect, the poet says to Maecenas: 'Never mind all this fancy astrological hokum—you don't have to be an astrologer to see how closely our destinies are tied together.'" West 1991, on the other hand, argues inter alia against the widespread belief "that Horace did not know or care about his own horoscope"; he reads the shifting tone of *C.* 2.17, its mix of humor and seriousness, especially well. Cf. also Reckford 1997, 604–5, on Horace's playful/serious punning on *Horatius/hora*, here as elsewhere: "As Kidd [1982, 91] has shown, Horace alludes at *Odes* 2.17.17–19 to the *horoscopos*, changing the more usual *natalis dies* to *natalis hora*, and speaks with a doubly assumed (experiential and nominal) authority about the *hora*."

23. Cf. Coffey 1976, 238n58: "Housman has shown [*CQ* 7 (1913) 18–21, = *Clas. Papers* 2.852f.] that lines 45–51 may be interpreted in precise astrological terms; Persius' model, Hor. *C.* 2, 17, 15–24 is less exact. Unlike Horace, Persius the Stoic would presumably have accepted astrology." Persius's playful language may take on a further dimension from Cornutus's studies of *allegoresis* in theology, in which

ancient wisdom preserved in poetry became overlaid with much spurious mythology: cf. Tate 1929; also Most 1989, 2027–28, on Cornutus's close attention to syllables, sounds, and etymology.

24. The intertextuality is complex. As Kissel (1990, 723–26), sees it, Terence presumably adapts a scene from Menander's *Eunuchos*; Horace uses Terence; Persius goes back to Menander for the Greek names and probably conflates Menander, Terence, and Horace. In so doing, he evokes the mechanical repetitiousness of comic actions; cf. Bergson, in *Le Rire*. Cf. also Cicero's use of comedy to depict lovers' folly in *Tusc.* 4.31.66–35.76, with passages from Trabea and Caecilius and then, climactically and most effectively, from Terence, *Eun.* 14–18. Note also the lover Phaedria's uncertain movement toward Thais's house and away again, and back again—a nice sequel to the pull back and forth of those two dominatrices, *Avaritia* and *Luxuria*, at *Sat.* 5. 132–56.

25. Obscenities, more or less implicit: (a) *limen ad obscenum*, not just the "threshold" of the house; (b) extending itself (as obscene jokes are wont to do) to the much-debated *Chrysidis udas / ebrius ante fores* (165–66); and (c) with a hint of threat to the lover's masculinity (*rem patriam frangam*—more than money and reputation at stake!). Cf. also 173–74, *si totus et integer illinc / exiera*s, and the sexual dangers implied earlier, for young Persius, at 32–33.

26. In his *Paradoxa Stoicorum*, 33–41, Cicero uses his rhetorical gifts to make the paradox, "Only the wise man is free" (= "Every fool is a slave") attractive to Roman sensibilities: *Quid est enim libertas? Potestas vivendi ut velis . . .* following one's own *voluntas*, doing nothing under compulsion (34). Slavery is redefined, not in the usual legal sense, but as *oboedientia fracti animi et abiecti et arbitrio carentis suo . . .* (35). Examples include: being ordered around by a woman; desiring statues, silver, houses, et cetera; desiring special fish to eat; legacy-hunting; desiring honors and command—all this with fears arising from a bad conscience (36–41). Cf. Newman 1989, 1489, on Seneca, *Ep.* 47.1 (*immo conservi*): "Suddenly the notion of the whole is reversed; the slave is not becoming more like his master, but the master has instead become like the slave." Cf. also Epict. 2.1.26–28; 4.1.51–59, 144–50, on manumission versus true freedom. We should remember that L. Annaeus Cornutus, the addressee of *Satire* 5, was a freedman, perhaps of the elder Seneca; more likely, Nock suggests (1931, col. 996), of Lucan's father, Annaeus Mela. Cf. also Seneca, *Ep.* 37.4 (what *stultitia* endures): *Hos tam graves dominos, interdum alternis imperantes, interdum pariter, dimittit a te sapientia, quae sola libertas est.* Inwood 2005, 37, translates, "These masters are very severe, sometimes giving orders by turns, sometimes in concert with each other," but Persius brings out the further element of confusion. Cf. also Rudd 1976, 80–81, on Persius's reminiscence of Horace, *Serm.* 2.7.82 at *Sat.* 5.128–29; also M. Aur. *Med.* 7.3, *sigillaria neurospastoumena*, "little marionettes, dancing and jerking on their strings" (Rutherford 1989, 149n1), tracing the comparison back to Plato, *Lg.* 1.644de, 10.903d).

27. Cf. Hooley 1997, 206–29, on Persius's *Satire* 3 as a "responsive countercreation" (208) to Horace's *Satires* 2.3; "not so much a shift away from irony as an unsettling of customary Horatian indicators of that irony" (211), so that diatribe becomes "functional" again and can be taken seriously, though not "simply" seriously (216).

28. McCarthy 2000, 27.

29. Satiric attacks on superstition in Lucretius, Horace, and Persius probably go back to Lucilius: cf. 484–89M.: grown-ups fear ghosts and goblins the way children fear bronze statues, as if they were alive. On the ugliness of superstitious practices in Persius, cf. Plaza 2006, 100n100 (fat and inflation; also 90–104, on swollenness generally). Persius's view of religion and superstition probably owed much to Cornutus's teaching of cultural history and use of allegorical interpretations (n. 23, above). If he followed Posidonius, he would have envisioned, for example, two stages of Judaism: the first, a healthy reaction against the beliefs of Egyptians, Libyans, and Greeks; the second, a decline into superstition (cf. Nock 1931, col. 1000). On *allegoresis*, cf. Long and Sedley 1987, 323: "Note, however, that the standard Stoic response to the inadequacy of primitive theological notions is not rejection but allegorical reinterpretation. Hence the thunderbolt, a prime example of those divine terrors, is retained by Cleanthes (T2), but as a symbol of the creativity of fire. Likewise he may well have argued that fear of the supernatural is a primitive forerunner of a very proper wonder at the divine."

30. Pope, *Epilogue to the Satires, Dialogue I*, 57–60.

31. Several essays in Elsner and Masters 1994 trace the role of literature and rhetoric—Tacitus and Suetonius, primarily—in creating the generally accepted portrait of Nero as corrupt, depraved, and irresponsible. Will he be rehabilitated as a misunderstood artist? For want of better evidence, I follow the traditional view as set forth in, for example, Cizek 1972, Griffin 1984, and Rudich 1993.

32. For the trial of Antistius in 62 A.D. under the *maiestas* law, cf. Tacitus, *Ann.* 14.48–49. "He wrote libelous poems on Nero and recited them in public at a dinner given by the respectable senator M. Ostorius Scapula . . . an openly dissident gesture, performed within a narrow dissident environment . . . and probably a secret informer" (Rudich 1993, 56). Cizek 1972, 146, suggests that Nero "used the pretext of scurrilous verses against him to intimidate the growing opposition, although, as Suetonius reports, he usually treated such verses indulgently" *vel contemptu omnis infamiae, vel ne fatendo dolorem irritaret ingenia (Nero, 39.3)*. Thrasea's protest was tactful; it still employed *dissimulatio*, but it was evidently, according to Tacitus, an expression of freedom: *libertas Thraseae servitium aliorum rupit* (49).

33. As Rudich puts it (1993, 95): after Nero "renounced friendship with Lucan and forbade public recitation of his poems" (Tac., *Ann.* 15.49), he was "left with the choice of keeping entirely silent and composing "for the drawer," with an eye toward posthumous fame only, or of acquainting a narrow circle of friends and sympathizers with his current writing orally or by circulation of a small number of manuscripts." There may have been conspiracies before 65: cf. Tac. *Ann.* 14.65.2; Pagan 2004, 73–75, argues that Tacitus may have downplayed earlier tendencies "so as to consolidate the conspiracies into one narrative piece" (75).

34. Perhaps there was more. Sullivan 1978 defends the scholiast's attribution of lines 99–102 to Nero, probably from his poem entitled *Attis* or *The Bacchantes* at the *Ludi Iuvenales* of 59 A.D. (Dio 62.20; note the date's appropriateness for Persius's inspiration). But as Morford says (1985, 2016–17), lines 99–102 are probably not by Nero, but "more likely to be the satirist's parodies of the sort of poetry that was favoured by Nero."

35. Cf. Griffin 1984, 156, on the identifying of hostile allusions to Nero in extant contemporary works: "There is no reason to doubt that such allusions exist, some

intended by the author, some invented by malevolent readers or imagined by the Emperor himself." For the danger of the "Caligula" passage (which concerns the triumph of an anonymous "Caesar" until Caesonia is named), we may read back from Bartsch's remarks (1994, 159–60) on Pliny's claim in his (ambiguous) *Panegyricus* that one can now speak out honestly, can denigrate past rulers, whereas "Domitian punished all criticism of his predecessor Nero because he knew himself to be 'doing the same things' and saw in such criticism a veiled attack upon his own person—or at least knew that it would be so interpreted by its audience, who presumably were well aware of the similarities." Intentional or not, "in practical terms it was the audience's reaction that transformed a given statement into an act of opposition or an *ad hominem* slur" (66); "At all times, the blend of allusion, obscurity, and disclaimers was a delicate balancing act that could go wrong and sometimes did" (97). Cf. also D. Griffin (1994, 138–41) on how satire flourishes under constraint, repression, and fear, and how satirists who could not speak out directly might be driven into innuendo, suspicion of which itself becomes a subject of satire. Differently (and this may apply to Persius), an era of ambiguity and simulation "reinforces strategies to reestablish the real, to prove the sincerity of one's intentions, to demonstrate the authenticity of discourse and one's meaning" (Bartsch, 185).

Cucciarelli (2005, 76–77) suggestively reconsiders the "Midas" question in *Satire* 1. "The story [of Midas's replacement by everybody] perhaps originates with a misunderstanding of a commentator's gloss on verse 121. But if, as is probable, the story was first circulated just after, or even contemporaneously with, the book's initial publication, it must still count as a valuable testimony to the open 'legibility' of the text of Persius within, or near, its original setting. The inevitability of certain readers finding an allusion to Nero, the consequent risk of censure, and the necessity of an intervention into the text, work to bring the satires of Persius inside the anti-imperial frame of the opposition. Perhaps the senatorial, Stoic circles in which Persius lived and wrote were inevitably inclined to interpret his poems in a political key. They may have wished to see a political act, a denunciation, in Persius's attempting to muzzle a genre that had been set up to express free speech: 'but for me it's forbidden to mumble?' But apart from tendentious interpretations (perhaps willful mis-appropriations), free speech of an overtly political kind does not appear in Persius' satires. Only philosophical 'freedom,' the emancipation of the individual from the constraints of vice and desire."

36. Most 1989, 2041–42, following Griffin and Sullivan, questions whether there existed any clear-cut Stoic opposition to Nero "or any well-defined literature of opposition as contrasted with the poetry of patronage." As Long (1983, 987) says, "If Stoicism was a threat to tyrannical rulers, this stemmed from its general principles rather than a doctrinal opposition to autocracy. Taking the world as a whole to be like a well-ordered state, the Stoics taught that nothing is of ultimate value to a man except his moral integrity."

37. Cf. Syme's fine account of Thrasea (1958, 554–61), mainly following Tacitus. In his view, philosophical teachings influenced Thrasea less than "the dignity of the governing class, personal honour, and the paramountcy of free speech" (558). Thrasea was "not rigorous or obstinate. . . . He was both sensible and humane." (561n8). Cf. also Rudich 1993, 38: with Agrippina's murder "his stance of *dissimula-*

tio came to an end"; he "hastened to save his own *dignitas* embodied in his individual *libertas*, his inner freedom of thought and action."

38. Musonius and Thrasea : Epict.1.1.27, cited by Lutz 1947, 149. Similarly, Rutherford (1989, 72) notes the steadying influence of philosophical advisers in Tacitus's account of the death of Rubellius Plautus in 62: *ductoresque sapientiae, Coeranum Graeci, Musonium Tusci generis constantiam opperiendae mortis pro incerta et trepida vita suasisse.* For Musonius's continuing influence after his death through his son-in-law Artemidorus and his pupils, including Euphrates and Minicius, cf. Griffin 2007, 455–58, 461–63.

39. Tacitus is characteristically skeptical about the value of Thrasea's dramatic protest, walking out of the senate after Agrippina's death: *sibi causam periculi fecit, ceteris libertatis initium non praebuit.* (*Ann.* 14.12.1). But cf. Villeneuve 1918, 32–43: although Tacitus sometimes reproaches the Stoics for their desire for fame and their useless sacrifices, "Il est necessaire, à certaines époques, que la dignité humaine ait ses martyres." Cf. Epict. 1.2.22 on Helvidius Priscus and the "purple thread."

40. Seneca's comment, *De tranq. animi* 4.6, is similar: *si a prima te rei publica parte fortuna summoverit, stes tamen et clamore iuves et, si quis fauces oppresserit, stes tamen et silentio iuves. Numquam inutilis est opera civis boni; auditus visusque, voltu, nutu, obstinatione tacita incessuque ipso prodest.*

41. Cf. *Vita*, 30–32: *idem decem fere annis* [I translate, "from about the age of ten"] *summe dilectus a Paeto Thrasea est, ita ut peregrinaretur quoque cum eo aliquando, cognatam eius Arriam uxorem habente.* Also, 47–48: Among Persius's unpublished writings that, after his death, Cornutus advised his mother to destroy were a few verses honoring the elder Arria, Thrasea's mother-in-law, who stabbed herself first to encourage her hesitating husband ("*Paete, non dolet*"). If Persius wrote a travel-poem, *hodoporikon*, in the grand tradition of Lucilius and Horace, it may have described a journey with Thrasea. Rudich (1993, 61–62) asks why Persius's mother destroyed these early works, by Cornutus's advice (*Vita*, 48–49): they might have been endowed with an *animus nocendi*—so, to protect the family? (Cizek 1972, 64–65, suggests that Persius in his own person may have linked Cornutus's circle with Thrasea's.)

42. Tacitus, *Ann.* 16.34.2–3 describes how, just before Thrasea received the notice to die, he had gathered many distinguished men and women in his gardens, and was apparently talking with Demetrius the Cynic about the soul's fate and the separation [in death] of spirit and body. Although Tacitus's scene is too Socratic to be altogether convincing, it surely followed many such discussions in Thrasea's gardens: of philosophy, and probably politics, too.

43. Cf. Cizek 1972, 184: Persius's *Satires*, published in 63 or 64, would have strengthened the opposition to Nero, encouraged a spirit of revolt.

44. Weinbrot 1982, 373–74.

45. In his *Discourse of Satire* (1692, in Chambers and Frost 1974), Dryden mainly follows Casaubon, giving a balanced judgment of Persius's merit, which he finds "not equal, in the main, to that of Juvenal or Horace, and yet in some things to be preferred to both of them" (50–51). He jokes about Persius's stylistic obscurity and misses his wit, yet praises his philosophical consistency and seriousness and "a spirit of sincerity in all he says" (51–57). On Dryden's treatment of Persius and its influence, cf. D. Griffin 1994, 19–21. Dryden, he says, wanted it all: "Juvenalian wit and

'Majesty,' Persean moral rigor, and Horatian finesse" (21). "Even in his praise of Persius, Dryden in fact does not offer the moral philosophy or style of Persius's satires for imitation; he emphasizes only their thematic unity and bipolar moral plan. It is thus on a strikingly narrow foundation, a highly selective reading of Persius, that Dryden constructs his powerful, prescriptive theory." For Persius as odd man out, cf. Hooley 2004, 218: "To later ages, Persius' middle position, transitional in the reader's passage from one kind of satire to another, evolved to something like 'middling,' being neither the one or other excellent example of the genre." On the continuing interest in Persius, however, throughout the seventeenth and eighteenth centuries, see Frost 1968–1969 and Dessen 1978; see also the many fine translations up to, and emphatically including, our own time.

46. Weinbrot 1982, 26.

47. Again, I owe this suggestion to my perceptive anonymous reader.

CHAPTER FOUR
LIFE, DEATH, AND ART

1. For a general view, cf. Scullard 1967, 146–51; for a more detailed historical sketch, Terrenato 1998, especially interesting on the critical events after 80 B.C. Cicero's letter (*Fam.* 13.4) to L. Valerius Orca, chair of a commission that might have reorganized the territory radically, "emphasizes as positive qualities both long duration in time and probity (*tam grave, tam firmum, tam honestum municipium*), which should earn the Volaterrans a moral right not to be disrupted. The coalescence of the two concepts is subsumed in the adjective '*firmum*,' with its double meaning of 'steadfast' and 'stable, unmovable' " (107).

2. Lawrence [1932] 1986, 139.

3. Ibid., 146.

4. For photographs and discussions, cf. Mansuelli 1965, 174 and plate 53; Sprenger-Bartoluni 1977, 166 and plates 286–87; *Volterra* 1985, 43 and plate 47 (portraits with typical features, only apparently realistic).

5. Plin, *Ep.* 3.16.

6. There are two funeral inscriptions involving Persii in *CIL* 11.2. One is given by an Aulus Persius Severus (a suggestive *cognomen*) for his wife, Vergilia Saturna; another for a boy of the same name, son of (probably the same) Aulus, who died aged eight years, three months, nineteen days.

7. Terrenato 1998, 109.

8. A scholiast at *Sat.* 2.1 notes that Plotius Macrinus (the dedicatee of *Satire 2*, but not mentioned in the *Vita*) had sold Persius a piece of land on good terms: *alloquitur Macrinum sane hominem eruditum et paterna se affectu diligentem, qui in domo Servilii didicerat, a quo agellum comparaverat indulto sibi pretio aliquantulo* (*Comm. Cornuti*, edd. Clausen-Zetzel). Might there be an ironic compliment to the generous Macrinus in Persius's play on *Macrine* (1)—*non tu prece poscis emaci* (3)— *spem macram* (35) ?

9. Cf. *Epict.* 3.21.40–46, cited by Hadot 1998, 190, on the value of life's ordinary actions: "Eat like a human, drink like a human, get spruced up, get married, have children, live the life of a citizen."

10. Bo points out (at line 7) that in winter, then as still today, the Ligurian sea-shore was much frequented by old and sick people. Near Luna (Roman Lunae, modern Luni, founded 181 B.C.) and the thin Ligurian stretch of coast north of Pisa, there is indeed a large inlet with high cliffs around it, a protected harbor for the Roman fleet (as well as for Persius). Persius's *meum mare* (7) may refer to a place where he long felt at home, perhaps a piece of land that his mother, Fulvia Sisenna, brought her second husband as a part of her dowry (*schol. ad* vi.6). At the time when Persius wrote *Satire* 6, it probably belonged to some relative.

11. If Kissel is right, Persius may be contrasting his dear but real *Portus Lunae* with the "Harbor of the Moon" described by Ennius as a kind of Elysian Fields; cf. his dream of Homer and reincarnation, at which Persius scoffs (as Lucretius did before him). Land and sea, and the shore where they meet, or protected bay, belong to our own world of life and death.

12. Freudenburg (2001, 195f.) and I (in my Spring 1999 Martin Lectures) developed this nice formulation independently.

13. For the shipwrecked man, cf. also Pers. 1.88–91, with its echoes of Horace, *Ars. P.* 19–21, 102–3 (and, behind Horace, Lucr., *DRN.* 3.221–25). As Fiske (1913, 23) says, Horace was discussing stylistic needs; "Persius, however, connects his fig-ure of the pathetic mariner with a plea for simplicity and sincerity." Does the ship-wrecked man in *Satire* 1 overweigh or deconstruct the one in *Satire* 6? Or should we see the two in balance, as reflecting complementary truths of compassion and fraud? Note also how Persius himself will be reduced to an image, of Mercury in a painting (62–63).

14. *In luminis oras*: cf. *DRN.* 1.22, 170, 179; 2.577; 5.1455; and esp. 5.222–27, the newborn babe like a shipwrecked sailor: *tum porro puer, ut saevis proiectus ab undis navita.*

15. On *Satire* 6 and its relation to Horace's *Ep.* 2.2, see Hooley 1997, 154–74, esp. 157, 162. Horace probably intended *Ep.* 2.2 as his poetic epilogue. The *Ars Poetica* was probably earlier (cf. Reckford 2002, n. 9); the *Carmen Saeculare* and *Odes* 4 came later, in 17 and 13 B.C., respectively, and *Ep.* 2.1, the literary report to Augustus, also around 13. Taken together, the long Epistles of Book 2 make up Horace's literary "last will and testament": artistic, personal, and Roman.

16. Two Horatian motifs meet in *Satire* 6: (a) anxiety about what one's heir will say—cf. Horace, *Ep.* 1.5.13–14 (cited by Morford 1984, 66): *Parcus ob heredis curam nimiumque severus / adsidet insano* . . . , here joined with *Ep.* 2.2.190–92; and (b) the greedy or reckless heir, often reacting against a miserly father: *C.* 2.3.17–20, 2.14.25–28, 3.24.54–61, 4.7.19–20; also, and very important for Persius, *Serm.* 2.3.122–23, 142–57, 224–38.

17. The initial mention of "Caesar" at 6.43 (*missa est a Caesare laurus*) must have made people think of Nero, even though this Caesar turns out to be Gaius (Cali-gula), husband of Caesonia, celebrating his fake German triumph; cf. Tacitus's ac-count of triumphal honors accorded Nero in 55 A.D. (*Ann.* 13.8), in 58 (*Ann.* 13.41), and in 61(?) (*Ann.* 15.18); also Suet. *Nero*, 13.1–2. Trevor Luke suggests to me that the *laurus* at 6.43 might especially recall the *litterae laureatae*, probably written by Seneca, that were sent to Rome, justifying Agrippina's murder (Tac. *Ann.* 14.11). "What does seem clear," says Griffin (1984, 233), "is that Nero came to find the burden of expected military glory as hard to bear as Gaius and Claudius had."

"What is characteristic of [Tacitus's] Neronian narrative is the travesty of Roman conceptions of military glory. Thus Nero's entry to Rome after the murder of his mother in 59 resembles that of a *triumphator*" (230); and later, Nero's return from victory in the Greek games resembles a parody of a Roman triumph, such as a satirist would have been glad to invent. Cf. Griffin, 209; Edwards 1994, 90; Champlin 2003, 219–21; Beard 2007, 271n37.

18. Freudenburg's fine discussions of Horace's *Satire* 1.1 (1993, esp. 192–93; 2001, 27–44, esp. 32) connect the attack on unlimited greed familiar from diatribe with Horace's new idea and practice of satire. Freudenburg (2001, 35–38) also develops Putnam's suggestion (1995) that "Horace resembles the shepherd-poet of Eclogue 10 in knowing precisely when and how to set limits to his poetic work" (Freudenburg's wording). For the contented or discontented dinner-guest, cf. Bion-Teles; Lucr., *DRN*. 3.935–39; Hor., *Serm*. 1.1.117–20, *Ep*. 2.2.213–16.

19. The statement in *Vita* 42–44 is puzzling: *scriptitavit et raro et tarde; hunc ipsum librum inperfectum reliquit. Versus aliqui dempti sunt ultimo libro, ut quasi finitus esset.* Did Persius write more verses after the ending we have? Did he leave them in place, perhaps in protest against closure? Did he mark them for deletion? Or did Cornutus do this for him (cf. Morford 1984, 65)? I cannot believe that Cornutus, who "edited the book lightly" (*leviter contraxit, Vita* 44), would have made any significant change in *Satire* 6. The abrupt ending would take on added significance if Persius had meant to go on, perhaps had sketched a start of a seventh satire (cf. Harvey 1981, 202–3) but decided, being close to death, to cut it short—even as Atropos with her shears cuts short a promising young life.

20. Boswell 1799, 2.300–301 (9 May 1773).

21. Leach (1978) speaks of the "common task of self-definition" found in Virgil's *Eclogues*, Horace's *Sermones* 1, and Tibullus's first book of elegies, their shared "strong emphasis upon the achievement of an artistic identity through the completion of a poetic book"; cf. also Zetzel 1980 on *Serm.* 1: "The poems are carefully ordered, so that the interpretation of each one is in some way affected by its position in the book, and conscious irony and ambiguity are the hallmarks of the work as a whole and in its parts" (72–73). The order of Persius's *Satires* is disputed, though *Satire* 1 is generally agreed to be late; I incline now to Villeneuve's ordering (1918, 186): 2, 3, 4, 5, 6, 1. But, as Van Sickle (1980, 5) reminds us, a reader, after finishing the papyrus book roll, might roll it back and read it backwards, "an opportunity to review the work in reverse order and to compare beginning and end." *Satire* 6 might thus be read both as an ending and as a new beginning.

22. See my discussion above, n. 19.

23. I thought that, in a lost folder, I had taken this quotation from Reydams-Schils 1998 or an early version of Reydams-Schils 2005, but neither she nor I could locate it. If I made it up, congratulations to myself; otherwise, sincere apologies to the as yet undiscovered author.

24. Life as a game: Epict. 1.24.20 ("*Ouketi Paisdô!*"); cf. 1.25.7–8, 2.16.37; contrast the merely childish behavior of children (2.16.25, 28) and of "grown-ups" (2.16.39: It's time to be weaned, eat solid food, not cry for mammas and nurses; cf. *Sat.* 3. 16–18). Cf. also Dobbin 1998, 204, on M. Aur., *Med.* 3.7–13: "Regarding life as a play, or game, helps clarify the basic distinction between what is in our power and what is not. The roles, or rules of the game, are dictated by forces beyond

our control, and are therefore not in our power. But it is within our power to play the game (or part) well."

25. Cf. Reckford 2002, on many facets of "childish" and "childlike" behavior in *Epistles* 1 and 2.2.

26. Korzeniewski (1970, 203) notes the imaginative leap from the infant (2.31–40) to the self-frustrating wish for old age (41, ending in *senectae*), suggesting the lifelong sweep of folly.

27. Shakespeare, *As You Like It* II.vii.143–44; cf. also 163–66, the return to "second childishness and mere oblivion."

28. I largely concur with Relihan's argument (1989, 145–46) "that the language of Persius' *Satire* 1 is a private language, a language of self-communion; that his satires are in the main constructed as dialogues within the author's self; that the *Satires* are not primarily directed toward an external audience." I disagree, however, with his subsequent assertion that "there is a coherent progression within the book of satires that culminates in the rejection of the profession of satirist," or "that the topic of the *Satires* as a book is how Persius fails to be a satirist" (146).

29. Lines 9–11 are somewhat unclear, but it seems that people who have allegedly grown up, leaving children's games behind, are engaging in silly, childish activities (*puerilitas*), while assuming a pose of old-fashioned moral strictness (*severitas*). In the case of older men, the contradiction would suggest more or less conscious hypocrisy. With youths, there would be the suggestion of acting or becoming old before their time (cf. *senium*, 26). Bramble (1974, 142–43) follows Némethy (1903) in seeing the hypocritical old men as *cinaedi*, who continue to do what the boys did as *pueri delicati* before they became men. Possibly so; the point remains, that "Persius implies the opposite of what he says (we have not in fact 'grown up')." His main model is Horace, *Ars P.* 109–10, where *patres severi* become literary dilettantes. Might the confusion here with which Persius's interpreters struggle reflect something of that other confusion, the mix-up of ages and behaviors, that he is satirizing?

30. As Beikircher (1969, 42) points out with regard to *Sat.* 6.16, *senium* can refer either to the weakness of old age or to melancholy (*Gram*), worry; Beikircher rightly takes the two together, as worry that ages you prematurely. Note the connection between *minui senio* (16) and *tu bona incolumis minuas?* (37). At 1.26 (*en pallor seniumque*), Kissel (1990) compares Hor., *Ep.* 1.18.47 (*inhumanae senium depone Camenae*) and *Ep.* 2.2.82–83 (*insenuitque libris et curis*). Here we see, in Horace, (a) the popular view of poets as pale, strange figures leading unhealthy lives, acting or becoming old before their time; and (b) a self-ironic protest about the really serious hard work of writing well. For *minui senio*, Harvey (1981) compares Hor., *C.* 2.16.30, *longa Tithonum minuit senectus*. Does Persius console himself with the thought that he won't grow old and bent in body or in spirit?

31. Although the Stoics were more interested in feelings than the Cynics (Hadot 1969, 131–35), they paid most attention to preliminary emotional responses: not *adfectus*, but *principia proludentia adfectibus* (Sen., *De Ira* 2.2.5). What they cared about was "more like motivations than like emotions" (Brennan 2005, 91); the affective side of passions was generally played down (Inwood 1985, 144–45; and see Inwood's fine essay on "Seneca and Psychological Dualism," 23–64). Seneca, *De Ira* 2.2–4 gives our fullest Stoic account of the progress of passion, if not checked, from (a) first, involuntary motions, then (b) joined with judgment, an act of volition,

to (c) rushing headlong, beyond our control. So it's best to extirpate anger alto-
gether from the start: *careamus hoc malo purgemusque mentem et exstirpemus radicitus*
... (3.42.1). Aristotelian moderation and control simply won't work.

32. Constant effort and strain: Cicero, *Tusc.* 2.22–24 (*contentio, intentio*); cf. Vil-
leneuve 1918, 29, "L'effort continuel . . . la perpetuelle surveillance de soi"). Many
positive Stoic terms in Seneca, *De Vita Beata* (*compositum ordinatumque* , 8.3; *concors,
consensit, concinuit,* 8.15) may imply the pressure on nonsages to attain total self-
agreement with no dissenting voice, no hesitation or reluctance to act as one should.
But Persius describes how Cornutus and he balanced concentrated study with
healthy relaxation (5.42–44, "laxamus seria"). Would poetry-writing, too, have alle-
viated the stricter "intentionality" of his Stoic life?

33. Cf. Cic., *Pro Murena* 29–31, where Cicero pokes fun at Cato's Stoicism (*doc-
trina . . . paulo asperior et durior, quam aut veritas aut natura patitur*), with its lack of
forgiveness, compassion, *humanitas*—though he was joking then, "playing to the
gallery" (*De Fin.* 4.74). As Snyder has suggested (1980, 119, developing ideas of
"atomology" first advanced by Friedländer), at *DRN.* 638–44 *inversis sub verbis* "may
hint . . . at Lucretius' own use of verbal play in the nearby lines, . . . including
gravis/Graios (640), the implied *stolidi/Stoici* at 641, and the subtle earlier play on
[*Hera*]*kleitos/clarus*." Cf. also Reckford 1997, 597, and, among later developments,
Shakespeare, *Shrew* 1.1.30, "stock," cited by Brennan 2005, 6.

34. Cf. Long 1982, 986: "Neither of them [Epictetus, Marcus Aurelius], it may
seem, adequately perceived the creative power of human emotions, the charm of
spontaneous behavior, or the delight of aesthetic experience."

35. It is ironic but suggestive that our English word "apathy" comes from
apatheia, the Stoics' ideal "freedom from passion." White 1995 discusses the
"Penitent's Paradox," the problem of grief at our lack of wisdom or inadequate
moral progress (244; Chrysippus advised, not grieving, but new effort at self-
improvement); also, he notes that Chrysippus may have recommended premedita-
tion of ills (Cic., *Tusc.* 3.52, etc.), though "preoccupation with life's darker side
easily leads to depression." (238). Cf. Asmis 1989, 2247, on "a tension in Marcus'
thought between faith in the goodness of the world and a sense of futility," "his
pessimistic belief that the things of this world, including human life, are deeply
flawed." Squillante Saccone (1995) makes good intuitive suggestions about Persi-
us's struggle with *accidia* (35, 40) and melancholy (*passim*), as also about the uses of
humor and aggressive irony as escape from suffering.

36. Cf. Sherman 2005, 85–86: "Can there be a controlled way of being morally
angry and of expressing it in a way that has both social utility and personal *reparative
benefit*?" [italics mine]. Also 96–97, on the problems of using "dissociation in pursuit
of wholeheartedness," and 105f. [despite Sherman's great appreciation of Stoicism,
especially for soldiers] on the value today of feeling outrage, compassion, and fear.

37. According to the *Vita,* 51, Persius died *stomachi vitio*: of an ulcer, or a cancer?
Dan Hooley reminded me (in a private communication, 12 August 2002) that "*sto-
machus* could of course be anything from the throat on down. In any case, an early
death by such means would almost certainly mean chronic pain in later stages."
Cucchiarelli (2001, 199n46) suggests that *vitio stomachi* must have been someone's
educated guess, based on Persius's Lucilian aggressiveness. I wonder whether it was
not rather a psychosomatic reality, induced in some part by repressed anger and

frustration, to which Persius gave voice in the *Satires*; cf. the inner pain powerfully indicated at *Sat*.5.115–17 (*Sin tu . . . astutam vapido servas in pectore volpem*: recall the story of the Spartan boy) and 129–30 (*sed si intus et in iecore aegro nascuntur domini*). Cf. also Squillante Saccone 1995, 26, on Persius's death, the effect of bile in the stomach and diaphragm, and many physical references in his poetry.

38. Sorabji (2000, 294; cf. also 76–77) suggests that the Stoics ignore catharsis because of "the view which Seneca puts that the theatre, and the arts in general, do not stir up emotions at all, but only first movements." I suggest, rather, that the Stoics could see tragedy or comedy—or satire—as (a) stirring up the "first beginnings" of emotions; (b) airing them in a limited, conditional, and playful fashion— after which correct judgment would reassert itself and take over; and thus (c) bringing repressed feelings to consciousness (what I call "emotional self-recognizance") so they can be dealt with by reliable cognitive means. For a related but unorthodox Stoic view that Posidonius may have held, see Colish 1990, 46n117: "Since the passions are irrational by nature, he argues, they cannot be affected by the application of a rational means of control. They can be dealt with only by non-rational means. . . . Posidonius' strategy for allaying the passions is to inflame them in the belief that they possess only a limited amount of energy and that they can be forced in this way to burn themselves out. The passions are to be manipulated and exhausted by such devices as music, poetry, and the imagination."

39. On Stoic views of poetry, cf. DeLacy 1958; Nussbaum 1994, 351: "For unlike Epicureans and Skeptics, unlike Plato as well, they have a high regard for poetry, holding that it can play a valuable role in promoting self-recognition, and especially in confronting the spectator with the vicissitudes and uncertainties of life." But vigilance is needed; cf. Plutarch, *How the Young Person Should Listen to Poetry*, 15D (like Odysseus tied to the mast, not like his sailors). Chrysippus quoted Euripides so lavishly that one person, asked what he was reading, said, "The *Medea* of Chrysippus." (Diog. Laert. 7.180).

40. Religion: *DRN*. 1.63–65; lovers, *DRN*. 4. 1076–81; and cf. Elder's reminder (1954, 92) of how "A whole psychic landscape can be distilled in such a phrase as *atrae formidinis ora* (4.173)."

41. Cf. Segal 1990, 14–15, 30–31, on how Lucretius "ventures more deeply into those fears and experiences which Epicurus dismisses"; Nussbaum 1994, 195–201, on Lucretius's diagnostic argument, in which irrational fears are revealed through irrational behavior, subjective condition, and occasions of acknowledgment. Differently, Michels 1955, 163, 166: "The element in Lucretius' feeling about death which has sometimes been interpreted as suppressed fear is actually the same *horror* that is part of the divine *voluptas* he experiences in the contemplation of the infinite and eternal *maiestas cognita rerum*."

42. Kenney, 83 (with refs.) on *DRN*. 3. 59–86: "The idea that avarice and ambition, with all their attendant crimes, are motivated by fear of death seems to be L's own extension of the Epicurean thesis that it was desire for security . . . that drove men to seek fear and status."

43. Shakespeare, *Measure for Measure*, III.i.117–21, continuing with religious fears, Dantesque images of punishment after death ("And the delighted spirit / to bathe in fiery floods . . . ").

44. Cf. Pythagoras's advice, cited by Epict. 3.10.2–3, to review the day's actions, badly or well done, before going to sleep: rebuke yourself for the bad, take pleasure in the good.

45. Cf. Plato, *Rep.* 330d–331b: A man with many bad deeds on his conscience is afraid as he gets nearer death, often awakens from sleep frightened, as children do.

46. Images of drowning and falling (*Sat.* 3.32–34, 41–42) were imaginatively linked by Lucretius, *DRN.* 3.465–66 (the man in a coma; cf. Segal 1990, 88); drowning also at 3.828–29, *in nigras lethargi mergitur undas* (black being the color of death). Persius rings changes on what may have been a familiar Stoic illustration of the futility of trying to stop passion in midcourse: it is like trying to stop yourself when you've fallen off a cliff (*qui se ex Leucata praecipitaverit*, Cic. *Tusc.* 4.18.41), or when you are being carried out to sea, *in altumque provehitur* (4.18.42); similarly, Seneca, *De Ira* 1.7.4: beginnings are in our power, but then we plunge headlong (*ut in praeceps datis corporibus nullum sui arbitrium est* . . . ; cf. Inwood 2005, 51, citing Chrysippus, *SVF.* 3.462). For Persius, Squillante Saccone (1995, 115–16) suggests a fear of falling into error and evil, but also sees fear of falling as a key obsession of the melancholic, "il segnale dell' angoscia provocata della caduta nella malinconia." Cf. also Hooley 2004, 233: the self's "inward geography" in Persius "is almost always tinged with language of a kind of psychic vertigo and despair"; "That vertiginous *imus, imus praecipites*, when read straight, has the feeling of real despair" (243).

47. Stoic ideas of death and the afterlife are diverse, contradictory. Cf. Hoven 1971; also Asmis 1989, 2250–51, on the different possibilities contemplated by Marcus Aurelius in different places, and compared (2251n99) to other Stoic views. Cleanthes: all souls persist until the world-conflagration; Chrysippus: only the souls of the wise do so; Panaetius: the soul persists after death; Epictetus: the soul doesn't survive the body's death. If the soul is an organized whole, says Marcus, it will either be exstinguished (*sbesthênai* = absorbed into the whole, into the "seminal *logoi*" in the cosmos), or change to another place or condition (*metastênai*); or if there are atoms moving at random, it will be scattered (*skedasthênai*). What matters, however, is not what one thinks or wishes would happen after death, but being prepared to obey the god's will in this, as in all else; cf. Epict. 3.24.95–103. See also Newman 1989, 1512–13, on M. Aur. *Med.* 5.4: "Life is not [as in the usual commonplace] a journey towards death; rather death is simply a point along that journey where we stop and become part of the Nature which produced and nourished us. . . . Death is not an end, but simply a process, a transition."

48. Cf. Lucr. *DRN.* 1.222–23 (penetration through empty spaces within, *per inania*, and dissolution); 3.982–83, *divum metus urget inanis mortalis casumque timent quem cuique ferat fors* [where we might read *inanis* as accusative plural, modifying *mortalis*, as well as nominative singular, modifying *metus*]; 3.998, *nam petere imperium quod inane est nec datur umquam*, . . . ; 5.1431, *in curis consumit inanibus aevum*.

49. Cf. Brunt 1974, 14, on Marcus Aurelius: "To Stoics fame was at best one of the secondary goods, which a man rationally prefers to its opposite but on which he should not set his heart: virtue is its own reward. Marcus continually insists on the worthlessness of reputation, contemporary or posthumous or both; not only on this general ground but also because it is inevitably ephemeral and conferred by men of false principles, whose judgment deserves no respect. . . . On fame he protests too much. Here and there he lets out that he did pay regard to or fear what

was said of him. . . . In any case the mere frequency of his allusions to fame shows how much it was in his mind."

50. Cf. Sorabji 2000, 186–87: one can have "strong, determined, and intense motivation" so long as one understands the true value of things; also 171, on the Stoic image of the archer: what matters in life is not hitting the target, but aiming rightly. Still, I wish Persius could have read Quintilian's praise, *multum et verae gloriae quamvis uno libro Persius meruit* (*Inst.* 10.1.94; though Quintilian still admires Lucilius greatly and rates Horace highest).

51. In Italian, alongside *riconoscimento* ("recognition, acknowledgment, identification"), there is *riconoscenza* ("gratitude, thoughtfulness"); in French, *reconnaissance* denotes recognition, discovery, gratitude, thankfulness, review, acknowledgment, reward, and the like. So I would like to think of my own writing as a *vol de reconnaissance*.

EPILOGUE
FROM PERSIUS TO JUVENAL

1. As Courtney (1980, 2–3, 9) sees it, Juvenal was probably himself a poor client who lived in a humble part of Rome (cf. Martial 12.18); later, his circumstances probably improved. For reading Juvenal, Braund 1988 and 1996 are most helpful. Henderson 1997 reperforms the wild humor of *Satire* 8 in a typically funny but also serious tour de force, playing different kinds of reading, different levels of interpretation, against one another.

2. Throughout this epilogue, I use Niall Rudd's translation (in Rudd and Barr, 1991), colloquial and lively, yet close to Juvenal's verse-structure and rhythms. The reader might also consult Peter Green's freer translation (1967, rev. 1998) for its fun and verve, and Braund's more literal, though still colloquial and humorous, prose version (with facing texts) in her 2004 Loeb volume.

3. Chambers and Frost 1974, 63.

4. Cf. Braund 1996, 105, on Juvenal's debt at 1.142–46 to Persius, *Sat.* 3.98–106: "*turgidus* in the initial position (J. 143; Pers. 3.98) and *hinc* introducing the consequences (J. 144; Pers. 3.102) signal the imitation." Cf also Courtney, 113. For "crudum pavonem" (143), cf. also Horace, *Ep.* 1.6.61 (one of Persius's chief models), *crudi tumidique lavemur*. As Keane says (2006, 97), "While Persius' tale serves as an illustration of madness, Juvenal puts a moralistic and essentially legal twist on the story with the declaration 'Your punishment awaits you' (*poena tamen praesens*, 142)."

5. *Plaudendum* for *plangendum*: Courtney 1980, 115. Cf. also Courtney, 26: "*amicus*, one of the most frequently occurring words in Juvenal (309 times). But on the majority of its occurrences in him the word is ironical, a suitable final stab to end a paragraph (1.146, 5.113 [cf. 108] and 173) or a refrain or complaint (3. 87, 101, 107, 112, 116, 121; all ending the line)." (And add, at 5.173, ending Book 1.)

6. Dickens 1954, 59.

7. Dryden 1974, 54. I note happily that Martindale's parenthetical reading (2005b, 293) agrees with mine: "(the sexual connotations of the language are evi-

dent, and indeed traditional in satire)"; happily, too, that his chosen example of "traditional" (n. 10) is Persius's *Satire* 1.

8. Braund 1996, 121.

9. Again, reading back from Juvenal, we may find homosexual suggestions in Pers. *Sat.* 1.9–11, the serious, hypocritical pose (*nostrum illud vivere triste*, 9; *cum sapimus patruos*, 11) contrasted with the careless, childish behavior; this in turn leads to Persius's wider diagnosis of poetic and personal dysfunction at Rome.

10. Lind 1957, 245–56, includes Brooks's fine translations of the *Choliambics* and *Satires* 1, 3, and 6; passage quoted from 246–47.

11. Expense and futility: Rudd 1976, 85, argues that Juvenal "almost certainly borrowed" from Tacitus, *Dial.* 9.3: "[A] poet who wants to recite has to round up an audience: he is out of pocket because he must borrow a house (*domum mutuatur*), get the room ready, hire seats (*subsellia conducit*), and distribute programmes"; "Juv. gives the material a comic elaboration." I read *Sat.* 7.37–47 as alternately positive and negative: (A1) 37–38, *ipse facit versus* . . . ; (B1) 39–42, *at si dulcedine* . . . ; (A2) 43–44, *scit dare libertos* . . . ; (B2) 45–47, *nemo dabit* . . . ; so, I think, *dare* at 43 suggests a false hope that will be frustrated for the dependent writer. Behind these verses we recall Pers. *Sat.* 1.53–54, *calidum scis ponere sumen, scis comitem horridulum trita donare lacerna*: pathetically inadequate gifts, but gifts nonetheless. But in Juvenal, nobody gives—only a loan at best (*commodat*, 40), and what he knows (*scit*) how to do, he mostly does for his own benefit.

12. But cf. Rudd 1976, 92–93, on *Sat.* 7.29, *hederis et imagine macra*: an emaciated bust, like the emaciated poet; if we compare *quorum . . . sequaces* in Persius's prologue, "we find that Juvenal's *macra* helps turn ironical humour into sardonic wit."

13. Cf. Jenkyns 1982, 178–79: "What he means, in prosaic terms, is that the boys' copies of the school classics are grimy with use and the smoke of the lamps; but his way of putting it is such that for a second we see Virgil and Horace themselves, those noble Augustans, discolored and covered with smuts." Juvenal emphasizes the material conditions of writing: the tablet with its yellow parchment (23), the historian's endless papyrus rolls (100–102); cf. *Sat.* 7.22–29, earlier, where Juvenal cynically advises the poet to give up and burn his writings, or leave them as food for bookworms (*positos tinea pertunde libellos*, 26)—anticipating the destructive work, in any case, of an uncaring Nature.

14. On the perishability of things we struggle for (*tituli*, busts, statues, etc.), cf. Henderson 1997, esp. on *Sat.* 8.1–5: medallion-portraits, waxen masks, busts or heads (28); "fallen idols," statues smashed or mutilated (39–41); the "imagery of *imagines*" throughout *Satire* 8 (84).

15. Cf. Hooley 1997, 201: "The imperative *cedo* elides the hard road to such poise and accomplished virtue; between it and the habits of mind the satire so painstakingly examines is virtually everything. Is, then, an ethical composure analogous to Horace's vision of inner, pastoral peace possible? Persius does not say no. He merely points out its distance from our world and ourselves."

BIBLIOGRAPHY

Abel, K. 1986. "Die dritte satire des Persius als dichterisches Kunstwerk." In *Kontinuität und Wandel. Lateinische Poesie von Naevius bis Baudelaire. F. Munari zum 65. Geb.tag*. Hildesheim: 143–87.

Anderson, W. S. 1982. *Essays on Roman Satire*. Princeton.

Asmis, E. 1989. "The Stoicism of Marcus Aurelius." ANRW 2.36.3, 2228–52.

Bald, R. C. 1970. *John Donne: A Life*. Oxford.

Barchiesi, A., and A. Cucchiarelli. 2005. "Satire and the poet: the body as self-referential symbol." In Freudenburg: 207–23.

Bartsch, S. 1994. *Actors in the Audience: Theatricality and Doublespeak from Nero to Hadrian*. Cambridge, Mass., and London.

———. 1997. *Ideology in Cold Blood: A Reading of Lucan's Civil War*. Cambridge, Mass., and London.

Barthes, R. 1975. *The Pleasure of the Text*. Translated by Richard Miller. New York.

———. 1985. *The Grain of the Voice: Interviews 1962–1980*. Translated by Linda Coverdale. Berkeley and Los Angeles.

Batstone, W. 2006. "Provocation. The point of Reception Theory." In Martindale and Thomas: 14–20.

Baumlin, J. S. 1986. "Donne's Christian Diatribes: Persius and the Rhetorical Persona of 'Satyre III' and 'Satyre V.' " In C. Summers and T. Petworth, eds., *The Eagle and the Dove: Reassessing John Donne*. New York: 92–105.

Beard, M. 2007. *The Roman Triumph*. Cambridge, Mass., and London.

Beikircher, H. 1969. *Kommentar zur VI. Satire des A. Persius Flaccus*. Vienna.

Bernstein, M. 1986–87. " 'O Totiens Servus': Saturnalia and Servitude in Augustan Rome." *Critical Inquiry* 13: 450–74.

Bo, D., ed. 1969. *A. Persi Flacci Saturarum Liber*. Turin.

———. 1991. "Una vexatissima quaestio: Lucilio, Lucrezio e Persio I 1–2." In *Studi di filologia classica in onore di Giusto Monaco, III: Letteratura Latina dall' età di Tiberio all' età del basso impero*. Palermo: 1095–1105.

Boswell, J. 1799. *Life of Johnson*, ed. G. B. Hill. 3d ed., New York.

Bowditch, P. L. 1996. "The Horatian Poetics of Ezra Pound and Robert Pinsky." *CW* 89: 451–57, 466–77.

———. 2001. *Horace and the Gift Economy of Patronage*. Berkeley.

Bramble, J. C. 1974. *Persius and the Programmatic Satire*. Cambridge.

———. 1982. "Martial and Juvenal." *Cambridge History of Classical Literature*, 2:597–623.

Braund, S. H. 1988. *Beyond Anger: A Study of Juvenal's Third Book of Satires*. Cambridge.

———, ed. 1989. *Satire and Society in Ancient Rome*. Exeter.

———. 1992. *Roman Verse Satire*. Oxford.

Braund, S. H. 1996. *The Roman Satirists and Their Masks*. London.

———. 2002. "Twenty-first Century Persius." *Arion* 9.3: 65–80.

———, ed. and trans. 2004. *Juvenal and Persius*. Cambridge, Mass., and London.

Brennan, T. 2005. *The Stoic Life. Emotions, Duties, and Fate*. Oxford.

Brink, C. O. 1963. *Horace on Poetry I: Prolegomena to the Literary Epistles*. Cambridge.

———. 1971. *Horace on Poetry II: The "Ars Poetica."* Cambridge.

———. 1982. *Horace on Poetry III: Epistles Book II: The Letters to Augustus and Florus*. Cambridge.

Brooks, R. A. 1981. *Ennius and Roman Tragedy*. New York.

Brown, P. M. 1993. *Horace Satires I*. Warminster.

Brunt, P. A. 1974. "Marcus Aurelius in his Meditations." *JRS* 64: 1–20.

———. 1977. "From Epictetus to Arrian." *Athenaeum* 55: 19–48.

Burnett, A. P. 1983. *Three Archaic Poets*. London.

Cameron, A. 1995. *Callimachus and His Critics*. Princeton.

Cavallo, G. 1989. "Testo, Libro, Lettura." In G. Cavallo, P. Fedeli, and A. Giardina, eds., *Lo Spazio Letterario di Roma Antica II: La Circolazione del Testo*. Rome: 307–41.

Chambers, A. B., and W. Frost, eds. 1974. *The Works of John Dryden. IV: Poems 1693–1696*. Berkeley.

Champlin, E. 2003. *Nero*. Cambridge, Mass.

Christes, J. 1971. *Der Frühe Lucilius*. Heidelberg.

Citroni, M. 1989. "Musa Pedestre." In G. Cavallo, P. Fedeli, and A. Giardina, eds., *Lo Spazio Letterario di Roma Antica I: La Produzione del Testo*. Rome: 311–35.

———. 1990. "I Destinatari Contemporanei." In G. Cavallo, P. Fedeli, and A. Giardina, eds., *Lo Spazio Letterario di Roma Antica III: La Recezione del Testo*. Rome: 53–116.

———. 1991. "L'Autobiografia nella satira e nell' epigramma Latino." In idem, *La componente autobiografica nella poesia greca e latina fra realtà e artificio letterario*. Pisa: 275–92.

———. 1992. "Gli interlocutori del sermo Oraziano: gioco scenico e destinazione del testo." In G. Arrighetti and F. Montanari, eds., *Atti del Convegno Nazionale di Studi su Orazio*. Turin: 95–127.

———. 1995. *Poesia e Lettori in Roma Antica*. Rome.

Cizek, E. 1972. *L'Époque de Néron et ses Controverses Idéologiques*. Leiden.

Clark, G. 1995. *Augustine: Confessions, Books I–IV*. Cambridge.

Clarke, G., 1990. *T. S. Eliot: Critical Assessments*. 2 Vols. London.

Clausen, W. V. 1956. *A. Persi Flacci Saturarum Liber*. Oxford.

———. 1992. *A. Persi Flacci et D. Iuni Iuvenalis Saturae*, 2d ed. Oxford.

Clausen, W. V., and J. E. G. Zetzel. 2004. *Commentum Cornuti in Persium*. Munich and Leipzig.

Clayman, D. L. 1980. *Callimachus' Iambi*. Leiden.

Coffee, M. 1976. *Roman Satire*. London and New York.

Colish, M. L. 1990. *The Stoic Tradition from Antiquity to the Early Middle Ages. Vol. I: Stoicism in Classical Latin Literature*. Leiden.

Conington, J. 1893. *The Satires of A. Persius Flaccus*, 3d ed. rev. Oxford.

Conte, G. B. 1986. *The Rhetoric of Imitation: Genre and Poetic Meaning in Virgil and Other Latin Poets*. Ithaca and London.

————. 1994. *Latin Literature: A History.* Translated by J. B.Solodow. Revised by D. Fowler and G. W. Most. Baltimore and London.

Costa, C. D. N. 1994. *Seneca: Four Dialogues.* Warminster.

Courtney, E. 1980. *A Commentary on the Satires of Juvenal.* London.

Cucchiarelli, A. 2001. *La satira e il poeta: Orazio tra Epodi e Sermones.* Pisa.

————. 2005. "Speaking from Silence: the Stoic Paradoxes of Persius." In Freuden-burg: 62–80.

DeLacy, P. 1958. "Stoic Views of Poetry." *AJP* 69: 241–71.

Delius, H–U. 1978–79. "Luther und die Satiren des Persius." *Helikon* 18–19: 364–77.

Dessen, C. S. 1978. "An Eighteenth-Century Imitation of Persius, Satire I." *Texas Studies in Literature and Language* 20: 433–56.

————. 1996. *The Satires of Persius. Iunctura Callidus Acri.* 2d ed. London.

Dickens, C. 1910. "A Christmas Carol," in idem, *Christmas Books* [1852]. New York.

Dilke, O. A. W. 1981. "The Interpretation of Horace's 'Epistles,' " *ANRW* 2.31.3: 1837–65.

Dobbin, R. 1998. *Epictetus: Discourses Book 1.* Oxford.

Donaghue, D. 2000. *Words Alone. The Poet T. S. Eliot.* New Haven and London.

Dover, K. J. 1993. *Aristophanes: Frogs.* Oxford.

Dudley, D. R. 1937. *A History of Cynicism.* London.

Dupont, F. 1997. "*Recitatio* and the Reorganization of the Space of Public Dis-course." Translated by T. Habinek and A. Lardinois. In T. Habinek and A. Schiesaro, eds., *The Roman Cultural Revolution.* Cambridge: 44–59.

DuQuesnay, J. M. LeM. 1984. "Horace and Maecenas: The Propaganda Value of *Sermones 1.*" In Woodman and West: 19–58.

Edelstein, L. and Kidd, J. G. 1972. *Posidonius I: The Fragments.* Cambridge.

Edmunds, L. 1992. *From a Sabine Jar: Reading Horace, Odes 1.9.* Chapel Hill and London.

————. 2001. *Intertextuality and the Reading of Roman Poetry.* Baltimore and London.

Edwards, C. 1993. *The Politics of Immorality in Ancient Rome.* Cambridge.

————. 1994. "Beware of Imitations: Theatre and the Subversion of Imperial Iden-tity." In Elsner and Masters: 83–97.

————. 1997. "Self-Scrutiny and Self-Transformation in Seneca's Letters." *G and R* 44: 23–38.

Ehlers, W–W. 1990. "Zur Rezitation der Satire des Persius." In G.Vogt-Spira, ed., *Strukturen der Mündlichkeit in der römischen Literatur.* Tübingen: 171–81.

Elder, J. P. 1954. "Lucretius 1.1–49." *TAPA* 85: 88–120.

Eliot, T. S. 1950. *Selected Essays.* New York.

————. 1957. *On Poetry and Poets.* London.

————. 1971. *The Waste Land: A Facsimile and Transcript of the Original Drafts Includ-ing the Annotations of Ezra Pound,* ed. Valerie Eliot. New York.

Elsner, J., and J. Masters, eds. 1994. *Reflections of Nero: Culture, History, and Represen-tation.* Chapel Hill and London.

Fantham, E. 1996. *Roman Literary Culture. From Cicero to Apuleius.* Baltimore and London.

Farrell, J. 1991. *Vergil's Georgics and the Traditions of Ancient Epic: The Art of Allusion in Literary History*. New York and Oxford.

———. 2005. "Intention and Intertext." *Phoenix* 59: 98–111.

Fedeli, P. 1989. "I Sistemi di Produzione e Diffusione." In G. Cavallo, P. Fedeli, and A. Giardina, eds., *Lo Spazio Letterario di Roma Antica II: La Circolazione del Testo*. Rome: 343–78.

Feeney, D. 2002. "UNA CUM SCRIPTORE MEO: Poetry, Principate, and the Traditions of Literary History in the Epistle to Augustus." In Woodman and Feeney: 172–87.

Ferri, R. 1993. *I dispiaceri di un epicureo*. Pisa.

Fish, S. 1980. *Is There a Text in This Class? The Power of Interpretive Communities*. Cambridge, Mass.

Fiske, G. C. 1913. "Lucilius, the *Ars Poetica* of Horace, and Persius." *HSCP* 24: 1–36.

———. [1920] 1971. *Lucilius and Horace. A Study in the Classical Theory of Imitation*. Westport, Conn.

Fitzgerald, W. 2000. *Slavery and the Roman Literary Imagination*. Cambridge.

Flintoff, E. 1982. "Food for Thought. Some Imagery in Persius Satire 2." *Hermes* 110: 341–54.

Forster, E. M. 1936. *Abinger Harvest*. London.

Foucault, M. 1988. *The Care of the Self*. Translated by R. Hurley. New York.

Fowler, D. 2000. *Roman Constructions: Readings in Postmodern Latin*. Oxford.

Freudenburg, K. 1990. "Horace's Satiric Program and the Language of Contemporary Theory in *Satires* 2.1." *AJP* 111: 187–203.

———. 1993. *The Walking Muse: Horace on the Theory of Satire*. Princeton.

———. 2001. *Satires of Rome: Threatening Poses from Lucilius to Juvenal*. Cambridge.

———. 2002. "SOLUS SAPIENS LIBER EST: Recommissioning Lyric in *Epistles I*." In Woodman and Feeney: 124–40.

———, ed. 2005. *The Cambridge Companion to Roman Satire*. Cambridge.

Frischer, B. 1991. *Shifting Paradigms: New Approaches to Horace's Ars Poetica*. Atlanta.

Frost, W. 1968–69. "English Persius in the Golden Age." *Eighteenth Century Studies* 2.2: 77–101.

Gamel, M–K. 1998. "Reading as a Man: Performance and Gender in Roman Elegy." *Helios* 25: 79–95.

Gardner, H. [1950] 1959. *The Art of T. S. Eliot*. New York.

———. 1973. "*The Waste Land*: Paris 1922." In North 2001: 72–89.

Gärtner, U. 2001. "Lucilius und die Freundschaft." In Manuwald: 90–110.

Gentili, B. 1984. *Poesia e Pubblico nella Grecia Antica*. Rome.

Gildersleeve, B. L. 1903. *The Satires of A. Persius Flaccus*. New York.

Gill, C. 1998. "Personhood and Personality: The Four-Personae Theory in Cicero, *De Officiis* I." In J. Annas, ed, *Oxford Studies in Ancient Philosophy* 6: 169–99.

Gold, B. 1992. "Openings in Horace's *Satires* and *Odes*: Poet, Patron, and Audience." *YCS* 29: 161–85.

———. 1994. "Humor in Juvenal's Sixth Satire: Is it Funny?" In S. Jakel and A. Timonen, eds., *Laughter Down the Centuries*. Turku: 1:95–111.

Goldberg, S. M. 2005. *Constructing Literature in the Roman Republic: Poetry and its Reception*. Cambridge.

Gordon, L. 1988. *Eliot's New Life*. New York.

———. 1999. *T. S. Eliot: An Imperfect Life*. New York.

Gowers, E. 1993. *The Loaded Table: Representations of Food in Roman Literature*. Oxford.

———. 1994. "Persius and the Decoction of Nero." In Elsner and Masters 1994: 131–50.

———. 2003. "Fragments of Autobiography in Horace *Satires* I." *CA* 22: 55–91.

Gratwick, M. S. 1982. "The Satires of Ennius and Lucilius," *CHCL* 2: 156–71.

Green, P. 1967. *Juvenal: The Sixteen Satires*. New York.

Greenblatt, S. 1980. *Renaissance Self-Fashioning: From More to Shakespeare*. Chicago.

Griffin, D. 1994. *Satire: A Critical Reintroduction*. Lexington, Ky.

Griffin, M. T. 1976. *Seneca: A Philosopher in Politics*. Oxford.

———. 1984. *Nero: The End of a Dynasty*. New Haven and London.

———. 1996. "Cynicism and the Romans: Attraction and Repulsion." In R. B. Branham and M–O. Goulet-Cazé, eds., *The Cynics*. Berkeley and Los Angeles: 190–204.

———. 2007. "The Younger Pliny's Debt to Moral Philosophy," *HSCP* 103: 451–81.

Grimes, S. 1972. "Structure in the Satires of Persius." In D. R.Dudley, ed., *Neronians and Flavians: Silver Latin I*. London and Boston: 113–54.

Gruen, E. S. 1992. *Culture and National Identity in Republican Rome*. Ithaca.

Gunderson, E. 2005. "The Libidinal Rhetoric of Satire." In Freudenburg: 224–40.

Habinek, T. 2005. *The World of Roman Song: From Ritualized Speech to Social Order*. Baltimore and London.

Hadot, I. 1969. *Seneca und die Griechisch-Römische Tradition der Seelenleitung*. Berlin.

Hadot, P. 1998. *The Inner Citadel. The Meditations of Marcus Aurelius*. Translated by M. Chase. Cambridge, Mass., and London.

Hagendahl, H. 1958. *Latin Fathers and the Classics*. Göteborg.

———. 1967. *Augustine and the Latin Classics*. Stockholm.

Halpern, D. 1995. *Who's Writing This? Notations on the Authorial I with Self-portraits*. Hopewell, N.J.

Harrison, G. 1987. "The Confessions of Lucilius (Horace *Sat*. 2.1.30–34): A Defense of Autobiographical Satire?" *CA* 6: 38–52.

Harrison, G. W. M., ed. 2000. *Seneca in Performance*. London.

Harrison, S. J., ed. 1995. *Homage to Horace: A Bimillenary Celebration*. Oxford.

———. 2007. *Generic Enrichment in Vergil and Horace*. Oxford.

Harvey, R. A. 1981. *A Commentary on Persius*. Leiden.

Havel, V. 1989. "The Power of the Powerless." Translated by P. Wilson. In Havel, *Living in Truth*, ed. J. Vladislav. London and Boston: 36–122.

Henderson, J. 1989. " Not 'Women in Satire' but 'Satire Writes Woman.' " In Braund 1989: 89–125, 139–49.

———. 1991. "Persius' Didactic Satire: The Pupil as Teacher." *Ramus* 20: 123–48.

———. 1997. *Figuring Out Roman Nobility. Juvenal's Eighth Satire*. Exeter.

Henderson, J. 1999. *Wtiting Down Rome: Satire, Comedy, and other Offences in Latin Poetry.* Oxford.

Hendrickson, G. L. 1894. "The Dramatic *Satura* and the Old Comedy at Rome." *AJP* 15: 1–30.

———. 1900. "Horace, *Serm.* I.4: A Protest and a Program." *AJP* 21: 121–42.

———. 1928a. "The First Satire of Persius." *CP* 23: 97–112.

———. 1928b. "The Third Satire of Persius." *CP* 23: 332–42.

Hense, O. [1909] 1969. *Teletis Reliquiae.* Hildesheim and New York.

Henss, D. 1955. "Die Imitationstechnik des Persius." *Philologus* 99: 277–94.

Herington, J. 1985. *Poetry Into Drama: Early Tragedy and the Greek Poetic Tradition.* Berkeley, Los Angeles, and London.

Hershbell, J. P. 1989. "The Stoicism of Epictetus: Twentieth Century Perspectives." *ANRW* II.36.3: 2148–63.

Hester, M. T. 1982. *Kinde Pitty and Brave Scorn: John Donne's* Satyres. Durham, N.C.

Highet, G. 1949. *The Classical Tradition.* New York and London.

Hillman, J. 1979. "*Senex* and *Puer.*" In *Puer Papers.* Irving, Tex.: 3–53.

Hinds, S. 1998. *Allusion and Intertext. Dynamics of Appropriation in Roman Poetry.* Cambridge.

Hirth, H. J. 1985. *Horaz: Der Dichter der Briefe.* Hildesheim, Zurich, and New York.

Hooley, D. M. 1997. *The Knotted Thong: Structures of Mimesis in Persius.* Ann Arbor.

———. 2004. "Persius in the Middle." In S. Kyriakidis and F. De Martino, eds., *Middles in Latin Poetry.* Bari: 217–43.

Housman, A. E. 1913. "Notes on Persius." *CQ* 7: 12–32.

Hoven, R. 1971. *Stoïcisme et Stoïciens Face Au Problème de l'Au-delà.* Paris.

Hunter, R. 1996. *Theocritus and the Archaeology of Greek Poetry.* Cambridge.

Hutchison, A. N. 1970. "Constant Company: John Donne and his Satiric Personae." *Discourse* 13: 354–63.

Inwood, B. 1985. *Ethics and Human Action in Early Stoicism.* Oxford.

———. 2005. *Reading Seneca: Stoic Philosophy at Rome.* Oxford.

Jahn, O., ed. 1843. *Auli Persii Flacci Saturarum Liber.* Leipzig.

Jenkinson, R. 1973. "Interpretations of Persius' Satires III and IV." *Latomus* 32: 521–49.

Jenkyns, R. 1982. *Three Classical Poets: Sappho, Catullus, and Juvenal.* Cambridge, Mass.

Johnson, W. A. 2000. "Toward a Sociology of Reading in Classical Antiquity." *AJP* 121: 593–627.

Johnson, W. R. 1992. "The Death of Pleasure: Literary Critics in Technological Societies." In G. K. Galinsky, ed., *The Interpretation of Roman Poetry: Empiricism or Hermeneutics?* Frankfurt: 200–214.

———. 1993. *Horace and the Dialectic of Freedom: Readings in Epistles 1.* Ithaca and London.

Kallendorf, C. 2006. "Virgil, Milton, and the Modern Reader." In Martindale and Thomas: 67–79.

Kaster, R. A. 1995. *Suetonius De Grammaticis et Rhetoribus.* Oxford.

Keane, C. 2002a. "Satiric Memories: Autobiography and the Construction of Genre." *CJ* 97: 215–31.

———.2002b. "The Critical Contexts of Satiric Discourse." *CML* 22: 7–31.

———. 2006. *Figuring Genre in Roman Satire*. Oxford.

Kennedy, D. F. 1992. " 'Augustan' and 'Anti-Augustan': Reflections on Terms of Reference." In A. Powell, ed., *Roman Poetry and Propaganda in the Age of Augustus*. Bristol: 26–58.

Kenner, H. 1973. "The Urban Apocalypse." In Litz: 23–49.

Kernan, A. 1959. *The Cankered Muse: Satires of the English Renaissance*. New Haven.

Kidd, D. A. 1982. "Astrology for Maecenas." *Antichthon* 16: 88–96.

Kidd, J. G. 1988. *Posidonius II: The Commentary*. Cambridge.

Kilpatrick, R. S. 1986. *The Poetry of Friendship: Horace, Epistles I*. Edmonton.

———. 1990. *The Poetry of Criticism: Horace, Epistles II and Ars Poetica*. Edmonton.

Kindstrand, J. F. 1976. *Bion of Borysthenes*. Uppsala.

King, R. J. 1998. "Ritual and Autobiography: The Cult of Reading in Ovid's *Tristia* 4.10." *Helios* 25: 99–119.

Kirby, J. T. "Toward a Rhetoric of Poetics: Rhetor as Author and Narrator." *Journal of Narrative Technique* 22: 1–22.

Kissel, W. 1990. *Aulus Persius Flaccus Satiren*. Heidelberg.

Klingner, F., ed. 1970. *Q. Horati Flacci Opera*. Leipzig.

Knox, B. 1996. "Author, Author." *Philosophy and Literature* 20: 76–88.

Korzeniewski, D. 1970. "Die zweite Satire des Persius." In D. Korzeniewski, ed., *Die römische Satire*. Darmstadt: 199–210.

Krenkel, W. 1970. *Lucilius Satiren* . Leiden.

Labate, M. 1981. *Quinto Orazio Flacco Satire*. Milan.

LaFleur, R. A. 1981. "Horace and Onomasti Komodein: The Law of Satire." *ANRW* II.31.3: 1790–1826.

LaPenna, A. 1959. *Persio Satire*. Milan.

———. 1992. "Orazio e la relativizzazione della morale." In *Atti del Convegno Nazionale di Studi su Orazio*. Turin: 43–72.

———. 1993. *Saggi e studi su Orazio*. Florence.

Laurenti, R. 1989. "Musonio, maestro di Epitteto." *ANRW* II.36.3: 2105–46.

Lawrence, D. H. 1932. *Etruscan Places*. London: repr. 1986, Siena.

Leach, E. W. 1978. "Vergil, Horace, Tibullus: Three Collections of Ten." *Ramus* 7: 79–105.

Lee, G., and W. Barr. 1987. *The Satires of Persius*. Liverpool.

Lefèvre, E., 2001. "Lucilius und die Politik." In Manuwald: 139–49.

Lind, L. R., ed. 1957. *Latin Poetry in Verse Translation*. Boston.

Littlewood, C. 2002. "*Integer Ipse*? Self-knowledge and Self-representation in Persius *Satires* 4." *Phoenix* 56: 56–83.

Litz, A. W., ed. 1973. *Eliot in His Time: Essays on the Occasion of the Fiftieth Anniversary of* The Waste Land. Princeton.

Long, A. A. 1982. "Epictetus, Marcus Aurelius." In T. J.Luce, ed., *Ancient Writers II: Greece and Rome*. New York: 985–1102.

———. 2002. *Epictetus. A Stoic and Socratic Guide to Life*. Oxford.

Long, A. A., and D. N. Sedley. 1987. *The Hellenistic Philosophers*. Cambridge.

Lutz, C. E. 1947. "Musonius Rufus: 'The Roman Socrates.' " *YCS* 10: 3–147.

———. "The Symbol of the Y of Pythagoras in the Ninth Century." In idem, *The Oldest Library Motto and Other Library Essays*. Hamden, Conn.

Macleod, C. 1977. "The Poet, the Critic, and the Moralist: Horace, *Epistles* 1.19."
    CQ 27: 359–76.

———. 1979. "The Poetry of Ethics: Horace, *Epistles I*." *JRS* 69: 16–27.

———. 1986. *Horace: The Epistles*. Rome.

Malamud, M. 1996. "Out of Circulation? An Essay on Exchange in Persius' Sat-
    ires." *Ramus* 25: 39–64.

Mansuelli, G. A. 1965. *The Art of Etruria and Early Rome*. Translated by C. E. Ellis.
    New York.

Manuwald, G., ed. 2001. *Der Satiriker Lucilius und seine Zeit*. Munich.

Maresca, T. E. 1966. *Pope's Horatian Poems*. Columbus.

Markus, D. D. 2000. "Performing the Book: The Recital of Epic in First-Century
    c.e. Rome." *CA* 19: 138–79.

Marmorale, E. V. 1956. *Persio*. Florence.

Martindale, C. 1993a. *Redeeming the Text: Latin Poetry and the Hermeneutics of Recep-
    tion*. Cambridge.

———. 1993b. "Introduction." In Martindale and Hopkins: 1–26.

———. 2005a. *Latin Poetry and the Judgment of Taste: An Essay in Aesthetics*. Oxford.

———. 2005b. "The Horatian and the Juvenalesque in English letters." In Freu-
    denburg: 284–98.

———. 2006. "Introduction: Thinking Through Reception." In Martindale and
    Thomas: 1–13.

Martindale, C., and D. Hopkins, eds. 1993. *Horace Made New*. Cambridge.

Martindale, C., and R. F. Thomas, eds. 2006. *Classics and the Uses of Reception*.
    Oxford.

Marx, F. 1904–5. *C. Lucilii Carmina Reliquiae*. Leipzig.

Mason, H. A. 1963. "Is Juvenal a Classic? An Introductory Essay." In Sullivan 1963:
    93–176.

McCarthy, K. 2000. *Slaves, Masters, and the Art of Authority in Plautine Comedy*.
    Princeton and Oxford.

McDermott, E. A. 1982. "Horace, Maecenas, and Odes 2.17." *Hermes* 110:
    211–28.

McGann, M. J. 1969. *Studies in Horace's First Book of Epistles*. Brussels.

Medine, P. E. 1976. "Isaac Casaubon's *Prolegomena* to the Satires of Persius: An
    Introduction, Text, and Translation." *ELR* 6: 271–98.

Merrill, P. F. 1991. *Deception and Perception in the Sixth Satire of Persius*. Ph.D. Diss.,
    University of North Carolina.

Merwin, W. S., and W. S. Anderson. 1961. *The Satires of Persius*. Bloomington.

Michels, A. K. 1955. "Death and Two Poets." *TAPA* 86: 160–79.

Miller, P. A. 1998. "The Bodily Grotesque in Roman Satire: Images of Sterility."
    Arethusa 31: 257–83.

———. 2005. *Latin Verse Satire. An Anthology and Critical Reader*. London and
    New York.

Moles, J. 2002. "Poetry, Philosophy, Politics and Play: *Epistles I*." In Woodman and
    Feeney: 141–57.

Morford, M. 1984. *Persius*. Boston.

———. 1985. "Nero's Patronage and Participation in Literature and the Arts."
    ANRW II.32.3: 2003–31.

———. 2001. "*Sum Petulante Splene: Cachinno*: The Humor of Persius." *CB* 77: 35–49.

Morgan, M. H. 1909. *A Bibliography of Persius*. Cambridge, Mass.

Most, G. W. 1989. "Cornutus and Stoic Allegoresis: A Preliminary Report." *ANRW* II.36.3: 2014–65.

———. 1992. "*Disiecti membra poetae*: The Rhetoric of Dismemberment in Neronian Poetry." In R. Hexter and D. Selden, eds., *Innovations of Antiquity*. New York and London: 391–419.

———. 1998. " 'With Fearful Steps Pursuing': Hopes of High Talk with the Departed Dead." *TAPA* 128: 311–24.

Muecke, F. 1979. "Horace the Satirist: Form and Method in *Satires* 1.4." *Prudentia* 11: 55–68.

———. 1990. "The Audience of/in Horace's *Satires*." *AUMLA* 74: 34–47.

———. 1995. "Law, Rhetoric, and Genre in Horace, *Satires* 2.1." In Harrison: 203–18.

———. 1997. *Horace: Satires II*. Warminster.

Nauta, R.R. 1994. "Historicizing Reading: The Aesthetics of Reception and Horace's 'Soracte Ode.' " In I. F. J. DeJong and J. P.Sullivan, eds., *Modern Critical Theory and Classical Literature*. Leiden: 207–30.

Nehamas, A. 1998. *The Art of Living: Socratic Reflections from Plato to Foucault*. Berkeley, Los Angeles, and London

Némethy, G., ed, 1903. *A. Persii Flacci Satirae*. Budapest.

Newman, R. J. 1989. "*Cotidie meditare*. Theory and Practice of the *meditatio* in Imperial Stoicism." *ANRW* II.36.3: 1473–1517.

Nisbet, R. G. M. 1963. "Persius." In Sullivan: 39–71.

Nisbet, R. G. M., and M. Hubbard. 1978. *A Commentary on Horace: Odes, Book II*. Oxford.

Nock, A. D. 1931. "Kornutos." *RE Suppl.* 5: cols. 995–1005.

North, M., ed. 1991. *T. S. Eliot: The Waste Land*. New York and London.

Nussbaum, M. C. 1994. *The Therapy of Desire*. Princeton.

———. 2002. "The Incomplete Feminism of Musonius Rufus, Platonist, Stoic, and Roman." In M. C. Nussbaum and J. Sihvola, eds., *The Sleep of Reason*. Chicago and London: 283–326.

Oakley, J. P. 1998. *A Commentary on Livy Books VI–X. Vol. II: Books VII–VIII*. Oxford.

Oldfather, W. A. 1925. *Epictetus*. Cambridge, Mass., and London.

Oliensis, E. 1995. "Life After Publication: Horace, *Epistles* 1.20." *Arethusa* 28: 209–24.

———. 1998. *Horace and the Rhetoric of Authority*. Cambridge.

Oltramare, A. 1926. *Les origines de la diatribe Romaine*. Lausanne.

O'Neill, J. N. 1994. *Place in Horace: An Examination of Social Hierarchies in Horace, Epistles I*." Ph.D. Diss., Harvard University.

Pagan, V. E. 2004. *Conspiracy Narratives in Roman History*. Austin.

Paratore, E. 1968. *Biografia e Poetica di Persio*. Florence.

Pasoli, E. 1982. *Tre Poeti Latini Espressionisti: Properzio, Persio, Giovenale*. Rome.

Pasoli, E. 1985. "Attualità di Persio." *ANRW* II.32.3: 1813–43.

Peterson, R. G. 1972–73. "The Unknown Self in the Fourth Satire of Persius." *CJ* 68: 205–9.

Pinsky, R. 1979. *An Explanation of America*. Princeton.

Plaza, M. 2006. *The Function of Humour in Roman Verse Satire: Laughing and Lying*. Oxford.

Porter, D. H. 2002. "Playing the Game: Horace, *Epistles* 1." *CW* 96: 21–60.

Porter, J. J. 2006. "Foucault's Antiquity." In Martindale and Thomas: 168–79.

Puelma Piwonka, M. 1949. *Lucilius und Kallimachos*. Frankfurt. Repr. 1978: New York and London.

Putnam, M. 1995. "Pastoral Satire." *Arion* 3: 303–16.

———. 2001. "The Loom of Latin." *TAPA* 131: 329–39.

Quinn, K. 1982. "The Poet and His Audience in the Augustan Age." *ANRW* II.30.1: 75–180.

Raine, C. 2006. *T. S. Eliot*. Oxford.

Rainey, L. 2005. *Revisiting The Waste Land*. New Haven and London.

Randolph, M. C. 1939. *The Neo-Classic Theory of the Formal Verse Satire in England, 1700–1750*. Ph.D. Diss., University of North Carolina.

———. 1941. "The Medical Concept in English Renaissance Satiric Theory: Its Possible Relationships and Implications." *SP* 38: 125–57.

Raschke, W. 1987. "*Arma Pro Amico*: Lucilian Satire at a Crisis of the Roman Republic." *Hermes* 115: 299–318.

Reckford, K. J. 1962. "Studies in Persius." *Hermes* 90: 476–504.

———. 1969. *Horace*. New York.

———. 1987. *Aristophanes' Old-and-New Comedy. Volume I: Six Essays in Perspective*. Chapel Hill and London.

———. 1991. "Horace Revisited." *Arion* 3d series, 1: 209–22.

———. 1997. "Horatius: The Man and the Hour." *AJP* 118: 583–612.

———. 1998. "Reading the Sick Body: Decomposition and Morality in Persius' Third Satire." *Arethusa* 31: 337–54.

———. 1999a. "Only a Wet Dream? Hope and Skepticism in Horace, *Satires* 1.5." *AJP* 120: 525–54.

———. 1999b. "Persius." In *Dictionary of Literary Biography*, vol. 211, *Ancient Roman Writers*, ed. W. W. Briggs. Detroit, San Francisco, and London: 208–13.

———. 2002. "*Pueri ludentes*: Some Aspects of Play and Seriousness in Horace's *Epistles*." *TAPA* 132: 1–19.

Relihan, J. C. 1989. "The Confessions of Persius." *ICS* 14: 145–67.

———. 1991. "Pardoning Persius' Laughter." *Mnem.* 44: 433–35.

Reydams-Schils, Gretchen. 1998. "Roman and Stoic: The Self as a Mediator." *Dionysius* 14: 35–62.

———. 2005. *The Roman Stoics: Self, Responsibility, and Affection*. Chicago.

Richlin, A. 1992. *The Garden of Priapus: Sexuality and Aggression in Roman Humor*. Rev. ed. Oxford.

Rosen, R. M. 1988. *Old Comedy and the Iambographic Tradition*. Atlanta.

———. 1992. "Mixing of Genres and Literary Program in *Herodas 8*." *HSCP* 94: 205–18.

———. 2007. *Making Mockery: The Poetics of Ancient Satire*. Oxford.

Roth, P. 1988. *The Counterlife*. New York.

Rostagni, A. 1944. *Suetonio De Poetis e Biografi Minori*. Turin.

Rubino, C. A. 1985. "Monuments and Pyramids: Death and the Poet in Horace, *Carmina* 3.30." *CML* 5: 99–111.

Rudd, N. 1966. *The Satires of Horace*. Cambridge.

———. 1970. "Persiana." *CR* 20: 282–88.

———. 1973. *Horace: Satires and Epistles. Persius: Satires*. London.

———. 1976. *Lines of Inquiry: Studies in Latin Poetry*. Cambridge.

———. 1986. *Themes in Roman Satire*. Norman, Okla., and London.

Rudd, N., and W. Barr. 1991. *Juvenal: The Satires*. Translated by Niall Rudd. Introduction and notes by William Barr. Oxford.

Rudich, V. 1993. *Political Dissidence Under Nero: The Price of Dissimulation*. London and New York.

Rutherford, R. B. 1981. "Horace, *Epistles* 2.2: Introspection and Retrospective." *CQ* 31: 375–80.

———. 1989. *The Meditations of Marcus Aurelius: A Study*. Oxford.

Schlegel, C. M. 2000. "Horace and His Fathers: *Satires* 1.4 and 1.6." *AJP* 121: 93–119.

———. 2005. *Satire and the Threat of Speech: Horace's* Satires, *Book 1*. Madison.

Scholz, U. W. "Der frühe Lucilius und Horaz." *Hermes* 114: 335–65.

Scullard, H. H. 1967. *The Etruscan Cities and Rome*. Baltimore and London.

Segal, C. 1989. "Poetic Immortality and the Fear of Death: The Second Proem of the *De Rerum Natura*." *HSCP* 92: 193–212.

———. 1990. *Lucretius on Death and Anxiety: Poetry and Philosophy in the* De Rerum Natura. Princeton.

Selden, R. 1978. *English Verse Satire, 1590–1765*. London.

Sherman, N. 2005. *Stoic Warriors: The Ancient Philosophy Behind the Military Mind*. Oxford.

Skinner, M. B. 1993. "Catullus in Performance." *CJ* 89: 61–68.

Slater, N. W. 1990. *Reading Petronius*. Baltimore and London.

Snyder, J. M. 1980. *Puns and Poetry in Lucretius'* De Rerum Natura. Amsterdam.

Sorabji, R. 2000. *Emotion and Peace of Mind: From Stoic Agitation to Christian Temptation*. Oxford.

Sosin, J. D. 1999. "Lucretius, Seneca, and Persius 1.1–2." *TAPA* 129: 281–99.

Sprenger, M., and G. Bartoloni. 1977. *Die Etrusker: Kunst und Geschichte*. Munich.

Squillante Saccone, M. 1985. "La Poesia di Persio alla luce degli studi piu recenti (1964–1983)." *ANRW* II.32.3: 1781–1812.

———. 1995. *Persio: Il linguaggio della malinconia*. Naples.

Stack, F. 1985. *Pope and Horace: Studies in Imitation*. Cambridge.

Stadter, P. A. 1980. *Arrian of Nicomedia*. Chapel Hill.

Starr, R. J. 1991. "Reading Aloud: Lectures and Roman Reading." *CJ* 86: 337–43.

Steiner, G. 1989. *Real Presences*. Chicago.

Striker, G. 1996. *Essays on Hellenistic Epistemology and Ethics*. Cambridge.

Sullivan, J. P., ed. 1963. *Critical Essays on Roman Literature: Satire*. London.

———. 1972. "In Defense of Persius." *Ramus* 1: 48–62.

———. 1978. "Ass's Ears and Atthises: Persius on Nero." *AJP* 99: 159–70.

Sullivan, J. P. 1984. "Preface." In R. E. Braun, *Persius Satires*. Lawrence.

———. 1985. *Literature and Politics in the Age of Nero*. Ithaca and London.

Syme, R. 1958. *Tacitus*. Vol. II. Oxford.

Tandoi, V. 1965. "*Morituri Verba Catonis*." *Maia* 17: 315–39.

Tarrant, R. J. 1985. *Seneca: Thyestes*. Atlanta.

Tartari Chersoni, M. 2005. "Echi Aristofanei in Persio? (4.33–41: per una rilettura)." *GIF* 57: 115–29.

Tate, J. 1929. "Cornutus and the Poets." *CQ* 23: 41–45.

Terrenato, N. 1998. "*Tam Firmum Municipium*: The Romanization of Volaterrae and its Cultural Implications." *JRS* 88: 94–114.

Thomas, R. F. 1999. *Reading Virgil and His Texts: Studies in Intertextuality*. Ann Arbor.

Thormählin, M. 1978. *The Waste Land: A Fragmentary Wholeness*. Lund.

Traina, A. 1992. "Orazio e Aristippo: Le *Epistole* e l'arte di convivere." In *Atti del Convegno nazionale di studi di Orazio*: 205–18. Turin.

Ullman, B. L. 1914. "Dramatic 'Satura'". *CP* 9: 1–23.

———. 1920. "The Present Status of the *Satura* Question." *SP* 4: 379–401.

Van Sickle, J. 1980. "The Book Roll and Some Conventions of the Poetic Book." *Arethusa* 13: 5–42.

Vasaly, A. 1993. *Representations: Images of the World in Ciceronian Oratory*. Berkeley, Los Angeles, and London.

Villeneuve, F. 1918. *Essai sur Perse*. Paris.

[Volterra]. 1985. *Volterra und die Etrusker: Archaeologische Kostbarkeiten aus dem Museo Guarnacci in Volterra*. Freiburg.

Wagenvoort, H. 1956. *Studies in Roman Literature, Culture and Religion*. Leiden.

Walters, J. 1998. "Making a Spectacle; Deviant Men, Invective, and Pleasure." *Arethusa* 31: 355–67.

Warmington, E. H. 1938. *Remains of Old Latin. Vol. III: Lucilius, The Twelve Tables*. Cambridge, Mass., and London.

Waszink, J. H. 1963. "Das Einleitungsgedicht des Persius." *WS* 76: 79–91.

Watson, L. C. 1995. "Horace's Epodes. The Importance of Iambos." In Harrison 1995: 188–202.

Wehner, B. 2004. *Die Funktion der Dialogenstruktur in Epiktets Diatriben*. Stuttgart.

Wehrle, W. T. 1992. *The Satiric Voice: Program, Form and Meaning in Persius and Juvenal*. Hildesheim.

Weinbrot, H.D. 1982. *Alexander Pope and the Traditions of Formal Verse Satire*. Princeton.

West, D. 1991. "*Cur Me Querelis* (Horace, *Odes* 2.17)." *AJP* 112: 45–52.

Wheeler, A. J. 1992. *English Verse Satire from Donne to Dryden: Imitation of Classical Models*. Heidelberg.

White, P. 1993. *Promised Verse: Poets in the Society of Augustan Rome*. Cambridge and London.

White, S. A. 1995. "Cicero and the Therapists." In J.G.F. Powell, ed., *Cicero the Philosopher: Twelve Papers*. Oxford: 219–46.

Whitehead, J. K. 1996. "Towards a Definition of Etruscan Humor." *Etruscan Studies* 3: 9–32.

Whitmarsh, T. 2006. "True Histories: Lucian, Bakhtin, and the Pragmatics of Reception." In Martindale and Thomas: 104–15.

Wiesen, D. S. 1964. *St. Jerome as a Satirist*. Ithaca.

Williams, C. 1999. *Roman Homosexuality: Ideologies of Morality in Classical Antiquity.* New York and Oxford.

Wilson, E. 1952. "A Defence of Persius." [1927]. In idem, *The Shores of Light.* New York: 267–73.

Winkler, M. M. 1993. *The Persona in Three Satires of Juvenal.* Hildesheim, Zurich, and New York.

Witke, C. 1970. *Latin Satire: The Structure of Persuasion.* Leiden.

Woodman, T. 1974. "EXEGI MONUMENTUM: Horace, *Odes* 3.30." In T. Woodman and D. West, eds., *Quality and Pleasure in Latin Poetry.* Cambridge: 115–28.

Woodman, T., and D. Feeney, eds. 2002. *Traditions and Contexts in the Poetry of Horace.* Cambridge.

Woodman, T., and J. Powell, eds. 1992. *Actor and Audience in Latin Literature.* Cambridge.

Wray, D. 2001. *Catullus and the Poetics of Roman Manhood.* Cambridge.

Zetzel, J. E. G. 1977. "Lucilius, Lucretius, and Persius 1.1." *CP* 72: 40–42.

———. 1980. "Horace's *Liber Sermonum*: The Structure of Ambiguity." *Arethusa* 13: 59–77.

GENERAL INDEX

Accius, 46
Adams, Henry, 110–111
Agrippina, the Younger, 29, 32, 125
Alcibiades. *See* Socrates
allusion and intertextuality, 12, 183–84nn20, 21
Anderson, William, 81,110
Archilochus, 29,32–33
Aristophanes, 10, 27–28, 32, 46, 49–50, 60, 90, 141, 157; and Persius, 50–51, 141, 150, 191n59, 192nn63, 65
Aristotle, 28–29
Armstrong, David, 112
Arria, the Elder, 134, 208n41; the Younger, 16
Arrian, 96–98; *Arrian's Discourses of Epictetus. See* Epictetus, *Discourses*
Augustine. *See* Saint Augustine
Augustus, 38n48, 102, 196n22, 201n2
author: renewed interest in, 16–17, 182n17; "implicated," 108

Bakhtin, Mikhael, 182n17, 202nll
Barthes, Roland, 68, 182n17, 184nn22, 23
Bartsch, Shadi, 206n35
Bassus, Caesius, 9, 54, 62, 136–37, 145, 150, 160, 182n14
Baumli, James, 1–2
Bion of Borysthenes, 32–33, 68, 189nn34–36
Bo, Domenico, 11
Borges, Jorge Luis, 181n6
Bourdieu, Pierre, 13–14, 37
Braund, Susanna, 12, 216n1
Brooks, Robert A., 14, 168–69, 198n36, 217n10

Caecina family, 132–33
Caesonia, wife of Caligula, 141
Caligula (Gaius Caesar), 141, 206n35, 210n17
Callimachus: choliambs, 29; *iamboi*, 8, 29–30, 53, 188nn23–24, 192n67; literary standards, 34, 39, 53, 170–71

Casaubon, Isaac, 9, 54, 62, 182n14
Cato, Marcus, the Younger, 86–87, 91, 118nn32, 34
Catullus, 8, 31, 102–3, 201n2; use of choliambs, 53
Christian Fathers, 61–62
Chrysippus, 100, 130, 143–44; etymologizing, 198n36; and Euripides, 214n39; on poetry, 152; on premeditation of ills, 213n35
Cicero, and *cicer*, 121; on true and false glory, 158–59; quotes poetry, 152; and Stoic paradoxes, 205n26; help for Volterra, 209n1
Citroni, Mario, 12
Clark, Gillian, 86
Claudius Agathinus, 93
Clausen, Wendell, 11, 18
Cleanthes, *Hymn to Zeus*, 195n9
comedy: Greek Old Comedy, 10, 14, 28, 32, 50, 159; New Comedy, 32
Conington, John, 11
Cornutus, Annaeus, 16, 103, 108–9, 206n29; a freedman, 205n26; exile, 125; *allegoresis* and theology, 195n9, 204n23, 206n29; Persius's bequest to, 130; P's confession to, 112–20; P's tribute to, 108; advises destroying P's early work, 208n41; and P's *libellus*, 145, 211n19
Cratinus, 32, 49–50
criticism and theory, 11–14; New Criticism, 11, 87, 182n16; performance theory, 12, 183n18; reader reception theory, 12–13, 183–84nn20–22; reader response theory, 12, 183n18
Cucciarelli, A., 207n35

Dante, 82, 91, 93
Demetrius the Cynic, 199n42, 208n42
diatribe, 189n35
Dickens, Charles: *A Christmas Carol*, 91, 164–65; *Our Mutual Friend*, 24, 186n14
Domitian, 206n35

INDEX LOCORUM